Professional .NET for Java Developers with C#

Jack Lunn
Dr P G Sarang
Erick Sgarbi
John Timney
Stephen Watt

Wrox Press Ltd. ®

Professional .NET for Java Developers with C#

© 2002 Wrox Press

All rights reserved. No part of this book may be reproduced, stored in a retrieval system, or transmitted in any form or by any means, without the prior written permission of the publisher, except in the case of brief quotations embodied in critical articles or reviews.

The authors and publisher have made every effort during the preparation of this book to ensure accuracy of the material. However, the information contained in this book is sold without warranty, either express or implied. Neither the authors, Wrox Press, nor its dealers or distributors will be held liable for any damages caused or alleged to have been caused either directly or indirectly by this book.

First printed November 2002

Published by Wrox Press Ltd,
Arden House, 1102 Warwick Road, Acocks Green,
Birmingham, B27 6BH, UK.
Printed in the USA
ISBN 1-86100-791-4

Trademark Acknowledgments

Wrox has endeavored to adhere to trademark conventions for all companies and products mentioned in this book, such as the appropriate use of capitalization. Wrox cannot, however, guarantee the accuracy of this information.

Credits

Authors
Jack Lunn
Dr P G Sarang
Erick Sgarbi
John Timney
Stephen Watt

Project Manager
Nicola Phillips

Commisioning Editor
Dan Richardson

Technical Editors
Ewan Buckingham
Richard Deeson

Managing Editor
Laurent Lafon

Technical Reviewers
Chris Crane
Cristof Falk
Ben Galbraith
Don Lee
Phil Powers de George
David Schultz

Production Coordinator
Neil Lote

Cover Design
Natalie O'Donnell

Series Editor
Dan Richardson

Proof Reader
Chris Smith

Indexer
Martin Brooks

About the Authors

Jack Lunn

Jack Lunn is a Visiting Instructor of Computer Information Systems at Anderson College in Anderson, South Carolina. Prior to taking up teaching, Jack spent two years as a professional Java programmer. He escaped with his dignity barely intact, although he failed to secure a multi-million dollar house in California before the company's stock plummeted.

In addition to his work with the college, Jack spends time consulting for local clients, playing racquetball, or hanging out with his wife and two-year-old son, Robert. His wife is expecting another child in December. Jack has a Masters degree in Computer Science from Clemson University and may be reached through his web site at www.productiveEsolutions.com or via e-mail at jacklunn@yahoo.com. Jack wrote chapters 6 and 8 of this book.

Dr P G Sarang

With more than 20 years of IT experience, Dr Sarang specializes in architecting and designing solutions. A CEO of ABCOM Information Systems Pvt, Dr Sarang is responsible for training and project development on Java, CORBA, and Microsoft platforms. During his long career, Dr Sarang has developed a number of successful products and has completed several industry assignments. He is a regular speaker at many international conferences and regularly contributes technical articles to well reputed international journals and magazines. He has co-authored several books for Wrox on Java, J2EE, e-commerce, and .NET, and contributed chapters 2 and 3 of this book.

Thanks to Chandan Parulkar and Rahul Bhirud for providing valuable assistance in code development and my special thanks to Girish Nadkarni of Wrox India, who introduced me to the company, and provided very valuable support during all the work I have since done.

I would like to dedicate my contribution to this book to my wife Nita, and my son Sanket.

Erick Sgarbi

Erick was introduced to computers in the early 80's learning how to program Sinclair Basic on a ZX Spectrum where he enjoyed creating computer games with his brothers. He was also very much involved in school science projects on the subject of rocket engineering, a direct inspiration from his father.

For the last several years, Erick has dedicated himself to software development and consulting, working with languages such as Java, Visual C++, Visual Basic, and others. Now Erick is focusing on .NET Technologies by designing applications for Mobile and Smart devices in distributed environments emphasizing his time on web enabled solutions.

He is also author and contributor for AspToday.com and MSDNA. Erick wrote chapters 4 and 10, and can be reached at erick@ihug.com.au.

I would like to thank my family for their support and especially to my father for encouraging me to learn lots of interesting technologies since a young age. My special thanks to Wrox press for presenting me with the opportunity to share my knowledge and experience on this book and my articles at AspToday.com.

Above all, I would like to thank my best friends in the whole world, Christopher Moreira and Patrick Moreira for their continuous support; without you guys I would never be able to be the person I am today, thank you.

John Timney

John lives with his lovely wife Philippa in the small town of Chester-Le-Street in the north of England. He is a postgraduate of Nottingham University having gained an MA in Information Technology, following both a BA Honours Degree and Postgraduate Diploma from Humberside University and before that, a Higher National Diploma from Luton University. John specialises in Internet solutions across a range of technologies. His technical expertise has earned him a Microsoft Most Valuable Professional (MVP) award. His hobbies include Martial Arts and John has Black Belts in two different styles of Karate (if he says that's how to do something it's probably a good idea to believe him!). Another interest is of course writing, and John has contributed to a number of Wrox Press books relating to J2EE and .NET. He is author of chapters 5 and 7.

I would like to offer a dedication to my wife Pippa for being my best friend for so long. To my parents Anne and John, and to Brenda and Steve, have a happy and long retirement.

Stephen Watt

Steve Watt lives in Austin, Texas but hails from the sunny shores of Cape Town, South Africa. He holds the MC3D, MCDBA, MC3E, MCT, and MCP + I certifications, and runs Aikona Technologies, specialists in .NET and J2EE component development. Steve has spent most of his time consulting in South Africa, the Middle East, and the USA. In his spare time, he enjoys playing rugby, surfing, and spending time with his family and friends. He wrote chapters 1, 9, and 11, and can be reached at steve@aikona.com.

My thanks goes out to my lovely wife Kenda, who managed everything while I disappeared from view. Thank you for your love, support, and patience. A big thank-you to my Staffordshire bull terrier, Pearl, who insists on barging into my study for some affection just when I am trying to concentrate the most. To my father, Dave Watt, for his support and encouragement for any project I have ever undertaken. Last but not least, to my best friend, my Rock of Ages, Jesus.

Table of Contents

Introduction   1

Who Is This Book For?   2
What Does This Book Cover?   2
What Do I Need To Use This Book?   3
Conventions   4
Customer Support   4
    How to Download Sample Code for this Book   4
    Errata   5
    E-mail Support   5
    p2p.wrox.com   6
        Why This System Offers the Best Support   6

Chapter 1: Platform Architecture   9

What is Microsoft .NET?   10
    .NET Enterprise Servers   11
    Microsoft .NET Smart Clients   12
    Microsoft .NET XML Web Services   12
    Microsoft .NET Developer Tools   13

XML Web Services   13
    XML Web Services and SOAP   13
        Building XML Web Services with .NET   14
    WSDL, DISCO, and UDDI   14

The .NET Framework   15
    Advantages of the .NET Framework   15
        Application Reliability   16
        New Architectural Model   16
        Multi-language Support   16
        New Language Features   17
        Support for Smart Clients   17
        Metadata Support   17
        No Touch (XCopy) Deployment   17
        Internal Naming   18
        Security   18
        Application Integration   18
        Standardization   18
        Improved Data Access   18

Table of Contents

ASP.NET	19
Windows Forms	20
The Common Language Runtime	20
Type Safety	21
The Common Type System	21
Common Language Specification (CLS)	23
The JIT Compiler and MSIL	23
Managed Code	23
The Base Class Libraries	24
Application Models Inside the Class Libraries	25
Assemblies and Manifests	25
Support for Different Platforms and Architectures	26
Transaction Support	26
Future Implications of .NET	27
A Comparison between J2EE and .NET	27
J2EE Counterattack on .NET	28
The Microsoft Defense	29
Summary	29
Chapter 2: Development Tools	**31**
Notepad and csc.exe	31
The Console Application	32
Running the Application	32
Visual Studio .NET	33
Web Forms	33
Windows Forms	33
XML Support	33
Web Services	33
Creating a Windows Application	33
Adding Components	35
Setting Control Properties	36
Writing Up the Button_Click Event Handler	37
Building and Running the Application	38
Creating Web Applications with VS.NET	39
Creating a New Project	39
Designing the User Interface	41
Writing Code	41
Deploying and Running the Application	42
Creating an ASP.NET Web Service	42
Creating a New Project	42
Wizard Generated Files	43
Writing the Web Method	44
Running the Web Service	45
Creating a Consumer Application	46
Invoking the Web Method	47

Table of Contents

Debugging in Visual Studio.NET	48
Breakpoints	48
Watches	48

WebMatrix — 49

The Interface	49
Web Matrix Features and Language Support	50
Design	50
Toolbox	52
Custom Controls and My Snippets	53
Properties	54
Classes Tab	54
Community	55
Coding and Development	55
Running an Application	56

Dreamweaver MX — 57

The Interface	57
Documents and Templates	58
Features and Language Support	59

SharpDevelop — 59

Templates	60

Summary — 61

Chapter 3: Language Syntax — 63

Source File Conventions — 64

File Naming	64
Top-level Declarations	64
Top-level Declarations in Java	65
Top-level Declarations in C#	65

Language Syntax — 66

Primitive Data Types	67
Converting and Casting	68
Value and Reference Types	70
Boxing and Unboxing	71
Operators	71
The checked and unchecked Operators	72
The is Operator	73
The sizeof Operator	74
typeof and GetType	74
Flow Control	76
Branching Statements	76
Looping Statements	77

Class Fundamentals — 78

Access Modifiers	78
The sealed Modifier	78
The readonly Modifier	79
The Main() Method	80

iii

Table of Contents

Other Methods	81
Passing by Reference	81
Using an Indeterminate Number of Parameters	83
Properties	84

Structs — 85

Arrays in C# — 86

The One-Dimensional Array	86
Initialization	86
Multi-Dimensional Arrays	87
Initialization	88
Jagged Arrays	88
The System.Array Class	88

Inheritance and Derived Classes — 89

Typecasting to a Base Class	91
The base Keyword	91
Selecting Constructors	92
Method Overriding	93
Virtual Methods	93
Method Overriding with the new Modifier	94
Abstract Classes	96
Interfaces	97
Implementing Multiple Interfaces	98
Operator Overloading	98

Exceptions — 101

Advanced C# Techniques — 102

Indexers	102
Attributes	104
Delegates	105
Re-assigning Delegates	106
Invoking Delegates	106
Garbage Collection	108
Safe and Unsafe Code	108
The unsafe Keyword	108
The fixed Keyword	109

Summary — 110

Chapter 4: Data Access — 113

The Structure of ADO.NET — 114

ADO.NET Managed Providers	116
Connection Class	118
Command Class	118
DataReader Class	119
The DataAdapter Class	119
The DataSet Class	120
DataTableCollection	122
DataRelationCollection	123

Table of Contents

Filtering and Sorting DataSets	**124**
Getting Practical	**125**
Fetching Data	127
Manipulating Data	129
Simple DataSet Example	129
Using Tables and Relations	131
Modifying Data	134
ADO.NET Events	143
Connection Events	143
DataAdapter Events	144
DataTable Events	144
ADO.NET Exceptions	**146**
Outputting DataSets' Content	**149**
XML	149
Serialization	152
Summary	**154**
Chapter 5: Dynamic Web Applications	**157**
Page Requests and How They Work	**159**
ASP.NET Page Events	**160**
HTML Server Controls	**161**
Web Server Controls	**172**
Validation Controls	**201**
Inline or Code-Behind?	**211**
Principles of Code Behind	213
ASP.NET and JSP	214
Summary	**215**
Chapter 6: Advanced Dynamic Web Applications	**217**
Running the Examples	**217**
Data-Bound Controls in ASP.NET	**218**
Properties	218
Collections	219
DataTables	221
Deleting Records	232
Managing Session and Application State	**234**
Session State	234
The mode Attribute	234
The cookieless Attribute	234
The timeout Attribute	234

v

Table of Contents

    The Shopping Cart Page   235
    Application State   242

Building Custom Controls   244
    A Basic Custom Control   245
    A Derived Custom Control   248

A Composite Custom Control   252

Summary   259

Chapter 7: ASP.NET Web Services   261

Creating ASP.NET Web Services   262
    Invoking a Web Service   263
        BufferResponse   263
        CacheDuration   264
        Description   264
        EnableSession   264
        MessageName   265
        TransactionOption   265
    Creating an ASP.NET Web Service   265
    Testing ASP.NET Web Services   268
    Consuming a Web Service   269
    Using External Web Services in .NET Clients   274

Web Service Chaining   277

Summary   277

Chapter 8: Windows Forms and Smart Clients   281

A Simple Windows Forms Application   281
    Looking Behind the Scenes   283
    Working with Properties   284
    Adding a Control to the Form   286
        Code for the Button   287
    Layout Options for Controls   288
        The Anchor Property   288
        The Dock Property   289
    Event Handling   290
    Completing the Application   291
        RadioButton and GroupBox   292
        Listing Options   294
        Capturing User Input   296
    Building the Application   301

Smart Clients   302
    Making the Assembly   302
    Publish the Assembly   303
    Trust the Assembly   303
    Creating the Loader   303

Testing the Smart Client	305
Updating the Smart Client	305

Data-Bound Controls for WinForms — 308

Binding to Single Elements	309
Binding to Multiple Elements	310

Summary — 311

Chapter 9: Enterprise Components — 313

J2EE Support for Enterprise Applications — 313

The J2EE Platform	314
The J2EE Runtime Infrastructure	315
J2EE Container Architecture	315
The J2EE APIs	317
J2EE Technologies	318
Component Technologies	319
Service Technologies	320
Communication Technologies	320
J2EE Deployment	321

.NET Support for Enterprise Applications — 321

The System.EnterpriseServices Library	322
COM+ Overview	323
The Component Services Manager	324
Transactions	326
Just-in-Time Activation (JIT Activation)	326
Security	327
Object Pooling and State Management	327
Component Queuing	328
Event Support	328
Component Load Balancing	328

Putting COM+ into Practice — 329

Writing your ServicedComponent	329
Configuring your Assemblies	332
Compiling the Application	333
Adding Object Pooling and JIT Activation Support	333
Writing the Client Application	334

Summary — 336

Chapter 10: .NET Remoting — 339

Remote Objects Architecture — 340

RMI	340
.NET Remoting	341

Exploring .NET Remoting — 342

The Remoting Namespace	343
Serialization in .NET	343

Table of Contents

Marshalling Concepts	346
Marshal-By-Reference	347
Marshal-By-Value	347
Marshal-By-Value Versus Marshal-By-Reference	348
Channels	348
Formatters	349
Activation	349
Server-side Activation	350
Client-side Activation	355
Call Context	358
Leases and Sponsors	360
Leasing	360
Sponsors	363
Tracking and Logging	365
Building a Remoting Application	**369**
Delegates and Event Remoting Issues	370
Building the Chat Server	372
Configuration files	372
Server Application	373
Building the Server Assembly (Remote Server Object)	374
The Client Application	381
Summary	**386**
Chapter 11: Interoperating with Existing Code	**389**
Interoperating with Java	**389**
Microsoft Biztalk Server	390
Integration Using Web Services	390
Microsoft Visual J#	391
Creating a Visual J# Application	391
The Java Language Conversion Assistant (JLCA)	394
The Binary Converter Tool	397
A Comparison between Java, J#, and C#	398
Interoperating with COM	**400**
Accessing a COM Component from .NET	400
Runtime-Callable Wrappers	401
Generating Managed Metadata Using tlbImp.exe	401
Accessing the COM Component in C#	403
Late Binding and Early Binding	404
Releasing COM Objects from Memory	405
Incorporating ActiveX Controls in .NET Applications	405
Summary	**406**
Index	**409**

Table of Contents

Introduction

Microsoft is very excited about its .NET initiative, and seems convinced the rest of the world will be compelled to buy licenses and propel it to dominance. There's no doubt that the .NET Framework represents a radical departure from the traditional Microsoft model. .NET is fully object oriented, and it offers a consistent approach to the entire gamut of programming problems. As its name suggests, the Framework provides a highly network-aware model, with strong support for techniques such as remoting, web services, XML, and others, like the new so-called Smart Client paradigm.

One factor behind this overhaul and unification of just about all of Microsoft's programming tools is the threat represented by Java. Java is a well-supported, non-proprietary language, and its elegance and full object orientation helped power it to greater success than Visual Basic in just a few years. Bill and his empire felt obliged to strike back.

Well-publicized legal actions have been brought by Microsoft's competitors accusing the Redmond giant of abusing its monopoly position, such as attempting to stymie Java's growth by manipulating the JVM included with Windows to support non-standard language constructs, in contravention of the terms of Sun's General Public License (GPL) for Java. The courts eventually agreed with Sun, and forbade Microsoft updating its JVM beyond its then current state, at v1.4.1.

Given that Microsoft cannot create a Windows-specific Java language, and as its marketing is based heavily on creating and maintaining reliance on its operating system, it developed their own C# language that shares many of the features and benefits of Java. Although Microsoft claim C# is derived from C++ rather than Java, there are many aspects of the new language that strongly echo Java, giving Java developers a good headstart, and making C# the logical entry path to the .NET model.

Introduction

Who Is This Book For?

If you are a Java developer, and you'd like to find out more about C# and the .NET Framework, this book is for you. C# has many parallels with Java, and this book takes advantage of this to introduce the new language and programming model. Frequent examples highlight the differences and similarities between Java and C#. There's no need to have any particular package such as Visual Studio .NET to use this book: all code is presented for use with the freely downloadable command-line compilers and tools.

What Does This Book Cover?

The book starts by covering essential fundamental architectural and syntactical issues that all .NET developers need to grasp, before moving on to more advanced techniques for professional developers. We show how to implement Windows desktop applications, web applications, data access, remoting, Smart Clients, and interoperability.

The book's chapters can be summarized as follows:

Chapter 1 – *Platform Architecture:* Starts the ball rolling with an introduction to the .NET Framework. We look at the components that together make up the Framework, namely the Common Language Runtime, the class libraries, and ASP.NET. We look at .NET's advantages, and compare and contrast it with J2EE.

Chapter2 – *Development Tools:* Even though the tools for compiling and running any .NET application are freely available from Microsoft, some powerful development environments are available, which can greatly enhance your productivity. We look at the most important of these in this chapter.

Chapter 3 – *Language Syntax:* In this chapter, we cover the essentials of the C# language. We draw some useful parallels with corresponding Java syntax and create some simple examples as we examine basics such as operators, loops, methods, and exceptions, finishing with a look at the C#-specific features of indexers, attributes, and delegates.

Chapter 4 – *Data Access:* Almost every application makes use of data held in some kind of data store, be it a full-scale database or a formatted text file, such as XML. This chapter introduces the techniques .NET supports for accessing data from our applications, showing how to display it, edit it, and delete it.

Chapter 5 – *Dynamic Web Applications:* We introduce the basics of creating web applications in the .NET world, investigating the events that drive ASP.NET applications and the controls that we have on hand when creating our web UI. We create examples to demonstrate controls, ranging from the regular HTML controls through to the more sophisticated .NET server controls.

Chapter 6 – *Advanced Dynamic Web Applications:* Expanding on what we learned in the previous chapter, this chapter covers more advanced techniques. We look at data binding in web applications, which can be a great way to quickly display and interact with data on a web page. We also investigate Application and Session state to allow applications to retain important information as users move from page to page. We round off with a look at User Controls, which allow us to extend the standard web controls and create our own.

Chapter 7 – *ASP.NET Web Services:* Unlike the Java environment, the .NET platform is strongly oriented towards XML Web Services. In this final web chapter, we look at how easy .NET makes web service development thanks to ASP.NET's built-in support. We create and deploy a simple example that interacts with a backend database, and show how the command line tools can be used to generate code for interacting with web services.

Chapter 8 – *Windows Forms and Smart Clients:* The great thing about the .NET Framework is that we can use the exact same language and very similar techniques for web development as for desktop development. In this chapter, we create a fully-featured Windows desktop application in Notepad, compiling it on the command line. We then modify this standalone desktop application to transform it into a Smart Client – Microsoft's name for desktop applications that have built-in deployment and updating capability, bringing the central control of web applications to the desktop.

Chapter 9 – *Enterprise Components:* There are many aspects of the J2EE environment specifically geared towards large, distributed, enterprise-caliber applications, and .NET capabilities are at least as powerful. This chapter familiarizes you with the .NET features and classes that are particularly relevant to enterprise application programmers.

Chapter 10 – *.NET Remoting:* The Java mechanism for running code remotely is known as RMI (Remote Method Invocation), and is mirrored in .NET's remoting technology. These techniques allow us to access code on remote machines seamlessly, which can form a key part of distributed solutions for the enterprise. There are many technical subtleties that a developer must understand in order to implement remoting solutions, and this chapter covers them all.

Chapter 11 – *Interoperating with Existing Code:* When moving over to a new technology such as .NET, most businesses will have a sizable library of legacy components. To make the transition smoothly, it's crucial to be able to make use of such existing code, and in this chapter, you'll find out how to access both Java and COM components in your .NET applications.

What Do I Need To Use This Book?

This book was written with Java developers who want to experiment with C# in mind. For that reason, we've endeavored to minimize the tools required to run the samples. The great majority of the code can be run using the command line compilers and tools that come with the freely downloadable .NET SDK. The SDK can be found by clicking **Microsoft .NET Framework SDK** under the **Software Development Kits** option in the left-hand navigation bar of the MSDN download area at:

> http://msdn.microsoft.com/downloads/default.asp

In order to run the SDK, you must have Windows NT, 2000, or XP installed on your machine.

For the web applications, including web services, you will need IIS installed on a Windows 2000 or XP machine *before* installing the .NET Framework. IIS is an optional component on Windows 2000 and XP Professional, and is installed in a separate step after the operating system has finished installing. If you need to, you can install IIS via the Add/Remove Programs dialog in Windows Control Panel.

Conventions

We've used a number of different styles of text and layout in this book to differentiate between different kinds of information. Here are examples of the styles used and an explanation of what they mean.

Code has several fonts. If we're talking about code in the text, we use a non-proportional font like this: for...next. If it's a block of code that can be typed as a program and run, then it will also appear within a gray box:

```
<asp:TextBox id="txtNameBox" runat="server" />
<asp:Button id="btnSubmit" onclick="btnSubmit_Click"
                    runat="server" Text="Click Here!" />
```

Sometimes we'll see code in a mixture of styles, like this:

```
Private Sub calDates_SelectionChanged(ByVal sender As System.Object, _
        ByVal e As System.EventArgs) Handles calDates.SelectionChanged
    lblMessage.Text = _
        "Current Date: " & calDates.SelectedDate.ToLongDateString()
End Sub
```

When this happens, the code with a white background is code we are already familiar with; the line highlighted in gray is a new addition to the code since we last looked at it.

Advice, hints, and background information come in this type of font.

> **Important pieces of information are placed inside boxes like this.**

Bullets appear indented, with each new bullet marked as follows:

- **Important Words** are in a bold type font.
- Words that appear on the screen, or in menus like **File** or **Window**, are in a similar font to the one you would see on a Windows desktop.
- Keys that you press on the keyboard, such as *Ctrl* and *Enter*, are in italics.

Customer Support

We always value hearing from our readers, and we want to know what you think about this book: what you liked, what you didn't like, and what you think we can do better next time. You can send us your comments, either by returning the reply card in the back of the book, or by e-mail to feedback@wrox.com. Please be sure to mention the book title in your message.

How to Download Sample Code for this Book

Visit the Wrox site at http://www.wrox.com/, and locate the title through our **Find a Book** facility. Open the book's detail page and click the **Download Code** link. Alternatively, click the DOWNLOAD CODE link at the top of the Wrox homepage, and select the book in the textbox there.

Introduction

Before you download the code for this book, you may register your book by providing your name and current e-mail address. This is a purely optional step which allows us to contact you should issues with the code download arise, or should the code download package be updated at a later date. Be assured that Wrox will never pass any details supplied during registration to any third party. Full details are contained in our Privacy Policy, linked to from the download page.

Download files are archived using WinZip, and need to be extracted with a decompression program such as WinZip or PKUnzip. The code is typically arranged with a suitable folder structure, so ensure your decompression software is set to use folder names before extracting the files.

Errata

We've made every effort to make sure that there are no errors in the text or in the code. However, no one is perfect and mistakes do occur. If you find an error in one of our books, such as a spelling mistake or a faulty piece of code, we would be very grateful to hear about it. By sending in errata, you may save another reader hours of frustration, and of course, you will be helping us provide even higher quality information. Simply e-mail the information to support@wrox.com, where your information will be checked and posted on the errata page for the title, or used in subsequent editions of the book.

To view errata on the web site, go to http://www.wrox.com/, and locate the title through the Find a Book search box. Clicking the View errata link that appears below the cover graphic on the book's detail page brings up a list of all errata for that book reported to date.

E-mail Support

If you wish to directly query a problem in the book with an expert who knows the book in detail then e-mail support@wrox.com, with the title of the book and the last four numbers of the ISBN in the subject field of the e-mail. A typical e-mail should include the following things:

- ❑ The **title of the book**, **last four digits of the ISBN** (7914), and **page number** of the problem in the Subject field.
- ❑ Your **name**, **contact information**, and the **problem** in the body of the message.

We **won't** send you junk mail. We need the details to save your time and ours. When you send an e-mail message, it will go through the following chain of support:

- ❑ Customer Support – Your message is delivered to our customer support staff, who are the first people to read it. They have files on most frequently asked questions and will answer anything general about the book or the web site immediately.
- ❑ Editorial – Deeper queries are forwarded to the technical editor responsible for that book. They have experience with the programming language or particular product, and are able to answer detailed technical questions on the subject.
- ❑ The Authors – Finally, in the unlikely event that the editor cannot answer your problem, they will forward the request to the author. We do try to protect the author from any distractions to their writing; however, we are quite happy to forward specific requests to them. All Wrox authors help with the support on their books. They will e-mail the customer and the editor with their response, and again all readers should benefit.

Introduction

The Wrox Support process can only offer support to issues that are directly pertinent to the content of our published title. Support for questions that fall outside the scope of normal book support is provided via the community lists of our http://p2p.wrox.com/ forum.

p2p.wrox.com

For author and peer discussion join the P2P mailing lists. Our unique system provides **programmer to programmer**™ contact on mailing lists, forums, and newsgroups, all in addition to our one-to-one e-mail support system. If you post a query to P2P, you can be confident that it is being examined by the many Wrox authors and other industry experts who are present on our mailing lists. At p2p.wrox.com you will find a number of different lists that can help you, not only while you read this book, but also as you move on and develop your own applications.

To subscribe to a mailing list just follow these steps:

1. Go to http://p2p.wrox.com/
2. Choose the appropriate category from the left menu bar
3. Click on the mailing list you wish to join
4. Follow the instructions to subscribe and fill in your e-mail address and password
5. Reply to the confirmation e-mail you receive
6. Use the subscription manager to join more lists and set your e-mail preferences

Why This System Offers the Best Support

You can choose to join the mailing lists or you can receive them as a weekly digest. If you don't have the time, or facilities, to receive the mailing list, then you can search our online archives. Junk and spam mails are deleted, and your own e-mail address is protected by the unique Lyris system. Queries about joining or leaving lists, and any other general queries about lists, should be sent to listsupport@p2p.wrox.com.

Introduction

Platform Architecture

Since the announcement of the **Microsoft .NET** platform in 2000, information has been flowing fast and furiously from the software giant. Such a large flow of information has meant that it has sometimes been difficult to collate and digest what is important and what is not. The .NET moniker has been added to a large number of products and technologies, including:

- .NET Enterprise Servers (such as SQL Server and Exchange Server)
- Windows .NET Server
- Visual Studio .NET
- .NET Framework

In this chapter we'll explain exactly what the .NET platform is, and what technologies and products it consists of. Then we'll move on to the **.NET Framework**, which is a key part of the .NET strategy and the focus of much of this book. Finally, we'll discuss the differences between the **Java 2 Enterprise Edition (J2EE)** and Microsoft .NET platforms.

Microsoft .NET seeks to pick up on the strengths of Java and improve on its weaknesses, as well as add a whole lot of other cool features. As a lot of the fundamental concepts are the same you'll have a good understanding of how Microsoft .NET works by the end of the chapter.

Specifically, in this chapter, we'll cover:

- What Microsoft .NET is
- The .NET Framework
- A comparison between J2EE and .NET

What is Microsoft .NET?

The Microsoft .NET strategy was implemented in response to:

- The decreasing cost of communications
- The increase in client processing capabilities
- The increased use of the Internet as a medium in which to run software applications

Microsoft wanted to create a platform that could be used to run software applications that make use of the powerful processing capabilities of the client as well as the extensive communication capabilities of the Internet. The standard *n*-tier approach to using distributed capabilities left a lot to be desired, as there was always a lot of power on the client that was left unharnessed.

The solution Microsoft eventually came up with was a very loosely-coupled and distributed architecture, supported by a core set of technologies for connecting all applications over the Web using **W3C standardized XML Web Services**, whilst making as much of use of client processing power as possible. We will take an in-depth look at each of these parts of Microsoft .NET as we proceed through the chapter.

Microsoft .NET is comprised of four core components:

- .NET Enterprise Servers
- .NET Smart Clients
- XML Web Services
- Developer Tools

All of these components run over a set of technologies known as the .NET Framework, which consists of three core components:

- The **Common Language Runtime (CLR)**
- The **.NET Class Libraries**
- Microsoft **ASP.NET**

These three components are largely the foundation on which the .NET strategy is implemented. We will be following up with more information on each of these at a later stage in this chapter.

The following diagram illustrates how XML Web Services are the glue that keeps the architecture together in the Microsoft .NET platform:

Platform Architecture

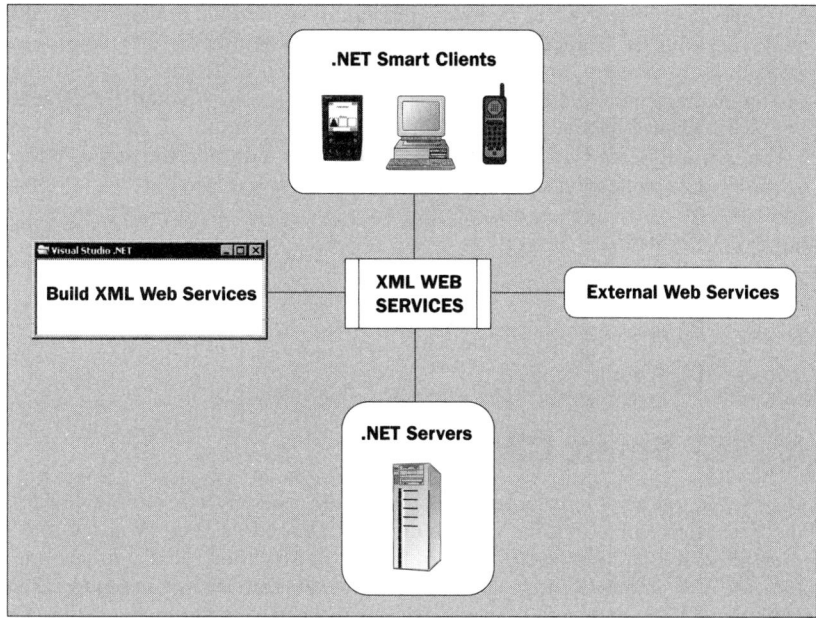

.NET Enterprise Servers

The server infrastructure for .NET currently consists of the Windows 2000 Server family, the .NET Enterprise Server family and the Windows .NET Server family.

The .NET Enterprise Server family consists of:

- Microsoft Application Center 2000
- Microsoft Biztalk Server 2000
- Microsoft Commerce Server 2000
- Microsoft Content Management Server 2001
- Microsoft Exchange Server 2000
- Microsoft Host Integration Server 2000
- Microsoft Internet Security and Acceleration Server 2000
- Microsoft Mobile Information 2001 Server
- Microsoft SharePoint Portal Server 2001
- Microsoft SQL Server 2000

Windows .NET Server is currently still in development and is intended to become the platform of choice for deploying your .NET applications. The .NET Server family provides improved server reliability, availability, scalability, and manageability with added performance and tuning features. Alongside remote management and internationalization support, security and authentication have also been improved with support for Smart Card and the Kerberos v5 protocol. At the time of going to press the .NET Server was in Release Candidate 1. The .NET Server Editions, much like Windows 2000, are structured towards your application's needs. They consist of:

- Windows .NET Standard Server
- Windows .NET Enterprise Server
- Windows .NET Datacenter Server
- Windows .NET Web Server

Microsoft .NET Smart Clients

Smart Clients is a fairly general term used to refer to personal computers, mobile devices, and embedded devices. Microsoft Windows XP, Windows XP Embedded, and Windows CE .NET will be empowering these devices to be accessible to and be part of Microsoft .NET applications and also to make use of the .NET Framework's managed, secure execution environment. Smart Clients are able to make use of Windows Forms for their user interface and they are able to leverage the .NET Framework to download additional or updated components, as needed, via the web. XML Web Service support is also part of their inherent design, which we will learn more about in the next section.

You can find more information about Smart Clients in Chapter 8.

Microsoft .NET XML Web Services

XML Web Services are the new architecture for developing software in Microsoft. NET. The idea is to break your application down into components and select which ones you would like to provide a **Simple Object Access Protocol (SOAP)** interface into. Since SOAP is a **World Wide Web Consortium (W3C)** standard, applications on any supporting platform can therefore talk to with your component.

For more information on SOAP and other W3C standards, check out the W3C homepage at http://www.w3c.org.

The basic idea is that future applications will be made by a process of "Lego engineering". By calling logic from other people's SOAP-enabled components (that they have agreed to expose to you), you can stick all the SOAP-enabled blocks together to create your application.

For those of you who like to minimize the amount of work you do writing an application, this architecture will set you speedily on your way to obtaining component reusability nirvana.

We discuss XML Web Services in the .NET world in Chapter 7.

Microsoft .NET Developer Tools

A key objective of .NET was to make it overtly tool friendly – thus with some cool new re-engineering, Visual Studio 6 became Visual Studio .NET. The goal was to take the Visual Basic **Rapid Application Development (RAD)** experience and extend it to all the development tools and languages, equipping them with a multitude of RAD features, such as Drag and Drop, Wizards, Design Time Controls, and the Simple Window Interaction Model.

Visual Studio .NET offers strong support for XML Web Services. It achieves this by enabling developers to assemble .NET applications from existing Visual Studio 6 applications using upgrade wizards. You can also use Design Time Controls to SOAP-enable your application with a click of a property. Support for attributal programming allows you to provide meta-data for the runtime in your source code, which in turn provides you with the means to ensure the correct runtime semantics for your application. This can save you valuable time as a developer.

The tool's core strengths come from the underlying support within the Common Language Runtime, a core part of the .NET Framework. The tool actually interoperates with key components of the runtime during development, greatly minimizing the risk of runtime exceptions. Additionally, Microsoft has developed the **Visual Studio Integrators Program** (VSIP) which provides an implementation standard for compiler and language vendors to extend Visual Studio .NET, by adding their own languages to those already supported.

Chapter 2 provides a rundown of the most important tools available to .NET developers.

XML Web Services

After the advent of the *n*-tier web application, most developers were left with a choice between implementing browser-based applications or designing distributed thick client applications where the logic was shared across several tiers. The former offered ease of deployment with little client-side logic, while the latter required additional maintenance but provided powerful client-side logic.

One of the issues additionally plaguing the latter architecture was what developers aptly termed, 'DLL hell'. This involved components with the same name overwriting each other, causing version inconsistencies and more likely than not, crippling applications.

The .NET task at hand was to develop a happy medium between the two architectures – power on the client, coupled with ease of deployment on the server. Enter XML Web Services...

XML Web Services and SOAP

SOAP is at the heart of XML Web Services. It enables applications to communicate with XML over HTTP. A SOAP-enabled component can make a **SOAP Request** to another SOAP-enabled component, which in turn can reply with the data in a **SOAP Response** that contains the data that your component requested.

The process can also be reversed. That is, your application can consist of SOAP-enabled components that outside applications can make requests to in order to use your component logic. In fact, you could build an application using your own SOAP components as well as a few from disparate applications around the Web. Microsoft describes this as **aggregation**, **integration**, and **consumption**.

SOAP is a fairly flexible protocol, in that if applications are using it as their means of communication, the two parties can come together in agreement and define what part of the SOAP Messages are intrinsic and which are not. During the course of time, the two partners can start utilizing more and more of what they are sending to each other. This allows the two parties to quite comfortably set the pace of their application integration as well as provide a means for more complex applications to communicate seamlessly with simple ones.

> The W3C (World Wide Web Consortium) is frequently mentioned in our explanation of the .NET web services architecture. This highlights the fact that .NET applications can integrate with web services that *do not run on the .NET platform, or even on Windows machines,* thanks to the *open standards* on web services that the W3C maintains. It is quite possible to create a .NET web service that communicates with a web service running on the J2EE platform.

Building XML Web Services with .NET

.NET facilitates the breaking down of an application into identifiable SOAP-enabled components. In a nutshell, the platform leverages the Web for communications, with SOAP as the W3C standard communication protocol, and XML as the W3C standard data format. Thus when you SOAP-enable your components, other applications that are SOAP enabled can communicate with them using the SOAP protocol over the Web. Applications designed in this format are universally known as web services.

The platform also provides an infrastructure and toolset that has been specifically designed for XML Web Service application development.

In keeping with the goal of implementing RAD support wherever possible, the developer does not really have to know much about composing and consuming SOAP messages – that can be left to Visual Studio .NET, or other development tools. Microsoft has made it as easy as clicking a box to SOAP-enable a selected component – everything required is automatically generated by the IDE. The toolset lives up to its name by letting you visually compose the majority of your applications.

At present, it is still 'early days' and there aren't a large number of web services out there ready to be consumed by .NET applications. Microsoft is presently working alongside companies to identify the sorts of web services that are needed both now and in the future. An important thing to keep in mind is that if you are using someone else's SOAP-enabled component in your application, you normally have little control over that component. In my personal opinion, there are going to be agreements that will have to be designed and signed off so that someone doesn't pull the rug from under your application's feet when you least expect it. Definitely a design issue to ponder over during your next system reboot.

WSDL, DISCO, and UDDI

Web Services Description Language (WSDL) is a standard that is used to specify the functionality of an XML Web Service. WSDL describes how SOAP Messages need to be composed if your web service is to accurately consume them by detailing information such as what parameters and data types are acceptable.

There are two mechanisms available for the discovery of your web service:

- **SOAP Discovery Specification (DISCO)** is a lightweight discovery specification. It enables you to build a discovery document detailing all web services that are available at your URL. It also enables interested parties to query your URL for the discovery document in order to find out what web services you offer. DISCO exists as an alternative to UDDI which some view as a less viable approach.

- **Universal Description, Discovery, and Integration (UDDI)** is a registry, of which there are several available on the web. Once a registry is located, you can register your web service with it. People can then interrogate the directory to locate the information or web services they require. For more information on the UDDI specification, go to http://www.uddi.org/.

In brief, DISCO is a good option if you already know the URL for the web services that you are interested in. UDDI is an alternative that enables searching of directories for web services that meet your particular requirements.

The .NET Framework

The .NET Framework consists of four core components: ASP.NET, Windows Forms, the Base Class Libraries, and the Common Language Runtime (CLR). These components are the foundation on which the .NET Strategy is implemented.

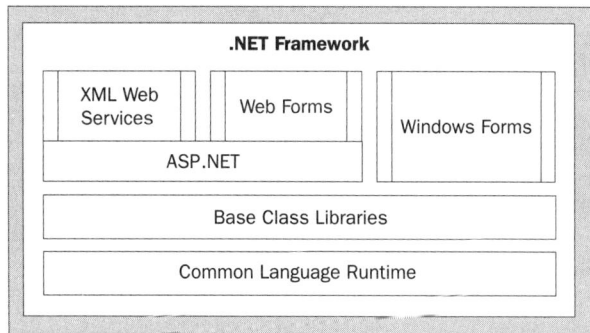

Advantages of the .NET Framework

The major advantages of the .NET Framework are:

- Application reliability
- New architectural model
- Multi-language support
- New language features
- Support for Smart Clients
- Metadata support
- "No Touch" (XCopy) deployment

Chapter 1

- Internal naming
- Security
- Application integration
- Standardization
- Improved data access

We'll discuss each of these advantages in turn.

Application Reliability

The .NET Framework uses features first developed in Windows 2000 to improve application stability – particularly improving compilation and caching techniques to improve application performance.

Many of the issues in modern applications are due to memory leaks or poor memory handling. The .NET Framework incorporates a high-performance garbage collector that manages memory by releasing unused memory while requiring very little processing and memory for itself. This results in better overall application performance and reliability.

New Architectural Model

Compared to traditional software on Windows, a different architectural approach has been taken in order to minimize application development and maintenance efforts. Just to mention one change, the Base Classes present a unified library from which all software developers can draw upon, regardless of what type of application they are trying to build and what Microsoft technologies they are using to build it. So if you spend most of your time writing software for .NET Smart Clients and then move to developing XML Web Services, the differences will be minimal aside from a few new class libraries you will have to learn. If you are a Java developer this will seem fairly logical, but this has not always been the case with Microsoft development.

Multi-language Support

One of the core features of the .NET Framework is multi-language support. Presently, over 24 languages have been written for the .NET platform. Believe it or not, even Assembler.NET is supported (so you can create an XML Web Service in assembler!).

A form of the Java language is supported in J#. NET, however Sun's common Java APIs are replaced with the .NET Base Class Libraries and C# remains the preferred language for development in the Framework. Java support is simply provided so that Java developers can move comfortably and quickly onto the CLR. Another tool for speeding up migration is the **Java Language Conversion Assistant** which is provided as a tool that can convert from Java code to C# code. This is available from:

http://msdn.microsoft.com/vstudio/downloads/tools/jlca/default.asp

The idea behind all of this is that a programmer can build an application in the .NET Framework by utilizing the supported language of their choice. Microsoft's view is that in one case a particular problem may be best solved using Visual Basic .NET while another problem may be better tackled with C#. This also means that you can write part of your application in COBOL .NET and part of it in C#.

New Language Features

The runtime environment has been designed so that your code is **type safe**. This feature enables easy integration of code between the different .NET languages. Exceptions are now handled in exactly the same way that they are in Java, through the ever faithful `try...catch...finally` blocks.

This may seem obvious to us Java people, but a lot of folks moving up the ladder to .NET from traditional ASP or Visual Basic were previously stuck with rather clumsy exception handling that in a way would be like coding a `try...catch` block for every single statement that may be problematic.

The Visual Basic language has been further improved and now carries full support for object-orientation and inheritance. Chapter 3 elaborates a little more on these features in the context of C#, although the principle is the same in VB.NET.

Support for Smart Clients

A common programming model is also supplied for writing both web applications and smart clients that can be deployed on anything from your personal computer to mobile phones and Personal Digital Assistants (PDAs).

Metadata Support

We can create self-describing components via metadata that is packaged into the binary file along with the code. This allows for additional information, such as dependencies, to be provided. Since this metadata is auto-generated from the source code at compile time, we don't have to worry about versioning, as it will always be up to date.

Now that the runtime has access to this component information it can dynamically generate a cache of information describing all the components on the system. If this cache ever becomes damaged the runtime can intuitively rebuild it. Furthermore, this enables every component to describe what it contains as well as what it depends on.

For example, if I write an application and pass it on to you and you are having issues getting it to run, you can have a look to see what dependencies are not being met. This eases the debugging process somewhat as this metadata can be linked to the help and documentation functionality. Since the help information is being read directly from the component the metadata is always synchronized.

As metadata allows us to know about our components, the Windows Registry is no longer required for locating them, which in turn lays the foundation for the ease of deployment of applications and components in .NET.

No Touch (XCopy) Deployment

No touch deployment is the term Microsoft gives the feature that enables Windows-based application components to be updated by a web server accessible to your end users. Deployment has been made even easier by automatic versioning of components and application cognizance of this fact. Registering applications has been done away with, which minimizes the previously frequent system restarts. In fact, deploying applications is now so easy, it can be achieved with the old DOS `XCOPY` command; hence this form of deployment is referred to as XCopy deployment in many circles.

Chapter 1

A lot is said about Windows constantly having to be rebooted, but a lot can also be said about Java application engines having to be restarted every time you make a configuration or code change so that the application can read in the new changes. This new deployment mechanism seeks to minimize the configuration changes that you will have to undertake.

Internal Naming

The .NET Framework includes a very strong internal naming system. This means that if one application overwrites a shared library, then an existing application that depends on the old shared library can actually repair itself. This is accomplished by your application checking its shared files on initialization, and if it discovers that one of those files has changed, it can autonomously ask the runtime to obtain a version it knows is compatible.

Security

The .NET security models were developed specifically for application integration over the Internet. Features include obtaining information on where an application originates, what its digital signature is and what the application is trying to accomplish. The .NET Framework can then use this information in conjunction with pre-set resource security policies to make highly granular access level decisions at runtime.

Application Integration

Application integration is a huge part of .NET, for this Microsoft wants the language of communication to be SOAP and all application executables to be XML Web Services. Web Services are at the core of the Framework and Microsoft has have developed COM Interop technology to enable your existing Win32 Applications to be accessible to .NET via a COM Interop wrapper. Tools have been provided to enable further integration such as the **Visual Basic Upgrade Tool** (for going from VB 6.0 to .NET; see Chapter 11) and the Java Language Conversion Assistant for porting Java apps over into C#. The JLCA ports as much of your Java code over as possible, however not everything is supported in .NET and for that which is un-portable, the tool provides links to whitepapers and documentation that deal with porting those particular topics to .NET.

Standardization

Furthermore, in order to keep the open standards banner flying high, Microsoft has submitted specifications for C# and a subset of the .NET Framework called the **Common Language Infrastructure** (CLI) to the ECMA Standards Body for standardization. These specifications represent the participation of six other ECMA partners, including HP-Compaq and Intel, and are currently on track to be considered by the ECMA General Assembly later this year for formal approval.

ECMA is a standards body founded in 1961, whose goal is to standardize information and communication systems to enable faster economic and social growth in world markets. Approval for Microsoft would most likely mean increased third party support, implementation and adoption and move .NET to the realm of a widely implemented standard, much like HTTP or TCP/IP.

Improved Data Access

The .NET technology for data access is Microsoft ADO.NET. Using ADO.NET, developers can work with an XML-based cache of the data they seek, rather than having to directly read or write to the database. ADO.NET was specifically designed with disconnected data-access in mind – previously you would have to obtain a recordset and convert that recordset to XML for use in your web application; as ADO.NET can skip this step, it saves quite a bit of time.

ASP.NET

The function of **ASP.NET** in the .NET Framework is to give us a programming model that provides higher-level components and services aimed specifically at creating XML Web Services and applications. This model has its own set of libraries within the **.NET Base Class Library**.

The following diagram shows how Web Applications and Web Services run on top of the ASP.NET Runtime and Infrastructure Services:

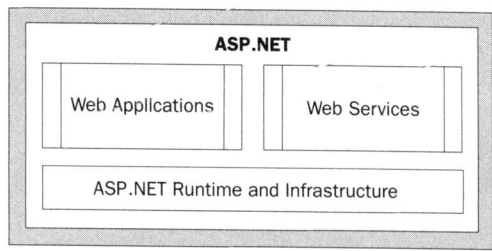

Web Service development has been structured so that design-time controls can be used for developing services quickly and easily. There is a set of server-side controls that are quite similar to standard browser UI components excepting that they run on the server while providing the UI to the browser. In addition there is a set of web controls for those requiring additional complex functionality. The controls have been designed to exhibit client-side intelligence, in that they are able to determine the type of browser that is making the request and return an appropriate UI. For example, a WAP-enabled cell phone will be returned WML as opposed to DHTML. This definitely saves time in programming a consistent interface to any kind of supported client. The proverbial thorn in the web developer's side, session-state management, has been greatly improved upon, even to the extent of supporting clustering and process recycling.

ASP.NET has its own HTTP runtime, which is **not the same as the CLR**. This runtime is multithreaded and asynchronously processes all incoming HTTP Requests. The advantage of it being multithreaded is that one HTTP Request will not tie up the runtime if it is waiting on a resource.

Unlike traditional ASP, due to the multi-language support of .NET, ASP.NET pages do not have to be written in VBScript or Jscript, they can be written in any .NET-supported language.

You can find more information ASP.NET, and how it compares to Java Server Pages, in Chapters 5 and 6.

Windows Forms

Windows Forms are a set of classes within the Base Class Libraries that enable you to build smart-client or Windows-based desktop applications. The idea extends upon the foundation of rapidly building forms-based applications that was laid down with Microsoft Visual Basic. If you have been working with Java Swing or the AWT to build your client front ends, wait until you see this!

This is Microsoft Rapid Application Development (RAD) technology at its best. You can literally whip up a very powerful GUI in about five minutes of dragging and dropping an extensive set of ActiveX Controls (much like Client Java Beans). Adding your application logic is really easy, as with Visual Studio .NET you can create your event handling logic by simply double-clicking on one of your User Interface controls. Once that is done you just simply write code that can draw upon functionality provided by the WinForms class libraries within the event handlers.

Another facet of Windows Forms is that they (like all components of the .NET Framework) have an inherent support of XML Web Services, so writing a desktop or handheld client application that uses XML Web Services to interact with SOAP enabled server components is a piece of cake.

The Common Language Runtime

The **Common Language Runtime (CLR)** is perched neatly on top of the Windows OS and since all .NET Languages are compiled into an intermediate language (IL) that runs on the CLR it is responsible for the run-time conversion of the application into native code. Since the CLR supports more than 24 languages (and counting...), and multiple languages can be used within the same application, another facet the CLR handles is language integration.

The following diagram illustrates the main components of the CLR:

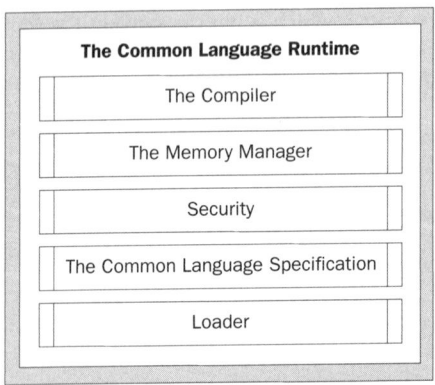

At run time, the CLR provides a set of integral automated services that are designed to make the developer's life easier. These services include memory management, class loading, garbage collection, exception handling, the underlying threading model, and security.

At development time, the CLR makes the developer's life easier by providing handlers for lifetime management, type-naming, cross-language exception handling, delegate-based event management, dynamic binding, and reflection.

In Java, we don't have to worry about memory management or garbage collection since it is automated for us; however, this is a significant leap forward from developing Windows DNA applications. A contentious issue that is often referred to regarding garbage collection in Java, is that the collector cannot be depended upon or forced to clean up objects that are holding memory once you are done with them; those decisions are made by the garbage collection algorithm.

> *An interesting point to note is that since garbage collection can be such a contentious issue, there is also a version of the garbage collector specifically designed for multi-processor architectures. This version of the garbage collector is meant to provide better throughput than using one designed for single processors on a multi-processor box.*

The .NET Framework enables the developer to develop detailed security policies that enable them to apply or deny an extensive and flexible set of privileges to resources and tasks. Because the CLR is responsible for the actual execution of the code it can make run-time decisions on how to enforce these security policies based on criteria such as where the code came from and digital signatures.

Type Safety

One other aspect of the .NET Framework is that it is **type safe**. This means that the .NET Framework tightly controls types so that each variable is marked as being a distinct type. Each type is defined with the **Common Type System** (CTS), which specifies what the type can and cannot do.

This prevents unsafe casting from one data type to another, which is an important aspect when implementing multiple languages in a Framework, as even simple things like a String in Visual Basic are not the same as a String in Visual C++.

The Common Type System

The Common Type System (CTS) defines rules for creating types and also specifies two standard sets of data types, **value types** and **reference types**.

Usually, value data types (which refer to variables and enumerations you declare in your code) are placed on the **stack** and reference data types (which hold object references) are place on the **heap**. If a value data type is declared as a field within a reference type it is then placed on the heap. This is actually quite similar to the way memory is managed in Java.

Data types are object-oriented and are all derived from System.Object in the Base Class Library. Runtime services are used by the .NET compilers to define, create, and execute these data types (as opposed to using a tool- or language-specific method). The fact that all types are common between all the languages enables integration between all the supported languages in .NET. This allows classes written in one language to inherit from classes written in another, and is also why we can catch an exception in a C# class that is thrown by a VB.NET component.

The example below illustrates the data type hierarchy:

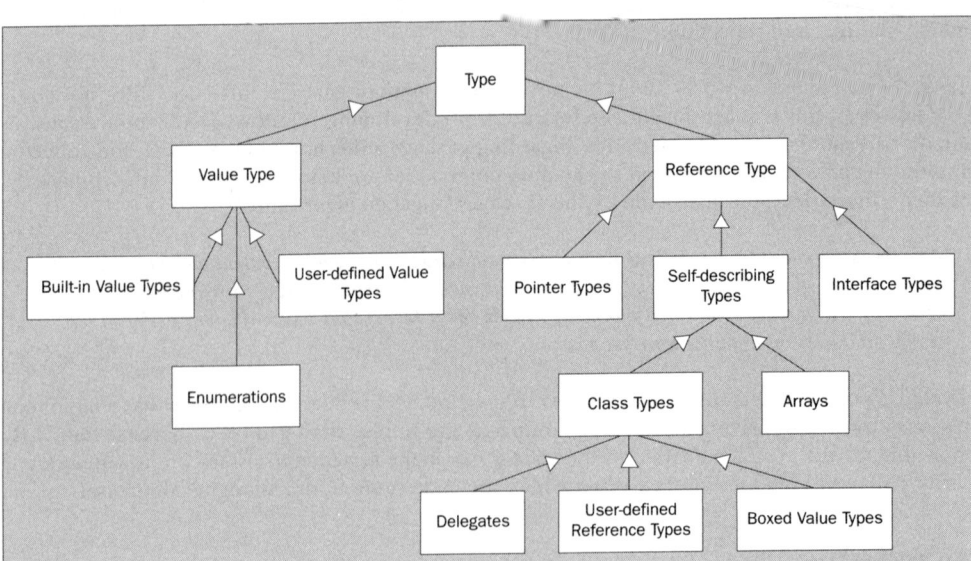

Here's a quick summary of the types. We'll consider value types first:

Value Type	Base class for all value types
Built-in value types	The standard primitive type representing numbers, Boolean values or characters
User-defined value types	Types that have been defined in source code and stored as a value type
Enumerations	Sets of enumerated values

Now the reference types:

Reference Type	Base class for all data types that are accessed through a reference
Self-describing Types	Data types that provide information about themselves for the benefit of the garbage collector
Pointer Types	Pointers, when used in unmanaged code
Interface Types	Interfaces
Class Types	Types that are self-describing but are not arrays
Arrays	Type that contain an array of objects
Delegates	Types that hold references to methods

Reference Type	Base class for all data types that are accessed through a reference
Boxed Value Types	Value types that are temporarily wrapped up in a reference so that they can be stored on the heap
User-Defined Reference Type	Types that have been defined in source code and stored as a reference type

We investigate the difference between value and reference types further in Chapter 3.

Common Language Specification (CLS)

The **Common Language Specification (CLS)** defines a set of language features intrinsic to the .NET Framework. This is the core specification describing what your language needs to adhere to, to compile and execute on the .NET Framework. Visual Basic .NET is a good example of a language that doesn't fully support all the features of MSIL and the Common Type System even though it is fully compliant with CLS. Thus as long as your language is CLS-compliant, the amount of MSIL and CTS you want to support is up to you.

> *If you need to write code that does not support the CLS don't fret. The code will compile, although the MSIL generated is not guaranteed to be language interoperable.*

The JIT Compiler and MSIL

Microsoft Intermediate Language (MSIL) contains the definition of the instruction language and in a general view, is the .NET equivalent to Java Byte Code.

When you compile an application in VB.NET it is actually being compiling to MSIL, which at run time will be compiled by the **just-in-time (JIT) compiler** into native code. For a Java developer, this should be a familiar concept.

The JIT compiler is actually pretty smart though; instead of compiling your whole application into native code on startup, which would involve a wee bit of a wait, it compiles sections of your application, as they are needed. A compiler on demand so to speak.

Managed Code

Code that runs on the .NET Framework is known as **managed code**, and this term describes how the .NET runtime oversees its activities, allocating memory and freeing resources at appropriate intervals automatically (**garbage collection**). The Framework also takes responsibility for ensuring the code does not perform any illegal or dangerous operations, such as accessing the system area of memory.

To this end, it prevents certain operations that it considers risky, including pointer manipulation. Such operations are still possible, however, and in fact the C# language does support pointers. To allow pointer operations, we need to disable type safety checking by marking code with the `unsafe` keyword. Note that such blocks are still managed code, in that they are run under the aegis of the .NET runtime, and so resources are freed automatically when objects go out of scope. See Chapter 3 for more on this keyword.

Chapter 1

The Base Class Libraries

The base class libraries are object-oriented and hierarchically structured to reflect this. At present they are fairly comprehensive and are constantly being added to by Microsoft with the end goal being that the developer can use the library to solve any given development problem.

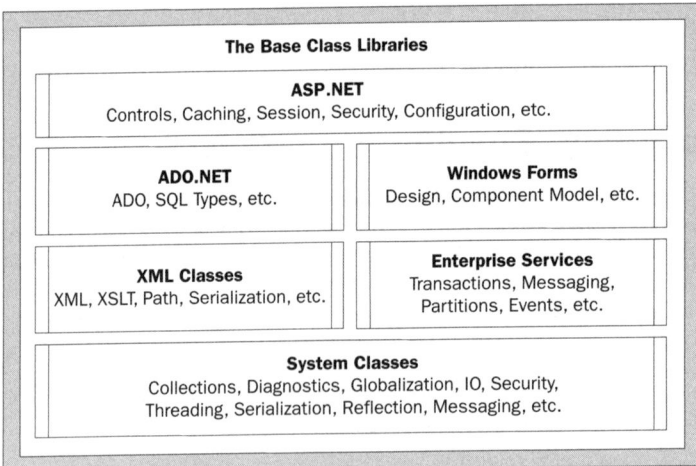

This diagram illustrates some of the key class libraries within the Base Class Library.

The Base Class Library is available to every supported .NET language. Since the developer doesn't actually interact with the runtime, they use this library, which in turn uses the runtime. Some of the key classes are:

- ❑ COM Interoperability
- ❑ Data Access (ADO.NET)
- ❑ Directory Access (replaces ADSI)
- ❑ File System Access
- ❑ Graphics (GDI +)
- ❑ .NET Attributes and Reflection
- ❑ Networking
- ❑ Accessing the Registry
- ❑ Windows-based Services

The objective of the naming standard in the library has been to describe each class as accurately as possible. The naming standard is very similar to naming your classes and packages in Java. The Microsoft 'Dot' Classes (`Microsoft.ComServices`) are what Microsoft has designed and put in the libraries; other vendors could add libraries in the future and they would have their company name in front (`Wrox.CodeSamples`). Keep in mind though, that, just as when creating package names in Java, the actual convention is really up to you.

Another key design aspect that should not be overlooked is that since the libraries are object-oriented, if a particular class doesn't quite have the functionality of what you are looking for, you can inherit from that class's super-classes higher up in the hierarchy and write your own similar class from scratch.

> *Previously, Visual Basic developers used the Visual Basic runtime, Visual C++ developers used the MFC and ATL framework and Visual J++ developers used the Windows Foundation Classes. The .NET Framework unifies all these different classes into the Base Class Library. This in turn makes every supported .NET language an equal player in the .NET Framework since they all have access to the same resources to accomplish a given task.*

Application Models Inside the Class Libraries

These class libraries are what you would expect in the core Sun Java library, and encompass collections, input/output, data types, numerical classes, graphics, threading, networking, globalization, cryptography, data access, and reflection, among others. There are even debugging classes that a development environment can use. For enterprise applications, one can find classes for transactions, events, partitions, and messaging.

There are libraries specifically for .NET applications and building XML Web Services. The WinForms application model (`System.Windows.Forms`) is tightly coupled in design and allows for building more traditional Windows GUI applications. It contains powerful UI components where you can extend ActiveX controls and other windows to create transparent, layered, and floating windows.

The WebForms programming model is loosely coupled and disconnected in design, and allows for building web applications with generally low trust between client and server.

The `System.Data` and `System.Xml` libraries provide data-access ability for SQL queries and for taking the data returned from SQL and very quickly and easily turning it into XML, or HTML that can then be projected to the client to create a UI. This can be for both connected and disconnected data-access models and these libraries are heavily integrated with XML allowing you to view and manipulate your data either as hierarchical XML or as a relational structure. This definitely saves you time from rendering your recordset into XML.

`Microsoft.ComServices` is the library for creating .NET wrappers for existing Win32 COM+ functionality. It enables the developer to leverage automatic transactions, object pooling, and other features, such as queuing.

> *Basically, the further into the architecture you go, the more you may notice that what lies behind all these technologies can be quite different. However, Microsoft has attempted to present them all to the developer in as unified and consistent a manner as possible.*

Assemblies and Manifests

An **assembly** can be one or several files with the core files being executables (`.exe`), Dynamic Linked Libraries (`.dll`) or both. The assembly will contain a **manifest**, which describes the contents of the assembly. The manifest contains the assembly metadata and type metadata. Assembly metadata describes the assembly's properties and external references to other assemblies. Type metadata describes the classes, methods, and properties that are inside the assembly.

We learned earlier that metadata was used by the .NET Framework for describing the component. The metadata within an assembly usually contains the following information:

- Assembly file list
- Referenced assemblies
- Type reference information
- Version information

Assemblies are available in two formats, shared and private.

Private assemblies usually ship with software such as an executable with a number of accompanying libraries and are intended only to be used by that software. The system guarantees that only the intended application may load the accompanying libraries.

Shared assemblies usually would accompany a common library that is intended for use by multiple applications. In order to avoid a recurrence of 'DLL Hell' more precautions are taken to avoid issues such as name collisions (where types from different applications have the same name) and the risk of a newer version of an assembly overwriting an earlier one. Shared assemblies are thus placed inside, and managed by, the global assembly cache (GAC), which is a special folder sub-tree on the file system.

Support for Different Platforms and Architectures

As we mentioned previously there is a standard currently in development with ECMA for a run-time environment based upon .NET called the Common Language Infrastructure.

Once this has become a standard, a runtime could be developed for other platforms – Linux for example. Then applications that run on the CLI on .NET would also be executable upon the Linux version of the CLI.

Transaction Support

Microsoft introduced the Component Object Model (COM) in 1992 as the object model for building reusable components in Windows. COM was later extended into COM+, which was an amalgamation of Microsoft Transaction Server, Distributed COM (DCOM), and several other component services. COM+ is largely used in Windows applications to provide database and object connection pooling and process management. Microsoft .NET uses COM+ as an integral part of the Framework as it provides the component services for building distributable middle-tier applications, which in itself is a core part of the .NET strategy.

> *Most Windows applications incorporate COM to a very large degree and Microsoft has actually made .NET backwards compatible by allowing you to transparently call a .NET Framework component from a COM object written in Visual Studio 6. This works identically in reverse using Visual Studio .NET*

In keeping with ease of use, a .NET Framework developer can make use of COM+ transaction support in their application by simply copying the components that require the functionality into a specific folder. The .NET Framework will then automatically add the components to the COM+ transaction monitor. All of this is done without the developer having to know anything about how COM+ works.

Future Implications of .NET

In my opinion, historically, no new technology has ever stormed the marketplace to such an extent that all other technologies dropped off the face of the earth. XML Web Services offer application developers the ability to select which components they would like to expose as web services, so that moving to .NET XML Web Services can be done at the speed the decision-making parties are comfortable with.

This seems to point to the fact that in the Microsoft realm, there are still going to be standard Windows/Windows DNA applications around for a while, and probably a more gradual move to .NET.

I do feel that there are going to be more and more social or contractual agreements set up between parties interested in leveraging each other's applications and it will be interesting to see how the business model evolves to profit from this. I expect access to web services be sold in a similar manner to licensed software. Will it depend on usage? Reliability, maybe?

A Comparison between J2EE and .NET

Both Sun and Microsoft consider that there is an inordinate amount of 'plumbing' that goes into building web services. Both companies feel that applications should run within a container that handles functionality such as transactions, message queuing, load balancing, and interacting with XML. The difference between the two strategies is therefore a particular vendor's implementation and design of the container.

Firstly, it is important to understand that .NET is first and foremost a **product strategy aiming to become a standard**. J2EE is different in that is **already a standard**, which application server vendors can conform to. Examples of these include IBM WebSphere, Jboss, and BEA WebLogic.

The table below should put things into a rough perspective:

Feature	.NET Implementation	J2EE Implementation
Middleware	Microsoft, with the potential for more to join after ECMA standardization of the Common Language infrastructure	Numerous vendor implementations such as BEA, IBM, Apache, etc.
Runtime Environment	The Common Language Runtime	Java Runtime Environment
Server Side Components	.NET Managed Components	Enterprise Java Beans and Servlets
Data Access	ADO.NET	SQLJ and JDBC
W3C SOAP, WSDL and UDDI Standards	Supported	Supported
Web Service Implementation	.NET Framework	JAXP or 3rd-Party Implementation

Table continued on following page

Feature	.NET Implementation	J2EE Implementation
Dynamic Web Pages	ASP.NET	Java Server Pages
Legacy Support	Microsoft Host Integration Server 2000	J2EE Connector Architecture (JCA)
Platform Support	Presently, only on Microsoft Platforms but plans are afoot for ECMA Standardization for core components of the .NET Framework	Platform agnostic

J2EE Counterattack on .NET

We've now covered the principal strong points of the .NET platform over Java. Both camps have issues regarding the way the other camp have architected their Frameworks, and there is a lot that can be said about Java, so for objectivity's sake I would like to discuss a few of the concerns being raised by the J2EE community about .NET

First and foremost, .NET ties us to the Windows platform. Although plans are afoot to standardize core components of the CLR, there is no actual present alternative implementation.

Support for Electronic Business using eXtensible Markup-Language (ebXML) is notably absent in Microsoft .NET. This is an industry standard that is an extension of the SOAP Specification being piloted by the UN/CEFACT and OASIS. It is a specification to enable complex business transactions using XML, that is, transactions that are more complex than the average SOAP message. While J2EE offers ebXML support, Microsoft offers BizTalk for Business-to-Business communication and one has to wonder whether if will come to the table while BizTalk is still operating with proprietary SOAP extensions.

Although this is really a matter of personal opinion, a lot of members in the J2EE community feel that technology maturity is an important card to have in your hand in this day and age. With J2EE being widely used and .NET being a new technology, they feel that the onus should be placed on Microsoft to prove that the .NET technology is all it says it is.

Legacy support is another contentious issue. The J2EE community feels that the J2EE Connector Architecture (JCA) is superior to MS Host Integration Server 2000 in that the community is developing new adapters into legacy systems all the time, while with Host Integration Server you are tied to what Microsoft provides, and when it provides it.

One riposte from the Java community I find particularly amusing concerns the multi-language support of .NET, comparing it to the Tower of Babel mentioned in the book of Genesis in the Bible. In the story of the Tower of Babel, a huge tower is being built to reach the sky, and development goes along fine while all parties speak the same language. However, at one point, for some reason I forget, the creator decides to cause all parties involved to start speaking different languages, with the result that all parties lose their common organization, and are unable to complete the project.

This really seems to echo the sentiment resounding from certain members of the J2EE community who take the view that multiple languages increase the complexity of a given problem. Some commentators hold the view that it is nice to be able to write an application in your language of choice, or the language that your development team are most familiar with, yet they feel that it is a bad idea to mix more than one language in a single application since it requires additional complexity, maintenance, and overhead.

That seems to me a matter of personal preference but also a possible guideline on how and when to use multi-language support.

The Microsoft Defense

Microsoft views multi-language support as the key feature that Java J2EE does not have. The fact that absolutely everything in .NET is interoperable via XML is seen as an added bonus, and in addition Microsoft feels that Java lacks the support for web services that it provides.

Microsoft has provided a framework for enabling, as a Web Service, absolutely anything that is executable – even a Windows Service. The tool for building web services is another key feature it holds to be superior. Microsoft maintains that Visual Studio .NET is the best development tool on the market hands down, for any kind of application development. This is key in MS's view, as the IDE is what the developer works with on a day-to-day basis, and it has a real ability to enhance productivity.

Summary

Microsoft .NET is all about building Web Services, in a type-safe, multi-language environment that provides you with a great tool for getting your applications quickly to the market.

The underlying system services handle a lot of the 'plumbing' that usually takes developers a considerable amount of time debugging, and the .NET Framework with Visual Studio .NET makes development just plain easy.

I am sure that you are going to have a lot of fun reading through the following chapters in the book and seeing just how easy all of this really is. I am personally rather glad that Microsoft has come out with .NET; whether you like it or not, it has definitely brought some innovation to the market which will keep all the other vendors on their toes – which can only be a good thing for us developers.

Regardless of how you, the J2EE community, may feel about Microsoft, it is hard to refute that it has always been great at providing tools and technologies that are really easy to use. I am sure that once you've gone through the examples in the following chapters, you will share the same sentiment about its latest technology strategy.

Happy coding.

Development Tools

A range of development tools have been produced to assist developers creating software on the .NET Framework. The aim of this chapter is to introduce some of the options available to you, namely:

- Notepad
- Visual Studio .NET
- Web Matrix
- Macromedia DreamWeaver MX
- Sharp Develop

In this chapter, we'll give you a quick insight into the appearance, capabilities, and features of all of these. However, of most interest to us are Notepad and Visual Studio .NET, as these are the environments that we will be using throughout the remainder of this book to develop our examples, and illustrate concepts. For these two we'll go into a little more detail, and demonstrate working 'Hello World' type examples, that you can follow if you wish to get up to speed before moving on to language syntax in Chapter 3.

Let's begin with the oldest, simplest (and some would say best) development environment around – Notepad coupled with a command-line compiler!

Notepad and csc.exe

Notepad provides:

- Simplicity of interface
- Total control of how your code is structured

Notepad (or another text editor of your choice) is the most common tool used by most of Java programmers. Fortunately, like Java, .NET does not mandate the use of any specific development tool, and you can simply write your code in a text file, save it with the correct extension, compile with the appropriate compiler (or deploy if necessary), and run. In this section we will create a simple 'Hello World' console application to demonstrate.

The Console Application

This is a simple console application that says hello to the person whose name is passed as command-line argument, or prints a "Hello World!" message on the console if no argument is passed.

Enter the following program as a text file and save it with a `.cs` extension. Unlike Java, the name of the `.cs` file need **not** be same as the name of the public class in the file. Let us save this file as `TestApp.cs`.

> Be careful not to pick up a `.txt` affix to your file while saving – Notepad will do this automatically in the Save dialogue, unless you choose All files in the Save as type box.

```
using System;

public class MyFirstConsoleApplication
  {
    static void Main(string[] args)
    {
      if (args.Length == 0)
        Console.WriteLine("Hello World !");
      else
        Console.WriteLine("Hello "+ args[0] +" !");
    }
  }
```

Running the Application

You can now compile the above application using the `csc` compiler from the command prompt:

> `csc TestApp.cs`

This generates a `TestApp.exe` file in the folder from which the command was run. Run the application by invoking the executable from command prompt:

```
C:\>csc TestApp.cs
Microsoft (R) Visual C# .NET Compiler version 7.00.9466
for Microsoft (R) .NET Framework version 1.0.3705
Copyright (C) Microsoft Corporation 2001. All rights reserved.

C:\>TestApp Mike
Hello Mike !

C:\>TestApp
Hello World !

C:\>
```

Visual Studio .NET

Visual Studio .NET is Microsoft's complete Integrated Development Environment (IDE) for creating the whole span of .NET applications. Using this tool you can create everything from ASP.NET web applications, to VB.NET and J# desktop applications, with XML web services in between. It supports the complete range of .NET languages, and allows them to share common tools and facilities for the creation of mixed language solutions.

Visual Studio .NET is a vast IDE, and easily a book in itself (it is, in fact – *Effective Visual Studio .NET*, ISBN 1-86100-696-9). We'll be using Visual Studio .NET throughout this book, but we've got a lot to cover in this chapter, so for the moment, we'll only give you a quick overview. You'll find more details of how to design and build, in the relevant chapters throughout the book.

Web Forms

Web Forms is an ASP.NET technology that allows you to create programmable web pages using the drag-and-drop design facility, and then write the code for the event handlers afterwards. The web forms can be viewed on any browser, and on any platform, as they render themselves as browser-targeted HTML and script code.

Windows Forms

Windows Forms is a .NET Framework-based technology used for Windows application development. Rich and sophisticated Windows applications can be developed using extensible sets of classes provided by the .NET Framework. It also provides a simple drag/drop architecture for GUI building.

XML Support

XML (Extensible Markup Language) provides techniques for describing structured data. Visual Studio .NET provides tools for designing XML schemas and editing XML documents. It also provides inbuilt support for data transfer between different tiers of an *n*-tier application. Even its database access is provided through XML documents, allowing unprecedented flexibility in the manner, and structure, in which you can store and retrieve your information.

Web Services

Web services are a new technology that allows an application to call methods on remote objects using XML SOAP over HTTP. Web service applications are not tied to any particular component technology and can be accessed by any language, component model, or platform. Visual Studio .NET provides wizards that help you create the proxies required for effective web service communication quickly and easily.

To introduce you to a few of the features of Visual Studio .NET we will now consider the development of a simple application.

Creating a Windows Application

In this section we will learn how to use the Visual Studio .NET IDE to create a Windows-based "Hello World" application, rather similar to the one we create previously in Notepad.

First of all, start up Visual Studio .NET, and select the **New Project** menu option in the **File** menu to create a new project. This will open the **New Project** dialog box shown below. Select **Visual C# Projects**. (We will use C# to create all the projects discussed in this chapter.)

> Note: When you create a new project in Visual Studio, first it creates a new solution to house the project. You can also add projects to existing solutions.
>
> Solutions are containers of related projects and associated items that can build into a complete application. It allows you to work on multiple related projects in a single IDE instance.

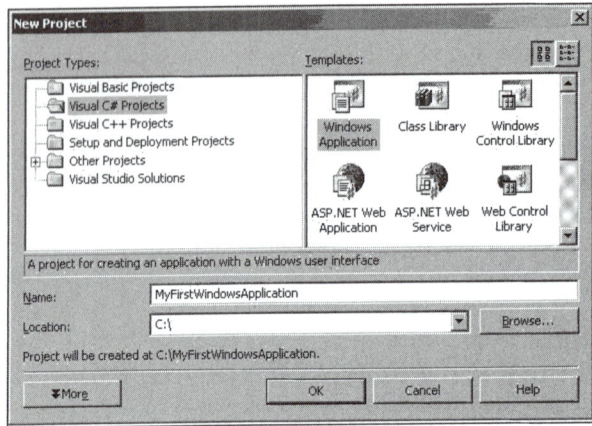

You will find several types of project under this option. Select **Windows Application** and supply a name for the application that you are creating. Click **OK**.

Visual Studio .NET will generate a new project, complete with all necessary auxiliary files. It also adds a blank form named **Form1.cs** and generates the source code for it:

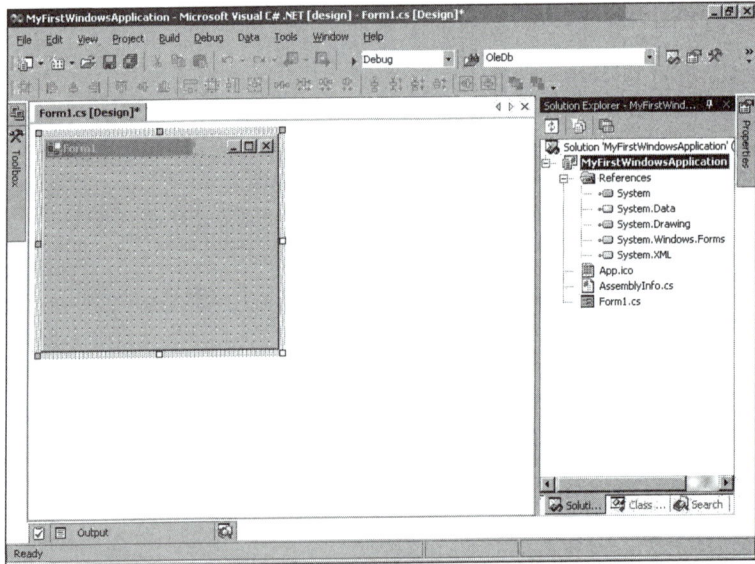

Development Tools

The highlighted window on the right-hand side is the **Solution Explorer**. It shows details about the projects in the current solution.

The IDE also creates an `AssemblyInfo.cs` file that describes the project's assembly and versioning information. The Common Language Runtime uses the information stored in this file for type resolution.

Finally, Visual Studio .NET adds the `System`, `System.Data`, `System.Drawing`, `System.Windows.Forms`, and `System.XML` namespace references to your form by default.

> A namespace is similar to a Java package. Namespaces are discussed further in the next chapter.

Adding Components

Visual Studio .NET allows you to conduct almost all of your design work in a 'point-and-click' manner, by dragging components onto your form from the Toolbox. To do this, open the Toolbox by simply moving the mouse over the Toolbox icon in the IDE (alternatively you can select the **Toolbox** menu option in the View menu). You will see a palette as shown here:

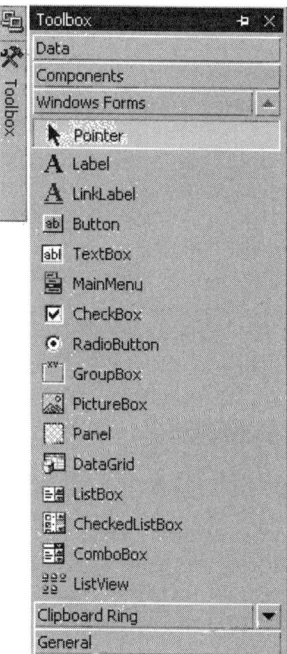

The Toolbox contains several components for developing GUIs. Simply select the component and drag it onto your form. Alternatively, double-click items, and they will be added to the top-right corner of the currently selected container on the form.

35

Chapter 2

For our application we will put a `TextBox` and a `Button` on the form:

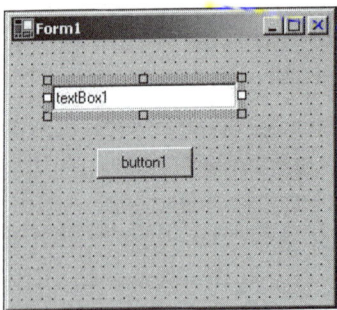

Setting Control Properties

Every control exposes several properties that can be set using the Properties window in Visual Studio .NET at design time. You can open the this window using the **Properties** icon, by pressing *F4,* or by selecting the **View | Properties Window** menu option:

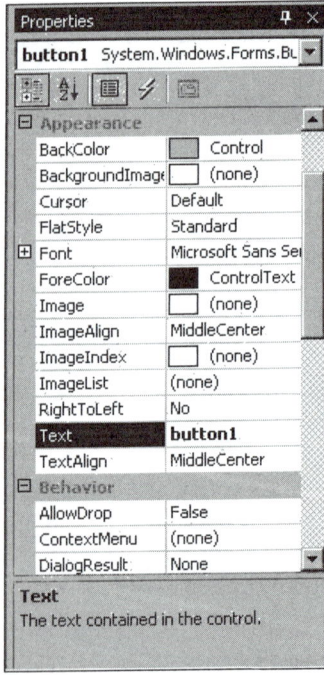

In this window, change the `Text` property of the `Button` to `Click Me`. Behind the scenes, this will change the `Text` property of the `Button` control, as we'll see in Chapter 8.

> All objects, including the page itself, have properties that can be accessed through the **Properties** window.

Development Tools

Writing Up the Button_Click Event Handler

Our application will simply display **Hello World!** in the textbox when we click the button. For this to happen, we need to define an event handler for the `Click` event of the Button control.

As you probably know, events are the way that one object is able to provide notification to another that something has happened. Event handlers are the code that is executed by objects to deal with events that arise.

Visual Studio .NET provides a very easy way to do this. Select the **Events** icon in the **Properties** window and provide the handler name for the `Click` event as shown in the following screenshot:

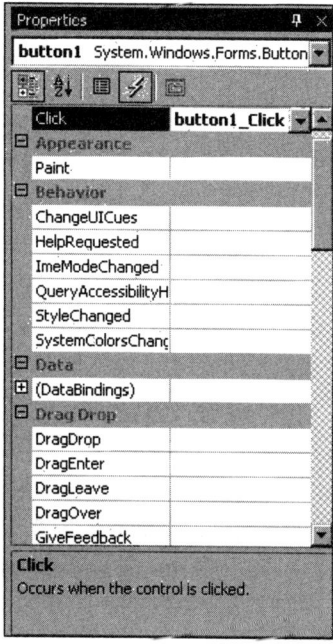

When you press *Enter* this will display the event handler as shown in following screen. Alternatively double click on the button and it will automatically add the `button1_click` event handler in `Form1.cs` file:

```
private void button1_click(object sender, System.EventArgs e)
{

}
```

Visual Studio .NET does the registration of the event handler with the `Click` event automatically for you. If you look higher up in the code page that has appeared, you will find code similar to the fragment below:

```
button1.Click += new System.EventHandler(this.button1_Click);
```

Chapter 2

Now that the handler has been created, we are in a position to add our "Hello World" logic by entering the following information between the braces of the event handler:

```
textBox1.Text = "Hello World !";
```

Your page should now look something like this:

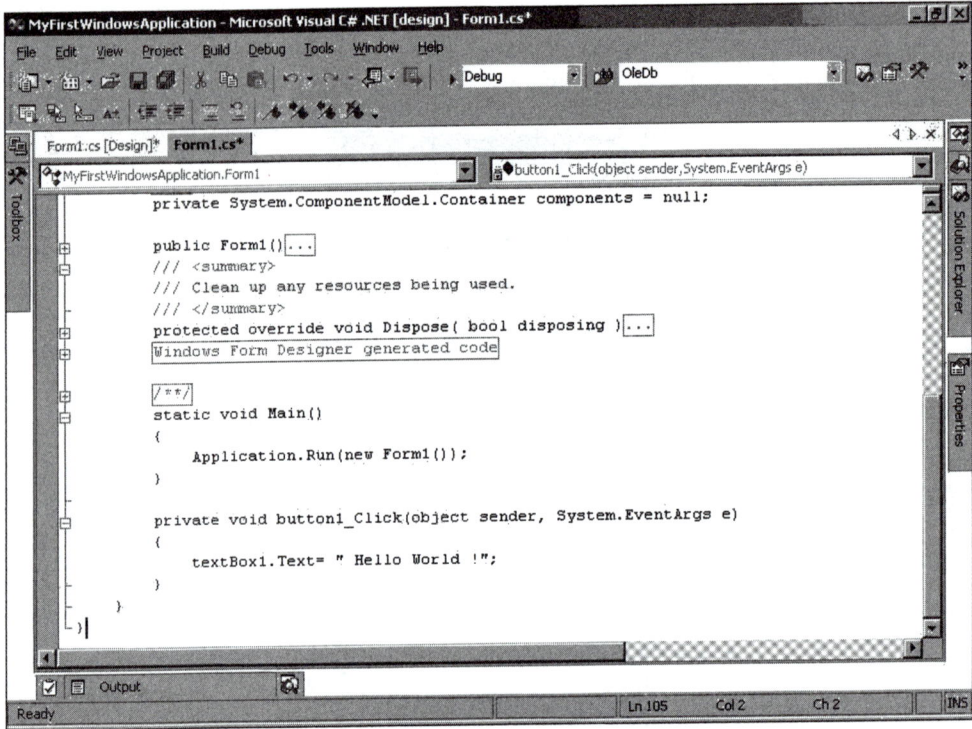

Building and Running the Application

Now that we've created our GUI, and hooked it up to our logic, all that remains is to build and run our application. To do this, select the Build | Build Solution menu option to build the application or alternatively press *Ctrl+Shift+B*.

Once the application is built successfully you can run it by selecting Start *(or pressing F5)*. This will also build the application again if there have been any modifications since the last build. Once this is done, the application will run in **Debug** mode. You can select Start without Debug (or press *Ctrl+F5*) to run without the debug safeguards.

If there are any errors while building your application, the task list box at the bottom of your screen will automatically appear, showing the list of errors along with their descriptions.

Hopefully, if you've followed the example correctly, your application will run properly, and look something like this when you click the button:

Development Tools

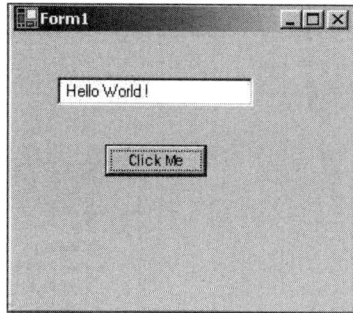

Hopefully this simple example will have given you an insight into how easy it is to develop Windows applications on the .NET platform using Visual Studio .NET. We'll move along quickly now, to see how easy it is to create applications for the Web.

Creating Web Applications with VS.NET

In this section we will create an ASP.NET application using the Visual Studio .NET IDE. This is the easiest, fastest, and most reliable way of creating ASP .NET web applications on the platform to date.

Visual Studio .NET provides:

- ❏ A visual designer for web pages with drag-and-drop controls and code views
- ❏ An intelligent code editor that includes statement completion, syntax checking, and other smart features
- ❏ Project management facilities for creating, managing, and deploying files on local and remote machines

Creating a New Project

You can create ASP.NET applications in the Visual Studio .NET IDE just as you would Windows applications. Open the **New Project** dialog box and select **ASP.NET Web Application**. This will create the web application on Microsoft's IIS server on your local system (http://localhost/) by default. Alternatively you can specify the name of the server on which you want to create the web application.

For these examples to run, you need to make sure IIS is installed, and up and running correctly.

At the time of project creation, Visual Studio .NET creates a folder with the name of your application in IIS's public web folder (by default `..\inetpub\wwwroot`) and copies the relevant files there. It also connects to your web server and creates a virtual folder for the application. Your client browser can access the web pages from this folder.

The following screenshot shows the `MyFirstWebApplication` opened in Visual Studio .NET along with the Solution Explorer showing all the wizard-generated files. By default it creates a `WebForm` with name `WebForm1.aspx` (just as it automatically generated `Form.cs` for us in the previous example):

39

Chapter 2

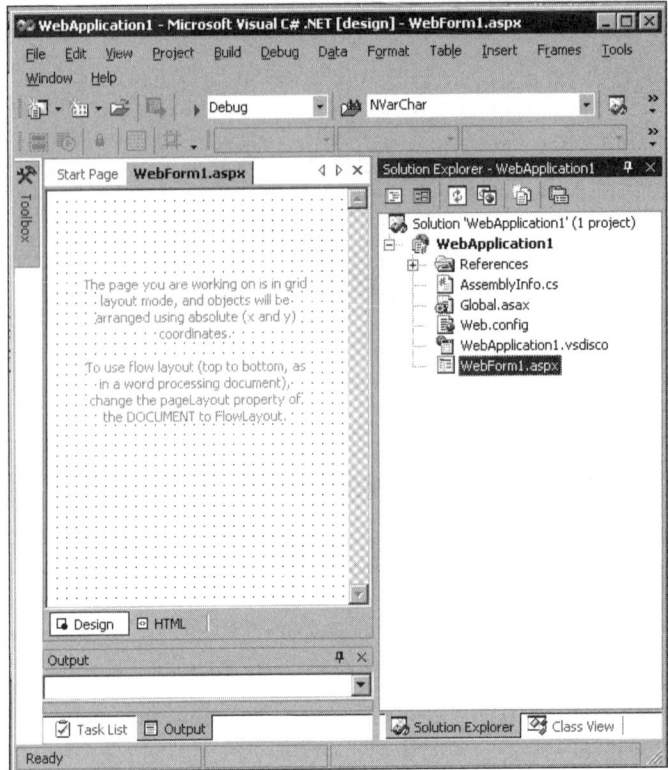

The wizard creates several files during the project creation process. These files are:

- **AssemblyInfo.cs** – This file contains general information about the assembly that is created for the project. Various assembly attributes such as AssemblyTitle, AssemblyDescription, AssemblyCopyright, AssemblyVersion, etc. are defined in this file.

- **[application name].vsdisco** – Refers to any web service added to the project. It is an XML file and contains informational links about an ASP.NET web service. We will talk about web services in detail in Chapter 7.

- **global.asax** – Similar to the original Global.asa file in ASP 3.0. This file is optional and if present contains the code for application-level event handlers. At runtime, this gets compiled to IL. If you modify this file, ASP.NET completes all current requests for the application and restarts the application domain after sending the Application_OnEnd event to existing listeners. At the next client request, the file is re-compiled to new IL code.

- **web.config** – This file consists of information related to application settings. These settings include assembly binding policy, remoting objects, custom channels, security, and other settings that the application can read at runtime.

- **[application name].aspx** – A Form where the user interface or HTML code is defined.

Development Tools

- ***[application name].aspx.cs*** – This is the code-behind file for the web form. You will not find this in the project list. When you right-click on the form in the design view and select **View Code** you will see this file. Alternatively you can click the **View Code** button in Solution Explorer.
- **App.ico** – This icon file contains the icon for your application. You can modify this file using Visual Studio .NET as it provides an excellent tool for creating graphical icons.

If you look back to the previous screenshot, you will see that it shows two tags at the bottom: **Design** and **HTML**. By default, the ASPX file is opened in **Design** mode. In **Design** mode you can design the web page by directly dropping the controls from the Toolbox. If you click on the **HTML** tag you'll see the HTML code generated for the current web form.

Designing the User Interface

You can create your user interface in just the same way as you did for your Windows application. Simply select controls from the Toolbox and drag them onto your web form. You can also modify their properties in the same manner:

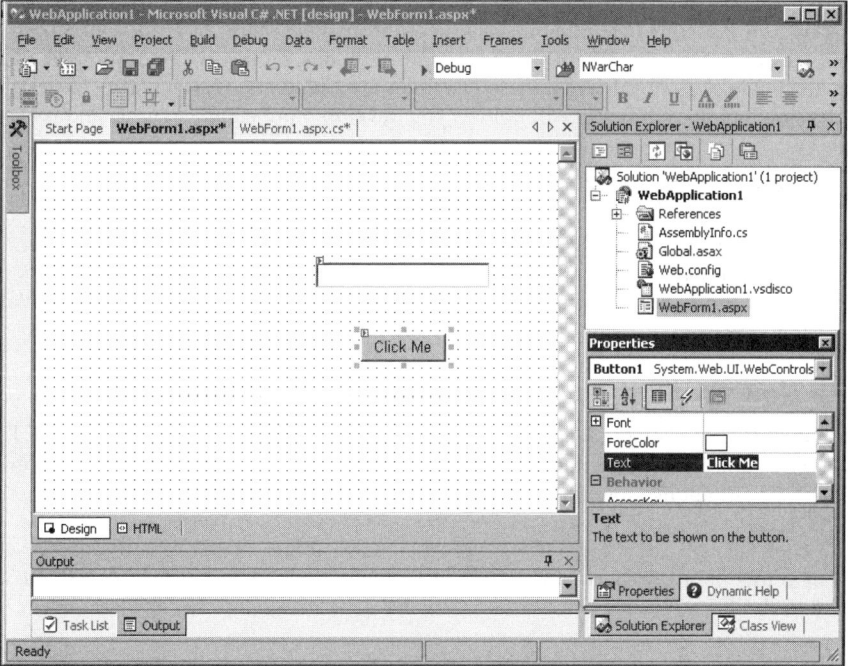

Writing Code

The next step is to add the program code in the **code behind page**, similarly to how we did in the previous example. The difference is that in ASP.NET, the HTML code that creates the controls is separate from the file that houses code for the controls. Hence the name "code behind", however it is possible to use inline ASP.NET code blocks within the HTML should you wish.

Back to our example – find the event handler for the `Button` control and add the following code:

```
private void Button1_Click(object sender, System.EventArgs e)
{
  TextBox1.Text = "Hello World !";
}
```

Deploying and Running the Application

Build the application with Visual Studio .NET by pressing *Ctrl+Shift+B*. This will build and deploy the application. Now you can run it by pressing *F5*, which will open the browser with the web form's URL:

http://localhost/[yourapplication's name]/WebForm1.aspx

The results are similar to the previous example, so we'll leave it to you to see how they are rendered in your browser. (Hint: try it on a PDA if you've got one, and look at the difference in the HTML. We'll discuss this more in Chapters 5 and 6.)

Hopefully by now you'll be beginning to see one of the great strengths of the Visual Studio .NET IDE. We've just created two very different types of application, but the way we've developed and executed them has been almost identical. True, these examples are trivial, but this similarity of design is a key feature of Visual Studio .NET, and will hold as you develop more complex applications as well.

Creating an ASP.NET Web Service

Let's create one more application with Visual Studio .NET, before moving on to briefly consider what other development environments are available for you on the .NET platform. Once again, create a new project in Visual Studio .NET, and under the **Visual C# Projects** type, select **ASP.NET Web Service**. This will, again, create your skeleton code, ready for you to begin development.

Creating a New Project

Open the **New Project** dialog in Visual Studio .NET. Select **Visual C# Projects | ASP.NET Web Service**. You will have to specify the name of your project and the URL for the web server where you want to deploy your application (the default is **http://localhost/** as before).

When you click **OK**, a Visual Studio .NET wizard creates a folder in the `../Inetpub/wwwRoot` directory of your system, and a corresponding virtual folder on IIS, just as for the ASP.NET web application we built earlier.

Development Tools

You're then presented with a screen that looks something like this:

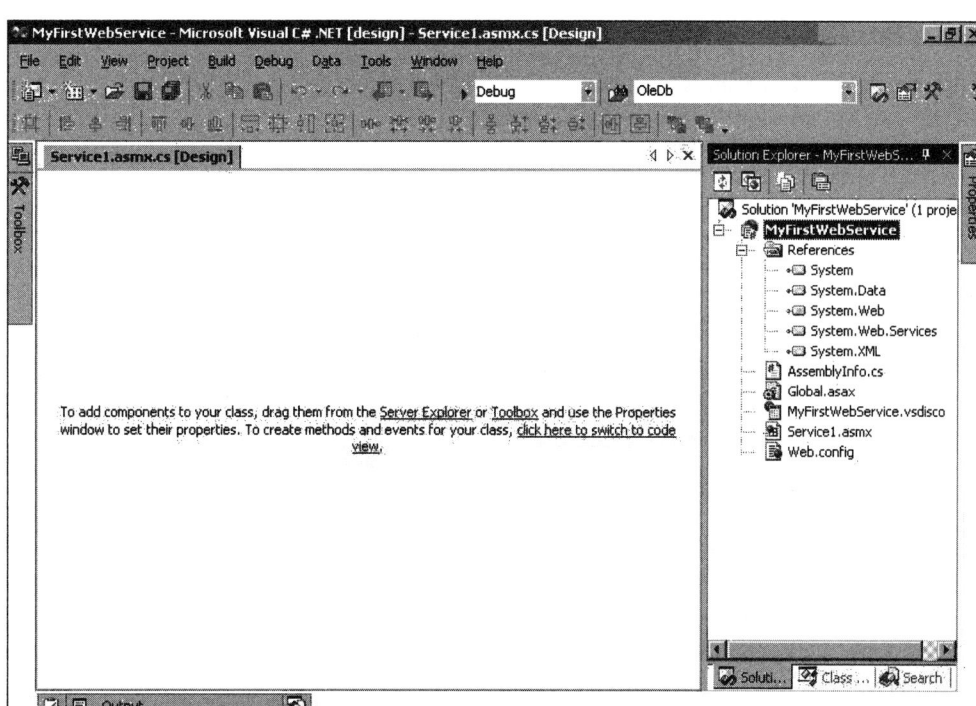

Wizard Generated Files

Once the project is created, you will find that the IDE has generated the following files:

- **AssemblyInfo.cs** – This file contains general information about the project assembly.
- **global.asax** – This is similar to the Global.asa file in ASP 3.0 Framework, and performs the same functions as for the ASP.NET web application.
- **Service1.asmx** – This file is important to us. We will modify this file to implement our service methods.
- **web.config** – This file consists of information related to application settings. The application settings are specific to each application. These settings include, session state configuration, assembly binding policy, remoting objects and custom channels. The application can read the settings from this file at runtime.
- **[yourapplicationname].vsdisco** – This file provides service location information in XML format.

43

Chapter 2

Writing the Web Method

As we saw in the previous screenshot, the IDE opens the ASMX file in design mode. But since web services do not have a GUI, we have to shift immediately to code view. Do that now, and adapt the pre-prepared web service as follows:

```
[WebMethod]
public string HelloWorld()
{
  return "Hello World";
}
```

Here's a screenshot of what it should look like:

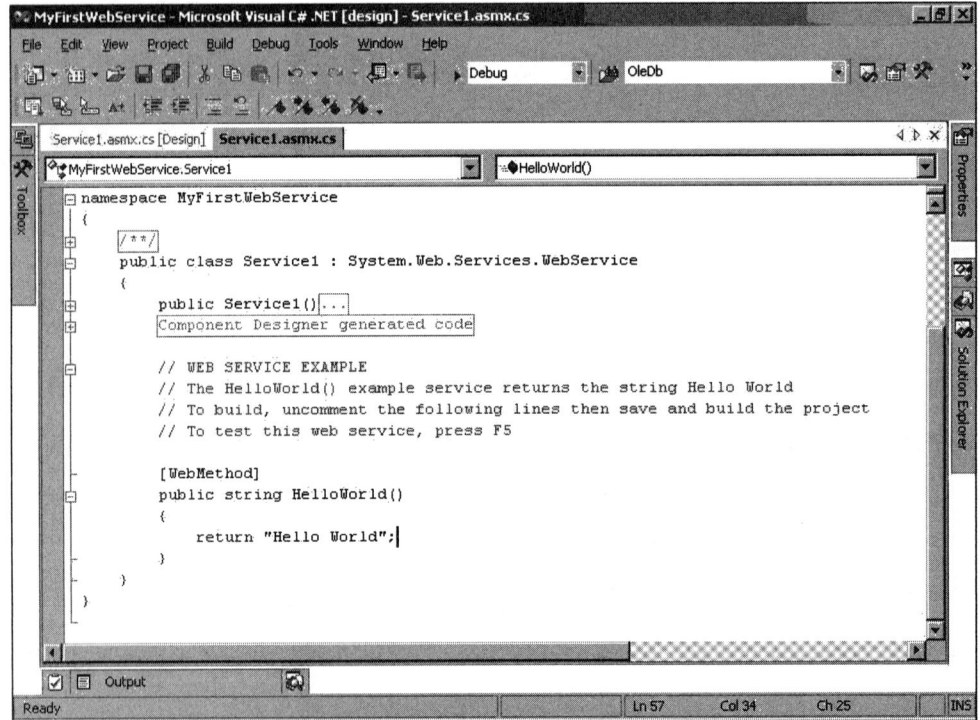

Note the [WebMethod] attribute at the top of the method definition, which tells the ASP.NET runtime that the subsequent method is a web method.

> *The IDE creates the* HelloWorld *web method by default. This simple web method that returns the message* Hello World *is initially commented, so uncomment it. VS.NET provides a button on the toolbar for uncommenting multiple lines at once.*

Running the Web Service

After you have designed and implemented the business logic for the service you can compile and deploy it on the server. Press *Ctrl+Shift+B* to build and deploy the service. Run the application by pressing *F5*:

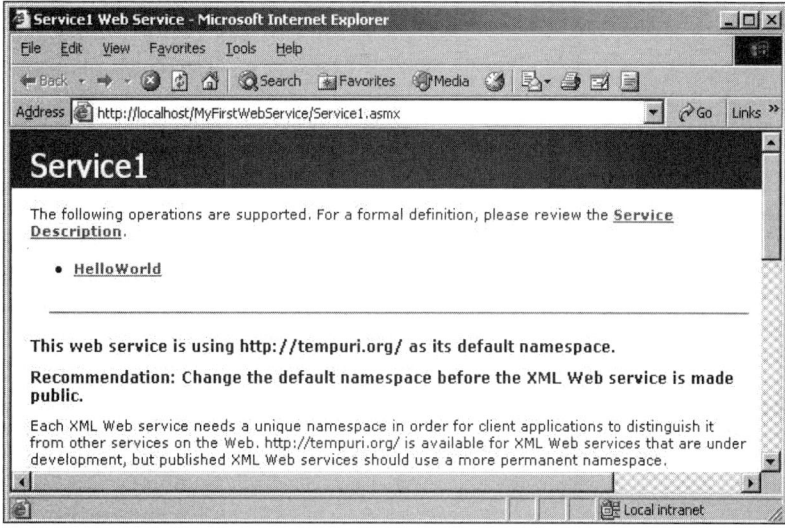

The Service1.asmx file contains the information about the service along with links to both the service and the service description (WSDL file).

Click the method name to test the service. The browser displays a new page with an **Invoke** button. The page will display textboxes for each parameter that the web method takes. Since the HelloWorld service doesn't take any parameters, only an **Invoke** button is displayed. Press the button to invoke the service:

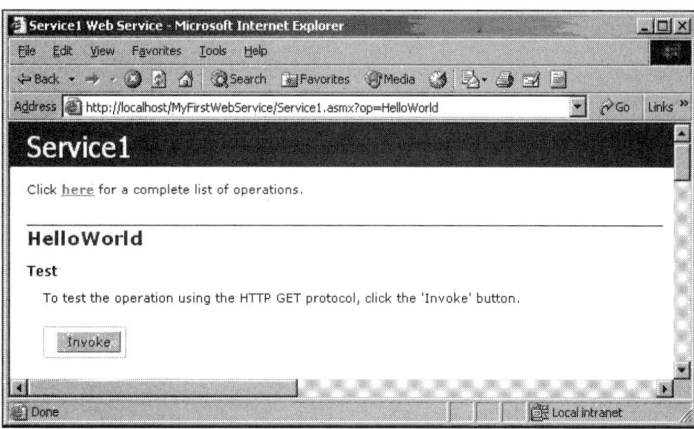

This calls the web service's method, and returns the result in XML format, as shown here:

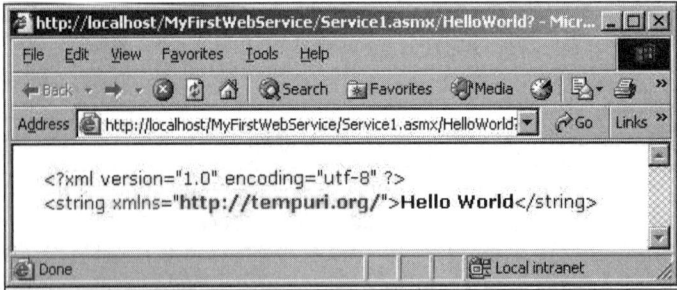

Creating a Consumer Application

Once a service is created and deployed, it may be registered with UDDI (Universal Description, Discovery, and Integration). One such directory where your exposed service may be registered for clients to locate is available at www.uddi.org. The UDDI directory maintains a link to your WSDL file that the client can download in order to request the desired service.

In this section, we will develop a GUI-based client application that consumes our web service.

Begin by creating a standard Windows application named **CSharpClient** and open Solution Explorer. Right-click on the **Reference** node, and select **Add Web Reference**.

This opens the Add Web Reference dialog. This can either connect directly to the UDDI registry to search for new web services, or you can specify the address of a known web service in the address box:

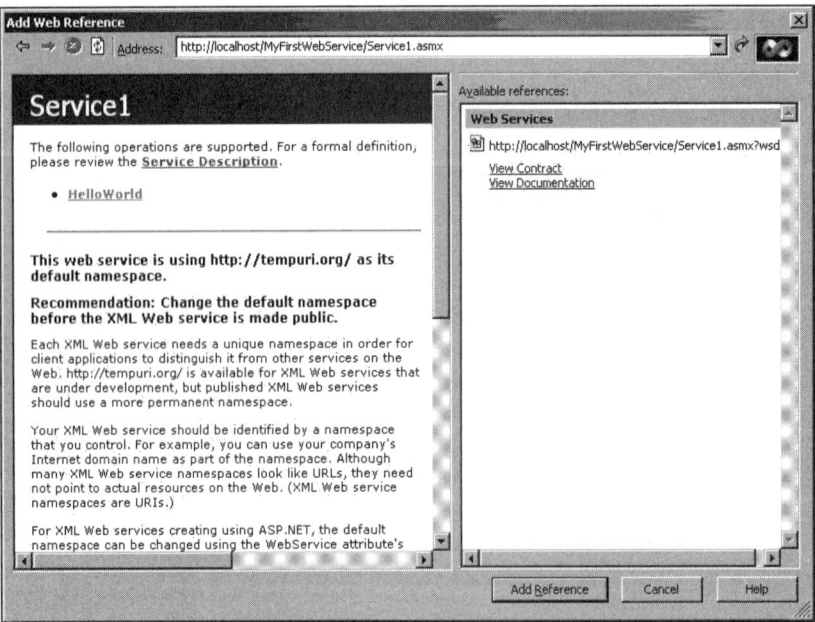

Development Tools

Navigate to your web service. The easiest way is to run the web service in another instance of VS.NET with *F5*, and copy and paste the URL from the browser address box. We then see details about our web service as shown in the above screenshot. Click on the **Add Reference** button to add a reference to the web service in your project. When you do, the IDE will add some new files to your project:

Invoking the Web Method

Now that you've created a reference to the web service, the next step is to invoke it. In our application we will simply add a button and a textbox to our Form. We will invoke the `HelloWorld` web service on button `Click` and display the result in the textbox as we did in the regular web application sample earlier.

Add the following code for the `button1_Click` event handler:

```
private void button1_Click(object sender, System.EventArgs e)
{
  localhost.Service1 s = new localhost.Service1();
  textBox1.Text = s.HelloWorld();
}
```

> Note `localhost` is the default name for the namespace containing web services on the local machine. If the web service is running on a remote machine, its URL, in reverse, will be used by default. The name can be changed to something more memorable through Solution Explorer if desired.

`Service1` is the name of the proxy class. You just need to create the instance of the proxy class and invoke the method on it.

Now run the application by pressing *F5*.

Once the application has been built, you should see something resembling the following. The web service has been consumed by your client, and displayed in the textbox:

47

Debugging in Visual Studio.NET

In the previous section, we discussed application development using Visual Studio .NET. In this section, we will have a brief discussion of debugging. The Visual Studio .NET IDE uses traditional principles and processes including setting breakpoints and examining the values of variables. This is very similar to how things were done in its predecessor, Visual Studio 6.0.

Breakpoints

You can set a breakpoint on any line of program code. The easiest way is to click on the gray margin area on the left of the code editor window. This will highlight the adjacent code line in red, indicating a breakpoint has been set. Alternatively select the line and press *F9*. The following screenshot shows a breakpoint added for the first line in the `btnAdd_Click` method. To remove this breakpoint click on the same position in the shaded area, or select the line and press *F9* again.

```
private void btnAdd_Click(object sender, System.EventArgs e)
{
    int num1= Int32.Parse(txtNumber1.Text);
```
At Form1.cs, line 121 character 4 ('WindowsApplicationDebug.Form1.btnAdd_Click(object sender,System.EventArgs e)', line 3)
```
    txtSum.Text= sum.ToString();
}
```

Sometimes setting a simple breakpoint may not be adequate; and you may need to use conditional breakpoints. These will stop execution only if a given condition is satisfied.

To do this select the Debug | New Breakpoint menu option. This opens the **New Breakpoint** dialog box that provides several options for setting conditional breakpoints. Once the breakpoint is set the program execution will halt at the particular line where the condition is met.

Watches

While in break mode, the simplest way to see the values of program items is to move the mouse cursor over the desired variable in the code editor; its value will then appear in a pop-up Tooltip. Alternatively use the **Watch window** by selecting Debug | Windows | Watch:

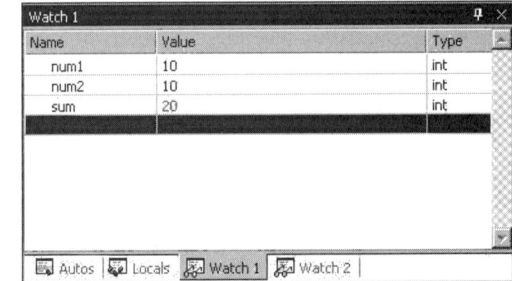

The window has three tabs: Autos, Locals, and Watch. Autos monitors last the few variables that were accessed by the program. Locals monitors all variables accessible to the currently running method, while Watch monitors any variables that you have explicitly added.

Development Tools

That concludes our coverage of Visual Studio .NET, arguably the most comprehensive .NET development tool available at the present time. We will now go on to quickly discuss some of the other development environments that are available to you.

WebMatrix

As we mentioned in the previous sections, Microsoft provides an excellent development tool in the form of Visual Studio .NET for all-round .NET development. However, it's a large package, and can be quite expensive in some configurations.

Microsoft Web Matrix on the other hand is a free download, and designed for web-based application development. It supports the ASP.NET runtime as well as some .NET languages (such as C# and VB.NET). It is available from http://www.asp.net/webmatrix/

The Interface

The interface is very similar to Visual Studio .NET, with minor changes. The main difference is that Web Matrix supports only web application development while Visual Studio .NET also supports Windows and console applications.

When you open Web Matrix, and get past the splash screen, you'll see the following options:

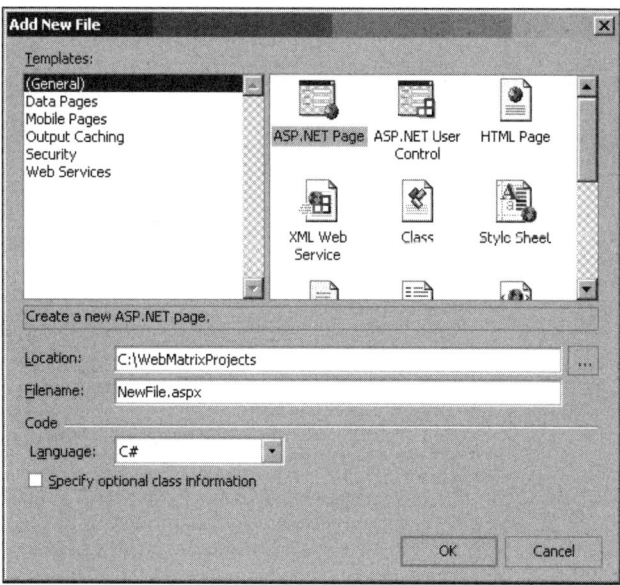

Before starting a project in Web Matrix, check the documentation to make sure that it has the functionality to complete the processes that you require.

Chapter 2

Web Matrix Features and Language Support

Web Matrix provides simplified document formats for web-based development. The supported languages for ASP.NET development are C# and VB.NET. **As of the time of writing C# and VB.NET are the only supported languages for the Web Matrix tool.** For this discussion we will split Web Matrix's features into the following two sections:

- Design
- Coding

Design

Let's begin by looking at the design features that are provided by the tool. In brief they are:

- Workspace
- Toolbox
- Properties

At first glance, these may look quite familiar because they're modeled on the layout of Visual Studio .NET. We'll discuss them briefly now:

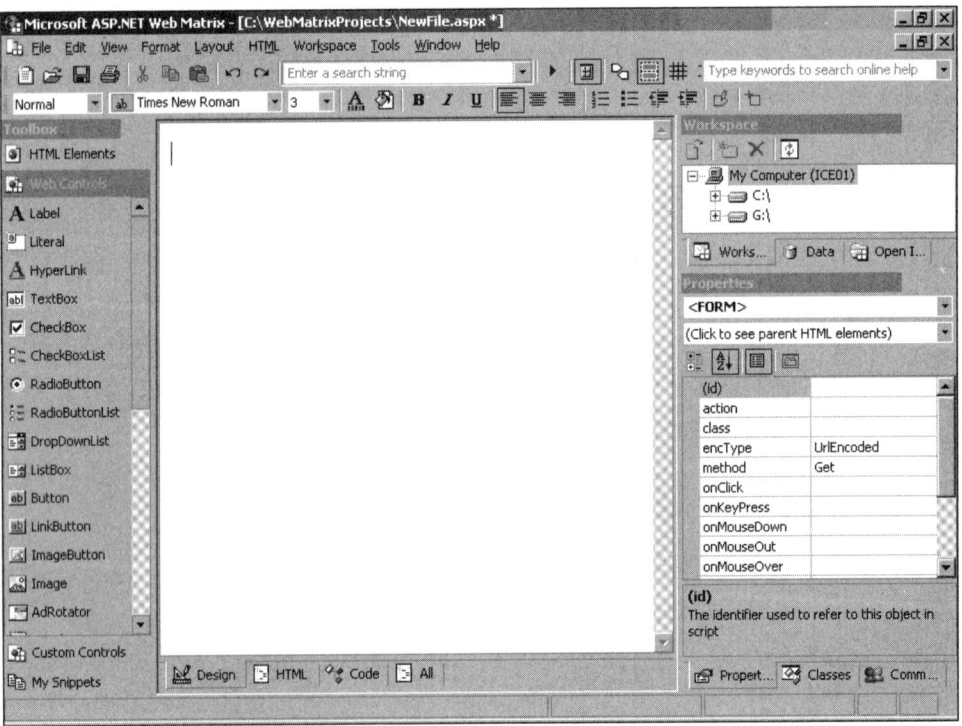

Development Tools

The top right window in the above screenshot is the Workspace window. It has three tabs: **Workspace**, **Data** and **Open Items**:

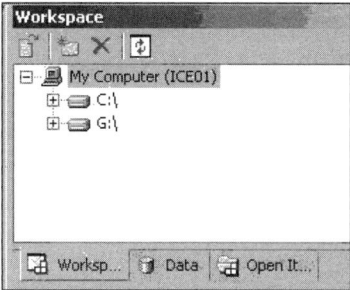

The workspace is the machine on which the developer is working. The **Data** tab represents the connections made by the tool to any databases and **Open Items** lists the project files currently in use.

Data Tab

Using the **Data** tab we can configure any database servers that are available. The tab provides us with items (represented using icons) such as **New Connection**, **New Items**, **Edit**, **Query**, **Delete** and **Close Connection**.

> *Web Matrix's connections and interfaces are quite intuitive, and the details of their operation are beyond the scope of what we can achieve in this brief chapter. However, if you're interested in using Web Matrix as a development tool, you might find it useful to download the free Wrox Press PDF book from the http://www.asp.net/webmatrix/ homepage.*

51

Open Items Tab

The open items tab lists all files currently in use:

Toolbox

The Toolbox contains the GUI controls and components that can be used for creating an ASP.NET application. It has four subsets **HTML Elements, Web Controls, Custom Controls,** and **MySnippets**. Controls can be dragged-and-dropped onto the Form in just the same way as in Visual Studio .NET:

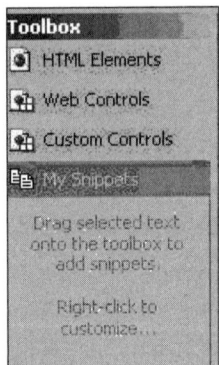

Development Tools

The contents of the first two menus are self explanatory, and don't differ significantly from Visual Studio .NET. Bear in mind that the controls marked HTML aren't dynamic, while those marked Web Controls are ASP.NET controls, and therefore are dynamic:

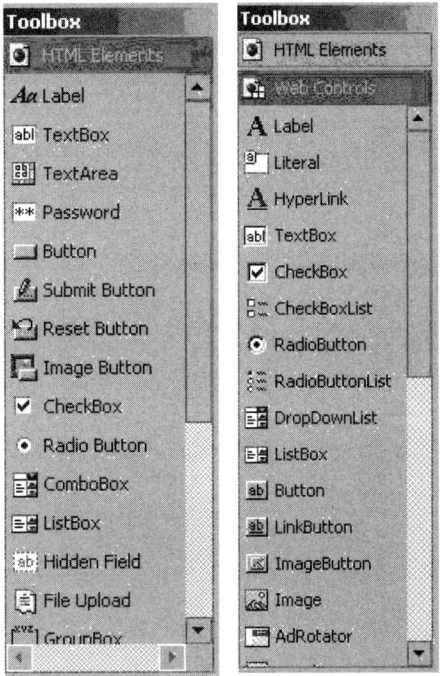

Custom Controls and My Snippets

These tabs represent the controls designed and created by you, the developer. the **My Snippets** tab provides a place where we can store code or other text for easy access later. Simply drag-and-drop selected text onto the Snippets tab. This is a unique feature of Web Matrix, which isn't available in its big brother, Visual Studio .NET, at the moment:

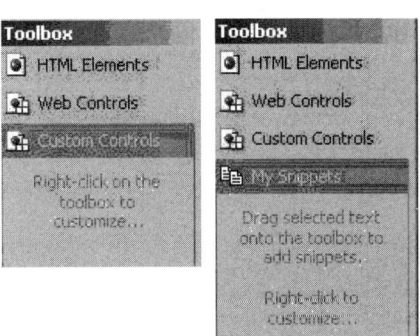

53

Properties

Just as with Visual Studio, the Properties window details the settings defined for a particular control, and you can manipulate property values from this pane. The window has three tabs, Properties, Classes, and Community:

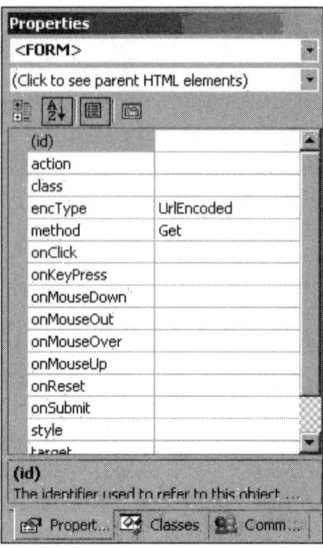

Classes Tab

The Classes tab provides information about all the available classes in the .NET Framework. We can view the namespace or class details using the first icon (Show Type Members) in the Classes tab:

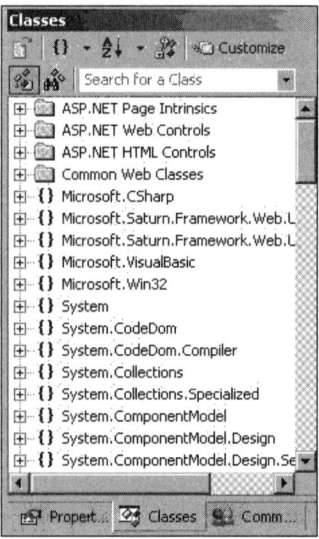

Development Tools

Community

Community is Web Matrix's online help. It provides information and links about the tool, different forums, and various newsgroups:

Coding and Development

After selecting a particular document template, the tool displays a window where we can design our interface and write its code. In this case, we have just added some text:

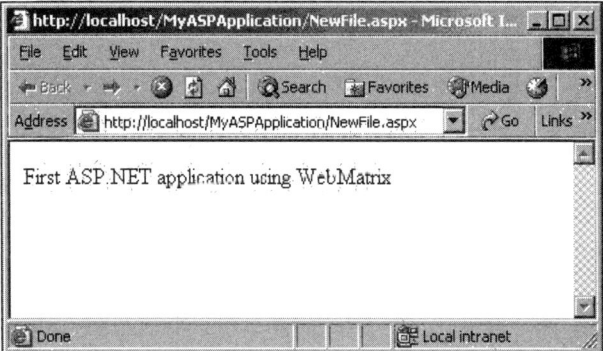

This window is created when we create a new document using the **File | New | General | ASP.NET Page** menu option. As you can see in the next screenshot the window has four tabs: **Design**, **HTML**, **Code**, and **All**. **Design** is the area where we drop our controls, **HTML** is the HTML code that is automatically generated for us, **Code** is the process logic that we have to provide for our application to work, and **All** displays both the **HTML** and **Code** tabs at once.

This is self-explanatory when you use the tool, so we won't deal with it in any more detail here. However, we will pause for just a moment, to notice that unlike Visual Studio .NET, Web Matrix doesn't use code-behind pages for its files. Instead, it places the script logic at the head of the file, with the HTML after it; as demonstrated in this screenshot of the **All** tab:

55

Chapter 2

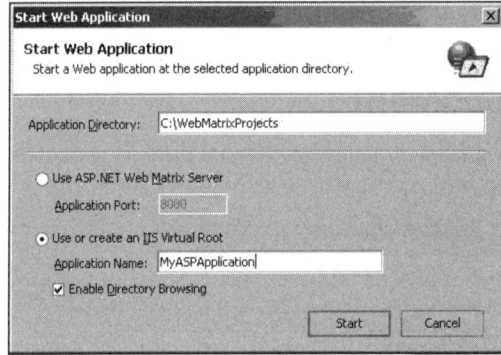

Running an Application

You can run an application by selecting View | Start, or by pressing *F5*. The tool then displays a window where we can configure our application's deployment settings:

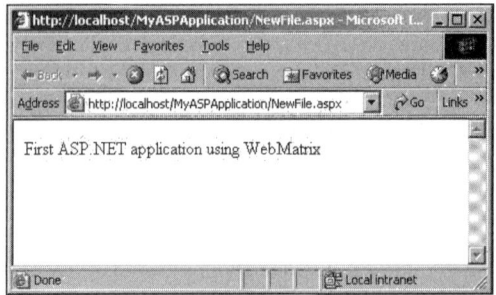

In the above screenshot we have two deployment options: Web Matrix Server, or Internet Information Server (IIS).

Web Matrix Server is a lightweight web server for developing and testing ASP.NET applications. It serves most web content including ASP.NET pages and XML web services.

As we started developing our examples on IIS, earlier in the chapter, we will continue to use it here. If we run our application, this is what we see in our browser:

Development Tools

We've covered the major contributions to .NET from Microsoft, now. But before we conclude this chapter you might be interested in a couple of alternative solutions that are available from other providers.

Dreamweaver MX

Dreamweaver MX is the latest version of Dreamweaver from Macromedia. It provides a development environment very similar Visual Studio .NET. Like WebMatrix, this tool concentrates on Web Development, rather than Windows application development. The tool includes features such as rapid web application development, code-editing support and visual layout tools.

The main feature of this tool is support for the .NET Framework along with the two main languages C# and VB.NET. The tool also supports languages like HTML, JavaScript, VBScript, Java, VB, ASP.NET, ColdFusion, JSP, PHP, XML, WML, EDML, and TLD. It also has a rich set of templates that can be used in fast development of web applications or a web site.

The Interface

The Dreamweaver MX development interface is shown below:

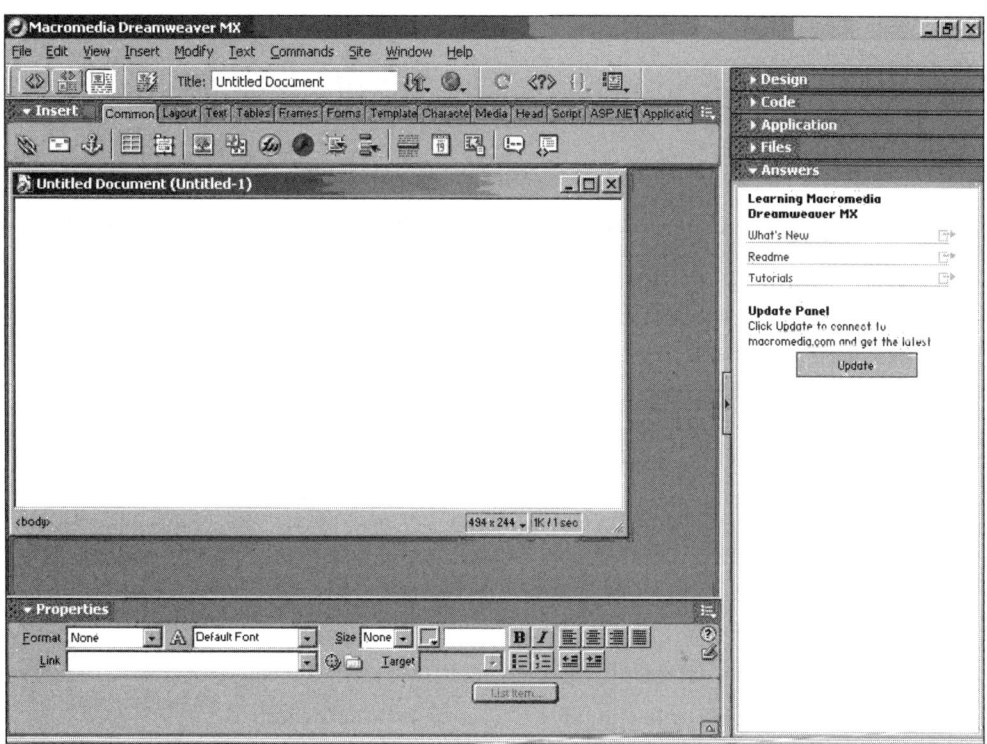

Documents and Templates

Like WebMatrix, DreamWeaver provides several templates for easy development of web applications:

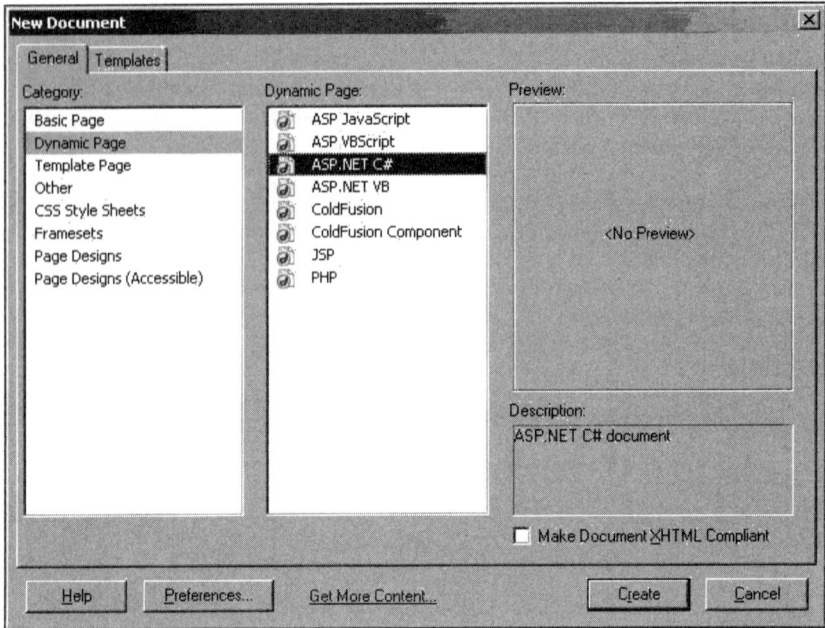

Dreamweaver supports an extremely rich list of documents. They are divided into categories as follows:

- **Basic Page** defines pages such as HTML, HTML Template, Library Item, CSS, JavaScript, and XML,
- **Dynamic Page** defines pages such as ASP JavaScript, ASP VBScript, ASP.NET C#, ASP.NET VB.NET, ColdFusion, ColdFusion Components, JSP, and PHP.
- **Template Page** defines templates for all the above listed pages in the Dynamic page category with the addition of HTML Template.
- **Other** provides different types of documents such as ActionScripts, ActionScripts Communications, ActionScripts Remote, C-Sharp, CSS, EDML, Java, JavaScript, Text, TLD, VB, VBScript, WML, and XML.
- **CSS Style Sheets** contains different types of style-sheets definitions that can be used in the interface development.
- **Framesets** provides different styles of frameset for the web site interface.
- **Page Designs** provides different types of page designs for the web site.

Development Tools

At the time of writing Dreamweaver MX is able to support the .NET Framework with C# and VB.NET only. For these languages, an ASP.NET template is available in the tools **Template Page** section:

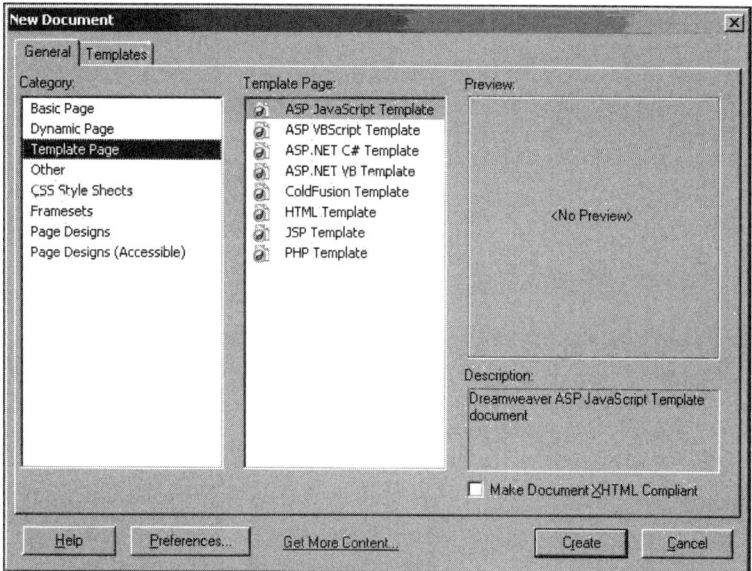

Features and Language Support

Dreamweaver targets a slightly different audience from Visual Studio .NET – one that is primarily web-oriented, and interested in maximising their users' experience of their web sites. For this reason it offers a variety of custom tags and features tailored to that audience, which do not appear in Visual Studio .NET.

Further information on Dreamweaver is beyond the scope of this book. If you would like to learn more, Macromedia has a great deal of information about its product here:

http://www.macromedia.com/software/dreamweaver/

SharpDevelop

In the previous sections we've looked at proprietary .NET development tools from Microsoft and Macromedia. Now, to finish up this chapter, we're going to look at a tool provided by the Open Source Community. **SharpDevelop** is released under the GNU General Public License and is sponsored by AlphaSierraPapa.com. It is available for free download here, along with its source code:

http://www.icsharpcode.net

Chapter 2

This tool is simple an editor that supports development within the .NET and Java Frameworks. The runtime for the editor is collected from the environmental settings of your system. It's interface looks like this:

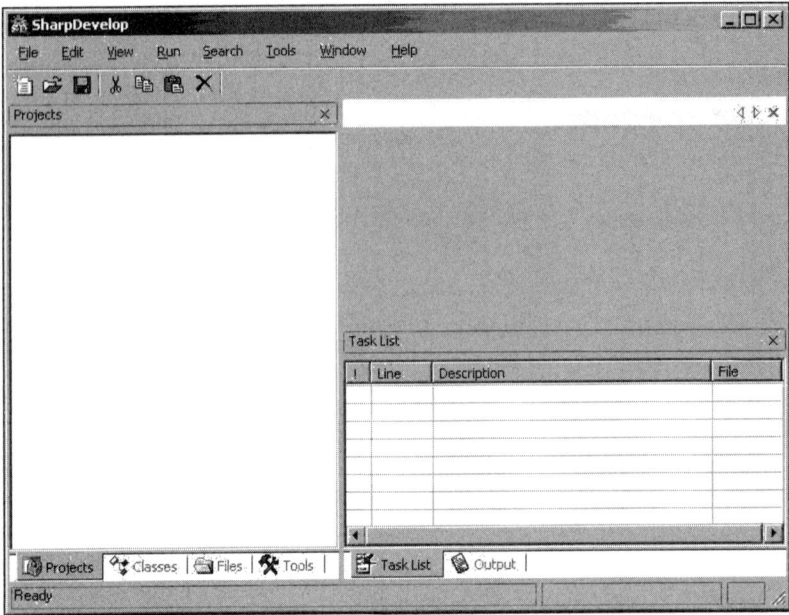

Templates

The tool provides templates for developing .NET applications with C# and VB.NET. It also provides a Java template. Here are the options:

- The C# Project provides template documents such as Console Project, Empty C# console application, Empty C# Windows application and Windows forms project.
- In the Java Project template we can have an Empty Java project, or a Java AWT Application project.
- SharpDevelop provides a single Blank Combine template.
- A VB.NET Project template consists of documents such as Empty VB Project and a VB Forms Application.

This editor is not as friendly, or easy to use, as its proprietary equivalents, and doesn't support the same degree of drag-and-drop functionality. However, its operation is quite neat, and it is easy to learn and get to grips with.

There are help forums to assist you in using SharpDevelop at the following address:

http://www.icsharpcode.net/OpenSource/SD/Forum/

Summary

To summarize, we have looked at the following environments in some detail:

- Notepad and `csc.exe` – this is without doubt the simplest development environment. You are able to do everything you can do with the other environments, but you have to explicitly code everything yourself.

  We'll be using Notepad in places through the remainder of the book where the Visual Studio .NET execution is trivial, but it is important to understand the not-so-trivial processes that are occurring 'behind the scenes'.

- Visual Studio .NET – the most comprehensive of the IDEs that we considered. It is Microsoft's primary development environment, and allows you to create a wide range of applications, in any of the .NET languages.

  We'll be using Visual Studio .NET throughout the remainder of the book in order to create the majority of our applications.

- WebMatrix – WebMatrix is a free download, and focuses entirely on creating web sites and web services. It contains its own internal web server, which makes it very useful for those wishing to code .NET web sites, without having access to IIS.

  We won't be using WebMatrix, or the remaining two IDEs, in this book. They are included for information only.

We also briefly considered:

- Dreamweaver MX – with a more comprehensive IDE than WebMatrix, Dreamweaver MX supports web development in a wide range of languages. Currently only C# and VB.NET are supported from the .NET platform, however.

- SharpDevelop – is Open Source GNU GPL software. It supports development in both .NET and Java, and may become more important in the future if the Mono project succeeds in porting .NET onto Linux (www.go-mono.org).

Hopefully this whistle-stop tour of some of the available IDEs has been of interest to you. Throughout this book we'll be demonstrating concepts using a mix of Visual Studio .NET and Notepad, as appropriate. The IDE that you choose to use, is, however, entirely up to you.

3
Language Syntax

Microsoft's new C# language resembles Java in many ways, and it is probably the best of the .NET Framework's languages for Java programmers who wish to migrate quickly.

> *As mentioned in the previous chapter, the .NET J# language is effectively Java for the .NET platform. It supports all the Java features and APIs as well as .NET APIs. However, because of Sun's court case against Microsoft, the API support is limited to JDK version 1.1.4. On the other hand, C# provides many additional features over J#, and C# is likely to become the preferred language for the development of .NET applications.*

In this chapter, we'll run through the similarities and differences between the two languages, in order to get a grasp of what's involved when migrating to .NET. The key similarities between Java and C# are:

- Both Java and C# are 100% object oriented.
- Both Java and C# have their roots in C++, and share features with that language.
- Both languages compile to an intermediate code rather than pure machine code. Java compiles to what is known as bytecode, while C# compiles to Microsoft's Intermediate Language, IL.
- Java bytecode is executed by an application called the Java virtual machine (JVM). Similarly, compiled C# programs are executed by the Common Language Runtime, or CLR.
- Exception handling in C# is very similar to Java, with some minor differences. C# handles run-time errors (also called exceptions) with the `try...catch` construct, just as in Java. The `System.Exception` class is the base class for all C# exception classes.
- Like Java, C# is strongly type checked. The compiler detects where types are used in a way that may cause errors at run time, and allows the programmer to provide error handlers in such places.
- Like Java, C# uses an event-driven programming model quite different from the procedural model of C and many other programming languages.

Chapter 3

- Like Java, C# provides automatic garbage collection, freeing the programmer from keeping track of allocated resources.
- Neither Java nor C# support multiple inheritance: both provide interfaces as an alternative.

Let's now look at the important differences that we'll cover in this chapter:

- Use of `main` method – A Java program compiles even if the `main` method is not declared, provided the source class is used as a super class.

    On the other hand, a C# source file does not compile without a `Main` method declaration and throws a compile-time error.

- Unlike Java, C# supports the `goto` statement, allowing execution to branch to a labeled statement.
- Multithreading in C# is much simpler than Java. Synchronization is implemented using the standard `Monitor` and `Mutex` C# classes.
- The C# language introduces the new concepts of **indexers**, **attributes**, and **delegates**. These are discussed later in the chapter.
- Like C++, C# supports operator overloading, allowing the developer to assign methods which provide custom behavior when standard operators are used on the class. Java does not support this, although both Java and C# support method overloading and overriding.

Source File Conventions

There are some differences in the file naming conventions and structure of source programs in the two languages that we need to be aware of.

File Naming

The naming convention for files containing C# classes is a little different to Java. Firstly, in Java, all source files have a `.java` extension. Each source file contains one top-level public class declaration, and the class name must match the filename. In other words, a class called `Customer` declared with public scope must be defined in a source file with the name `Customer.java`.

C# source code on the other hand is denoted by the `.cs` extension. Unlike Java, source files *can* contain more than one top-level public class declaration, and the filename doesn't need to match any of the classes' names.

Unlike Java, C# allows you to declare multiple public classes in a single file.

Top-level Declarations

In both Java and C#, source code begins with a few top-level declarations in a certain sequence. There are only a few differences in the declarations made in Java and C# programs.

Top-level Declarations in Java

In Java, we can group classes together with the `package` keyword. A packaged class must use the `package` keyword in the first executable line of the source file. Any `import` statements required to access classes in other packages appear next, and then comes the class declaration, like so:

```
package <Package name>;
import <package hierarchy>.<class name>;
class Customer
{
   .
   .
   .
}
```

Top-level Declarations in C#

C# uses the concept of **namespaces** to group logically related classes through the `namespace` keyword. These act similarly to Java packages, and a class with the same name may appear within two different namespaces. To access classes defined in a namespace external to the current one, we use the keyword `using` followed by the namespace name, as shown below:

```
using <namespace hierarchy>.<class name>;
namespace <namespace name> {
  class Customer
  {
     .
     .
     .
  }
}
```

Note that `using` statements may quite legally be placed inside a namespace declaration, in which case such imported namespaces form part of the containing namespace.

Java does not allow multiple packages in the same source file, while C# does allow multiple namespaces in a single `.cs` file:

```
namespace WroxData
{
  public class GetDetails
  {
      .
      .
      .
  }
      .
      .
      .
}
```

```
namespace WroxGraphics
{
  public class ShowDetails
  {
    .
    .
    .
  }
  .
  .
  .
}
```

Fully Qualified Names and Namespace Aliases

We can access classes in a .NET or user defined namespace without a `using` reference for that namespace, by giving the **fully qualified name** for the class, such as `System.Data.DataSet`, or `WroxData.GetDetails` in the above example.

Fully qualified names can get long and unwieldy, and in such cases, we can use the `using` keyword to specify a short name, or **alias**, to make our code more readable.

In the following code, an alias is created to refer to code written by a fictional company:

```
using DataTier = SmokeyInc.SQLCode.Client;
using System;

public class OutputSales
{
  public static void Main()
  {
    int sales = DataTier.GetSales("January");
    System.Console.WriteLine("January's Sales: {0}", sales);
  }
}
```

Note the syntax for `WriteLine()`, with `{x}` in the format string, where x denotes the position in the argument list of the value to insert at that position.

Language Syntax

In this section, we discuss the similarities and differences between the two languages. Some of the major differences are:

- Declaration of constants – Java uses the `final` keyword for this, while C# uses the keywords `const` or `readonly`.
- Compound data types – in Java, we can create compound data types as classes without methods using the `class` keyword, but C# offers `struct` for this purpose, as in C.

Language Syntax

- Destructors – C# allows us to create a destructor method that is called before instances of a class are destroyed. In Java, a `finalize()` method can be provided to contain code that cleans up resources before the object is garbage-collected. In C#, this function is provided by the class destructor. The destructor resembles a constructor with no arguments and a preceding tilde character ~.
- Function pointers – C# provides a construct called delegate to create a type-safe function pointer. Java does not have any such equivalent.

Primitive Data Types

C# provides all the data types that are available in Java, and adds support for unsigned numerals and a new 128-bit high precision floating-point type.

For each primitive data type in Java, the core class library provides a wrapper class that represents it as a Java object. For example, the `Integer` class wraps the `int` data type, and the `Double` class wraps the `double` data type.

On the other hand, all primitive data types in C# are objects in the `System` namespace. For each data type, a short name, or alias, is provided. For instance, `int` is the short name for `System.Int32` and `double` is the short form of `System.Double`.

The list of C# data types and their aliases is given below. As you will notice, the first 8 of these correspond to the primitive types available in Java. Note however that Java's `boolean` is called `bool` in C#:

Short Name	.NET Class	Type	Width (bits)	Range
byte	System.Byte	Unsigned integer	8	-128 to 127
int	System.Int32	Signed integer	32	-2,147,483,648 to 2,147,483,647
short	System.Int16	Signed integer	16	-32,768 to 32,767
long	System.Int64	Signed integer	64	-9223372036854775508 to 9223372036854775507
float	System.Single	Single-precision floating point type	32	-3.402823e38 to 3.402823e38
double	System.Double	Double-precision floating point type	64	-1.79769313486232e308 to 1.79769313486232e308
char	System.Char	A single Unicode character	16	Unicode symbols used in text

Table continued on following page

Short Name	.NET Class	Type	Width (bits)	Range
`bool`	`System.Boolean`	Logical Boolean type	8	True or false
`object`	`System.Object`	Base type of all other types (Reference types)		
`string`	`System.String`	A sequence of characters		
`sbyte`	`System.SByte`	Signed integer	8	-128 to 127
`ushort`	`System.UInt16`	Unsigned integer	16	0 to 65535
`uint`	`System.UInt32`	Unsigned integer	32	0 to 4294967295
`ulong`	`System.UInt64`	Unsigned integer	64	0 to 18446744073709551615
`decimal`	`System.Decimal`	Precise fractional or integral type that can represent decimal numbers with 29 significant digits	128	-2×10^{96} to 2×10^{96}

Because C# represents all primitive data types as objects, it is possible to call an object method on a primitive data type. For example:

```
int i=10;
Console.WriteLine (i.ToString());
```

This is achieved with the help of automatic **boxing** and **unboxing**.

Converting and Casting

Both Java and C# follow similar rules for automatic conversions and casting of data types.

Like Java, C# supports both **implicit** and **explicit** type conversions. In the case of widening conversions, the conversions are implicit. For example, the following conversion from `int` to `long` is implicit, as in Java:

```
int intVariable = 5;
long l =  intVariable;
```

The following table contains a complete list of implicit conversions in C#:

Source Type	Target Type
sbyte	short, int, long, float, double, or decimal
byte	short, ushort, int, uint, long, ulong, float, double, or decimal
short	int, long, float, double, or decimal
ushort	int, uint, long, ulong, float, double, or decimal
int	long, float, double, or decimal
uint	long, ulong, float, double, or decimal
long	float, double, or decimal
char	ushort, int, uint, long, ulong, float, double, or decimal
float	double
ulong	float, double, or decimal

We cast expressions that we wish to explicitly convert using the same syntax as Java:

```
long longVariable = 5483;
int intVariable = (int)longVariable;
```

The following conversions must be done explicitly:

Source Type	Target Type
sbyte	byte, ushort, uint, ulong, or char
byte	sbyte or char
short	sbyte, byte, ushort, uint, ulong, or char
ushort	sbyte, byte, short, or char
int	sbyte, byte, short, ushort, uint, ulong, or char
uint	sbyte, byte, short, ushort, int, or char
long	sbyte, byte, short, ushort, int, uint, ulong, or char
ulong	sbyte, byte, short, ushort, int, uint, long, or char
char	sbyte, byte, or short
float	sbyte, byte, short, ushort, int, uint, long, ulong, char, or decimal
double	sbyte, byte, short, ushort, int, uint, long, ulong, char, float, or decimal
decimal	sbyte, byte, short, ushort, int, uint, long, ulong, char, float, or double

Chapter 3

Value and Reference Types

C# supports two kinds of variable types:

- **value types** – these are the built-in primitive data types, such as `char`, `int`, `float`, and user defined types declared with `struct`.
- **reference types** – classes and other complex data types that are constructed from the primitive types. Variables of such types do not contain an instance of the type, but merely **a reference to an instance**.

Let's explore this a little further. If we create two value type variables, `i` and `j`, like so:

```
int i = 10;
int j = 20;
```

then `i` and `j` are completely independent of each other; they are given separate memory locations:

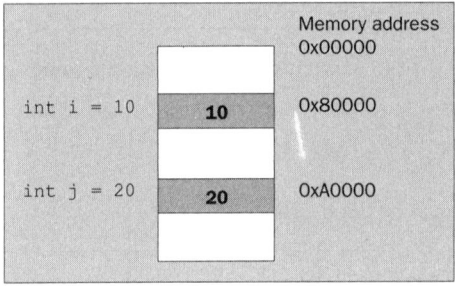

If we change the value of one of these variables, the other will naturally not be affected. For instance, if we have an expression such as this:

```
int k = i;
```

then there is still no connection between the variables. That is, if we then change the value of `i`, `k` will remain at the value that `i` had at the time of the assignment.

Reference types however act differently. For instance, we could declare two variables like so:

```
myClass a = new myClass();
myClass b = a;
```

Now because classes are reference types in C#, `a` is known as a reference to `myClass`. The first of the above two lines creates an instance of `myClass` in memory, and sets `a` to reference it. Thus, when we set `b` to equal `a`, it contains a duplicate of the reference to the class in memory. If we now change properties on `b`, properties on `a` would reflect these changes, because both point to the same object in memory, as shown in this figure:

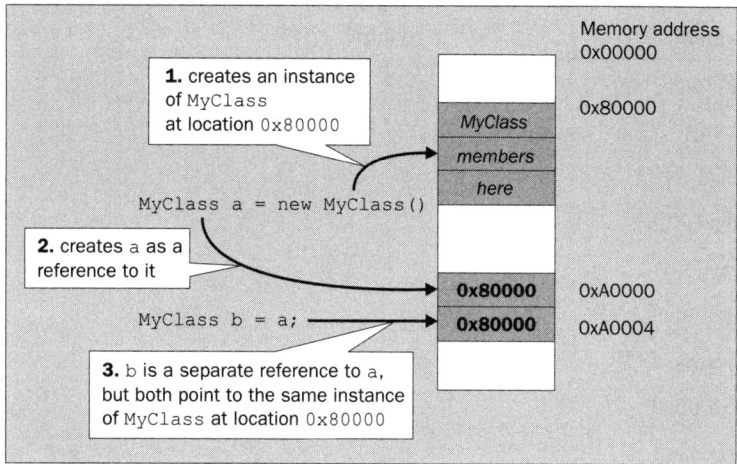

Boxing and Unboxing

The process of converting a value type to a reference type is called **boxing**. The inverse process, converting a reference type to a value type, is called **unboxing**. This is illustrated in the following code:

```
int valueVariable = 10;

// boxing
object obj = refVariable;

// unboxing
int valueVariable = (int) refVariable;
```

Java requires us to perform such conversions manually. Primitive data types may be converted into objects of wrapper classes by constructing such objects (boxing). Similarly, the values of primitive data types may be extracted from the objects of wrapper classes by calling an appropriate method on such objects (unboxing).

Operators

C# offers all applicable operators supported by Java, as listed in the following table. At the end of the table, you'll see some new operators available in C# but not Java:

Category	Symbol
Unary	++ -- + - ! ~ ()
Multiplicative	* / %
Additive	+ -
Shift	<< >>

Table continued on following page

71

Category	Symbol
Relational	`< > <= >=` `instanceof`
Equality	`== !=`
Logical AND	`&`
Logical XOR	`^`
Logical OR	`|`
Conditional AND	`&&`
Conditional OR	`||`
Conditional	`? :`
Assignment	`= *= /= %= += -= <<= >>= &= ^= |=`
Type of Operand	`typeof`
Size of Operand	`sizeof`
Enforce Overflow Checking	`checked`
Suppress Overflow Checking	`unchecked`

The only Java operator not available in C# is the >>> shift operator. This operator is present in Java as a consequence of the lack of unsigned variables in that language, for cases when right-shifting is required to insert 1s in the most significant bits.

C# however does support unsigned variables, and thus C# only needs the standard >> operator. This operator produces different results depending on whether the operand is signed or unsigned. Right-shifting an unsigned number inserts 0 in the most significant bit while right-shifting a signed number copies the previous most significant bit.

The checked and unchecked Operators

Arithmetic operations will result in overflow if the result is too large for the number of bits allocated to the data type in use. Such overflow can be checked or ignored for a given integral arithmetic operation using the `checked` and `unchecked` keywords. If the expression is a constant expression using `checked` (which is the default), an error would be generated at compile time.

Here's a simple example to illustrate these operators:

```
using System;
public class Class1
{
  public static void Main(string[] args)
  {
    short a = 10000, b = 10000;
```

```
      short d = unchecked((short)(10000*10000));
      System.Console.WriteLine(d);

      short c = (short)(a*b);
      System.Console.WriteLine(c);

      c = checked((short)(a*b));
      System.Console.WriteLine(c);
   }
}
```

In this code, the unchecked operator circumvents the compile time error that would otherwise be caused by the following statement:

```
      short d = unchecked((short)(10000*10000));
```

The next expression is unchecked by default, so we are not warned of overflow by an exception:

```
      short c = (short)(a*b);
```

We can force the expression to be checked for overflow at run time with the checked operator:

```
      c = checked((short)(a*b));
```

The is Operator

This operator determines whether the type of the object on the left hand side matches the type specified on the right:

```
   if (objReference is SomeClass) ...
```

In the following example, the CheckType() method prints a message describing the type of the argument passed to it:

```
using System;

public class ShowTypes
{
   public ShowTypes() {}

   public static void Main(string[] args)
   {
      CheckType (5);
      CheckType (10f);
      CheckType ("Hello");
   }

   private static void CheckType (object obj)
   {
      if (obj is int)
```

```
        {
            System.Console.WriteLine("Integer parameter");
        }
        else if (obj is float)
        {
            System.Console.WriteLine("Float parameter");
        }
        else if (obj is string)
        {
            System.Console.WriteLine("string parameter");
        }
    }
}
```

The sizeof Operator

The `sizeof` operator returns the size in bytes of the specified value type as illustrated by the following code:

```
public class Size
{
  public static void Main()
  {
    unsafe
    {
      System.Console.WriteLine("The size of short is {0}.", sizeof(short));
      System.Console.WriteLine("The size of int is {0}.", sizeof(int));
      System.Console.WriteLine("The size of double is {0}.",sizeof(double));
    }
  }
}
```

> Note that the code containing the **sizeof** operator has been placed in an **unsafe** block. This is because the **sizeof** operator is considered an unsafe operation due to its accessing memory directly. We return to the **unsafe** keyword towards the end of the chapter.

typeof and GetType

The `typeof` operator returns the type of the class passed to it as a `System.Type` object. The `GetType()` method is related, and returns the run-time type of a class or an expression. `typeof` and `GetType()` can be used in conjunction with reflection to find information about an object dynamically, as in the following example:

```
public class Customer
{
  string name;
  public Customer(){}

  public string Name
  {
    set
```

```
      {
        name = value;
      }
      get
      {
        return name;
      }
    }
  }

  public class TypeTest
  {
    public static void Main()
    {
      System.Type typeObj = typeof(Customer);

      System.Console.WriteLine("The Class name is {0}",
        typeObj.FullName);
      // Or use the GetType() method:
      //Customer obj = new Customer();
      //Type typeObj = obj.GetType();

      System.Console.WriteLine("\nThe Class Members\n=================\n ");
      System.Reflection.MemberInfo[] class_members = typeObj.GetMembers();
      foreach (System.Reflection.MemberInfo members in class_members)
        System.Console.WriteLine(members.ToString());

      System.Console.WriteLine("\nThe Class Methods\n=================\n");
      System.Reflection.MethodInfo[] class_methods = typeObj.GetMethods();
      foreach (System.Reflection.MethodInfo methods in class_methods)
        System.Console.WriteLine(methods.ToString());
    }
  }
```

If you run this program, it will produce output something like this:

This shows us the members that all classes inherit from `System.Object`, as well as revealing the way that C# represents `get` and `set` property accessors as `get_XXX()` and `set_XXX()` methods internally.

In the next example, we use `GetType()` to find the type of an expression at run time:

```csharp
public class TypeTest
{
  public static void Main()
  {
    int radius = 8;
    System.Console.WriteLine("Calculated area is = {0}",
                             radius * radius * System.Math.PI);
    System.Console.WriteLine("The result is of type {0}",
                             (radius * radius * System.Math.PI).GetType());
  }
}
```

The output of this program tells us that the result is of type `System.Double`, which is chosen because `System.Math.PI` is of this type.

Flow Control

Flow control statements are very similar in both languages, but there are some minor differences that I would like to cover in this section.

Branching Statements

Branching statements change the flow of program execution at run time according to certain conditions.

if, else, and else if

These are identical in both languages.

The switch Statement

In both languages, the `switch` statement provides conditional multiple branching operations. There is a difference though in that Java allows you to "fall through" a `case` and execute the next `case` unless you use a `break` statement at the end of the case. C# however *requires* the use of either a `break` or a `goto` statement at the end of each `case`, and if neither is present, the compiler produces the following error:

```
Control cannot fall through from one case label to another.
```

Beware though, that where a case doesn't specify any code to execute when that case is matched, control *will* fall through to the subsequent case. When using `goto` in a `switch` statement, we can only jump to another `case` block in the same switch. If we want to jump to the default case, we would use `goto default;` otherwise we'd use `goto case cond;` where `cond` is the matching condition of the case we wish to jump to. Another difference to Java's `switch` is that in Java, we can only switch on integer types, while C# lets us switch on a `string` variable.

For example, the following would be valid in C#, but not in Java:

```
switch (args[0])
{
  case "copy":
    .
    .
    .
    break;
  case "move":
    .
    .
    .
    goto case "delete";
    break;
  case "del":
  case "remove":
  case "delete":
    .
    .
    .
    break;
  default:
    .
    .
    .
    break;
}
```

The Return of goto

In Java, `goto` is a reserved keyword that is not implemented. However, we can use labeled statements with `break` or `continue` to achieve a similar purpose as `goto`.

C# does allow the `goto` statement to jump to a labeled statement. Note though that in order to jump to a particular label, the `goto` statement must be within the scope of the label. In other words, `goto` may not be used to jump into a statement block (although it can jump out of one), to jump out of a class, or to exit the `finally` block in `try...catch` statements. Be aware though that `goto` is discouraged in most cases, as it contravenes good object-oriented programming practice.

Looping Statements

Looping statements repeat a specified block of code until a given condition is met.

for Loops

The syntax and operation of `for` loops is the same in both languages:

```
for (initialization; condition; expression)
    statement;
```

foreach Loops

C# introduces a new loop type called the `foreach` loop (similar to Visual Basic's `For Each`). The following program code illustrates the use of the `foreach` statement to output the contents of an array:

```
public static void Main()
{
  int[] arr1= new int[] {1,2,3,4,5,6};
  foreach ( int i in arr1)
  {
    Console.WriteLine("Value is {0}", i);
  }
}
```

We look at arrays in C# in more detail later.

while and do...while Loops

The syntax and operation of `while` and `do...while` statements is same in both the languages:

```
while (condition)
{
  //statements
}
```

As usual, don't forget the trailing `;` in `do...while` loops:

```
do
{
  //statements
}
while(condition);
```

Class Fundamentals

As Java programs can be applications or applets, the `main()` method is not mandatory. A Java application must expose one and only one `main()` method. The `main()` method must be declared `public` so that the Java Virtual Machine has access to it, and it must also be declared `static` so that it can be invoked without instantiating the class. `main()` takes a `String` array argument representing the command line arguments specified by the user.

Access Modifiers

Modifiers are pretty much the same as those in Java, with several small differences that we will cover here. Each member of a class or the class itself may be declared with an access modifier to define the scope of permitted access. Classes that are not declared inside other classes can only specify the `public` or `internal` modifiers, while nested classes, like other class members, can specify any of the following five:

- `public` – visible to all
- `protected` – visible only from derived classes

- `private` – visible only within the given class
- `internal` – visible only within the same assembly
- `protected internal` – visible only from derived classes within the same assembly

The public, protected, and private Modifiers

These access modifiers have the same purpose and meaning as in Java. A `public` modifier makes the member available anywhere both inside and outside the class. A `protected` modifier indicates that access is limited to within the containing class or classes derived from it. A `private` modifier means that access is only possible from within the containing type.

The internal Modifier

An `internal` item may only be accessed within the current assembly. An assembly in the .NET world equates roughly to Java's JAR file; it represents the building blocks from which other programs can be constructed.

The protected internal Modifier

A `protected internal` item is only visible to types derived from the containing class that lie within the current assembly.

In C#, the default access modifier is `private`, while Java's default is package scope.

The sealed Modifier

A class with the `sealed` modifier on its class declaration can be thought of as directly opposite to an `abstract` class – it cannot be inherited. We might mark a class as `sealed` to prevent other classes overriding its functionality. Naturally, a `sealed` class cannot be abstract. Also note that `structs` are implicitly sealed; therefore, they cannot be inherited. The `sealed` modifier is equivalent to marking a class with the `final` keyword in Java.

The readonly Modifier

To define a constant in C#, we use the `const` or `readonly` modifier in place of Java's `final` keyword. The distinguishing factor between the two modifiers in C# is that `const` items are dealt with at compile time, while `readonly` fields are set up at runtime. This can allow us to modify the expression used to determine the value of a `readonly` field at runtime.

This means that assignment to `readonly` fields may occur in the class constructor as well as in the declaration. For example, the following class declares a `readonly` variable called `IntegerVariable` that is initialized in the class constructor:

```
public class ReadOnlyClass
{
  private readonly int IntegerConstant;

  public ReadOnlyClass ()
  {
    IntegerConstant = 5;
  }
```

```
      // We get a compile time error if we try to set the value of the readonly
      //   class variable outside of the constructor
      public int IntMember
      {
        set
        {
          IntegerConstant = value;
        }
        get
        {
          return IntegerConstant;
        }
      }

      public static void Main(string[] args)
      {
        ReadOnlyClass obj= new ReadOnlyClass();

        // We cannot perform this operation on a readonly field
        obj.IntMember = 100;
        System.Console.WriteLine("Value of IntegerConstant field is {0}",
                         obj.IntMember);
      }
    }
```

Note that if a `readonly` modifier is applied to a `static` field, it should be initialized in the `static` constructor of the class.

The Main() Method

Every C# application must contain one, and only one, `Main()` method specifying where program execution is to begin. Note that in C#, we capitalize the method name.

`Main()` can only return `int` or `void`, and has an optional string array argument to represent command line parameters:

```
    static int Main (string[] args)
    {
      .
      .
      .
      return 0;
    }
```

The `string` array parameter that contains any command-line arguments passed in works just as in Java. Thus, `args[0]` specifies the first command-line parameter, `args[1]` denotes the second parameter, and so on. Unlike C++, the `args` array does not contain the name of the EXE file.

Other Methods

When you pass parameters to a method, they may be passed by value or by reference. Value parameters simply take the value of any variable for use in the method, and hence the variable value in the calling code is not affected by actions performed on the parameters within a method.

Reference parameters on the other hand point to a variable declared in the calling code, and thus methods will modify the contents of that variable when passed by reference.

Passing by Reference

In Java, method parameters that refer to an object are always passed by reference, while primitive data type parameters are passed by value.

In C#, all parameters are passed by value by default. To pass by reference, we need to specify one of the keywords `ref` or `out`. The difference between these two keywords is in the parameter initialization. A `ref` parameter must be initialized before use, while an `out` parameter does not have to be explicitly initialized before being passed, and any previous value is ignored.

> **Be aware that when reference types are used as parameters for a method, the reference is itself passed by value. However, the reference still points to the same object in memory, and so changes made to the object's properties will persist after the method exits. But, as the reference is itself passed by value, should it be changed inside the method to point to a different object, or even a new one, the reference would be restored to point to the original object once the method completes, even if the original object were unassigned.**

The ref Keyword

We specify this keyword on a parameter when we want the called method to permanently change the value of variables used as parameters. What happens is that rather than passing the value of a variable used in the call, a reference to the variable itself is passed. The method then works on the reference, so that changes to the parameter during the method's execution are persisted to the original variable used as a parameter to the method.

The following code illustrates this in the `Add()` method, where the second `int` parameter is passed by reference with the `ref` keyword:

```
public class RefClass
{
  public static int Main(string[] args)
  {
    int total = 20;
    System.Console.WriteLine("Original value of 'total': {0}", total);

    // Call the Add method
    Add (10, ref total);

    System.Console.WriteLine("Value after Add() call: {0}", total);
    return 0;
  }
```

```
      public static void Add (int i, ref int result)
      {
        result += i;
      }
    }
```

The output of this simple example demonstrates that changes made to the `result` parameter are reflected in the variable, `total`, used in the `Add()` call:

Original value of 'total': 20
Value after Add() call: 30

This is because the `result` parameter references the actual memory location occupied by the `total` variable in the calling code. Be aware that a property of a class is not a variable, and cannot be used directly as a `ref` parameter.

> Note that the **ref** keyword must precede the parameter when the method is called, as well as in the method declaration.

The out Keyword

The `out` keyword has a very similar effect to the `ref` keyword, and modifications made to a parameter declared using `out` will be visible outside the method. The two differences from `ref` are that any initial value of an `out` parameter is ignored within the method, and secondly that an `out` parameter must be assigned to during the method:

```
public class OutClass
{
  public static void Main(string[] args)
  {
    int total = 20;
    System.Console.WriteLine("Original value of 'total': {0}", total);

    Add (33, 77, out total);

    System.Console.WriteLine("Value after Add() call: {0}", total);
  }

  public static void Add (int i, int j, out int result)
  {
    // The following line would cause a compile error
    //System.Console.WriteLine("Initial value inside method: {0}", result);
    result = i + j;
  }
}
```

In this case, the third parameter to the `Add()` method is declared with the `out` keyword, and calls to the method also require the `out` keyword for that parameter. The output will be:

Original value of 'total': 20
Value after Add() call: 110

So, to sum up, use the `ref` keyword when you want a method to modify an existing variable, and use the `out` keyword to return a value produced inside the method. It is generally used in conjunction with the method's return value when the method produces more than one result value for the calling code.

Using an Indeterminate Number of Parameters

C# allows us to send a variable number of parameters to a method by specifying the `params` keyword when the method is declared. The argument list can contain regular parameters also, but note that the parameter declared with the `params` keyword must come last. It takes the form of a variable length array, and there can be only one `params` parameter per method.

This feature has no equivalent in Java, and is in fact borrowed from C.

When the compiler tries to resolve a method call, it looks for a method whose argument list matches the method called. If no method overload that matches the argument list can be found, but there is a matching version with a `params` parameter of the appropriate type, then that method will be called, placing the extra arguments in an array.

The following example demonstrates this idea:

```csharp
public class ParamsClass
{
  public static int Main(string[] args)
  {
    Average ("List One", 5,10,15);
    Average ("List Two", 5,10,15,20,25,30);
    return 0;
  }

  public static void Average (string title, params int[] values)
  {
    int Sum = 0;
    System.Console.Write("Average of {0}: ", title);
    for (int i = 0; i < values.Length; i++)
    {
      Sum += values[i];
      System.Console.Write(values[i] + ", ");
    }
    System.Console.WriteLine(": {0}", (float)Sum/values.Length);
  }
}
```

In the above example, the method `Average` is declared with a `params` parameter of type integer array, letting us call it with any number of arguments. The output is shown here:

Average of List One: 5, 10, 15, : 10
Average of List Two: 5, 10, 15, 20, 25, 30, : 17.5

Note that we can specify a `params` parameter of type `Object` if we wish to allow indeterminate parameters of different types.

Properties

In C#, a property is a named member of a class, `struct`, or interface offering a neat way to access private fields through what are called the `get` and `set` **accessor methods**.

The following code snippet declares a property called `Species` for the class `Animal`, which abstracts access to the private variable called `name`:

```
public class Animal
{
  private string name;

  public string Species
  {
    get
    {
      return name;
    }
    set
    {
      name = value;
    }
  }
}
```

Often, the property will have the same name as the internal member that it accesses, but with a capital initial letter (such as `Name` in the above case), but I've avoided this here for clarity. Also, note the implicit parameter called `value` used in the `set` accessor – this has the type of the underlying member variable.

Accessors are in fact represented internally as `_getX()` and `_setX()` methods in order to maintain compatibility with the .NET languages which do not support accessors (as shown in the screenshot in the `typeOf` and `GetType()` section earlier in the chapter). Once a property is defined, it's then very easy to get or set its value:

```
Animal animal = new Animal()

// Set the property
animal.Species = "Lion"

// Get the property value
String str = animal.Species;
```

If property only has a `get` accessor, it is a **read-only** property. If it only has a `set` accessor, it is a **write-only** property. If it has both, it is a **read-write** property.

Structs

C# supports the `struct` keyword, another item that originates in C but is not available in Java. A `struct` can contain constructors, constants, fields, methods, properties, indexers, operators, and nested types in much the same way as a class. The important difference with a class is that `structs` are value types, while classes are reference types. This makes the `struct` the more efficient solution when creating arrays of objects, as an equivalent array of classes carries the space and time overhead from having to reference each class.

In the following example, we initialize a `struct` with the `new` keyword and also by initializing the members of an instance:

```
public struct CustomerStruct
{
  public int ID;
  public string name;

  public Customer(int customerID, string customerName)
  {
    ID = customerID;
    name = customerName;
  }
}

class TestClass
{
  public static void Main(string[] args)
  {
    // Declare a CustomerStruct using the default constructor
    CustomerStruct customer = new CustomerStruct();

    System.Console.WriteLine("Struct values before initialization");
    System.Console.WriteLine("ID = {0}, Name = {1}", customer.ID,
                             customer.name);
    customer.ID = 100;
    customer.name = "Robert";

    System.Console.WriteLine("Struct values after initialization");
    System.Console.WriteLine("ID = {0}, Name = {1}", customer.ID,
                             customer.name);
  }
}
```

When we compile and run the above code, it's output shows that `struct` variables are initialized by default. The `int` variable is initialized to 0, and the `string` variable to an empty string:

```
Struct values before initialization
ID = 0, Name =
Struct values after initialization
ID = 100, Name = Robert
```

Note though that were we to declare `customer` using the alternate notation, `CustomerStruct customer;`, its member variables would not be initialized, and trying to use them before setting them to values would generate a compile time error.

Arrays in C#

Arrays are ordered collections of items of the same data type that are accessed using the array name in conjunction with the offset from the start of the array of the desired item. There are some important differences in how arrays are declared and used in C# compared to Java that I will cover in this section.

The One-Dimensional Array

A one-dimensional array stores a fixed number of items in a linear fashion, requiring just a single index value to identify any one item.

In C#, the square brackets in the array declaration **must** follow the data type, and may **not** appear after the variable name as permitted in Java. Thus, an array of type integers is declared using following syntax:

```
int[] MyArray;
```

and the following declaration is **invalid** in C#:

```
int MyArray[];
```

Once we have declared an array, we use the `new` keyword to set its size, just as in Java:

```
int[] MyArray;            // declares the array reference
MyArray = new int[5];     // creates a 5 element integer array
```

We then access elements in a one-dimensional array using identical syntax to Java, noting that C# array indices are zero-based too:

```
MyArray [4]
```

So the above code accesses the last element of `MyArray`.

Initialization

Array elements may be initialized at creation using the same syntax as in Java:

```
MyArray = new int[5] {1, 2, 3, 4, 5};
```

> Unlike Java, the number of initializers must match the array size exactly.

We can use this feature to declare and initialize a C# array in a single line:

```
int[] TaxRates = {0, 20, 23, 40, 50};
```

This syntax creates an array of size equal to the number of initializers.

Initializing in a Program Loop

The other way to initialize an array in C# is to use the `foreach` loop. The loop below sets each element of an array to zero:

```
int[] MyLittleArray = new int[5];
foreach (int i in MyLittleArray) {
  MyLittleArray[i] = 0;
}
```

Multi-Dimensional Arrays

C# allows us to create regular multi-dimensional arrays that can be thought of as a matrix of values of the same type. Multi-dimensional arrays can be thought of arrays of arrays. However, the syntax in C# is a little different from that in Java, and in addition, C# introduces the **jagged array** – which is an array of non-identical arrays. We'll look at jagged arrays in a moment.

We declare a multi-dimensional rectangular array using following syntax:

```
int[,] My2DIntArray;
float[,,,] My4DFloatArray;
```

where `intArray` is the name by which every element can be accessed.

Note that the line `int[][] My2DintArray;` has a different meaning in C#, as we shall see shortly. Also, C# requires the square brackets to follow the type name, and they may not follow the identifier as permitted by Java.

Once declared, we allocate memory to the array like so:

```
int[,] My2DIntArray;         // declares array reference
My2DIntArray = new int[5,4]; // allocates space for 5x4 integers
```

Elements of the array are then accessed using the following syntax:

```
My2DIntArray [4,3] = 906;
```

As arrays are zero-based, this sets the element in the fifth column of the fourth row – the bottom right hand corner – to 906.

Initialization

Multi-dimensional arrays may be created, set up, and initialized in a single line by any of the following methods:

```
int[,] intArray = {     {1,2,3},
                        {4,5,6}     };

int[,] intArray = new int [2,3] {   {1,2,3},
                                    {4,5,6}     };

int[,] intArray = new int [,] {     {1,2,3},
                                    {4,5,6}     };
```

Initializing in a Program Loop

All the elements of an array may be initialized using a nested loop as shown here:

```
int[,] intArray = new int[5,4];
foreach (int i in intArray)
  foreach (int j in intArray[])
    j = 0;
```

Jagged Arrays

C# lets us create **jagged**, or non-rectangular, arrays, where each row contains a different number of columns. For instance, the following jagged array has four entries in the first row, and three in the second:

```
int[][] JaggedArray = new int[2][];
JaggedArray[0] = new int[4];
JaggedArray[1] = new int[3];
```

The System.Array Class

In .NET, arrays are implemented as instances of the `System.Array` class. This class provides several useful methods, such as `Sort()` and `Reverse()`.

The following program demonstrates how easy these methods are to work with. First, we reverse the elements of an array using the `Reverse()` method of the `Array` class, and then we sort them with the `Sort()` method:

```
using System;

public class ArrayMethods
{
  public static void Main()
  {
    // Create string array of size 5
    string[] EmployeeNames = new string[5];
    System.Console.WriteLine("Enter five employee names:");
```

```
    // Read 5 employee names from user
    for(int i=0;i<5;i++)
        EmployeeNames[i]= Console.ReadLine();

    // Print the array in original order
    System.Console.WriteLine("\n** Original Array **");
    foreach(string EmployeeName in EmployeeNames)
        System.Console.Write("{0}  ", EmployeeName);

    //print the array in reverse order.
    System.Console.WriteLine("\n\n** Values in Reverse Order **");
    System.Array.Reverse(EmployeeNames);
    foreach(string EmployeeName in EmployeeNames)
        System.Console.Write("{0}  ", EmployeeName);

    //print the array in sorted order.
    System.Console.WriteLine("\n\n** Values in Sorted Order **");
    System.Array.Sort(EmployeeNames);
    foreach(string EmployeeName in EmployeeNames)
        System.Console.Write("{0}  ", EmployeeName);
    }
}
```

Here's some typical output for this program:

```
Enter five employee names:
Paulie
Tony
Carlo
Vito
Luca

** Original Array **
Paulie Tony Carlo Vito Luca

** Value in Reverse order **
Luca Vito Carlo Tony Paulie

** Values in Sorted order **
Carlo Luca Paulie Tony Vito
```

Inheritance and Derived Classes

We can extend the functionality of an existing class by creating a new class that derives from the existing class. The derived class inherits the properties of the base class, and we can add or override methods and properties as required.

In C# inheritance is defined by the : operator, equivalent to extends in Java.

Chapter 3

Like Java, C# does not support multiple inheritance, meaning that classes can't inherit from more than one class. We can however use interfaces for that purpose in the same way as in Java, as we'll see in the next section.

The following code defines a class called `Point` with two private member variables x, y representing the position of the point. These variables are accessed through properties called X and Y respectively:

```csharp
public class Point
{
  private int x, y;
  public Point()
  {
    x = 0;
    y = 0;
  }

  public int X
  {
    get
    {
      return x;
    }
    set
    {
      x = value;
    }
  }
  public int Y
  {
    get
    {
      return y;
    }
    set
    {
      y = value;
    }
  }
}
```

We would derive a new class, called `ColorPoint` say, from the `Point` class like so:

```csharp
public class ColorPoint : Point
```

`ColorPoint` then inherits all the fields and methods of the base class, to which we can add new ones to provide extra features in the derived class according to our needs. In this case, we add a private member and accessors to add color to the point:

```csharp
using System.Drawing;

public class ColorPoint : Point
{
  private Color screenColor;
```

```
    public ColorPoint()
    {
      screenColor = Color.Red;
    }

    public Color ScreenColor
    {
      get
      {
        return screenColor;
      }
      set
      {
        screenColor = value;
      }
    }
  }
```

Note that the constructor of the derived class implicitly calls the constructor for the base class (or the superclass in Java terminology). In inheritance, all base class constructors are called before the derived class's constructors in the order that the classes appear in the class hierarchy.

Typecasting to a Base Class

As in Java, we can't use a reference to a base class to access the members and methods of a derived class even if the base class reference may contain a valid reference to an object of the derived type.

We can reference a derived class with a reference to the derived type implicitly:

```
  ColorPoint clrpt = new ColorPoint();
  Point pt = clrpt;
```

In this code, the base class reference, pt, contains a copy of the clrpt reference.

The base Keyword

We can access base class members in a subclass even when those base members are overridden in the superclass using the base keyword. For instance, we could create a derived class which contains a method with the same signature as in the base class. If we prefaced that method with the new keyword, we indicate that this is an all-new method belonging to the derived class. We could still provide a method for accessing the original method in the base class with the base keyword.

For instance, say our base Point class had a method called invert(), which swaps the x and y coordinates over. We could provide a substitute for this method in our derived ColorPoint class with code like this:

```
    public new void invert()
    {
      int holding = x;
      x = y;
```

Chapter 3

```
    y = holding;
    screenColor = Color.Gray;
}
```

As you can see, this method swaps x and y, and then sets the point's color to gray. We could provide access to the base implementation for this method by creating another method in `ColorPoint` such as this one:

```
    public void baseInvert()
    {
      base.invert();
    }
}
```

We would then invoke the base method on a `ColorPoint` object by calling the `baseInvert()` method.

```
ColorPoint clrpt = new ColorPoint();
clrpt.baseInvert();
```

Remember that we would get the same effect as this if we assigned a reference to the base class to an instance of `ColorPoint`, and then accessed its methods:

```
Point pt = clrpt;
pt.invert();
```

Selecting Constructors

Base class objects are always constructed before any deriving class. Thus the constructor for the base class is executed before the constructor of the derived class. If the base class has more than one constructor, the derived class can decide the constructor to be called. For example, we could modify our `Point` class to add a second constructor:

```
public class Point {
  private int x, y;

  public Point()
  {
      x = 0; y = 0;
  }

  public Point(int x, int y)
  {
    this.x = x;
    this.y = y;
  }
  .
  .
  .
}
```

92

We could then change the `ColorPoint` class to use a particular one of the available constructors using the `base` keyword:

```
public class ColorPoint : Point
{
  private Color color;

  public ColorPoint(int x, int y) : base (x, y)
  {
    color= Color.Red;
  }
  .
  .
  .
}
```

In Java, this functionality is implemented using the `super` keyword.

Method Overriding

A derived class may override the method of a base class by providing a new implementation for the declared method. To override a method of the base class, you may use any one of the following techniques. Property accessors as well as methods can be overridden in much the same way.

You may declare the base class method as `virtual` and override its definition in the derived class, or you could use `new` modifier to override a method originally defined in a base class.

Virtual Methods

A method that is to be overridden in a derived class is declared with the `virtual` modifier. In a derived class, the overridden method is declared using the `override` modifier.

The `override` modifier denotes a method or a property of a derived class that replaces one with the same name and signature in the base class. The base method, which is to be overridden must be declared as `virtual`, `abstract`, or `override`: it is not possible to override a non-virtual or static method in this way – see the next heading for that case. Both the overridden and the overriding method or property must have the same access level modifiers.

The following example shows a `virtual` method called `StepUp` that is overridden in a derived class with the `override` modifier:

```
public class CountClass
{
  public int count;

  // Constructor
  public CountClass(int startValue)
  {
    count = startValue;
  }
```

```
      public virtual int StepUp()
      {
        return ++count;
      }
    }

    class Count100Class : CountClass
    {
      // Constructor
      public Count100Class(int x) : base(x)
      {
      }

      public override int StepUp()
      {
        return ((base.count) + 100);
      }

      public static void Main()
      {
        CountClass counter = new CountClass(10);
        CountClass bigCounter = new Count100Class(10);
        System.Console.WriteLine("Value of count in base class = {0}",
                                  counter.StepUp());
        System.Console.WriteLine("Value of count in derived class = {0}",
                                  bigCounter.StepUp());
      }
    }
```

When we run this code, we see that the derived class's constructor uses the method body given in the base class, letting us initialize the count member without duplicating that code. Here's the output we get:

```
Value of count in base class = 11
Value of count in derived class = 110
```

Method Overriding with the new Modifier

We can't use the `override` keyword to override a method that is not declared `virtual`, but we can do so if we use the `new` keyword.

To demonstrate this, we'll write a class called `Employee` and derive another class called `SalariedEmp` from it. There are two methods in the `Employee` class, and we will override both using the techniques discussed:

```
using System;

public class Employee
{
  public virtual void show()
  {
    Console.WriteLine("- show method in base class");
  }
```

```csharp
    public void print()
    {
      Console.WriteLine("- print method in base class");
    }
  }

  public class SalariedEmp : Employee
  {
    public override void show()
    {
      Console.WriteLine("- show method in derived class");
    }

    public new void print()
    {
      Console.WriteLine("- print method in derived class");
    }
  }
```

The `show()` and `print()` methods now have a different effect depending on whether they are called on an `Employee` or a `SalariedEmp` object:

```csharp
  public class CallEmployees
  {
    public static void Main(string[] args)
    {
      Employee emp = new Employee();
      Console.WriteLine("Calling Employee methods:");
      emp.show();
      emp.print();

      SalariedEmp salemp = new SalariedEmp();
      Console.WriteLine ("\nCalling methods using derived class:");
      salemp.show();
      salemp.print();

      emp = salemp;
      Console.WriteLine ("\nCalling methods using base class:");
      emp.show();
      emp.print();
    }
  }
```

The program produces the following output:

```
Calling Employee methods:
- show method in base class
- print method in base class

Calling methods using derived class:
- show method in derived class
- print method in derived class
```

Calling methods using base class:
- show method in derived class
- print method in base class

As we see, the `show()` method of the derived class is being called in the last two cases regardless of the object reference used. This is because `show` is `virtual`, and at run time the object reference points to an instance of the derived class.

The `print()` method on the other hand is overridden by the `new` keyword. The base class `print()` method will always be called if the reference is a base class type, even if the reference points to an instance of a derived class.

Abstract Classes

An abstract class declares one or more methods or properties as `abstract`. Such methods do not have an implementation provided in the class that declares them, although an abstract class can also contain non-abstract methods, that is, methods for which an implementation has been provided. An `abstract` class cannot be instantiated directly, but only as a derived class. Such derived classes must provide implementations for all `abstract` methods and properties, using the `override` keyword, unless the derived member is itself declared `abstract`.

Note that C# has the same restriction as in Java: it is not possible to derive from more than one abstract class in a single derivation.

The following example declares an abstract `Employee` class. We also create a derived class called `Manager` that provides an implementation of the abstract `show()` method defined in the `Employee` class:

```
using System;
public abstract class Employee
{
  // abstract show method
  public abstract void show();
}

// Manager class extends Employee
public class Manager: Employee
{
  string name;
  public Manager(string name)

  {
     this.name = name;
  }

  //override the show method
  public override void show()
  {
     Console.WriteLine("Name : " + name);
  }
}
```

```
public class CreateManager
{
  public static int Main(string[] args)
  {

    // Create instance of Manager and assign it to an Employee reference
    Employee temp = new Manager("John Chapman");

    // Call show method. This will call the show method of the Manager class
    temp.show();
    return 0;
  }
}
```

This code invokes the implementation of show() provided by the Manager class, and prints the employee name on screen.

Interfaces

An interface is a sort of "skeleton class", containing method signatures but no method implementations. In this way, interfaces are like abstract classes that contain only abstract methods. C# interfaces are very similar to Java interfaces, and work in very much the same way.

All the members of an interface are public by definition, and an interface cannot contain constants, fields (private data members), constructors, destructors, or any type of static member. The compiler will generate an error if any modifier is specified for the members of an interface.

We can derive classes from an interface in order to implement that interface. Such derived classes must provide implementations for all the interface's methods unless the derived class is declared abstract.

An interface is declared identically to Java. In an interface definition, a property indicates only its type, and whether it is read-only, write-only, or read/write by get and set keywords alone. The interface below declares one read-only property:

```
public interface interfacename
{
  // method signatures
  void methodA();
  int methodB(float parameter1, bool parameter2);

  // properties
  int ReadOnlyProperty
  {
    get;
  }
}
```

A class can inherit from this interface, using a colon in place of Java's implements keyword. The implementing class must provide definitions for all methods, and any required property accessors:

```csharp
public class InterfaceImplementation : interfacename
{
  // fields
  private int count = 0;
  private int ID;

  // implement methods defined in interface
  public void methodA()
  {
    .
    .
    .
  }
  public int methodB(float parameter1, bool parameter2)
  {
    .
    .
    .
    return(integerVariable);
  }
  public int ReadOnlyProperty
  {
    get
    {
      return count;
    }
  }

  // add extra methods if required

}
```

Implementing Multiple Interfaces

A class may implement multiple interfaces using the following syntax:

```csharp
public class MyClass : interfacename1, interfacename2, interfacename3
```

If a class implements more than one interface where there is ambiguity in the names of members, it is resolved using the full qualifier for the property or method name. In other words, the derived class can resolve the conflict by using the full qualifier name for the method to indicate to which interface it belongs, as in `interfacename.MethodA`.

Operator Overloading

Like C++, C# allows us to overload operators for use on our own classes. This makes it possible for a user-defined data type look as natural and be as logical to use as a fundamental data type. For example, we might create a new data type called `Complex` to represent a complex number, and provide methods that perform mathematical operations on such numbers using the standard arithmetic operators, such as using the + operator to add two complex numbers.

To overload an operator, we write a function that has the name `operator` followed by the symbol for the operator to be overloaded. For instance, this is how we would overload + operator:

```
public static complex operator+(complex lhs, complex rhs)
```

All operator overloads are `static` methods of the class. Also be aware that if you overload the equality (==) operator, you must overload the inequality operator (!=) too.

The full list of operators that can be overloaded is:

- Unary operators: +, -, !, ~, ++, --, `true`, `false`
- Binary operators: +, -, *, /, %, &, |, ^, <<, >>, ==, !=, >, <, >=, <=

The next example creates a `Complex` class that overloads the + and - operators:

```
public class complex
{
  private float real;
  private float img;

  public complex(float p, float q)
  {
    real = p;
    img = q;
  }

  public complex()
  {
    real = 0;
    img = 0;
  }

  public void print()
  {
    Console.WriteLine("{0} + {1}i", real, img);
  }

  // Overloading '+' operator
  public static complex operator+(complex lhs, complex rhs)
  {
    complex sum = new complex();
    sum.real = lhs.real + rhs.real;
    sum.img = lhs.img + rhs.img;
    return (sum);
  }

  // Overloading '-' operator
  public static complex operator-(complex lhs, complex rhs)
  {
    complex result = new complex();
    result.real = lhs.real - rhs.real;
    result.img = lhs.img - rhs.img;
```

```
        return (result);
    }
}
```

This class allows us to create and manipulate two complex numbers with code such as this:

```
using System;

public class ComplexClass
{
  public static void Main(string[] args)
  {
    // Set up complex numbers
    complex A = new complex(10.5f,12.5f);
    complex B = new complex(8.0f,4.5f);
    complex C;

    // Print object A and B
    Console.Write("Complex Number A: ");
    A.print();
    Console.Write("Complex Number B: ");
    B.print();

    // Add A and B, print result
    C = A + B;
    Console.Write("\nA + B = ");
    C.print();

    // Subtract A and B, print result
    C = A - B;
    Console.Write("A - B = ");
    C.print();
  }
}
```

As the program demonstrates, we can now use the plus and minus operators on objects belonging to our complex class quite intuitively. Here is the output we would get:

Complex Number A: 10.5 + 12.5i
Complex Number B: 8 + 4.5i

A + B = 18.5 + 17i
A - B = 2.5 + 8i

> *Java does not support operator overloading, although internally it overloads the + operator for string concatenation.*

Exceptions

Exception handling in C# is very similar to that of Java.

Whenever something goes critically wrong during execution of a program, the .NET runtime creates an `Exception` object detailing the error. In .NET, `Exception` is the base class for all the exception classes. There are many classes derived from `Exception` class, including:

- `IndexOutOfRangeException` – an index greater than the size of an array or collection was used
- `NullReferenceException` – a property or method of a reference has been used before that reference has been set to a valid instance
- `ArithmeticException` – thrown when an operation results in overflow or underflow
- `FormatException` – an argument or operand was in an incorrect format

As in Java, when we have code that is liable to cause an exception, we place that code within a `try` block. One or more `catch` blocks immediately after provide the error handling, and we can also use a `finally` block for any code that we want to execute whether an exception is thrown or not.

Note that when using multiple `catch` blocks, the exceptions caught must be placed in order of increasing generality as only the first `catch` block that matches the thrown exception will be executed.

Also, C# doesn't require an argument for a `catch` block as Java does; in the absence of an argument, the `catch` block applies to any `Exception` class.

For example, while reading from a file, you may encounter a `FileNotFoundException` or an `IOException`, and we would want to place the more specific `FileNotFoundException` handler first:

```
try
{
  // Code to open and read a file
}
catch (FileNotFoundException fe)
{
  // Handle file not found exception first
}
catch (IOException ioe)
{
  // Now handle any other IO exceptions
}
catch
{
  // This block will catch all other exceptions
}
finally
{
  // Executed whether or not an exception occurs, often to release resources
}
```

We can create our own exception classes by deriving from `Exception`. For example, the following code creates an `InvalidDepartmentException` class that we might throw if, say, the department given for a new employee record is invalid. The class constructor for our user-defined exception calls the base class constructor using the `base` keyword, sending an appropriate message:

```
public class InvalidDepartmentException : System.Exception
{
  public InvalidDepartmentException(string Department) : base(
                    "Invalid Department: " + Department){ }
}
```

We could then throw an exception of this type with code such as this:

```
if (!(Department == "Sales" | Department == "Marketing"))
    throw new InvalidDepartmentException(Department);
```

Note that C# does not support the `throws` keyword, which is used in Java to declare that a method may throw a particular type of exception which must be handled by the calling code.

Advanced C# Techniques

C# is able to be more comprehensive as a language than its Java relative because C# is not constrained by the need to run on a variety of platforms. This opens up the opportunity for some more advanced features that wouldn't be easy to implement in Java, and we'll quickly look at some of those in this section.

Indexers

Indexers provide a way to access a `class` or `struct` in the same way as an array. For example, we may have a class that represents a single department in our company. The class could contain the names of all employees in the department, and indexers could allow us to access these names like this:

```
myDeptartment[0] = "Fred"
myDeptartment[1] = "Barney"
```

and so on. Indexers are enabled by defining a property with the following signature in the class definition:

```
public string this [int index]
```

We then provide `get` and `set` methods as for a normal property, and it is these accessors that specify what internal member is referred to when the indexer is used.

In the following simple example, we create a class called Department that uses indexers to access the employees in that department, internally represented as an array of strings:

```csharp
using System;

public class Department
{
  private string name;
  private const int MAX_EMPLOYEES = 10;
  private string [] employees = new string [MAX_EMPLOYEES];

  public Department(string deptName)
  {
    name = deptName;
  }

  public string this [int index]
  {
    get
    {
      if (index >= 0 && index < MAX_EMPLOYEES)
        return employees[index];
      else
        throw new IndexOutOfRangeException();
        //return "Error";
    }
    set
    {
      if (index >= 0 && index < MAX_EMPLOYEES)
        employees[index] = value;
      else
        throw new IndexOutOfRangeException();
        //return "Error";
    }
  }

  // Other methods and properties as usual
}
```

We can then create an instance of this class and access it as shown below:

```csharp
public class SalesDept
{
  public static void Main(string[] args)
  {
    Department sales = new Department("Sales");
    sales[0] = "Nikki";
    sales[1] = "Becky";
    System.Console.WriteLine("The sales team is {0} and {1}", sales[0],
                             sales[1]);
  }
}
```

Attributes

C# introduces a new mechanism for declaring information about methods called **attributes**. Extra information about a method (or other member) is placed inside declarative tags that precede the method definition. The information given by attributes can be retrieved at run time through reflection.

There are three types of attributes:

- **Conditional** – prevents the compilation of affected code unless the symbol specified has been defined by a directive. This attribute is most commonly used for debug builds.
- **DllImport** – accesses the core Windows API and other legacy functions implemented in the specified DLL.
- **Obsolete** – marks a method that has been superceded by a preferred method. The attribute can cause the compiler to generate either an error or a warning when the affected method is used.

A small example will demonstrate the ideas behind attributes:

```
#define DEBUG
using System;
using System.Diagnostics;
using System.Runtime.InteropServices;

class AttributeClass
{
  [DllImport("user32.dll")]
  public static extern int MessageBox(int parent, String text,
                                      String caption, int type);

  [Conditional("DEBUG")]
  public static void DebugMethod()
  {
    Console.WriteLine( "We are debugging");
  }

  [Conditional("DEBUG")]
  [Obsolete("This K&R sample is way past its sell-by", false)]
  public static void HelloWorld()
  {
    Console.WriteLine("Hello World");
  }

  [STAThread]
  static void Main(string[] args)
  {
    MessageBox(0,"Old Style MessageBox Call", "DllImport Sample", 0);
    DebugMethod();
    HelloWorld();
  }
}
```

Compiling this code generates a warning due to the `Obsolete` attribute, displaying the message specified in the first argument of the attribute. If we set the second argument of this attribute to `true`, we would get a compile time error rather than a warning, with the same message.

If we remove the initial directive defining the `DEBUG` token and recompile, our code will not invoke `DebugMethod()`.

Delegates

Languages such as C++, Pascal, and others support the concept of **function pointers** that permit us to choose which function we wish to call at run time.

Java does not provide any construct with the functionality of a function pointer, but C# does, through the `System.Delegate` class. A delegate instance encapsulates a method, that is a callable entity.

Unlike function pointers in other languages, a delegate contains the object reference as well as the method. For instance methods, the delegate consists of an instance of the containing class and a method on the instance. For static methods, a callable entity consists of a class and a static method on the class. Thus, a delegate may be used to invoke a function of any object, and delegates are object-oriented, type-safe, and secure.

There are three steps when defining and using delegates:

- Declaration
- Instantiation
- Invocation

We declare a delegate with the following syntax:

```
delegate void myDelegate();
```

This delegate can then be used to reference any function that returns `void` and does not take any arguments.

Similarly, to create a delegate for any function that takes a `string` parameter and returns a `long`, we would use the following syntax:

```
delegate long myDelgate(methodSignature);
```

We could then assign this delegate to any method with this signature, like so:

```
myDelegate operation = new myDelegate(methodName);
```

105

Re-assigning Delegates

Delegate objects are immutable, that is, the signature they match cannot be changed once set. However, we can point to another method as long as both have the same signature. For instance:

```
delegate myDelegate(int a, int b)
myDelegate operation = new myDelegate(Add);
operation = new myDelegate(Multiply);
```

Here, we reassign Op to a new delegate object so that Op then invokes the Multiply method. We can only do this if both Add() and Multiply() have the same signature.

Invoking Delegates

Invoking a delegate is fairly straightforward, simply substituting the name of the delegate variable for the method name:

```
delegate long myDelegate(int i, int j);
myDelegate operation = new myDelegate(Add);
long lresult = operation(10, 20);
```

This invokes the Add method with values 10 and 20, and returns a long result that is assigned to variable lresult.

Let's create a quick program to illustrate the creation, instantiation, and invocation of a delegate:

```
using System;

public class DelegateClass
{
  delegate long myDelegate (int i, int j);

  public static void Main(string[] args)
  {
    myDelegate operation = new myDelegate(MathClass.Add);

    Console.WriteLine("Call to Add method through delegate");
    long l = operation(10, 20);
    Console.WriteLine("Sum of 10 and 20 is " + l);

    Console.WriteLine("Call to Multiply method thru delegate");
    operation = new myDelegate(MathClass.Multiply);
    l = operation(1639, 1525);
    Console.WriteLine("1639 multiplied by 1525 equals " + l);

  }
}

public class MathClass
{
  public static long Add (int i, int j)
```

```
    {
      return (i+j);
    }

    public static long Multiply (int i, int j)
    {
      return (i*j);
    }

  }
```

The output we will get is this:

> Call to Add method through delegate
> Sum of 10 and 20 is 30
> Call to Multiply method through delegate
> 1639 multiplied by 1525 equals 2499475

As mentioned earlier, a delegate instance must contain an object reference. We got round this in the example above by declaring our methods as `static`, which means there's no need to specify an object reference ourselves. If a delegate refers to an instance method however, the object reference must be given like so:

```
MathClass obj = new MathClass();
myDelegate operation = new myDelegate(obj.Power);
```

where `Power` is an instance method of `MathClass`. So, if `MathClass`'s methods were *not* declared as `static`, we would invoke them through a delegate like so:

```
using System;

public class DelegateClass
{
  delegate long myDelegate(int i, int j);

  public static void Main(string[] args)
  {
  MathClass mathObj = new MathClass();
  myDelegate operation = new myDelegate(mathObj.Add);

    Console.WriteLine("Call to Add method through delegate");
    long l = operation(10, 20);
    Console.WriteLine("Sum of 10 and 20 is " + l);

    Console.WriteLine("Call to Multiply method thru delegate");
    operation = new myDelegate(mathObj.Multiply);
    l = operation(1639, 1525);
    Console.WriteLine("1639 multiplied by 1525 equals " + l);
  }
}
```

If you run this program, you'll get the same output as previously, when the methods were declared as `static`.

Garbage Collection

In C and C++, many objects require the programmer to allocate them resources once declared, before the objects may be safely used. Releasing these resources back to the free memory pool once the object is done with is also the responsibility of the programmer. If resources are not released, the code is said to leak memory, as more and more resources are consumed needlessly. On the other hand, if resources are released prematurely, loss of data, the corruption of other memory areas, and null pointer exceptions can result.

Both Java and C# prevent these dangers by independently managing the lifetime of all objects in use by an application.

In Java, the JVM takes care of deallocating memory by keeping track of the references to allocated resources. Whenever the JVM detects that a resource is no longer referenced by a valid reference, the resource is garbage-collected.

In C#, garbage collection is handled by the Common Language Runtime (CLR) with similar functionality to that of the JVM. The CLR garbage collector periodically checks the memory heap for any unreferenced objects, and releases the resources held by these objects.

Safe and Unsafe Code

A particularly interesting feature of C# is its support for non-type safe code. Normally, the CLR takes on the responsibility overseeing the behavior of IL (Intermediate Language) code, and prevents any shady-looking operations. However, there are times when we wish to directly access low-level functionality such as Win32 API calls, and we are permitted to do this, as long as we take responsibility for ensuring such code operates correctly. Such code must be placed inside `unsafe` blocks in our source code.

The unsafe Keyword

C# code that makes low-level API calls, uses pointer arithmetic, or carries out some other unsavory operation, has to be placed inside blocks marked with the `unsafe` keyword. Any of the following can be marked as `unsafe`:

- An entire method
- A code block in braces
- An individual statement

The following example demonstrates the use of `unsafe` in all three of the above situations:

```
class UnsafeClass
{
   unsafe static void PointyMethod()
   {
      int i=10;
      int *p = &i;
      System.Console.WriteLine("*p = " + *p);
      string address = "Pointer p = " + int.Format((int) p, "X");
```

```
      System.Console.WriteLine(address);
    }

    static void StillPointy()
    {
      int i=10;
      unsafe
      {
        int *p = &i;
        System.Console.WriteLine("*p = " + *p);
        string address = "Pointer p = " + int.Format((int) p, "X");
        System.Console.WriteLine(address);
      }
    }

    static void Main()
    {
      PointyMethod();
      StillPointy();
    }
}
```

In this code, the entire `PointyMethod()` method is marked `unsafe` because the method declares and uses pointers. The `StillPointy()` method marks a block of code as unsafe as this block once again uses pointers.

The fixed Keyword

In safe code, the garbage collector is quite free to move an object during its lifetime in its mission to organize and condense free resources. However, if our code uses pointers, this behavior could easily cause unexpected results, so we can instruct the garbage collector not to move certain objects using the `fixed` keyword.

The following code shows the `fixed` keyword being used to ensure that an array is not moved by the system during the execution of a block of code in the `PointyMethod()` method. Note that `fixed` is only used within `unsafe` code:

```
public class FixedClass
{
  public static void PointyMethod(char[] array)
  {
    unsafe
    {
      fixed (char *p = array)
      {
        for (int i=0; i<array.Length; i++)
        {
          System.Console.Write(*(p+i));
        }
      }
    }
  }
}
```

```
    static void Main ()
    {
      char[] array = { 'H', 'e', 'l', 'l', 'o' };
      PointyMethod(array);
    }
}
```

Summary

Though Microsoft and other vendors have introduced many languages for the .NET platform, C# is a language that closely resembles Java and is very well suited to developers wishing to migrate from J2EE to the .NET platform.

This chapter has compared and contrasted the two languages. In many ways, C# has the power of C++, the elegance of Java, and the ease of development of Visual Basic, and I hope that this chapter has demonstrated this.

The key advantages that C# offers over Java as a development language are:

- More flexible syntax than Java, with support for operator overloading and type-safe enumerations
- Support for 'dangerous' code through the `unsafe` keyword
- Interoperability with other .NET languages
- Access to the resources of the powerful .NET class library

The disadvantages are:

- Not suitable for all time-critical or high-performance applications
- Certain features such as inline function destructors guaranteed to run at particular points in the code are not available
- C# is of course not platform independent

Data Access

This chapter is going to cover data access using native .NET Framework classes. Where helpful, we'll draw parallels with JDBC as we examine the main issues a developer should be aware of when starting work with the .NET Framework and ADO.NET.

To give you an idea of the structure, the major topics covered in this chapter are:

- ADO.NET structure
- ADO.NET managed providers
- Simple connection to database
- Fetching data
- Manipulating data
- Using tables and relations
- Searching and sorting records
- ADO.NET data events
- ADO.NET data exceptions
- `DataSets` and XML
- `DataSets` and serialization

We'll take a practical approach to exploring the functionality of ADO.NET, by putting together several simple examples establishing the fundamental relationships between the .NET Framework and ADO.NET classes.

The Structure of ADO.NET

ADO.NET's predecessors were ADO and OLE DB. ADO was merely a wrapper of OLE DB to cater for complexities that OLE DB couldn't handle. As such, its architecture was rather loose, and not particularly well engineered – for example, both disconnected and connected models were housed within the same object, the `Recordset`.

In order to accommodate the diverse scenarios in which database functionality could be requested, old-style ADO's data must make an arduous journey across several interface layers, consuming resources as it goes. Even though ADO supported disconnected data sharing, it relied predominantly on a tightly coupled connection model, which resulted in every request creating a new connection to the data source. As you can imagine, this had a high impact on the application's performance.

ADO's limitations were acutely embarrassing to Microsoft in many areas, so when ADO.NET was designed, it was engineered specifically to avoid many of its predecessor's shortcomings. ADO.NET is **not** a wrapper around old ADO technology. It is a completely new data access technology, mainly housed in .the .NET Frameworks `System.Data.*` and `System.Xml` namespaces:

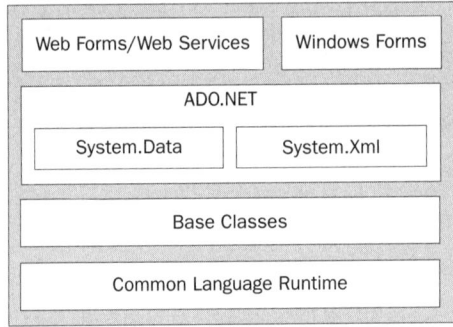

Database connections are resource intensive, particularly when establishing concurrent connections. A disconnected architecture minimizes this overhead by connecting with the data source for only a brief period of time. As well as reducing time per connection, this enables us to pass data freely between application tiers without worrying about the underlying connections. ADO.NET automatically produces serialized XML objects that can be streamed between components.

ADO.NET classes are found in the following namespaces:

Namespace	Description
`System.Data`	Represents the overall ADO.NET architecture
`System.Data.Common`	Classes to access a data source that are shared by a range of classes
`System.Data.OleDb`	Contains classes used by the .NET data provider for OLE DB data sources
`System.Data.SqlClient`	Classes used by the .NET data provider for SQL Server, specifically tuned for increased performance with SQL Server 7.0 and above

Data Access

Namespace	Description
System.Data.SqlTypes	Special classes for SQL Server native data types which can be used instead of System data types
System.Xml	Supports standard XML processing

Naturally, the names and contents of these namespaces differ from the packages that encapsulate the JDBC API; nevertheless, the concept is the same: classes that are used to perform a certain type of role are arranged together. The following diagram shows how ADO.NET's object model fits together:

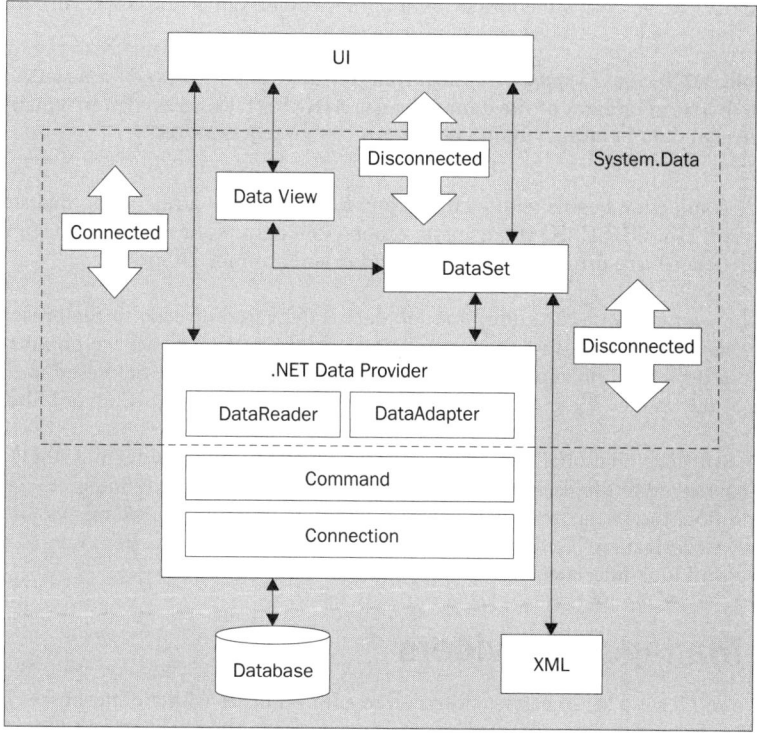

The key components of ADO.NET as shown in the above diagram are described next:

- ❑ DataSet – a relational structure conformant to XML Schemas. Can be seen as a collection of relational data, exposing several methods for access.
- ❑ .NET Managed Provider – the 'bridge' between the DataSet and the data store. It is broken up into the following classes:
    - ❑ Command – allows access to database commands, to return and modify data as well as to run stored procedures, or send and retrieve parameters.
    - ❑ Connection – establishes the underlying connection to the database.

115

- DataAdapter, provides functionality to populate and update the `DataSet` as well as maintaining synchronized updates between the `DataSet` and the data store.
- DataReader, provides a straight one-way forward-only connection to the data and it is regarded as the fastest way for data to be read from a database in ADO.NET.

- DataView – a customizable representation of the contents of a `DataSet`. It mainly supports functionality not present in a `DataSet` such as filtering and sorting.

The `DataReader` and `DataSet` represent the two distinct ways of accessing data: `DataReader` embodies the connected model, while the `DataSet` is disconnected. In general, `DataReader` performs better than a `DataSet`, due to the simple fact that it doesn't need to offer the complex and flexible structure of the `DataSet`. We will consider both of these objects in detail as we work through the chapter.

> In the old ADO, *cursor support* was required to track each instance of a `ResultSet` in order to perform updates of the data. Because ADO.NET was designed primarily with disconnected data in mind, cursors have been completely removed.

An ADO.NET connection begins with a connection being made to a relational data store, which can be SQL Server, OLE DB, ODBC, XML, or many others. Once this connection has been made, data can be taken from the data source using either a connected or a disconnected model.

When using the connected `DataReader` model, data is delivered directly to the presentation tier. Alternatively, we may wish to use disconnected architecture, in which case we populate a `DataSet` through a `DataAdapter`. Information stored in a `DataSet` can then be delivered to the user interface immediately, or interpreted by a `DataView` object if we wish to apply sorting and filtering.

The `DataSet` can store relational data and be shared between components in a single tier without having to be connected to the data source, giving it the potential to neatly integrate data from several sources. In addition, the `DataSet` is very XML-friendly, with built-in mechanisms for reading and writing directly to XML files. This means that `DataSets` provide an excellent way of interchanging data, which we will look into later on.

ADO.NET Managed Providers

A .NET data provider is a set of classes designed to communicate with a data source. In *n*-tier applications, the data provider manages the data flow between the backend and the presentation or middle layer of an application. Data providers are defined by interfaces residing in the `System.Data` namespace, as shown in the following hierarchy:

Data Access

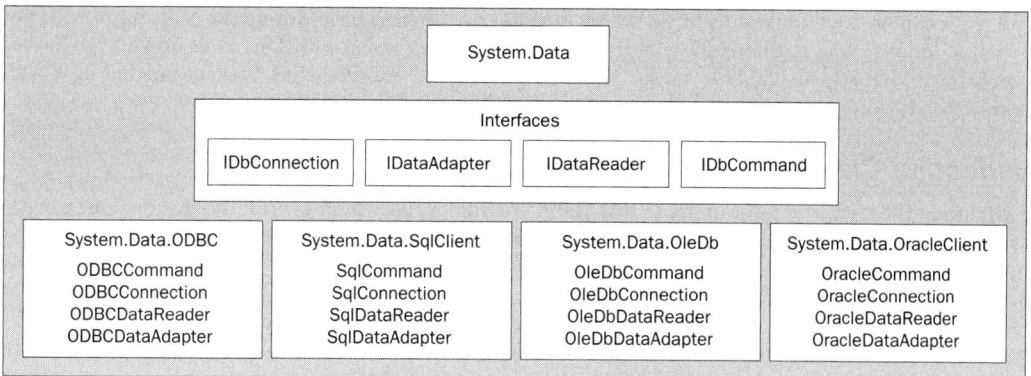

The managed providers distributed with the framework are `System.Data.SqlClient` and `System.Data.OleDb`; other providers are distributed as add-on components.

Different providers are available for different data sources to maximize efficiency for each data store. For example, if SQL Server is the backend database, the most efficient data provider will be `System.Data.SqlClient` because it is optimized for working with SQL Server. On the other hand, if our application uses another data source, including SQL Server 6.5 or earlier, we have to implement classes from the .NET OLE DB provider.

The great thing about the managed OLE DB data providers in .NET is that OLE DB providers for previous ADO versions can be reused, providing immediate support for a range of data sources in ADO.NET.

While OLE DB may seem a restricted way of accessing other database formats, specialized .NET classes are likely to be provided for an increasing number of systems as .NET becomes established. For instance, accessing Oracle data stores in .NET originally required either ODBC or OLE DB providers. Now however, native support is available, providing superior performance for Oracle databases, and making .NET a much more attractive platform for Oracle-based applications.

The ODBC.NET managed provider means that ADO.NET has native ODBC support, giving access to almost all legacy data that supports ODBC, such as AS400.

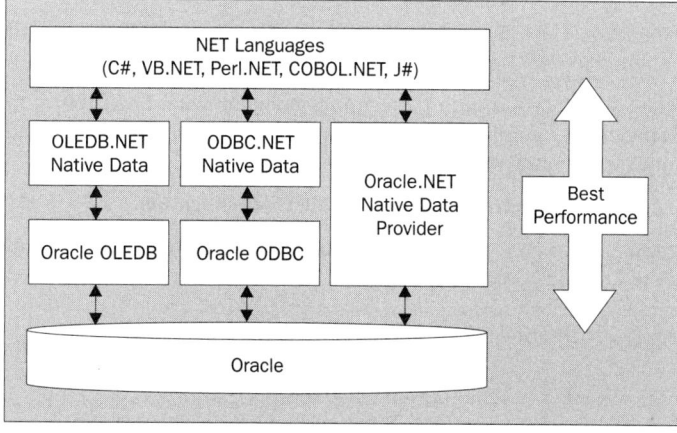

117

Chapter 4

In this chapter, we'll look at `System.Data.SqlClient`, which provides native SQL support. If you wish to follow along but don't have SQL Server, you can get hold of MSDE, a cut down SQL Server distributable, freely available from the MSDN web site, and bundled with packages including VS.NET and Office.

Connection Class

Mirroring the `Connection` interface that JDBC maintains, on which we call the `getConnection()` method to create a connection, ADO.NET uses classes that implement `IDbConnection`, such as `SqlConnection`.

The JDBC `Connection` class indicates the data source for a connection through the `ConnectionString` property, which gives the database name along with any other details required to connect.

.NET uses similar connection strings, and we could, for example, create a `SqlConnection` object with the following C# code:

```
SqlConnection myConn = new SqlConnection("initial catalog=SalesInfo;data
    source=localhost;uid=dataAdmin;pwd=reallySecretPassword");
```

Note that supplying a user ID and password in a connection string in this way is discouraged, and Microsoft recommends using Windows integrated security, where the current Windows logon is used for authentication. The username and password combination has been kept for compatibility with SQL Server 7.0 and below.

Command Class

An instance of the `Command` class represents the SQL statement or stored procedure that is to be executed against a particular database using a connection through a `Connection` object:

```
SqlCommand myCommand = new SqlCommand();
myCommand.Connection = myConn;
```

A `SqlCommand` object is executed by one of the following methods:

- `ExecuteReader()` – returns a `DataReader` object containing the records that match the query contained in the `CommandText` property.
- `ExecuteNonQuery()` – used for executing statements that don't return matching records. In SQL, this means all commands other than SELECT: INSERT, UPDATE, and DELETE. This method returns the number of rows affected.
- `ExecuteScalar()` – retrieves a single value from execution.
- `ExecuteXmlReader()` – returns an `XmlReader` populated with the results of the request stored in the `CommandText` property.

In JDBC, the `Statement` interface is used to execute SQL statements:

```
Statement myStatment = myConn.createStatement()
```

DataReader Class

`DataReader` provides a forward-only and read-only method of accessing data, and in many ways it is very similar to the JDBC `ResultSet`. The `DataReader` provides a connected link to a database, so it constantly occupies resources on the data server. Furthermore, because ADO.NET does not support cursors, no process other than reading and closing can be executed by the `DataReader`.

Unlike its predecessor in ADO, the `DataReader` class has no `EOF` (end of file) property to indicate that the end of records has been reached. Instead, the `Read()` method is called, reading in one record per call and returning `true`. If there are no more records, the method returns `false`.

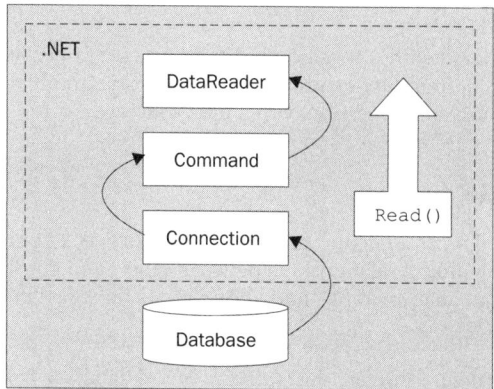

Even though ADO.NET provides support for disconnected access, it is good programming practice to use a `DataReader` whenever your data can be manipulated successfully with the connected model. This is primarily for enhanced performance.

A `DataReader` can be instantiated explicitly:

```
SqlDataReader dr = new SqlDataReader();
```

or by using the `ExecuteReader()` method on the `Command` object:

```
SqlDataReader dr = myCommand.ExecuteReader();
```

We will explore the `DataReader` and how to attach it to live data later in the chapter.

The DataAdapter Class

The `DataAdapter` is the bridge between the data source and the `DataSet`, but it is also responsible for managing the insertion, deletion, selection, and updating of records. To specify which type of task we wish it to perform, we create a `Command` object and assign it to the appropriate property on the `DataAdapter`. There are four properties to choose from, depending on the type of command we're executing: `DeleteCommand`, `InsertCommand`, `SelectCommand` and `UpdateCommand`:

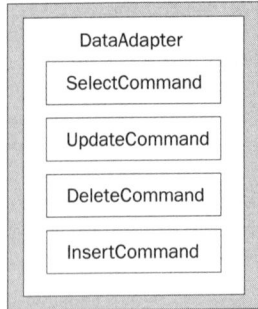

These properties are associated with Command objects that have properties containing the SQL statement to perform the required data manipulation. The Command objects are in turn associated with a Connection object that maintains a session with a data source.

The DataSet Class

The DataSet class is based on a collection of tables in memory. A DataSet can even store an entire database in the memory, including relationships between tables and constraints. This means that the DataSet supports relational 'map reading', and allows views on several tables or data sources without performing a database JOIN.

The DataSet's internal structure mirrors the structure of the database from where its data originates, providing an in-memory copy. This disconnected model functions in conjunction with a DataAdapter to exchange data with the database.

In JDBC, CachedRowSets have the same ability to store ResultSet data while detached from the data source. However, there are differences in the process. In .NET the DataAdapter first populates a DataSet by the DataAdapter's Fill() method. A JDBC CachedRowSet does not make use of adapters, and it uses its own populate() method to fill itself with data from a ResultSet. So, for the following Java statements:

```
CachedRowSet myCachedRowSet = new CachedRowSet();
myCachedRowSet.populate(myResultSet);
```

We would use the following in C#:

```
DataAdapter myDataAdapter = new DataAdapter();
myDataAdapter.SelectCommand = myCommand;
myDataAdapter.Fill(myDataSet);
```

> The Java **CachedRowSet** is a JavaBean-compliant complement to JDBC's **ResultSet**. **CachedRowSets** can be serialized, allowing them to be sent out to remote clients, updated, and transmitted back to a server. **DataSet** inherits from **MarshalByValueComponent**, which provides a basic implementation for transmitting itself to remote locations and implements **ISerializable**, which gives the ability to control its own serialization and deserialization. We'll return to these issues later on.

The `DataSet` can be used to update the database in the same fashion. Once data is altered in the `DataSet`, it can be passed back into the `DataAdapter` by calling the `Update()` method, which implicitly reflects all changes in the database.

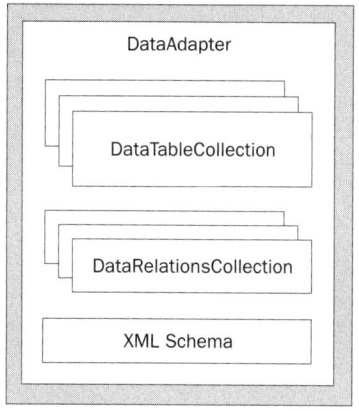

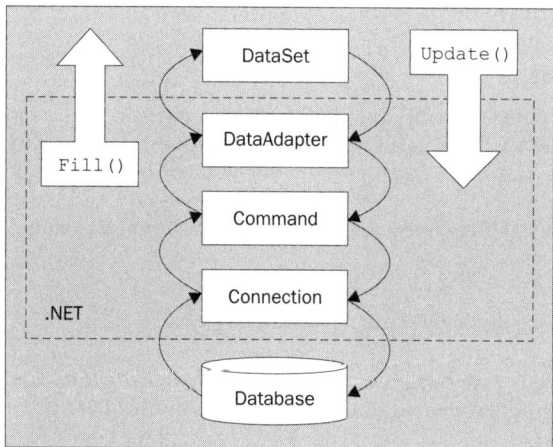

There are three main benefits that come from using a `DataSet`:

- A `DataSet` can hold as many tables as a database can contain, which provides us with a consistent in-memory relation model
- A `DataSet` has no dependency with the data source – it can perform any operation with the data without any permission from other processes
- A `DataSet` can read and write to a XML file, which can be a great benefit if integrating with other applications

Additionally, as long as the provider is native .NET, the `DataSet` can update and retrieve data from multiple data stores:

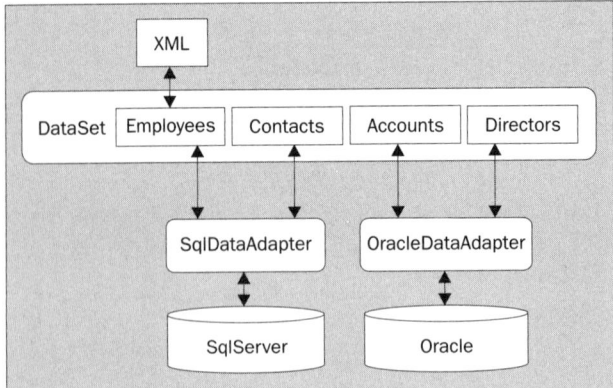

Let's have a look at the two top-level component classes of the `DataSet`: a `DataTableCollection` and a `DataRelationCollection`.

DataTableCollection

The `DataSet` holds its data as a collection of `DataTable` objects, which represent in-memory tables. They are contained in a `DataTableCollection` where they are defined by columns, rows, and constraints. These tables are accessed either by table name or by their index number in the collection.

For example, to retrieve a table named `Employees` from a `DataSet` named `myDataSet`, we may do so by table name:

```
DataTable myTable = myDataSet.Tables["Employees"];
```

Note that the table name is case sensitive. Alternatively, if we know that `Employees` is the first or only `DataTable` in the `DataSet`, we could retrieve it using an index of zero:

```
DataTable myTable = myDataSet.Tables[0];
```

A `DataTable` contains constraint objects and properties that provide the same relational integrity as found in the database table. This is achieved through the `DataColumn` class, which exposes properties to specify the type of contained data, and relations with other columns. We access a particular `DataColumn` in a `DataColumnCollection` in the same way as the `DataTable`: via the name of the column or the index in the collection. For example, we could instantiate a new column by name like this:

```
DataColumn myDataColumn = new DataColumn("ID");
```

This creates a column called `ID`. We can then assign a data type to that column:

```
myDataColumn.DataType = System.Type.GetType("System.Decimal");
```

Next, we add the `DataColumn` object to the `DataColumnCollection` of the `DataTable`:

```
myTable.Columns.Add(myDataColumn);
```

Finally, we set relational properties for the `DataColumn` like this:

```
myTable.Columns["ID"].AutoIncrement = true;
myTable.Columns["ID"].AutoIncrementSeed = 100;
myTable.Columns["ID"].AllowDBNull = true;
```

`DataRow` objects are contained in a `DataRowCollection`, which comprises the actual records in the table. Together with `DataColumns`, these conform to the schema defining the data. For example, we instantiate a new `DataRow` object like so:

```
DataRow myDataRow = new DataRow();
```

Now we assign values to it:

```
myDataRow["FirstName"] = "Jay";
myDataRow["LastName"] = "Sharp";
```

And finally, add it to the `Rows` collection of our `DataTable`:

```
myTable.Rows.Add(myDataRow);
```

As we continue through the chapter, we'll uncover the key methods and properties that allow `DataRows` to retrieve and modify data.

DataRelationCollection

A `DataRelationCollection` holds `DataRelation` objects to define a relationship between two `DataTables`, using `DataColumns` on each `DataTable` to create the relation. A relationship is established by a related column in both the parent and child `DataTable` that has a matching data type (thus reinforcing their relational data integrity).

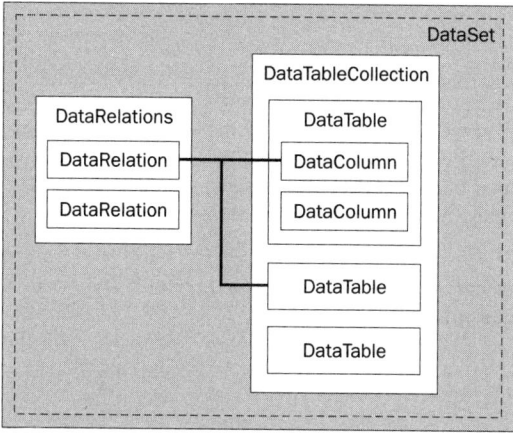

Once a relation is established between two tables, any modifications must satisfy the relationship if they are to be allowed.

For example, we could instantiate a new `DataRelation` object called `rel`, passing the constructor the name of the relation, the parent table key, and child table key:

```
DataRelation rel = new DataRelation("Details",
                myDataSet.Tables["Orders"].Columns["OrderID"],
                myDataSet.Tables["Order Details"].Columns["OrderID"]);
```

This establishes a relationship between the `OrderID` columns in the `Orders` table and `Order Details` table. We add the `DataRelation` to the `DataRelationCollection` of the `DataSet` with this code:

```
myDataSet.Relations.Add(myRelation);
```

Filtering and Sorting DataSets

The `DataView` provides a layer on top of the `DataSet` with the main purpose of facilitating connection with UI objects that provide functionalities such as filtering and sorting, as filtering and sorting are not built into the `DataSet`. The principal benefit of using the `DataView` is that we can populate an entire `DataSet` with `DataTables` and records, leaving filtering or sorting to the presentation tier, but avoiding future trips to the data store if we wish our data to be filtered or sorted differently.

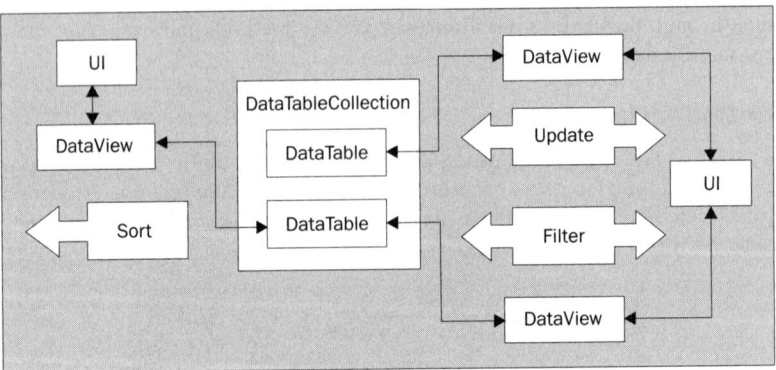

It is important to realize that we can only manipulate one `DataTable` per `DataView`, but that a `DataTable` can be associated with many `DataViews`. The `DataView` is capable of updating, adding, and deleting data, which can be controlled by properties such as `AllowDelete`, `AllowEdit` and `AllowNew`, providing an elegant means to modify data.

> The `DataView` class can only be used with the `DataSet` and is not available for use in conjunction with a `DataReader`.

Getting Practical

We are now going to cover some basic concepts of data access with ADO.NET, by exploring different approaches of data navigation and manipulation with reference to some Java code that performs the same function. We will use Microsoft SQL Server (v7.0 or higher) to manipulate records and tables from the sample Northwind database.

We'll create two simple console applications, one using JDBC and the other using ADO.NET, exposing some of the similarities between the two technologies.

> *To use SQL Server with JDBC, install the JDBC driver for SQL Server, available from the MSDN downloads site.*

Firstly let's start with the JDBC approach. We'll begin by determining if a connection is opened in the following file, called `SimpleConnection.java`:

```java
import java.sql.*;

public class SimpleConnection
{
  public static void main(String arg[])
  {
    Connection con;
    try
    {
      Class.forName("com.microsoft.jdbc.sqlserver.SQLServerDriver");
      String url =
        "jdbc:microsoft:sqlserver://SERVERNAME:1433;DatabaseName=Northwind";
      con = DriverManager.getConnection(url, "sa", "sa");
      if(!con.isClosed())
        System.out.println("Open");
    }
    catch(Exception e)
    {
      System.out.println(e);
    }
    finally
    {
      con.close
    }
  }
}
```

Remember to use the name of your server in the above code. When you run the program, you'll get the following output if connection was successful:

```
Command Prompt
C:\Pro C# for Java\Chapter 04>java SimpleConnection
Open
C:\Pro C# for Java\Chapter 04>
```

This example is nothing complicated, we're simply loading the database vendor driver and instantiating a JDBC `Connection` object by passing the username, password, and database URL. Let's now have a look at how the same task is accomplished using ADO.NET. Create a text file named `openSQL.cs`, and add the code described next.

Firstly, we must define the namespaces. Remember that unlike Java, .NET does not always have to use the `System` namespace in the way that `System.lang` is always there in Java. `System.Data.SqlClient` is the namespace that contains the classes used in ADO.NET:

```
using System;
using System.Data.SqlClient;
```

Now we can start our class, that comprises just the `Main()` method:

```
class SimpleConnection
{
  static void Main(string[] args)
  {
    try
    {
```

We need to set up a string that contains the connection parameters required for the constructor of a new `SqlConnection` object:

```
      string connStr = "data source=SERVERNAME;initial catalog=Northwind;"
                     + "integrated security=SSPI";
      SqlConnection sqlConn = new SqlConnection (connStr);
```

Once the `SqlConnection` object is instantiated, we can attempt to open the connection by explicitly calling the `Open()` method. We can then retrieve the connection status using the `State` property:

```
      sqlConn.Open();
      Console.WriteLine(sqlConn.State.ToString());
      sqlConn.Close();
```

We just need to finish up our `try...catch` block, and close the method and class:

```
    }
    catch(SqlException e)
    {
```

Data Access

```
      Console.WriteLine(e);
    }
  }
}
```

Compile the code with `csc.exe`, and run it. It produces very similar output to the Java equivalent:

```
Command Prompt
C:\Pro C# for Java\Chapter 04>csc openSQL.cs
Microsoft (R) Visual C# .NET Compiler version 7.00.9466
for Microsoft (R) .NET Framework version 1.0.3705
Copyright (C) Microsoft Corporation 2001. All rights reserved.

C:\Pro C# for Java\Chapter 04>openSQL
Open

C:\Pro C# for Java\Chapter 04>_
```

Fetching Data

When we talk about fetching data with JDBC, we know that a `ResultSet` can represent a table of records retrieved from a statement object that is generally created by executing a command against a database. When instantiated, a `ResultSet` has a default forward-only cursor and is not updateable. In this section, we'll look at two console programs that achieve the same result in JDBC and ADO.NET. Copy the Java code from the previous example to a new file called `Categories.java`, and add the lines highlighted below:

```java
import java.sql.*;

public class SimpleConnection
{
  public static void main(String arg[])
  {
    Connection con;
    try
    {
      Class.forName("com.microsoft.jdbc.sqlserver.SQLServerDriver");
      String url =
        "jdbc:microsoft:sqlserver://SERVERNAME:1433;DatabaseName=Northwind";
      con = DriverManager.getConnection(url, "sa", "sa");
      Statement st = con.createStatement();
      ResultSet rs = st.executeQuery("SELECT CategoryName FROM "
                                     + "CATEGORIES");
      while(rs.next())
      {
        System.out.println(rs.getString("CategoryName"));
      }
    }
    catch(Exception e)
    {
      System.out.println(e);
    }
```

```
      finally
      {
        con.close
      }
    }
  }
}
```

When you run the Java application you should see something like this:

```
C:\Pro C# for Java\Chapter 04>java Categories
Beverages
Condiments
Confections
Dairy Products
Grains/Cereals
Meat/Poultry
Produce
Seafood

C:\Pro C# for Java\Chapter 04>
```

To reproduce this functionality in ADO.NET, we use a `SqlDataReader` that behaves similarly to a default `ResultSet`; that is, it provides a read-only, forward-only stream of data. Copy the previous C# file as `Categories.cs`, and add the highlighted code:

```
using System;
using System.Data.SqlClient;

class SimpleConnection
{
  static void Main(string[] args)
  {
    try
    {
      string connStr = "data source=SERVERNAME;"
                    + "initial catalog=Northwind;"
                    + "integrated security=SSPI";
      SqlConnection sqlConn = new SqlConnection (connStr);

      sqlConn.Open();
      SqlCommand cd = new SqlCommand("SELECT * FROM CATEGORIES", sqlConn);
      SqlDataReader dr = cd.ExecuteReader();

      // Iterate through the stream one record at a time
      while (dr.Read())
      {
        Console.WriteLine(dr.GetString(1));
      }
      dr.Close();
      sqlConn.Close();
    }
    catch(SqlException e)
    {
```

```
          System.out.println(e);
      }
   }
}
```

All we do here is instantiate a `SqlCommand` object once our connection has been opened, by passing in a SQL `SELECT` statement along with the `SqlConnection` object. We then initialize a `SqlDataReader` object with the value returned from executing the `ExecuteReader()` method on the `SqlCommand` object. We can then iterate through the stream in a `while` loop, which continues until `Read()` returns `false`. Finally we close the `SqlDataReader`.

This C# application produces identical output to its Java equivalent:

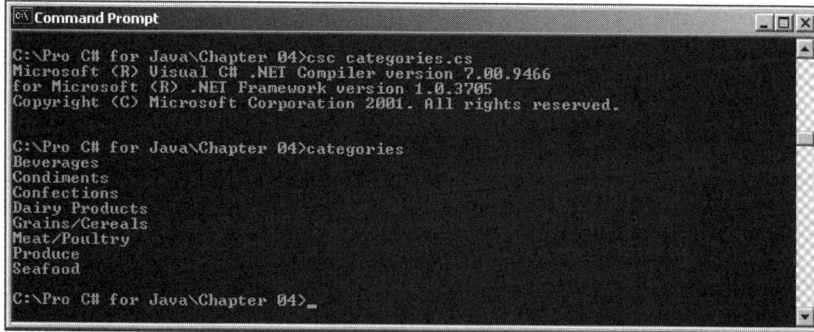

As you can see, it isn't hard to replicate basic JDBC functionality in .NET. Let's leave JDBC behind us now, and continue our exploration of ADO.NET in C#.

Manipulating Data

We can control and sort data much more easily with `DataSets`, which are arrangements of `DataTables` and `DataRows` corresponding to an underlying data source.

Simple DataSet Example

The following example demonstrates how to create a simple console application to connect to SQL Server using the .NET `SqlClient` managed provider. The code, in the file `Employees.cs`, shows how a `DataSet`, being completely independent of the data source, can be populated in the same fashion as a JDBC `CachedRowSet`. Our example will connect to the `Employees` table in the Northwind database and retrieve the first and last name of all employees:

```
using System;
using System.Data;
using System.Data.SqlClient;

   class SimpleDataSet
   {
     static void Main(string[] args)
     {
```

```csharp
string connStr = "data source=SERVERNAME;initial catalog=Northwind;"
               + "integrated security=SSPI;persist security "
               + "info=True;workstation id=guest;packet size=4096";

// Instantiate a Connection Object
SqlConnection sqlConn = new SqlConnection(connStr);

// Create the DataAdapter, DataSet, and Command objects
SqlDataAdapter myAdapter = new SqlDataAdapter();
DataSet myDataSet = new DataSet();
SqlCommand sqlSelectCommand = new SqlCommand();

// Create SQL Statement in CommandText Property of Command object
sqlSelectCommand.CommandText = "Select FirstName, LastName From"
                             + " Employees";

// Set Connection property of Command object
sqlSelectCommand.Connection = sqlConn;

// Assign Command object to DataAdapter
myAdapter.SelectCommand = sqlSelectCommand;

// Populate DataSet using SQL command in DataAdapter
myAdapter.Fill(myDataSet, "Employees");

Console.WriteLine("-----------------------");
Console.WriteLine("|First Name | LastName|");
Console.WriteLine("-----------------------");

// Iterate though "Employees" Table retrieving first and last names
foreach(DataRow emp in myDataSet.Tables["Employees"].Rows)
{
    Console.WriteLine(emp["FirstName"].ToString().PadRight(13) + " "
                    + emp["LastName"] );
}
   }
}
```

Here is the output of this simple program:

```
C:\Pro C# for Java\Chapter 04>employees

|First Name | LastName|

Nancy       Davolio
Andrew      Fuller
Janet       Leverling
Margaret    Peacock
Steven      Buchanan
Michael     Suyama
Robert      King
Laura       Callahan
Anne        Dodsworth

C:\Pro C# for Java\Chapter 04>
```

The approach used here is basically the same as that used with `SqlDataReader`. Note the `System.Data` namespace at the start of the file, which is where the `DataSet` class resides.

The first few lines of new code instantiate the objects we need for a basic `DataSet` interaction: the `DataSet` itself, and `SqlDataAdapter` and `SqlCommand` objects. The `SqlCommand` object contains the SQL command we wish to run on our database in the `CommandText` property. We use a `SELECT` statement that retrieves the first and last names from records in the `Employee` table. We also need to set the `Connection` property of the `SqlCommand` object to the `SqlConnection` that is to be used.

The next step is to set the `SelectCommand` property of the `SqlDataAdapter` to the `SqlCommand` object that we've just created. The `DataAdapter` will then manage the `SqlConnection` object associated with this `SqlCommand`, opening and closing the connection as required, removing the responsibility from the programmer to have to do so explicitly.

All the ground work is now complete, and we can populate our `DataSet` through the `SqlDataAdapter` by calling its `Fill()` method. We pass the `DataSet` and the name of the `DataTable` that will be created in the `DataSet` to hold our new data.

From this point on, we operate on the `DataSet` with no connection to the original data source whatsoever. When the final `foreach` loop iterates through all rows in the new `DataTable` (accessed through the `Rows` collection property), we write information held in the `DataSet` to the console without checking against the original data source.

> Note that we do not use the `DataSet` to directly access data, but instead use a reference to the appropriate `DataTable` within the `DataSet`.

Using Tables and Relations

Relational databases store data in a very structured and interrelated fashion. Referential integrity rules enforce constraints and minimize data redundancy.

A `DataSet` contains a collection called `DataRelationCollection` that holds relations, each relation being represented by a `DataRelation` object. A `DataRelation` describes a relationship between two tables linked by `DataColumn` objects – replicating the behavior of primary and foreign key pairs. It is also important to be aware that the `DataTables` are linked in a relational structure, where one is the parent table and the other the child.

The next example, `Relations.cs`, creates a relation between the `Order` and `Order Details` tables in the Northwind database and extracts records with an associative pattern. We start as usual:

```
using System;
using System.Data;
using System.Data.SqlClient;

class RelationExmaple
{
  static void Main(string[] args)
  {
    try
    {
      string connStr = "data source=SERVERNAME;initial catalog=Northwind;"
                     + "integrated security=SSPI";
```

```
// Instantiate a Connection Object
SqlConnection sqlConn = new SqlConnection(connStr);
```

We need to store both tables involved in the relation in the `DataSet`, and so we instantiate two `SqlDataAdapter` objects. One will be for the `Orders` table and the other for the `Order Details` table:

```
// Instantiate a DataAdapter for each database table
SqlDataAdapter sqlOrders = new SqlDataAdapter();
SqlDataAdapter sqlOrderDetails = new SqlDataAdapter();
```

Then we instantiate the `DataSet` and `Command` objects. We need a `SqlCommand` object for each `SqlDataAdapter`, passing the appropriate SQL SELECT statement to each. Note that the SQL statement must include the columns that we will access when we iterate through the `DataTable`, otherwise a `System.ArgumentException` will be thrown (we'll come back to exceptions in ADO.NET later on). Finally, we associate the `SqlConnection` to each `SqlCommand` object:

```
// Instantiate DataSet and Command objects
DataSet myDataSet = new DataSet();
SqlCommand sqlSelectOrders = new SqlCommand("SELECT OrderID FROM"
                             + " dbo.[Orders]");
SqlCommand sqlSelectDetail = new SqlCommand("SELECT OrderID,"
                             + " ProductID, UnitPrice, Quantity,"
                             + " Discount FROM dbo.[Order Details]");
sqlSelectOrders.Connection = sqlConn;
sqlSelectDetail.Connection = sqlConn;
```

At this point, we set each `SqlDataAdapter`'s `SelectCommand` property to the respective `SqlCommand` object so it runs the appropriate SQL command. After that, we can populate the `DataSet` with the two tables by calling the `Fill()` method on each `SqlDataAdapter`:

```
// Add each Command to appropriate DataAdapter
sqlOrders.SelectCommand = sqlSelectOrders;
sqlOrderDetails.SelectCommand = sqlSelectDetail;

// Fill DataSet with both database tables
sqlOrders.Fill(myDataSet, "Orders");
sqlOrderDetails.Fill(myDataSet, "Order Details");
```

To create a relation between two `DataTables` in a `DataSet`, we use the `DataRelation` class from `System.Data`. Firstly we create the relation using three arguments. The first argument is a string that names the relation, the second is the `DataColumn` corresponding to the primary key of the parent `DataTable`, and the last argument is the `DataColumn` corresponding to the foreign key in the child `DataTable`:

```
// Create a new DataRelation object
DataRelation relation = new DataRelation("Details",
            myDataSet.Tables["Orders"].Columns["OrderID"],
            myDataSet.Tables["Order Details"].Columns["OrderID"]);
```

We then add our `DataRelation` object to the `DataRelationCollection` of the `DataSet` by calling the `Add()` method on the `DataSet`'s `Relations` property:

```
// Add relation object to DataRelationCollection of DataSet
myDataSet.Relations.Add(relation);
```

Our code essentially produces a master detail report, displaying the order number for the master record, and showing the details from each subrecord. To accomplish this task, we use two nested `foreach` statements, the outer one iterating through the `OrderID`:

```
// Iterate Tables retrieving DataRows
foreach(DataRow drOrderID in myDataSet.Tables["Orders"].Rows)
{
  Console.WriteLine("Order ID: " + drOrderID["OrderID"]);
```

The second `foreach` statement iterates over all `DataRow` objects that are related to the parent table for the current loop, retrieving all details for the current order:

```
    foreach(DataRow drPrice in drOrderID.GetChildRows("Details"))
    {
      //Order Details
      Console.WriteLine("\tProduct ID: " + drPrice["ProductID"]);
      Console.WriteLine("\t\tUnit Price: $" + drPrice["UnitPrice"]);
      Console.WriteLine("\t\tUnit Discount: " + drPrice["Discount"]
                        + "%");
    }
```

This loop accesses all child rows using the `GetChildRows()` method on each `DataRow`. This method returns all `DataRows` in the `OrderDetails` `DataTable` where the `OrderID` field is related to the eponymous field in the `Orders` `DataTable`.

All that's left is to finish off our report, and close the class:

```
        Console.WriteLine("=====================================\n");
      }
    }
    catch(Exception e)
    {
      Console.WriteLine(e.Message);
    }
  }
}
```

If you compile and run the example, you should see many records go scrolling past:

```
Command Prompt
                Unit Price: $22.785
                Unit Discount: 0.02%
============================================
Order ID: 11081
        Product ID: 6
                Unit Price: $24.5
                Unit Discount: 0.02%
        Product ID: 14
                Unit Price: $22.785
                Unit Discount: 0.02%
============================================
Order ID: 11083
        Product ID: 6
                Unit Price: $24.5
                Unit Discount: 0.02%
        Product ID: 14
                Unit Price: $22.785
                Unit Discount: 0.02%
============================================
C:\Pro C# for Java\Chapter 04>
```

`DataRelations` can be very useful in many situations, including reporting, searching, and data navigation.

Modifying Data

We've now retrieved and read data from a database, but we haven't yet manipulated any of that data. We know that data is stored in `DataSets` in a relational fashion and that it can be easily accessed. However, we also know the `DataSet` is quite independent of the data source, so how can data be modified and reflected back to the database without having to update every record in a `DataSet` whether or not it's been changed?

The answer is **tracing**. Data is traced in an efficient fashion so that only modified records are updated. Take a look at the following diagram:

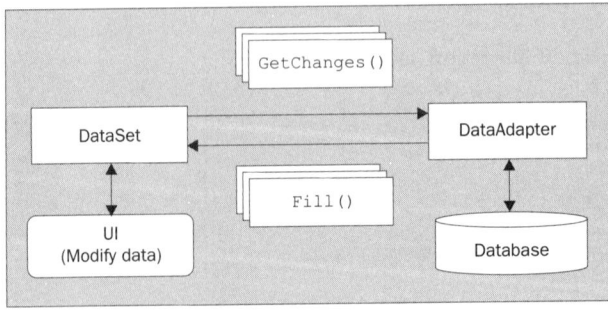

The `DataSet` automatically tracks changes that occur to its data, and the `DataAdapter` checks if the `DataSet` has changes before updating any data in the data source. If changes have occurred, the data adapter retrieves them, ignoring records that have not been changed, and updates the database accordingly.

The `DataSet` exposes a variety of methods related to tracing:

- `HasChanges()` – returns a `bool` indicating if changes have occurred.
- `GetChanges()` – returns a new `DataSet` containing only the changed records from the original `DataSet`.
- `AcceptChanges()` – commits all changes to the data since original state or last `AcceptChanges()` call.
- `RejectChanges()` – rejects and rolls back all changes since original data or since last `AcceptChanges()` call.

In the next example, we'll insert a new category and accompanying description to Northwind's `Category` table. This table details the foods this fine organization trades in.

This code, in the `NewCategory.cs` file, needs the `System.Data.SqlTypes` namespace, which defines a number of useful SQL Server data types. They provide a much safer way to deal with SQL databases, avoiding loss of data precision and other conversion errors. These classes mean that we do not need to convert between primitive types and `SqlTypes`, making our code run faster:

```
using System;
using System.Data;
using System.Data.SqlTypes;
using System.Data.SqlClient;

class InsertDataExample
{
  static void Main(string[] args)
  {
    try
    {
      string connStr = "data source=SERVERNAME;initial catalog=Northwind;"
                     + "integrated security=SSPI";

      // Instantiate a Connection Object and a DataSet
      SqlConnection sqlConn = new SqlConnection(connStr);
      DataSet myDataSet = new DataSet();
```

We instantiate two `SqlCommand` objects, the first to take care of the `SELECT` statement, and the second to deal with the `INSERT` statement:

```
      // Instantiate Command Objects
      SqlCommand SelectCommand = new SqlCommand();
      SqlCommand InsertCommand = new SqlCommand();

      // Set CommandText and Connection properties for each
      SelectCommand.CommandText = "SELECT CategoryID, CategoryName, "
                               + "Description, Picture FROM Categories";
      SelectCommand.Connection = sqlConn;
      InsertCommand.CommandText = "INSERT INTO Categories (CategoryName,"
                               + "Description, Picture) VALUES ("
                               + "@CategoryName, @Description, @Picture);"
```

Chapter 4

```
                        + " SELECT CategoryID, CategoryName, "
                        + "Description, Picture FROM Categories "
                        + "WHERE (CategoryID = @@IDENTITY)";
InsertCommand.Connection = sqlConn;
```

We can use a single `SqlDataAdapter` for both the insert and select operations by setting its `InsertCommand` and `SelectCommand` properties to the respective `SqlCommand` object:

```
// Instantiate a DataAdapter Object
SqlDataAdapter myDataAdapter = new SqlDataAdapter();

// Associate DataAdapter to Commands
myDataAdapter.InsertCommand = InsertCommand;
myDataAdapter.SelectCommand = SelectCommand;
```

Crucially, we need to add the parameters for the `INSERT` statement, adding them one by one to `InsertCommand`'s `SqlParameterCollection`. For each parameter, we pass a string representing the name of the parameter, followed by the data type, length, and name of the source column:

```
// Add parameters to InsertCommand.
myDataAdapter.InsertCommand.Parameters.Add("@CategoryName",
                SqlDbType.VarChar, 15, "CategoryName");
myDataAdapter.InsertCommand.Parameters.Add("@Description",
                SqlDbType.VarChar , 1073741823, "Description");
myDataAdapter.InsertCommand.Parameters.Add("@Picture",
                SqlDbType.Binary, 2147483647, "Picture");
```

Next we populate the `DataSet` using an overload of the `Fill()` method that takes the start and end index of records in the second and third parameters. We retrieve the first three records:

```
// Fill DataSet
myDataAdapter.Fill(myDataSet, 0, 3, "Categories");
```

Next we instantiate a `DataTable` that, as a reference type, acts like a pointer to the `DataTable` in the `DataSet`:

```
DataTable myDataTable = myDataSet.Tables["Categories"];
```

Now we can iterate over all `DataRows`, displaying the name and description of each category before changes:

```
foreach(DataRow dr in myDataTable.Rows)
{
  Console.WriteLine("Category Name: " + dr["CategoryName"]);
  Console.WriteLine("Description: " + dr["Description"] + "\n");
}
Console.WriteLine("Total Number of Categories: "
                + myDataTable.Rows.Count);
Console.WriteLine("-------------------------------");
```

In the next part of the code, we create a new `DataRow` using the `NewRow()` method on the `DataTable`. The new `DataRow` will be created matching existing rows in the `DataTable`. We assign values to the relevant columns, and add the `DataRow` to the `DataTable` using the `Add()` method on the `Rows` property:

```
// Create new Row
DataRow newRow = myDataTable.NewRow();

// Set values of fields
newRow["CategoryName"] = "Star Trek food";
newRow["Description"] = "Pipius claw, Alterian chowder, Zilm'kach, "
                     + "Romulan Otters' Noses...";

// Add new row to DataTable
myDataTable.Rows.Add(newRow);
```

Finally we update the database using the `Update()` method on the `DataAdapter`:

```
// Update Database
myDataAdapter.Update(myDataSet, "Categories");
```

To demonstrate what's been done, we loop through the `DataTable` once more, displaying the updated data:

```
      // Output the updated data
      foreach(DataRow dr in myDataTable.Rows)
      {
        Console.WriteLine("Category Name: " + dr["CategoryName"]);
        Console.WriteLine("Description: " + dr["Description"] + "\n");
      }
      Console.WriteLine("Total Number of Categories: "
                     + myDataTable.Rows.Count);
      Console.WriteLine("-------------------------------");

    }
    catch(Exception e)
    {
      Console.WriteLine(e.Message);
    }
  }
}
```

Data Access

137

If you compile and run the example, you should see this:

```
C:\Pro C# for Java\Chapter 04>newcategory
Category Name: Beverages
Description: Soft drinks, coffees, teas, beers, and ales
Category Name: Condiments
Description: Sweet and savory sauces, relishes, spreads, and seasonings
Category Name: Confections
Description: Desserts, candies, and sweet breads
Total Number of Categories: 3
------------------------------------------------------
Category Name: Beverages
Description: Soft drinks, coffees, teas, beers, and ales
Category Name: Condiments
Description: Sweet and savory sauces, relishes, spreads, and seasonings
Category Name: Confections
Description: Desserts, candies, and sweet breads
Category Name: Star Trek food
Description: Pipius claw, Alterian chowder, Zilm'kach, Romulan Otters' Noses...
Total Number of Categories: 4
------------------------------------------------------
C:\Pro C# for Java\Chapter 04>
```

I believe that covers just about all food categories now. An alternative approach would use a `Command` object's `ExecuteNonQuery()` method to insert, delete, or update the data source, by passing it the appropriate SQL statement.

The CommandBuilder Class

As we've seen, the `DataAdapter` does not automatically generate statements for database manipulation, and we need to create separate command objects, and associate them with the `DataAdapter`'s `Command` properties. This can be an unnecessary overhead for simple projects where there's no great need for customization.

For such cases, ADO.NET has two classes called `SqlCommandBuilder` and `OleDbCommandBuilder` that allow us to generate updating logic dynamically. They both work by registering themselves as a listener for the `RowUpdating` event of the `DataAdapter` which fires when data is modified. When the event occurs, `CommandBuilder` can examine the changes and generate the SQL statements required to persist them to the database.

> Note that `CommandBuilder` objects will not create any statements if the `SqlDataAdapter` does not have a **SELECT** statement that returns data assigned to the `SelectCommand` property.

The following example again uses the Northwind `Category` table, this time changing the `CategoryName` of the first record from **Beverages** to **Slurpables**, without writing a single UPDATE statement. We start off `UpdateCategory.cs` with the now familiar code:

```
using System;
using System.Data;
using System.Data.SqlTypes;
using System.Data.SqlClient;
```

```csharp
class CommandBuilderExample
{
  static void Main(string[] args)
  {
    try
    {
      string connStr = "data source=SERVERNAME;initial catalog=Northwind;"
                      + "integrated security=SSPI";

      // Instantiate a Connection object, a DataSet, and a DataAdapter
      SqlConnection sqlConn = new SqlConnection(connStr);
      DataSet myDataSet = new DataSet();
      SqlDataAdapter myDataAdapter = new SqlDataAdapter();
```

This time, rather than creating a separate `Command`, we'll pass a SELECT statement directly to the `SqlCommand` constructor as a string:

```csharp
      myDataAdapter.SelectCommand = new SqlCommand("SELECT * FROM"
                                  + " Categories", sqlConn);
```

Next, we instantiate the `SqlCommandBuilder` class, passing the `DataAdapter` to its constructor. From now on, the `SqlCommandBuilder` object will create several statements for any modified data:

```csharp
      SqlCommandBuilder CommandBuilder = new SqlCommandBuilder(
                                          myDataAdapter);
```

The next line populates the `DataSet`, then we move on to get the reference of the target `DataTable`, and a reference to the first `DataRow` in the `DataTable`:

```csharp
      // Fill DataSet
      myDataAdapter.Fill(myDataSet, "Categories");
      // Get DataTable reference
      DataTable myDataTable = myDataSet.Tables["Categories"];
      // Get DataRow reference
      DataRow existingRow = myDataTable.Rows[0];
      Console.WriteLine("Current name: " + existingRow["CategoryName"]);
```

Another important point when changing `DataRow` values is that we must call `BeginEdit()` prior to modifying any data. This places the `DataRow` in edit mode, suspending any validation events that may be set up. In our case, there are no validation rules but I'll include the `BeginEdit()` and `EndEdit()` calls for reference here:

```csharp
      existingRow.BeginEdit();
      existingRow["CategoryName"] = "Slurpables";
      existingRow.EndEdit();
      Console.WriteLine("\n\nCommand generated:");
```

The next line outputs the SQL statement generated by the `SqlCommandBuilder`:

```
                Console.WriteLine(CommandBuilder.GetUpdateCommand().CommandText);
                myDataAdapter.Update(myDataSet, "Categories");
                Console.WriteLine("\nNew name: " + existingRow["CategoryName"]);
            }
            catch(Exception e)
            {
                Console.WriteLine(e.Message);
            }
        }
    }
```

Running this example produces the following output:

```
C:\Pro C# for Java\Chapter 04>updatecategory
Current name: Beverages

Command generated:
UPDATE Categories SET CategoryName = @p1 , Description = @p2 , Picture = @p3 WHE
RE ( (CategoryID = @p4) AND ((CategoryName IS NULL AND @p5 IS NULL) OR (Category
Name = @p6)) )

New name: Slurpables
C:\Pro C# for Java\Chapter 04>_
```

Deleting Records

In the same way we add and modify a `DataRow`, we can delete it using the `DataRow`'s `Delete()` method. This method can be called from a reference to a `DataTable`:

```
myDataSet.Tables["Category"].Rows[3].Delete();
```

or by drilling into a `DataTable`:

```
myDataTable.Rows[3].Delete();
```

When updating the `DataSet` against the data source, the `GetChanges()` method will show that a `DataRow` has been deleted, and that data will be deleted from the database.

`CommandBuilder` reduces the amount of code we have to write, and also means that we don't have to worry about designing complex SQL statements.

Searching and Sorting Records

Filtering and sorting are fundamental functions for any database-based application. The `DataSet` does not expose any functionality for sorting and filtering records although a `DataTable` can select a few records, and even sort them by using the `Select()` method:

```
System.Data.DataRow[] drArray = myTable.Select("Date > '1/11/02'");
```

The problem with this approach is that it does not physically sort or filter records inside the container, and merely returns a `DataRow` array resulting from the filtering statement used. The underlying `DataTable` still contains the same records and unsorted values.

Data Access

Another method on `DataTable` returns the result from the expression given by the parameter. Called `Compute()`, this method returns an object containing the results of the expression, which in general is an aggregation. For example:

```
object obj = myTable.Compute("Sum(Debit)", "Debit > 1000"));
```

Yet another way to control expressions is provided by the `DataColumn`. We can add an extra `DataColumn` to a `DataTable` at runtime, such that the new `DataColumn`'s value is the result of an expression that we specify:

```
myTableColumns["Total"].Expression = "UnitPrice + TaxFee"
```

These approaches are suitable for small filtering and sorting tasks, but for presenting data, we must turn to `DataView`.

The `DataView` was designed primarily for binding data from a `DataTable` to a Windows Form or web application, but it also represents a good way to display different views of a `DataTable` without refreshing the source. In addition, `DataViews` can be bound to other components, providing a means for the user to update their contents, and such changes can then be registered back on the source `DataTable`.

Let's have a go at using a `DataView` to find a specific product from the `Products` table in the Northwind database.

Create a new text file called `ViewData.cs`. First we need the namespaces, then we start our class by setting up the connection details:

```csharp
using System;
using System.Data;
using System.Data.SqlClient;

class SearchExample
{
  static void Main(string[] args)
  {
    try
    {
      string connStr = "data source=SERVERNAME;initial catalog=Northwind;"
                   + "integrated security=SSPI";

      // Instantiate a Connection object, a DataSet, and a DataAdapter
      SqlConnection sqlConn = new SqlConnection(connStr);
      DataSet myDataSet = new DataSet();
      SqlDataAdapter myDataAdapter = new SqlDataAdapter("SELECT * FROM"
                                          + " CATEGORIES", sqlConn);
      // Fill DataSet
      myDataAdapter.Fill(myDataSet,"Categories");
```

Next, we instantiate a `DataView` object, referencing a `DataTable` inside the `DataSet`. We set its sort criteria by assigning a `DataColumn` name to the `DataView`'s `Sort` property:

```
            // Create DataView
            DataView myDataView = new DataView(myDataSet.Tables["Categories"]);
            myDataView.Sort = "CategoryName";
```

Then we pass the value that we want to match (which is `"Produce"` in this case) to the `Find()` method. This method returns an integer representing the index of the `DataRow` that contains this value in the specified column:

```
            int i = myDataView.Find("Produce");
```

If the `Find()` method returns -1, no matching record was found, otherwise we output the `DataRow` value, accessing it by the returned index:

```
        if(i != -1)
        {
          Console.WriteLine("Found record index " + i );
          Console.WriteLine("Name: " + myDataView[0]["CategoryName"]
                      + "\nDescription: " + myDataView[0]["Description"]);
        }
        else
        {
          Console.WriteLine("No records found");
        }
      }
      catch(Exception e)
      {
        Console.WriteLine(e.Message);
      }
    }
  }
```

If you compile and run this example, you should see something like:

```
C:\Pro C# for Java\Chapter 04>csc viewdata.cs
Microsoft (R) Visual C# .NET Compiler version 7.00.9466
for Microsoft (R) .NET Framework version 1.0.3705
Copyright (C) Microsoft Corporation 2001. All rights reserved.

C:\Pro C# for Java\Chapter 04>viewdata
Found record index 5
Name: Condiments
Description: Sweet and savory sauces, relishes, spreads, and seasonings

C:\Pro C# for Java\Chapter 04>
```

If we change the parameter used for the `Find()` method, using one that is not present in that column, we'll see something like this:

```
C:\Pro C# for Java\Chapter 04>viewdata
No records found

C:\Pro C# for Java\Chapter 04>
```

Data Access

Searching by the `Find()` method can be refined by using overloads that allow various keys to be specified for the search.

Filtering Records

`DataView` makes filtering very easy. We just use the `RowFilter` property to specify our filtering expression. Copy the previous example to `FilterData.cs`, and replace the `DataView` code with the following:

```
        // Create DataView
        DataView myDataView = new DataView (myDataSet.Tables["Categories"]);
        myDataView.Table = myDataSet.Tables["Categories"];
        myDataView.RowFilter = "CategoryName LIKE 'S*'";
        myDataView.Sort = "CategoryName";
        for(int i = 0;i < myDataView.Count -1; i++)
           Console.WriteLine(myDataView[i]["CategoryName"]);
    }
    catch(Exception e)
    {
        .
        .
        .
```

If you compile and run the new sample, you should get this:

```
C:\Pro C# for Java\Chapter 04>filterdata
Seafood
Slurpables

C:\Pro C# for Java\Chapter 04>
```

The main benefit of the `DataView` is that we can have multiple `DataView` objects, giving different perspectives of the same data source simultaneously.

ADO.NET Events

A `RowSet` in Java has the ability to respond to event notifications such as `rowSetListener` and `rowChanged`. In .NET, events are strongly supported by many ADO.NET classes and they are a great mechanism for improving the logic and robustness of our applications. We'll look at the most important events exposed by ADO.NET classes in this section. A class exposes properties named after each event that it supports, and to assign a handler to an event, we literally add the handler method to the appropriate property, as we shall see in this section's example. We'll also see how the handler method can use the event arguments object that it receives as a parameter to determine details about the event.

Connection Events

The `Connection` class fires the `StateChange` event when the connection changes state. It passes a `StateChangeEventArgs` object to the handler that contains data regarding to the event. Of this data, the `CurrentState` property, which indicates the latest state of the connection, is the most useful.

143

DataAdapter Events

The events that relate to `DataAdapter` concern updates performed on the database. The events are:

- `RowUpdating` – fired before a `DataRow` is updated
- `RowUpdated` – fired after a `DataRow` is updated

The event arguments object that this produces can determine, among other things, the type of statement that performed the update along with the `Command` object used, and the actual `DataRow` object involved in the process.

DataTable Events

The `DataTable` fires events as it listens for changes to its data and underlying schema. The information available to handlers for these events can be very useful when working with bound components, enabling us to keep the core backend logic separate from the presentation layer that triggers it.

The following example builds on the code in `UpdateCategory.cs`. Copy it to a new file called `DataTableEvents.cs`, and we'll implement a handler for both the connection change event, `StateChange`, and the `DataTable`'s `RowChanging` event.

Once we've instantiated the connection object, we add a handler for its `StateChange` event, which will be trigged when the connection changes status (principally when it is opened or closed):

```
.
.
.
// Instantiate a Connection Object, a DataSet, and a DataAdapter
SqlConnection sqlConn = new SqlConnection(connStr);
DataSet myDataSet = new DataSet();
SqlDataAdapter myDataAdapter = new SqlDataAdapter();

// Add event handler to Connection
sqlConn.StateChange += new StateChangeEventHandler(
    sqlConn_StateChange);

myDataAdapter.SelectCommand = new SqlCommand("SELECT * FROM"
                                      + " Categories", sqlConn);
SqlCommandBuilder CommandBuilder = new SqlCommandBuilder(
                                      myDataAdapter);
```

Similarly, once we've created the `DataTable` reference, we add a handler to its `RowChanging` event:

```
// Fill DataSet
Console.WriteLine("** Fill up DataSet **");
myDataAdapter.Fill(myDataSet,"Categories");

// Get DataTable reference
DataTable myDataTable = myDataSet.Tables["Categories"];
// Add event handler to DataTable
myDataTable.RowChanging += new DataRowChangeEventHandler(
    myDataTable_RowChanging);
```

```
            // Get DataRow reference
            DataRow existingRow = myDataTable.Rows[0];
            Console.WriteLine("Current name: " + existingRow["CategoryName"]);
            existingRow.BeginEdit();
            existingRow["CategoryName"] = "Beverages";
            existingRow.EndEdit();
            Console.WriteLine("** Update DataSet **");
            myDataAdapter.Update(myDataSet, "Categories");
            .
            .
            .
```

Here is the `sqlConn_StateChange` event handler method. As we've added it to the appropriate event on the `Connection` object, this method will be invoked whenever the connection changes state. All it does is output the new connection state:

```
      private static void sqlConn_StateChange(object sender,
            System.Data.StateChangeEventArgs e)
      {
         Console.WriteLine("\t(Connection Event [StateChange]): "
                     + e.CurrentState + "\n");
      }
```

The same principal applies to the other handler method, which will be invoked when a row is changed. It simply outputs the value of `CategoryName` for that `DataRow`, together with the action taken:

```
      private static void myDataTable_RowChanging(object sender,
                              System.Data.DataRowChangeEventArgs e)
      {
         Console.WriteLine("\tDataTable RowChanging Event --> Category={0} "
                     + "| Action = {1}\n", e.Row["CategoryName"], e.Action);
      }
   }
}
```

Here is the output we'll get from compiling and running the new code:

```
C:\Pro C# for Java\Chapter 04>datatableevents
** Fill up DataSet **
        (Connection Event [StateChange]): Open
        (Connection Event [StateChange]): Closed
Current name: Slurpables
        DataTable RowChanging Event --> Category=Beverages | Action = Change
** Update DataSet **
        (Connection Event [StateChange]): Open
        DataTable RowChanging Event --> Category=Beverages | Action = Commit
        (Connection Event [StateChange]): Closed
New name: Beverages
C:\Pro C# for Java\Chapter 04>
```

This gives some interesting insight into how the `DataAdapter` manages the connection to minimize connection time. We see that it opens a connection just for the duration of the `Fill()` method, closing it immediately after, and similarly when the database is updated.

ADO.NET Exceptions

A `SqlException` is thrown when the database returns a warning or error, but this class has many important members that can be examined to obtain significant information about the exception. The class hierarchy is as follows:

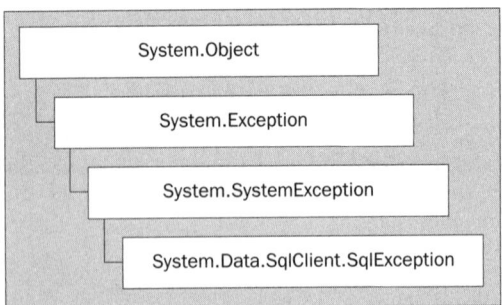

We've used `try...catch` constructs throughout this chapter, without handling any of the exceptions that may be caught, so now let's look at how we may deal with some of these errors.

Copy `openSQL.cs` and call it `error.cs`. Change its `try...catch` block to the following to cause an error by accessing a non-existent record from a `DataReader`:

```
try
{
  string connStr = "data source=SERVERNAME;initial catalog=Northwind;"
             + "integrated security=SSPI";
  SqlConnection sqlConn = new SqlConnection (connStr);

  sqlConn.Open();
  SqlCommand cd = new SqlCommand(
    "SELECT CategoryName FROM Categories", sqlConn);
  SqlDataReader dr = cd.ExecuteReader();

  Console.WriteLine(dr.GetValue(122));
  dr.Close();
}
catch (Exception e)
{
  Console.WriteLine("Message: " + e.Message);
  Console.WriteLine("Source: " + e.Source);
  Console.WriteLine();
  Console.WriteLine("Stack Trace: " + e.StackTrace);
}
```

Compiling and running the example produces the error message shown below:

```
C:\Pro C# for Java\Chapter 04>error
Message: Invalid attempt to read when no data is present.
Source: System.Data
Stack Trace:     at System.Data.SqlClient.SqlDataReader.PrepareRecord(Int32 i)
    at System.Data.SqlClient.SqlDataReader.GetValue(Int32 i)
    at SimpleConnection.Main(String[] args)
C:\Pro C# for Java\Chapter 04>
```

The first thing to note is that it was not a `SqlException` that was thrown, because the database did not return an error, rather it was an incorrect assignment in our code that caused the problem.

The `Exception` object contains valuable information regarding any problem we encounter. It allows us to look at the stack trace, revealing the trail of the methods called up to the error. In the above example, we see that `GetValue()` is called from within `Main()`, and that it itself calls a (private) method of the `DataReader` called `PrepareRecord()`, and it is this method that in fact threw the exception.

`SqlExceptions` are thrown when an error occurs at the .NET data provider level. For example, a `SqlException` would be thrown if we misspelled the statement in the `CommandText` property of a `Command` object, and tried to execute it. The `Exception` object for such exceptions exposes an `Errors` property which is a collection of `SqlError` objects. The `SqlError` class contains detailed information relevant to a warning or error generated by SQL Server.

SQL errors have a severity level contained in the `Class` property:

❑ 10 or less indicates problems triggered by inaccurate information provided by the user (or calling code)

❑ 11 to 16 are user-produced errors that can be rectified by the user

❑ 17 to 25 indicates software or hardware errors

When an error with a severity level of 17, 18, or 19 occurs, your application can continue, but it may be unable to execute further statements. The connection can remain open until the severity level reaches 20, at which point the CLR closes the connection.

The following code shows how we can extract information about the error that has occurred from the `SqlException`:

```
        catch (SqlException e)
        {
          Console.WriteLine("Source: " + e.Source);
          Console.WriteLine("Procedure: " + e.Procedure);
          Console.WriteLine("Line Number: " + e.LineNumber);
          Console.WriteLine("State: " + e.State);
          Console.WriteLine("Class: " + e.Class);
          Console.WriteLine("Error: " + e.Errors[0].ToString() + "\n");
        }
```

The last line here uses `ToString()` on the `SqlError` object to output the message returned by the `SqlException`.

Chapter 4

There are some points to note about the `SqlException` properties we're using:

- The `Procedure` property returns the line on the SQL statement or stored procedure rather than the method called from the .NET code
- `LineNumber` similarly refers to the T-SQL statement used, not the calling .NET code
- `State` is the status returned by the database, and is data source specific.

Let's change the code in `error.cs` to throw a SQL exception:

```
SqlCommand cd = new SqlCommand("SELECT CategoryName FROM"
                              + " CategoriesERROR", sqlConn);
```

Next add the `catch` block for `SqlException` shown above after the `try` block, but before the `catch` block for generic exceptions. If you compile and run the example now, this is what you'll see:

```
C:\Pro C# for Java\Chapter 04>sqlerror
Source: .Net SqlClient Data Provider
Procedure:
Line Number: 1
State: 1
Class: 16
Error: System.Data.SqlClient.SqlError: Invalid object name 'CategoriesERROR'.

C:\Pro C# for Java\Chapter 04>
```

The `Class` property value is 16, which indicates that the error was caused by the request – namely `CategoryERROR` was an incorrect target table. As the severity level is less than 20, the CLR has not closed the connection and it would be still possible to fix the error and try again.

We would get a more serious error if our connection string were invalid:

```
string connStr = "data source=DOESNOTEXIST;initial catalog=Northwind;"
               + "integrated security=SSPI";
```

If you compile and run with the above connection string, you'll get this:

```
C:\Pro C# for Java\Chapter 04>conerror
Source: .Net SqlClient Data Provider
Procedure: ConnectionOpen (Connect()).
Line Number: 0
State: 0
Class: 20
Error: System.Data.SqlClient.SqlError: SQL Server does not exist or access denied.

C:\Pro C# for Java\Chapter 04>
```

This error has a severity level of 20 meaning that the CLR will close the connection (or not open it). The error message returned is **SQL Server does not exist or access denied**, which is the standard error SQL gives when the `data source` parameter in the connection string refers to a database that either has a permission set too high or does not exist.

Outputting DataSets' Content

We have already seen that the `DataSet` is a particularly important class in ADO.NET and how it is structured using `DataTable` and `DataRow` objects. We are now going to explore how we can output the data held in a `DataSet` as XML or by serialization to a stream.

XML

The `DataSet`'s first language is XML: it uses XML natively, and this fluency makes the `DataSet` invaluable for XML-enabled solutions.

The `DataSet` exposes a set of key methods for reading and writing XML each with a variety of overloads for different input and output sources:

- `WriteXml()` – writes generic XML to a file or stream
- `WriteXmlSchema()` – writes XML schema elements to a file or stream
- `ReadXml()` – reads generic XML from a file or stream
- `ReadXmlSchema()` – reads XML schema elements from a file or stream
- `GetXml()` – returns XML from a file or stream as a string
- `GetXmlSchema()` – as above, but only suitable for reading schema elements

Copy `Categories.cs` to a new file called `WriteXML.cs`. We'll change the `try` block in its `Main()` method to save the information contained in the `DataSet` with the `WriteXml()` method. This method takes two parameters: the filename to use, and the writing mode, which uses the `XmlWriteMode` enumeration that resides in `System.Data`. In a later step, we'll then read the XML file into another `DataSet` in a second application:

```
sqlConn.Open();
SqlCommand cd = new SqlCommand("SELECT CategoryName, Description"
                              + " FROM Categories", sqlConn);
SqlDataAdapter myDataAdapter= new SqlDataAdapter();
myDataAdapter.SelectCommand = cd;
DataSet ds = new DataSet();
myDataAdapter.Fill(ds);

// Write XML data to a file including the schema
ds.WriteXml("C:\\DataSet.xml",XmlWriteMode.WriteSchema);
sqlConn.Close();
```

This will create the following XML file, including the inline schema at the start:

```
<?xml version="1.0" standalone="yes"?>
<NewDataSet>
  <xs:schema id="NewDataSet" xmlns=""
    xmlns:xs="http://www.w3.org/2001/XMLSchema"
    xmlns:msdata="urn:schemas-microsoft-com:xml-msdata">
    <xs:element name="NewDataSet" msdata:IsDataSet="true"
      msdata:Locale="en-AU">
      <xs:complexType>
```

```xml
          <xs:choice maxOccurs="unbounded">
            <xs:element name="Table">
              <xs:complexType>
                <xs:sequence>
                  <xs:element name="CategoryName" type="xs:string"
                    minOccurs="0" />
                  <xs:element name="Description" type="xs:string"
                    minOccurs="0" />
                </xs:sequence>
              </xs:complexType>
            </xs:element>
          </xs:choice>
      </xs:complexType>
    </xs:element>
</xs:schema>
<Table>
  <CategoryName>Beverages</CategoryName>
  <Description>Soft drinks, coffees, teas, beers, and ales</Description>
</Table>
<Table>
  <CategoryName>Condiments</CategoryName>
  <Description>Sweet and savory sauces, relishes, spreads, and
              seasonings</Description>
</Table>
<Table>
  <CategoryName>Confections</CategoryName>
  <Description>Desserts, candies, and sweet breads</Description>
</Table>
<Table>
  <CategoryName>Dairy Products</CategoryName>
  <Description>Cheeses</Description>
</Table>
<Table>
  <CategoryName>Grains/Cereals</CategoryName>
  <Description>Breads, crackers, pasta, and cereal</Description>
</Table>
<Table>
  <CategoryName>Meat/Poultry</CategoryName>
  <Description>Prepared meats</Description>
</Table>
<Table>
  <CategoryName>Produce</CategoryName>
  <Description>Dried fruit and bean curd</Description>
</Table>
<Table>
  <CategoryName>Seafood</CategoryName>
  <Description>Seaweed and fish</Description>
</Table>
<Table>
  <CategoryName>Star Trek food</CategoryName>
  <Description>Pipius claw, Alterian chowder, Zilm'kach, Romulan Otters'
              Noses...</Description>
</Table>
</NewDataSet>
```

If there were more tables and relations in the `DataSet`, each would be provided with a clear schema definitions.

Now we need an application to read the data, which we'll call `ReadXML.cs`. It can be very simple, as it doesn't need to worry about connecting to the data source:

```csharp
using System;
using System.Data;

class ReadCategories
{
  static void Main(string[] args)
  {
    try
    {

      DataSet ds = new DataSet();
      ds.ReadXml("C:\\DataSet.xml", System.Data.XmlReadMode.Auto);

      foreach(DataTable dt in ds.Tables)
        foreach(DataRow dr in dt.Rows)
        {
          for(int i = 0; i< dr.ItemArray.Length; i++)
          {
            Console.WriteLine(dr[i]);
          }
        }

    }
    catch(Exception e)
    {
      Console.WriteLine(e);
    }
  }
}
```

Compile and run this, and here's the output we'll see:

```
C:\Pro C# for Java\Chapter 04>readxml
Beverages
Soft drinks, coffees, teas, beers, and ales
Condiments
Sweet and savory sauces, relishes, spreads, and seasonings
Confections
Desserts, candies, and sweet breads
Dairy Products
Cheeses
Grains/Cereals
Breads, crackers, pasta, and cereal
Meat/Poultry
Prepared meats
Produce
Dried fruit and bean curd
Seafood
Seaweed and fish
Star Trek food
Pipius claw, Alterian chowder, Zilm'kach, Romulan Otters' Noses...

C:\Pro C# for Java\Chapter 04>
```

Chapter 4

This example demonstrates that we do not have to be connected to a database to use relational methodology to iterate through our data: we can access the data once it's in a `DataSet` just as if that data had come direct from the source database.

Serialization

Serialization is the process of converting object instances to a format that maintains the object's state. **Deserialization** is reverse process of reading objects that have already been serialized. We can use serialization to stream objects direct to other applications, or to store them for later retrieval.

In Java, classes that implement `System.io.Serializable` instantiate serializable objects. In .NET, classes implement the `ISerializable` interface, and have the ability to control their own serialization and deserialization.

The `DataSet` implements `ISerializable`, and also inherits from `MarshalByValueComponent` meaning that it supports .NET Remoting – which uses serialization for resource sharing on secure networks. Remoting is covered in depth in Chapter 10.

Let's now see the process of serialization and deserialization in action with a simple `DataSet` in the file called `Serialize.cs`. Firstly we need to import the namespaces for `MemoryStream` (a memory buffer), and `BinaryFormatter` (for serializing and deserializing):

```
using System;
using System.Data;
using System.IO;
using System.Runtime.Serialization.Formatters.Binary;

class SerializeDataSet
{
  static void Main(string[] args)
  {
    try
    {
      // Create a new DataSet and add tables
      DataSet myDataSet = new DataSet();
      myDataSet.Tables.Add("Accounts");
      myDataSet.Tables.Add("Marketing");
      myDataSet.Tables.Add("Management");
```

We'll have a separate method called `SerializeObject()` that will serialize the `DataSet` to a stream:

```
      // Serialize DataSet to a stream
      Stream serializedObject = SerializeObject(myDataSet);
```

We'll simply deserialize it straight away into a brand new `DataSet`, again using a separate method, called `DeserializeObject()`. It will return an `Object` which we can cast to `DataSet`:

```
      // Deserialize object and cast it as DataSet
      DataSet newDataSet = (DataSet)DeserializeObject(serializedObject);
      // Investigate deserialized object.
```

```
      foreach(DataTable dt in newDataSet.Tables)
        Console.WriteLine(dt.TableName);
    }
    // Exception handling is for wimps ;)
    catch(Exception e)
    {
      Console.WriteLine(e);
    }
  }
```

In `SerializeObject()`, we create a `MemoryStream`, which will be where our `DataSet` is serialized to:

```
    public static Stream SerializeObject(Object obj)
    {
      // Create a new MemoryStream object
      // (the CanWrite property should be set to true by default with the
      //  default constructor)
      MemoryStream myMemoryStream = new MemoryStream();
```

Once we have the stream, we pass it to a `BinaryFormatter`'s `Serialize()` method with the object to serialize:

```
      // Create a new instance of BinaryFormatter object
      BinaryFormatter bf = new BinaryFormatter();

      // Pass the MemoryStream instance and our object to be serialized
      //  to the BinaryFormatter Serialize() method
      bf.Serialize(myMemoryStream, obj);
```

Finally, we return the stream and close the method:

```
      return myMemoryStream;
    }
```

The `DeserializeObject()` method takes a stream, which is deserialized into the original object by a `BinaryFormatter`:

```
    public static object DeserializeObject(Stream sourceStream)
    {
      // Create a new BinaryFormatter instance
      BinaryFormatter bf = new BinaryFormatter();

      // Reset the memory stream position
      sourceStream.Position = 0;

      // Return deserialized object
      return bf.Deserialize(sourceStream);
    }
  }
```

If you compile and run the example you'll see something like this, demonstrating that when we serialize an object, we preserve its entire structure and values:

```
C:\Pro C# for Java\Chapter 04>serialize
Accounts
Marketing
Management
C:\Pro C# for Java\Chapter 04>
```

Summary

In this chapter, we've covered several aspects of data access under the .NET Framework. We've learned a little about the basic ADO.NET architecture, and looked into some of its powerful classes.

We've discovered the `DataSet`'s key role within the ADO.NET world. It is a very flexible container for data storage classes such as:

- `DataTable`
- `DataRow`
- `DataColumn`
- `DataRelation`

In many ways, ADO.NET echoes JDBC, and we looked at those as we looked into ADO.NET techniques for:

- Creating a connection
- Manipulating records
- Modifying data
- Applying relational integrity
- Searching, filtering, and sorting data

In the second half of the chapter, we had a brief look at some of the key events triggered by ADO.NET classes and moved on to ADO.NET exceptions. The SQL exception class details information relating to the data source level, rather than the CLR data access tier. The last thing we looked at was serialization, and we'll revisit this topic in Chapter 10.

Data Access

5

Dynamic Web Applications

This chapter introduces dynamic web application development with ASP.NET, the part of the .NET Framework that powers web applications including web services. You can think of ASP.NET as the .NET replacement for Active Server pages (ASP).

This chapter will not be about comparing JSP and servlets to ASP.NET, although some comparison is inevitable due to the nature of the topic. There is no real comparison between ASP.NET and JSP and a slightly different way of thinking is required for ASP.NET than for Java Server Pages (JSP) and servlets. For anyone needing a reminder, servlets provide a component-based method for building web-based applications under Java, and JSP can be considered the J2EE equivalent of Active Server Pages. JSP is an extension of the servlet technology created to support authoring and output of HTML in Java. It makes it easier to combine fixed or static template data with dynamic content.

There are major syntactical, architectural, and structural differences between ASP.NET and JSP, which will become apparent as you read on. Programming in ASP.NET is rather more like developing Java applications than JSP applications – especially in the way events are handled. You will however find that some of the objects you may have encountered in JSP have direct counterparts in ASP.NET (`Request`, `Session`, `Application`, and `Page` for instance). Also, you will see that the `TagLib` / `JavaBean` syntax used in JSP comes into play in ASP.NET.

Like ASP, both JSP and servlets tend to rely on intertwined presentation (HTML) and logic (Java) code. As such, development and maintenance can be difficult even in a small application, and a bit of a headache in a large enterprise application. To accomplish many of the same things, ASP.NET requires significantly less coding than any other web development technology which in itself reduces the problem of intertwined or 'spaghetti' coding. The greater part of this efficiency in code and design comes from the plethora of web controls that come with the language and a new way of thinking about how we, as developers, handle presentation and logic. Web controls are XML-based tags designed to produce a specific output given a specific input. We will discuss these controls in some depth in this chapter and introduce you to something called **code behind** a little later on.

Chapter 5

The shift to ASP.NET from its predecessor, ASP, is a bit of an evolutionary leap in terms of how it works behind the scenes. ASP.NET is a programming framework built on the CLR (Common Language Runtime) that can be used on a .NET-compliant server to build some very powerful web applications. Because the .NET Framework runtime supports many different languages, ASP.NET running on Internet Information Server (IIS), also supports many different languages, unlike any of the JSP engines. There are three supported straight out of the box – VB.NET, C#, and JScript.NET, but support is also available for many other languages including: Cobol, Perl, Python, Eiffel, SmallTalk, LISP, Scheme, Objective Camel, and many others. However, at the time of writing you can only run ASP.NET code on IIS servers on Windows 2000 or Windows XP. (Though you can run ASP.NET on Windows 98 and NT if you use the Web Matrix software's built-in web server, it doesn't support IIS.) In theory, ASP.NET could run on any platform should someone take the time to write the appropriate runtime. You might be interested in one open source migration already underway at www.go-mono.org.

One the surface, ASP.NET processes all code on the server in a similar way to a normal ASP or JSP application. When the ASP.NET code has been processed the server returns the resulting HTML to the client. If the client supports JavaScript, then ASP.NET will use appropriate JavaScript to enhance the client's browser experience. As the developer, you do not have to worry about putting much of this JavaScript together as it is done automatically behind the scenes using something called **.NET Controls**. At its simplest level, a .NET control is like an HTML tag with methods and properties.

So, now we have a little bit of background about ASP.NET, let's look at what we will be covering in this chapter. ASP.NET is a huge topic, and plenty of Wrox books such as *Beginning ASP.NET 1.0 with C#* (ISBN 1-86100-734-5) are available to help you take what you learn in the next few chapters further. In this chapter, we will be looking at:

- Page requests and how they work
- ASP.NET Page Events
- HTML Server Controls
- Web Server Controls
- Validation Controls
- Inline or Code Behind?
- ASP.NET and JSP

To successfully start utilizing ASP.NET for web development, it is important to understand how the ASP.NET page processing occurs, what makes an ASP.NET page tick, before we go on to look at how to put an ASP.NET page together and what the code might be like.

In order to run ASP.NET pages on IIS, you only need the .NET Common Language Runtime installed. This is not JSP – we don't need Tomcat or Jrun or some other third-party package, nor do we need a JDK – all that we require is provided with the .NET runtime. No need for source class files, JAR files, or packages, and it's a pretty uncomplicated install. IIS comes as standard with Windows 2000 and Windows .NET Server.

Create a directory under `C:\Inetpub\wwwroot` called `Chapter05` for the examples in this chapter, and give everyone permission to access it. All the examples files in this chapter use an `.aspx` file extension and should be saved to this directory.

Now let's move on to page requests and how they work in ASP.NET.

Page Requests and How They Work

If you have previously programmed web pages for IIS, you have probably used one of the ASP scripting languages to develop interactive web pages. ASP works by interpreting script, typically using VBScript, Jscript, PerlScript, or JavaScript. Every time the page is requested, IIS uses an interpreter to parse the script for each page request. When a remote client requests an ASP.NET page, the page is compiled into a DLL containing **Microsoft Intermediate Language** (MSIL) format code. MSIL is beyond the scope of this book, but it is important that you understand how ASP.NET pages actually end up being dealt with by the runtime.

In theory, the process for converting ASP.NET code to MSIL is somewhat similar to the way JSP pages are converted to servlets or bytecode on the first request. With ASP.NET, the first time you make a request for the page there is a performance hit as the page is compiled into MSIL (that's analogous to Java bytecode). Each subsequent request is much faster, similarly to JSP pages, which are compiled into servlets the first time they are accessed, and then each time the servlet is accessed, it is interpreted by the Java Virtual Machine. With ASP.NET, pages are precompiled into MSIL and then use JIT compiling like JSP.

Like Java, MSIL code can optionally be further translated into machine language at runtime using a Just In Time (JIT) compiler like NGEN.EXE (from the .NET SDK), or it can be interpreted straightaway by the runtime. Interpreting MSIL is not nearly as resource intensive as interpreting source code directly (as was the case in classic ASP) because a lot of the error checking has already been done.

Again, like Java, the compilation to MSIL enforces better programming practice by demanding that you adhere to more rigorous programming techniques, such as strong variable typing. An added benefit of ASP.NET over ASP is that the compiler checks the entire page for potential errors at first request, and catches many errors that an interpreter might let slip and may not become apparent for days.

So, there are a series of steps that occur behind the scenes when an ASP.NET page is requested, which are outlined below:

- ASP.NET first checks to see if there is already an up-to-date version of the IL code for the ASP.NET page
- If there is, this IL is given to the CLR, and the HTML output generated by the ASP.NET page is then sent to the remote client
- If, there is not, or the ASP.NET page's source code has changed since the last IL was generated, the ASP.NET page must be recompiled
- Depending on the language specified in the page directives, the proper compiler is instantiated and the IL created
- This IL is stored and used for all future requests

In ASP.NET, the IL compiled to native code is used when serving client requests during the course of the various page lifecycle events.

ASP.NET Page Events

In JSP, the JSP page implementation class file extends `HttpJspBase`, which in turn implements the `Servlet` interface. With JSP, the developer can describe initialization and destroy events by providing implementations for the `jspInit()` and `jspDestroy()` methods within their JSP pages. In ASP.NET you can choose to implement a few more methods to react to the various processing stages of the page than you can in JSP:

- `Page_Init` – This event is used to initialize values or connect any event handlers that you may have.

- `Page_Load` – This event can be used to perform a series of actions to either create your ASP.NET page for the first time or respond to client-side events that result from a post request to the page.

- `Page_DataBind` – The `DataBinding` event is raised when the `dataBind()` method is called just before the page attempts to load the page content. This allows you to connect HTML elements directly to data sources.

- `Page_PreRender` – This event is fired just before the output is rendered.

- `Page_Unload` – After a page has finished rendering, the `Page Unload` event will fire. This event is a good place to perform final cleanup work such as closing database connections that you should not simply leave for the garbage collector.

It is important not to confuse these page events with reactionary events, like click events, which we will be introduced to later. Typically, the method most developers will utilize is the `Page_Load` event, so let's take a quick look at it. There is no equivalent to the page load event in JSP: the closest event to it is the `jspInit()` event:

```
public void jspInit()
{
    //code goes here
}
```

The load event is just as simple to define in ASP.NET:

```
public void Page_Load()
{
    // code goes here
}
```

Like the JSP `init` event, `Page_Load` is typically used to perform form processing logic, data binding and any other initialization tasks that may be needed for controls and other page items. The example below demonstrates using `Page_Load` to initialize a value in something called a label web control (we will be discussing controls shortly):

```
<%@ Page Language="C#" Debug="true" %>

<html>
  <script runat="server">

  protected void Page_Load()
  {
    Result.Text = "Hello from Wrox";
  }
  </script>

  <body>
  <asp:Label id="Result" runat="server"/></br>
  </body>
</html>
```

In the above code, we have overridden the load event, which will fire before the page begins to process the actual page contents. We can carry out a small experiment with the order of precedence of events by making a small change to the `Label` tag, setting the `Text` property there also:

```
<asp:Label id="Result" Text="Hello from Microsoft" runat="server"/></br>
```

If we open the page with the above line added, we'll see that setting the `Text` property from within the `Load` event takes precedence over the actual tag value. So what exactly are these things called controls by the .NET Framework?

ASP.NET server controls are syntactically correct XML tags that either map directly to standard HTML elements, when they are referred to as HTML Server controls, or are unique to the .NET Framework. The latter are the web controls, and they output client-specific HTML to perform the behavior required, and include such sophisticated page items as the calendar control and the `DataGrid`. We will see these shortly, but first we'll discuss the HTML Server controls.

HTML Server Controls

One of the most important aspects of working with ASP.NET, and what I feel is one of the most significant differences between ASP.NET and JSP or servlets in developing web based applications is in the use of something called server controls. ASP.NET has changed the way you need to look at the use of HTML elements. The handling of HTML elements in J2EE is not the same as in ASP.NET and it is very important that you appreciate the different control sets.

HTML server controls in ASP.NET are HTML elements containing attributes that make them visible to methods on the server. Without the attributes they are simply HTML tags. By default, HTML elements on any Web Forms page (regardless of language) are not available to the server; they are treated as opaque text that is passed through to the browser from the scripting language chosen, whether they are served from JSP or ASP for example. However, by converting HTML elements to HTML server controls, in ASP.NET you expose them as elements you can program against on the server and make methods that very easily respond to events set against the control (such as the `Page_Load` event shown earlier).

The object model for HTML server controls maps closely to that of the corresponding HTML elements. HTML attributes are exposed in HTML server controls as properties. This is somewhat analogous to adding a JavaBean tag into your JSP page and exposing properties of the tag in your code.

Any HTML element on a page can be converted to an HTML server control by adding the appropriate attributes. As a minimum, an HTML element is converted to a control by the addition of the attribute `runat="server"`. This alerts the ASP.NET page Framework during parsing that it should create an instance of the control to use during server-side page processing. If you want to reference the control as a member within your code, you should also assign an ID attribute to the control.

- Set the control's `id` attribute (property) to a unique value for that page. It needs to be unique or it won't compile
- Set the `runat="server"` attribute to convert the HTML element to a .NET Server Control

```
<input id="Name" type=text size=40 runat="server">
```

The bottom line is that a .NET control will take all the properties and generate HTML from them, but we can control them programmatically. The controls themselves can be divided up based on their specific functionality. We could assume that given your background in J2EE web development we do not need to show how to define these standard HTML elements. However, when used as server controls the syntax may be slightly different, and in some instances, special server events exist for certain controls, which implies that properties exist to trigger these events.

To allow you to appreciate the different terminology used between JSP and ASP.NET, and to appreciate which HTML tag properties can be set dynamically we will provide an overview for them in the chapter, interspersed with some code examples.

For the purposes of the overview, we will present the controls in the manner shown below, with details outlining the permitted properties and methods supporting each server control:

```
<controltype
    property=value
    id=value
    runat="server" >
```

The control tags break down quite simply into syntactically correct XML tags outlining the control type and, where appropriate, the properties and methods attributed with the control. Based on the property description above, the equivalent control properties for an HTML `Hidden` input field example defined as a .NET control would look as shown below:

```
<input type="hidden"
    id="Hidden1"
    value="66"
    runat="server" >
```

Now that we have an understanding of syntax let's move into the HTML controls, starting with the `HtmlForm` control.

Forms

The `HtmlForm` control defines a standard HTML form tag. The values of controls within the form are posted to the server when the form is submitted. A common gotcha with using Form as a control in ASP.NET is that by default the action attribute is always set to the URL of the page itself. When the HTML `form` tag is defined as a server control, the action attribute cannot be changed; therefore, you can only post back to the page itself:

```
<form id="myFormID"
    method=POST | GET
    action="destination URL"
    runat="server" >
  Other server/html controls, input forms, etc. go here.
</form>
```

Text Editing

For editing text, we have a choice of the `HtmlInputText` control, and the `HtmlTextArea` control.

The `HtmlInputText` control displays text that can be edited by end users at run time, or changed programmatically:

```
<input type=text | password
    id="mytextID"
    maxlength="max no of characters"
    size="width of textbox"
    value="default text"
    runat="server" >
```

The `HtmlTextArea` control displays large quantities of text. It is used for multi-line text entry and display. When used as a server control, the `HtmlTextArea` control contains a special `ServerChange` event that is raised when the contents of the control change between posts to the server. It can be used for things like field validation:

```
<textarea id="myTextAreaID"
    cols="columns in the textarea"
    name="name passed to the browser"
    rows="the number of rows in the textarea"
    onserverchange="onserverchangeeventhandlercode"
    runat="server" >
  the text area text goes here
</textarea>
```

Buttons

For making things like standard button clicks happen in the browser, we have the `HtmlButton`, the `HtmlInputButton`, the `HtmlInputImage`, and the `HtmlAnchor` to choose from.

The `HtmlButton` control can contain any arbitrary HTML, and therefore it is very flexible in look and feel. The HTML `<button>` element is part of the HTML 4.0 specification. Therefore, the `HtmlButton` control is supported only in browsers supporting HTML 4.0 and above:

```
<button id="myButtonID"
    OnServerClick="on server click event handler"
    runat="server" >
  buttontext goes here
</button>
```

The `HtmlInputButton` performs a button-click task. It is used for standard button events such as `<input type=button>`, `<input type=submit>`, and the `<input type=reset>` HTML elements:

```
<input type=button | submit | reset
    id="programmaticID"
    OnServerClick="on server click event handler"
    runat="server" >
```

The `HtmlInputImage` button is much like a button, but displays a graphic. You can use the `HtmlInputImage` control to program against the traditional HTML `<input type=image>` element:

```
<input type=image
    id="myImageButtonID"
    src="path to image"
    align="image alignment"
    alt="alt text required"
    OnServerClick="on server click event handler"
    width="border width in pixels"
    runat="server" >
```

Anchors

The `HtmlAnchor` control enables web navigation from an anchor click. You can use the `HtmlAnchor` control to programmatically control an `<a>` HTML element. When used as a server-side control you need to embed the `HtmlAnchor` control inside the opening and closing tags of an `HtmlForm` control:

```
<a id="myHREFID"
    href="url to link to"
    name="bookmark name"
    OnServerClick="on server click event handler"
    target="frame or window in the page you have linked to"
    title="title to displayed in the browser"
    runat="server" >
  This is where you put the text of your link
</a>
```

An example of the anchor control in action:

```
<%@ Page Language="CS"%>
<html>
  <body>
    <form method="post" runat="server" ID="myForm">
      <a HRef="http://www.wrox.com" runat=server> Great Books at Wrox</a>
    </form>
  </body>
</html>
```

Dynamic Web Applications

The only real difference between this and the equivalent JSP code is the language declaration at the top, and the `runat=server` tags. Of course that is until you start interacting with the tag via something like the `on_load()` event or a `click()` event.

Select

To select items from a list you have the `HtmlSelect` control. By default, this control displays a drop-down listbox. If you allow multiple selections, then the control is displayed as a listbox:

```
<select id="mySelectID"
    OnServerChange="on server change event handler"
    DataSource="data binding source"
    DataMember="data member value"
    DataTextField="field to databind option ttext"
    DataValueField="field to databind option value"
    Multiple Items="collection of option elements"
    SelectedIndex="index of currently selected item"
    Size="the number of visible items"
    Value="current item value"
    runat="server" >
  <option>My Select value 1</option>
  <option>My Select value 2</option>
  <option>My Select value 3</option>
  .....etc
</select>
```

Graphics

For standard graphics display, we have the `HtmlImage` control. This control displays an image based on the standard HTML `<img>` element:

```
<img id="myImageID"
    alt="any alt text"
    align= top | middle | bottom | left | right
    border="border width"
    height="image height"
    src="the URL of the image to use"
    width="image width"
    runat="server" >
```

Hidden Fields

Hidden fields can be handled using the `HtmlInputHidden` control. It is also used to store state information for a form-server round trip. In ASP.NET, the system can automatically use something called **view state** to maintain state information for a control:

```
<input type="hidden"
    id="myHiddenFieldID"
    value="Some value"
    runat="server" >
```

Chapter 5

> A server control's view state is the accumulation of all its property values. In order to preserve these values across HTTP requests an ASP.NET server controls use this property to store the property values. The values are then passed as an encoded variable to an HTML hidden input element and posted back to the server as part of a form submission. In JSP you would typically have to manually store each property value in the session collection, in ASP.NET it is done automatically for you. Using view state in ASP.NET is not the same as using the ASP.NET **Session** object to store object state between page trips.

Binary

On/Off type HTML in ASP.NET is handled by the `HtmlInputCheckBox`, and the `HtmlInputRadioButton` controls.

The `HtmlInputCheckBox` control will create a checkbox based on the `<input type=checkbox>` HTML element that lets the user select a `true` or `false` state:

```
<input type=checkbox
    id="myCheckBoxID"
    checked
    runat="server" >
```

The `HtmlInputRadioButton` control displays a button that can be turned on or off to allow the user to select one item from a list of options. You can group multiple `HtmlInputRadioButton` controls together by setting the `Name` property to a value that is common to all `<input type=radio>` elements within that group:

```
<input type=radio
    id="myRadioButtonID"
    checked
    name="radiobuttongroup"
    runat="server" >
```

Tables

Without a table control rendering tables in JSP or servlets can be quite cumbersome. You will soon see how this improves tremendously, when we reach the web server controls section where the ASP.NET `Datagrid` control is discussed. However, for more traditional table rendering we have access to the `HtmlTable` control, and its siblings `HtmlTableRow` and `HtmlTableCell`.

As you can probably guess, `HtmlTable` actually allows you to program against the HTML `<table>` element:

```
<table id="myTableID"
    align=left | center | right
    bgcolor="bgcolor"
    border="border width in pixels"
    bordercolor="border color"
    cellpadding="spacing within cells in pixels"
    cellspacing="spacing between cells in pixels"
```

```
        height="table height"
        rows="collection of rows"
        width="table width"
        runat="server" >

Other table controls, such as TR and TD go here

   <tr>
    <td></td>
   </tr>

</table>
```

The `HtmlTableRow` control is used to program against the `<tr>` HTML element to represent a row in a table. In code, or manually you can control the background color, border color, and height of the row by setting the `BgColor`, `BorderColor`, and `Height` properties:

```
<tr id="myRowID"
    align="table content alignment"
    bgcolor="table bgcolor"
    bordercolor="border colour"
    height="table height"
    cells="collection of table cells"
    valign="vertical alignment of row content" >

    <td>cellcontent</td>
    <td>cellcontent</td>
    <td>cellcontent</td>

</tr>
```

The `HtmlTableCell` control maps to both the `<td>` and `<th>` HTML elements. A `<td>` element represents a data cell, while the `<th>` element represents a heading cell:

```
<td or th id="myTableCellID"
    align="alignment of content in the cell"
    bgcolor="bgcolor"
    bordercolor="bordercolor"
    colspan="the number of column cells to span"
    height="cell height"
    nowrap="True | False"
    rowspan=" the number of row cells to span "
    valign="vertical alignment options"
    width="cellwidth">
  CellContent
</td or /th>
```

Before we move on to the next control, let's take a look at a piece of simple `Table` code:

> As with all the examples in the chapter, choose an appropriate name for the example (**table1.aspx** for example) and save it in the **Chapter05** directory we created earlier. To run the example, simply type the path to the ASPX file in your web browser, such as **http://localhost/chapter05/table1.aspx**.

```
<%@ Page Language="C#" %>
<script runat="server">

  void Page_Load()
  {
    Table1.BgColor = "lime";
    Table1.Border = 2;
    Table1.BorderColor = "Blue";
  }

</script>

<html>
<head>
</head>
<body>
  <form runat="server">
    <h3>HtmlTable Example
    </h3>
    <table id="Table1" bordercolor="black" border="1" runat="server">
      <tbody>
        <tr>
          <td>
            Table Value 1
          </td>
          <td>
            Table Value 2
          </td>
          <td>
            Table Value 3
          </td>
        </tr>
      </tbody>
    </table>
  </form>
</body>
</html>
```

The `Table` tag can be scripted against using C# methods. Hence, loading the file produces output similar to that shown in the following screenshot, where the default properties we have coded against the `Table` element are changed in the `Page_Load()` event:

Dynamic Web Applications

Notice how we do not need to regenerate, or alter the string of HTML we are outputting. As it is now object based, we simply deal with the object properties in code.

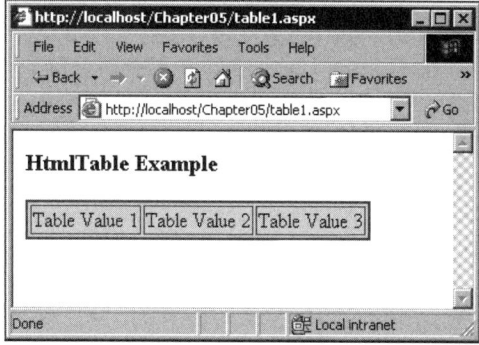

Multipart/Form-data handling

Moving on, one of the best and most sought-after additions to ASP.NET is the multipart/form-data handling built into it. JSP has had this for quite some time because the Net classes in Java cater for multipart/form-data handling relatively easily, and so building the appropriate code for upload is fairly straightforward. However in ASP, this has nearly always required a component, or at least a complex script file on the server. The client part of file upload is the specification of the `<input type=file>` tag in HTML. The tag is represented in ASP.NET by the `HtmlInputFile` control:

```
<input type=file
       id="myUploadFileID"
       accept="MIME encoding types"
       maxlength="maximum file path length"
       size="width of the file path textbox"
       postedfile=" uploadedfile"
       runat="server" >
```

Let's take a look at putting the upload server control into action, to produce the following simple screen and upload a file from a client browser to the web server:

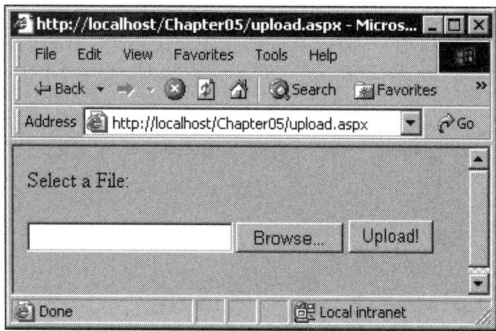

169

Chapter 5

The code will provide each file uploaded with a unique filename based on using the server tick count pre-pended to the filename and upon completion will display a simple summary to the end user. Although it is only an example, the demonstration will not show the server file path details to the end user as a simple security precaution. Here is the code:

```
<%@ Page Language="C#" Debug="true" %>

<html>
   <script runat="server">

      void UploadBtn_Click(Object sender, EventArgs e)
      {
//get a path to the current web directory
string strPath = Server.MapPath(Request.ServerVariables["Script_Name"]);
string[] pathdetails = strPath.Split(new char[]{'\\'});
strPath = "";
for (int i = 0; i < pathdetails.GetLength(0) - 1; i++)
{
    if(i < pathdetails.GetLength(0) - 1){
      strPath += pathdetails[i] + "\\";
    }
    else
    {
      strPath += pathdetails[i];
    }
}

//get just the filename of the uploaded file and tick stamp it
string strUploadedPath = MyFile.PostedFile.FileName;
string[] uploadPathdetails = strUploadedPath.Split(new char[]{'\\'});
strUploadedPath = uploadPathdetails[uploadPathdetails.GetLength(0) -1];

long tickStamp = DateTime.Now.Ticks;
string newFileName = (strPath + tickStamp + strUploadedPath);

// Save uploaded file to server
MyFile.PostedFile.SaveAs(newFileName);

         // Display information about posted file back to poster
         FileName.InnerHtml      = MyFile.PostedFile.FileName;
         MyContentType.InnerHtml = MyFile.PostedFile.ContentType;
         ContentLength.InnerHtml =
           MyFile.PostedFile.ContentLength.ToString();
         ServerFileName.InnerHtml  = tickStamp + strUploadedPath;
         FileDetails.Visible = true;

      }
   </script>

   <body bgcolor="lightblue">
      <form action="fileupload.aspx"
            method="post"
            enctype="multipart/form-data"
            runat="server">
```

```
            Select a File:<br><br>
            <input id="MyFile"
                   type="file"
                   runat="server">

            <input type=submit
                   value="Upload!"
                   OnServerclick="UploadBtn_Click"
                   runat="server">

            <br><br>

            <div id="FileDetails"
                 Visible=false
                 runat="server">
       <hr>
       Source FileName:    <span id="FileName" runat="server"/> <br>
       Server FileName:    <span id="ServerFileName" runat="server"/> <br>
       <hr>
       ContentType:        <span id="MyContentType" runat="server"/> <br>
       ContentLength:      <span id="ContentLength" runat="server"/>bytes
            </div>


        </form>
    </body>
</html>
```

Save the code as `upload.aspx` and request it in your browser. Once you have selected a file and clicked the upload button the file will be transferred and given a unique server name without requiring any components on the server other than the .NET Framework. With the exception of the file specifics, the result should look somewhat similar to that shown below:

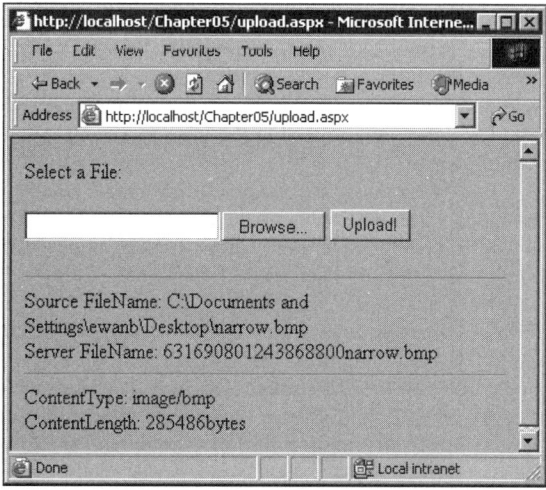

The last of the HTML controls to be aware of is the generic control `HtmlGenericControl`, which creates a basic object model for any HTML element converted to a control. As well as being used as a placeholder for other controls, it is also used to get access to a control for an HTML element not represented by a specific .NET Framework class, such as `<body>` and `<div>`:

```
<span | body | div | font | others
    id="myGenericID"
    runat="server" >
  The content between the tags
</span | body | div | font | others>
```

The next set of controls we'll look at are those specific to ASP.NET. These include some brand-new features like calendars, grids, and bound lists, which, due to their XML syntax are as easy to use as standard HTML. This type of control is referred to as a **web server control**. From a J2EE perspective, one way to think of web server controls is to consider them somewhat analogous to JavaBeans in that they are pre-provided add-ins that can intermingle with your code to produce a specific type of client-side output:

Web Server Controls

Web server controls were designed by Microsoft with a different emphasis from that of HTML controls. They do not map one-to-one to HTML server controls and are defined as abstract controls in which the actual HTML rendered by the control can be quite different from the model that you program against. They can be made up of other complex controls, and HTML controls. You can also build your own controls, which is covered in the next chapter of this book. The bulk of your web development in ASP.NET will be done using the web server controls.

The most important things that differentiate web server controls from HTML controls are:

- ❑ A rich yet common object model that provides type-safe programming capabilities.
- ❑ Automatic browser detection. The controls can detect browser capabilities and create appropriate output for both basic and rich (HTML 4.0) browsers. This means that the control actually changes the output depending of the browser type automatically for you without the need for you to add in any code, rendering the appropriate browser-level JavaScript required to trigger designated events.

It is worth noting that there is no standard out-of-the-box equivalent to these controls in JSP. To look for similar functionality you would have to use a third-party supplier like IBM, with its JSP format Bean Libraries.

All web server controls can be bound to a data source with very little work, so `DataGrids` can be simply bound to the contents of a database table for instance, or a `DropDownlist` can be automatically bound to an array of values. Like the HTML controls, there is a pre-defined set of web controls that come out of the box with ASP.NET. Like JSP bean developers, there are a million developers out there already extending the basic controls, or building new ones to extend the functionality available from the pre-defined set.

Next, we will take a look at the web server control syntax as we did with the HTML controls, again intermingling some of the descriptive text with some code snippets. One key thing to notice is the different way in which you define a web control, as opposed to the way in which you define an HTML control, as shown below:

```
<asp:Image id="image1" runat="server"
    AlternateText="Image Description"
    ImageAlign="left"
    ImageUrl="pict.jpg"/>
```

The main thing that stands out is the `asp:` prefix in front of what otherwise appears to be little more than an HTML control, and looks very much like a JavaBean declaration – that however is about where the similarity ends. Let's move on to the web controls in more detail. Another thing that we will introduce in this section is one or two of the server-side events that sit alongside the controls, such as the click event for buttons.

Label

The `Label` control in ASP.NET is used to display static text that the end user cannot edit. As its name suggests it is ideal for labels, or text strings:

```
<asp:Label id="myLabelID"
    Text="label"
    runat="server"/>
```

or:

```
<asp:Label id="myLabelID"
    runat="server">
  Text
</asp:Label>
```

Text Editing

For text editing, we have access to the `TextBox` control, which is an input control that lets the user enter common text. The default `TextMode` is to provide `Single` line textboxes only. You can, however, set the property to `MultiLine` (for multiple line input) or `Password` (single line mode only where characters typed are represented as *):

```
<asp:TextBox id="myTextboxI"
    AutoPostBack="True|False"
    Columns="characters"
    MaxLength="characters"
    Rows="rows"
    Text="text"
    TextMode="Single | Multiline | Password"
    Wrap="True|False"
    OnTextChanged="On Text Changed Method"
    runat="server"/>
```

173

Lists Selections

For list selections, we have access to the `DropDownList` control, which can be used to create a single selection drop-down list control. It automatically generates code in the HTML `select` tag format without you having to code any HTML. It can also be bound to a data source, such as an array, or a database table, and will automatically populate itself with the appropriate data:

```
<asp:DropDownList id="myDropDownID" runat="server"
    DataSource="<% databindingexpression %>"
    DataTextField="DataSourceField"
    DataValueField="DataSourceField"
    AutoPostBack="True|False"
    OnSelectedIndexChanged="On Selected Index Changed Method">

    <asp:ListItem value="value" selected="True|False">
      Text
    </asp:ListItem>

</asp:DropDownList>
```

Let's take a look at an example of the `DropDownList` in action. We will demonstrate how to declare a dropdown control, and then populate it with elements from code:

```
<%@ Page Language="C#" %>
<script runat="server">

  void Page_Load()
  {
  myDropDownList.Items.Add("A bit of text1");
  myDropDownList.Items.Add("A bit of text2");
  }

</script>


<html>
<head><title>DropListBox</title></head>

<body>

<form runat="server">

<asp:dropdownlist
id="myDropDownList"
runat="server"
/>

</form>

</body>
</html>
```

Of course we also have access to a `ListBox` control, which functions in a very similar manner to the `DropDownlist` but acts as a scrollable selection as opposed to a drop down selection:

```
<asp:ListBox id="myListboxID"
   DataSource="<% databindingexpression %>"
   DataTextField="DataSourceField"
   DataValueField="DataSourceField"
   AutoPostBack="True|False"
   Rows="rowcount"
   SelectionMode="Single|Multiple"
   OnSelectedIndexChanged="On Selected Index Changed Method"
   runat="server">

   <asp:ListItem value="value" selected="True|False">
    Text
   </asp:ListItem>

</asp:ListBox>
```

Again, the code is very like the `DropDownList` code, but in this instance we won't populate using the `On_Load` event:

```
<%@ Page Language="C#" %>
<html>
<head>

</head>
<body>
  <form runat="server">
   <asp:ListBox id="myListBoxID"
      Rows="2"
      SelectionMode="Multiple"
      Width="100px"
      runat="server">
     <asp:ListItem>ListBox Item 1</asp:ListItem>
     <asp:ListItem>ListBox Item 2</asp:ListItem>
     <asp:ListItem>ListBox Item 3</asp:ListItem>
     <asp:ListItem>ListBox Item 4</asp:ListItem>
   </asp:ListBox>
  </form>
</body>
</html>
```

Graphics

For graphics handling, the web controls provide the `Image` and the `AdRotator` controls.

The `Image` control simply displays an image. Quite often in traditional development, like JSP, images are used as buttons. In ASP.NET however there is an `ImageButton` control that provides better performance, so the image control should only be used for images:

```
<asp:Image id="myImageID" runat="server"
    ImageUrl="path to image"
    AlternateText="alt text string"
    ImageAlign="NotSet|AbsBottom|AbsMiddle|BaseLine|
        Bottom|Left|Middle|Right|TextTop|Top"/>
```

The `AdRotator` control is used for handling banner advertising in ASP.NET pages. It is a functionally efficient control that handles XML instructions to determine which images to display and how often. It is easy to use as shown below:

```
<html>
  <head>
    <title>J2EE adRotator Demo</title>
  </head>
  <body>
    <asp:AdRotator
        ID="adBannerTop"
        target="_blank"
        AdvertisementFile="Ads.xml"
        Runat="server" />
  </body>
</html>
```

You'll need an appropriate XML format advertisement file, which has the following syntax:

```
<?xml version="1.0" encoding="utf-8" ?>
<Advertisements>

  <Ad>
    <ImageUrl>image1.gif</ImageUrl>
    <NavigateUrl>www.wrox.com</NavigateUrl>
    <AlternateText>Go to wrox</AlternateText>
    <Keyword>aspx</Keyword>
    <Impressions>2</Impressions>
  </Ad>

  <Ad>
    <ImageUrl>image1.gif</ImageUrl>
    <NavigateUrl> www.microsoft.com</NavigateUrl>
    <AlternateText>Go to microsoft</AlternateText>
    <Keyword>aspx</Keyword>
    <Impressions>2</Impressions>
  </Ad>

</Advertisements>
```

If you were to run the ASPX for the adrotator example, the source code that is output shows how the control has converted the output to an anchor tag, easily understood by any browser:

```
<html>
  <head>
    <title>J2EE adRotator Demo</title>
```

```
        </head>
    <body>
        <a id="adBannerTop" href="/chapter6/www.microsoft.com" target="_blank"><img
src="/chapter6/image2.gif" alt="Go to microsoft" border="0" /></a>
    </body>
</html>
```

Binary Values

To handle binary on/off type values in the controls, we have access to the `CheckBox`, the `CheckBoxList`, the `RadioButton` and the `RadioButtonList` controls.

Starting with the `CheckBox` control, which creates a check box on the Web Forms page that allows the end user to switch the `CheckBox` between a `true` or `false` state:

```
<asp:CheckBox id="myCheckBoxID"
    AutoPostBack="True|False"
    Text="Label"
    TextAlign="Right|Left"
    Checked="True|False"
    OnCheckedChanged="On Checked Changed Method"
    runat="server"/>
```

You can make the `CheckBox` behave like a button and cause an automatic server `submit` on selection by setting the `AutoPostBack` property to be `True`, as shown here:

```
<asp:CheckBox id=myCheckBoxID runat="server"
    Text="CheckBox Example"
    AutoPostBack="True"/>
```

The next of these binary controls to consider is the `CheckBoxList` control, which is nothing more than a related set of `CheckBox` controls, and is declared as shown here:

```
<asp:CheckBoxList id="myCheckBoxList1"
    AutoPostBack="True|False"
    CellPadding="Pixels"
    DataSource='<% data binding expression %>'
    DataTextField="DataSource Field"
    DataValueField="DataSource Field"
    RepeatColumns="Column Count"
    RepeatDirection="Vertical|Horizontal"
    RepeatLayout="Flow|Table"
    TextAlign="Right|Left"
    OnSelectedIndexChanged="On Selected Index Changed Method"
    runat="server">

    <asp:ListItem value="value"
        selected="True|False">
    Text
    </asp:ListItem>

</asp:CheckBoxList>
```

As an example, you can use the `CheckBoxList` control to create a multi-selection checkbox group by populating it with `ListItem` entries:

```
<asp:CheckBoxList id="myCheckBoxListID"
    RepeatLayout="flow"
    runat="server">

    <asp:ListItem>CheckBoxListItem 1</asp:ListItem>
    <asp:ListItem>CheckBoxListItem 2</asp:ListItem>
    <asp:ListItem>CheckBoxListItem 3</asp:ListItem>

</asp:CheckBoxList>
```

The `RadioButton` Web Control creates an individual radio button as its output. Like HTML `RadioButton` controls you can group multiple radio buttons together if you specify the same `GroupName` for each `RadioButton` control. Grouping radio buttons together will only allow a single selection from the group:

```
<asp:RadioButton id="myRadioButtonID"
    AutoPostBack="True|False"
    Checked="True|False"
    GroupName="Group Name"
    Text="label"
    TextAlign="Right|Left"
    OnCheckedChanged="On Checked Changed Method"
    runat="server"/>
```

In the next example, we will demonstrate how to utilize the `AutoPostBack` option of a `RadioButton` control. We will also make use of a server parameter called `IsPostBack`, which determines if this is the first page delivery, or a delivery following a form submission. The parameter is often used to better control the processing within the `Page_Load` event to provide code optimization and improved performance:

```
<%@ Page Language="C#" %>
<html>
 <head>

    <script language="C#" runat="server">

      void Page_Load() {

        if (IsPostBack){

          if (myRadioID1.Checked) {
            Label1.Text = "You selected " + myRadioID1.Text;
          }
          else if (myRadioID2.Checked) {
            Label1.Text = "You selected " + myRadioID2.Text;
          }

        }
      }
```

```
    </script>

</head>
<body>

  <h2>RadioButton Example</h2>

  <form runat=server>

    <h4>Select A Radio Button:</h4>

    <asp:RadioButton id=myRadioID1 Text="Choice 1" GroupName="RadioGroup1"
AUtoPostBack="True" runat="server" /><br>

    <asp:RadioButton id=myRadioID2 Text="Choice 2" GroupName="RadioGroup1"
AUtoPostBack="True" runat="server"/><br>

    <p>
    <asp:Label id=Label1 font-bold="true" runat="server" />

  </form>

</body>
</html>
```

Selecting a particular `RadioButton` results in something similar to the following:

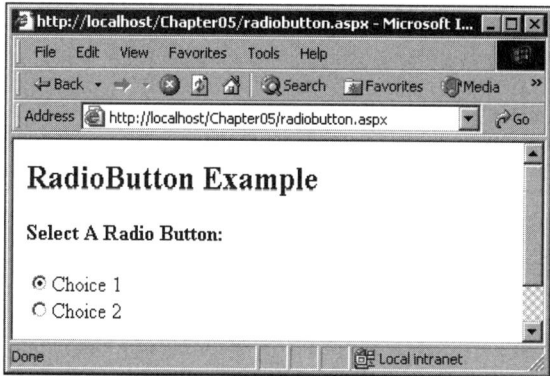

The final control in the binary on/off set is the `RadioButtonList` control, which is similar in functionality to the `CheckBoxList` control in that to specify the items for the `RadioButtonList` control a `ListItem` element is used for each entry:

```
<asp:RadioButtonList id="myRadioButtonListID"
    AutoPostBack="True|False"
    CellPadding="Pixels"
    DataSource="<% data binding expression %>"
    DataTextField="DataSource Field"
    DataValueField="DataSource Field"
    RepeatColumns="ColumnCount"
```

```
    RepeatDirection="Vertical|Horizontal"
    RepeatLayout="Flow|Table"
    TextAlign="Right|Left"
    OnSelectedIndexChanged="On Selected Index Changed Method"
    runat="server">

  <asp:ListItem Text="label"
    Value="value"
    Selected="True|False" />

</asp:RadioButtonList>
```

Calendar

The `Calendar` control is one of the most advanced controls in the web controls set. It displays one month and allows the end user to select dates and move to the next and previous months. It has parameters that allow the developer to specify whether the user can select a single day, a week, or a month, or to disable date selection entirely. The calendar control is just one example of the controls for which there is an equivalent JSP bean in the JSP third-party IBM Calendar Bean Suite. (The suite consists of six beans that aim at providing a set of calendar visual beans.) The ASP.NET calendar control operates 'out of the box' and is quite a complex control. As such we will only touch on it here; but a comprehensive evaluation of the control can be found in *Professional ASP.NET 1.0 Special Edition*, also by Wrox Press:

```
<asp:Calendar id="myCalendarID"
    CellPadding="pixels"
    CellSpacing="pixels"
    DayNameFormat="FirstLetter|FirstTwoLetters|Full|Short"
    FirstDayOfWeek="Default|Monday|Tuesday|Wednesday|
                    Thursday|Friday|Saturday|Sunday"
    NextMonthText="HTML text"
    NextPrevFormat="ShortMonth|FullMonth|CustomText"
    PrevMonthText="HTML text"
    SelectedDate="date"
    SelectionMode="None|Day|DayWeek|DayWeekMonth"
    SelectMonthText="HTML text"
    SelectWeekText="HTML text"
    ShowDayHeader="True|False"
    ShowGridLines="True|False"
    ShowNextPrevMonth="True|False"
    ShowTitle="True|False"
    TitleFormat="Month|MonthYear"
    TodaysDate="date"
    VisibleDate="date"
    OnDayRender="OnDayRenderMethod"
    OnSelectionChanged="On Selection Changed Method"
    OnVisibleMonthChanged="On Visible Month Changed Method"
    runat="server">

  <TodayDayStyle property="value"/>
  <DayHeaderStyle property="value"/>
  <DayStyle property="value"/>
  <NextPrevStyle property="value"/>
```

```
    <OtherMonthDayStyle property="value"/>
    <SelectedDayStyle property="value"/>
    <SelectorStyle property="value"/>
    <TitleStyle property="value"/>
    <TodayDayStyle property="value"/>
    <WeekendDayStyle property="value"/>
```

Given it functions out of the box, unlike the IBM Javabean, it is very easy to get it working with relatively little code and no knowledge of how to install components:

```
<%@ Page Language="C#" %>
<html>
 <head>

   <script language="C#" runat="server">

   protected void Date_Selected(object sender, EventArgs e)
   {
       Label1.Text = "The selected date is " +
            Calendar1.SelectedDate.ToShortDateString();
   }

    </script>

 </head>
 <body>

   <form runat=server>

    <asp:Calendar id="Calendar1"
      OnSelectionChanged="Date_Selected"
      SelectionMode="DayWeekMonth"
      Font-Name="Verdana"
      Font-Size="12px"
      NextPrevFormat="ShortMonth"
      SelectWeekText="week"
      SelectMonthText="month"
      runat="server">

    <TodayDayStyle Font-Bold="True"/>
    <DayHeaderStyle Font-Bold="True"/>
    <OtherMonthDayStyle ForeColor="gray"/>
    <TitleStyle BackColor="DarkGreen"
         ForeColor="white"
         Font-Bold="True"/>

    <SelectedDayStyle BackColor="Green"
            Font-Bold="True"/>
    <NextPrevStyle ForeColor="white"
          Font-Size="10px"/>
    <SelectorStyle BackColor="Green"
          ForeColor="white"
          Font-Size="9px"/>
    </asp:Calendar>
```

Chapter 5

```
        <asp:Label id=Label1 font-bold="true" runat="server" />

    </form>

</body>
</html>
```

Notice the use of the property `OnSelectionChanged` in the code. This is the first time we have come across this event in C#:

```
OnSelectionChanged="Date_Selected"
```

We have tied this property to a custom event handler method called `Date_Selected` in our script tags. This handler method, when activated, interrogates the `Calender1` values passed in the auto-submission by the form for the `selectedDate` property.

Notice that the event takes arguments, as many of the action events in .NET do. The first argument is the object that has raised the event. The second argument is an instance of the class that contains any specific event information; by default that would be `System.EventHandler()`. It is somewhat similar to adding an Action Listener in Java for a button, and we come back to the issue of wiring events to handlers in Chapter 8.

The result of loading and selecting a date should be similar to that shown below:

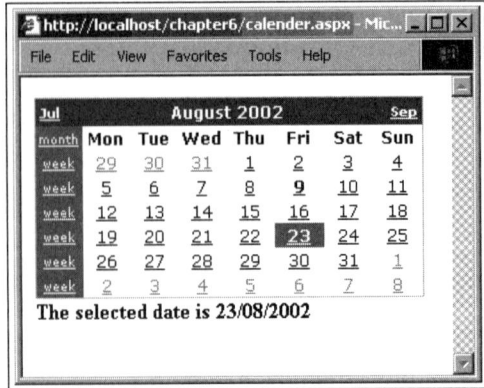

Buttons

Like HTML controls, web controls give access to a set of button-like objects. In the web controls, there are all types of buttons and each has a different purpose.

The `Button` control allows you to create a push button for a Web Form. There are two types of buttons that can be created using the `Button` control. A standard **submit** button (default) or a **command** button. You would normally create an event handler for the `Click` event to programmatically control the actions performed when the **submit** button is clicked:

```
<asp:Button id="MyButtonID"
            Text="label"
            CommandName="command"
            CommandArgument="commandargument"
            CausesValidation="true | false"
            OnClick="On Click Method"
            runat="server"/>
```

Typical use of the `Button` control is as follows:

```
<% @Page language="C#"%>
<html>
  <script language="C#" runat=server>
    private void btnclick_click(object sender, EventArgs e)
    {
      Label1.Text = "You clicked the button";
    }
  </script>
  <body>
    <form runat="server">
      <asp:Button Text="Click Here" id="btnClick"
                  onClick="btnclick_click" Runat=server />
      <asp:Label runat="server" id="Label1" />
    </form>
  </body>
</html>
```

with the `Button` in `Command` mode operating thus:

```
<%@ Page Language="C#" %>
<html>
  <head>
    <script language="C#" runat="server">
      void CommandButton_ClickEvent(Object sender, CommandEventArgs e)
      {
        Label1.Text = "You clicked the " + e.CommandName + " - "
            + e.CommandArgument + " button.";
      }
    </script>
  </head>
  <body>
    <form runat=server>
      <asp:Button id="ItemsButton1"
                  Text="Process 1000 Items"
                  CommandName="Process"
                  CommandArgument="1000"
                  OnCommand="CommandButton_ClickEvent"
                  runat="server"/>
      <asp:Button id="ItemsButton2"
                  Text="Process 2000 Items"
                  CommandName="Process"
                  CommandArgument="2000"
```

```
                OnCommand="CommandButton_ClickEvent"
                runat="server"/>
        <asp:Label id=Label1 font-bold="true" runat="server" />
    </form>
  </body>
</html>
```

The command example is a useful demonstration of how to utilize the **same click event** for different buttons, and could be enhanced with a switch statement, or similar.

The `LinkButton` control acts in the same way as a simple `Button` control, but has the appearance of a hyperlink. By default, a `LinkButton` control is a **submit** button, and you can provide an event handler for the `Click` event to programmatically control the actions performed when this submit button is clicked in the same way as you can for the `Button` control:

```
<asp:LinkButton id="myLinkButtonID"
            Text="label"
            Command="Command"
            CommandArgument="CommandArgument"
            CausesValidation="true | false"
            OnClick="On Click Method"
            runat="server"/>
```

or:

```
<asp:LinkButton id=" myLinkButtonID "
            Command="Command"
            CommandArgument="CommandArgument"
            CausesValidation="true | false"
            OnClick="On Click Method"
            runat="server">
    Text
</asp:LinkButton>
```

The last of the button type controls is the `ImageButton`. The `ImageButton` control enables you to handle user clicks on an image, which gives you functionality similar to that found in an image map in that it displays an image that responds to mouse clicks:

```
<asp:ImageButton id="myImageButtonID"
            ImageUrl="string"
            Command="Command"
            CommandArgument="CommandArgument"
            CausesValidation="true | false"
            OnClick="On Click Method"
            runat="server"/>
```

A simple example will explain this functionality better:

```
<%@ Page Language="C#" %>
<html>
  <head>
```

Dynamic Web Applications

```
    <script runat="server">
      void ImageButton_Click_Event(object Source, ImageClickEventArgs e)
      {
        Label1.Text="You clicked the Image at the " +
            "Coordinates: (" + e.X.ToString() + ", " +
            e.Y.ToString() + ")";
      }
    </script>
  </head>
  <body>
    <form runat="server">
      Click on the image.
      <br/>
      <asp:Label id="Label1" runat="server"/>
      <asp:ImageButton id="imagebuttonID"
                       AlternateText="My ImageButton"
                       ImageAlign="left"
                       ImageUrl="image1.gif"
                       OnClick="ImageButton_Click_Event"
                       runat="server"/>
    </form>
  </body>
</html>
```

Running the example and clicking on the image served produces these results:

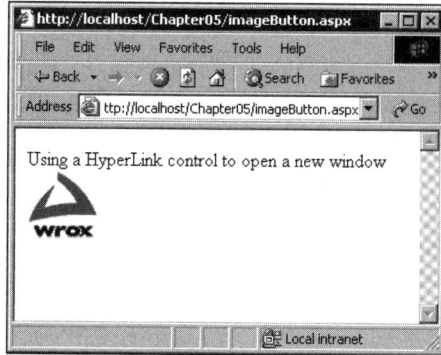

Navigation

There is only one control in the ASP.NET web controls set that is used for Navigation, and that is the `Hyperlink` control. You would use the `HyperLink` control to create a link that moves you to another page or another location on the same page. As with any `Hyperlink`, you can specify the frame or window to display the linked page by setting the `Target` property:

```
<asp:HyperLink id="HyperLink1"
               NavigateUrl="url"
               Text="HyperLinkText"
               ImageUrl="url"
               Target="window"
               runat="server"/>
```

or:

```
<asp:HyperLink id="HyperLink1"""
            NavigateUrl="url"
            ImageUrl="url"
            Target="window"
            runat="server">
   Text
</asp:HyperLink>
```

The code for this, as you can imagine, is quite straightforward:

```
<html>
  <head>
  </head>
  <body>
    Using a HyperLink control to open a new window
    <br/>
    <asp:HyperLink id="myhyperLinkID"
               ImageUrl="image1.gif"
               NavigateUrl="http://www.Wrox.com"
               Text="The Wrox Web Site"
               Target="_new"
               runat="server"/>
  </body>
</html>
```

Table Controls

Similar again to the HTML controls, there are three table elements available for handling table layout, the `Table` control, the `TableRow` control and the `TableCell` control. It relates in functionality to the `JSPTableFormat` bean found in the IBM Alphaworks JSP Format Bean Library.

The `Table` control allows you to build an HTML table and specify its characteristics or interact with them via code. It is worth noting that table rows and cells are controls in their own right, not properties of the `Table` control. The `Table` web server control has a richer set of properties than the HTML `Table` element:

```
<asp:Table id="Table1"
         BackImageUrl="url"
         CellSpacing="cellspacing"
         CellPadding="cellpadding"
         GridLines="None|Horizontal|Vertical|Both"
         HorizontalAlign="Center|Justify|Left|NotSet|Right"
         runat="server">
   <asp:TableRow>
     <asp:TableCell>
       Cell text
     </asp:TableCell>
   </asp:TableRow>
</asp:Table>
```

The `TableRow`, as you might expect represents a row in the `Table` control and allows you to manipulate it programmatically:

```
<asp:TableRow id="TableRow1"
              HorizontalAlign="Center|Justify|Left|NotSet|Right"
              VerticalAlign="Bottom|Middle|NotSet|Top"
              runat="server">
  <asp:TableCell>
    Cell text
  </asp:TableCell>
</asp:TableRow>
```

Finally, the `TableCell` control is available and represents a cell in a `Table` control:

```
<asp:TableCell id="TableCell1"
              ColumnSpan="colcount"
              RowSpan="rowcount"
              HorizontalAlign="Center|Justify|Left|NotSet|Right"
              VerticalAlign="Bottom|Middle|NotSet|Top"
              Wrap="True|False"
              runat="server">
    Cell text
</asp:TableCell>
```

Before we move on to the next control, let's take a look at a piece of `Table` code and compare the input code required to the actual output produced:

```
<html>
  <head>
  </head>
  <body>
    <p>
      <asp:Table id="Table1" runat="server" ForeColor="DarkGreen"
                 Font-Names="Arial" Align="Center">
        <asp:TableRow>
          <asp:TableCell BorderStyle="Solid">
            <asp:Label runat="server" ID="labelName">
              Stephanie Craddock
            </asp:Label>
          </asp:TableCell>
          <asp:TableCell BorderStyle="Solid">
            <asp:Label runat="server" ID="labelOccupation">
              Accountant
            </asp:Label>
          </asp:TableCell>
        </asp:TableRow>
      </asp:Table>
    </p>
  </body>
</html>
```

That's nothing like the way you would prepare the HTML code for a table in JSP or servlets. Here we have a `Table` control, with a `TableRow` control, and a number of `TableCell` controls containing `Label` controls. The output rendered by the ASP.NET engine for this is quite different from the source code that you provided, while in JSP it would in theory be identical to the source declarations.

As shown below, the server has rendered the output appropriately for the browser. In this case there is nothing we would not have expected, but it is nothing like the source code:

```html
<html>
  <head>
  </head>
  <body>
    <p>
      <table id="Table1" Align="Center" border="0"
          style="color:DarkGreen;font-family:Arial;">
        <tr>
          <td style="border-style:Solid;">
            <span id="labelName">Stephanie Craddock</span>
          </td>
          <td style="border-style:Solid;">
            <span id="labelOccupation">Accountant</span>
          </td>
        </tr>
      </table>
    </p>
  </body>
</html>
```

Panel

The `Panel` control is available to assist with layout. It creates a borderless division on the form that serves as a container for other controls and renders HTML `<div>` elements as its output. It is especially useful for programmatically displaying and hiding groups of controls:

```
<asp:Panel id="myPanelID"
           BackImageUrl="url"
           HorizontalAlign="Center|Justify|Left|NotSet|Right"
           Wrap="True|False"
           runat="server">
   Other controls can be declared here
</asp:Panel>
```

Another benefit of the `Panel` control is that it is quite useful as a container when you want to dynamically add controls at run time, as the example below demonstrates, or simply hide and show other controls than reside within it:

```
<%@ Page Language="C#" %>
<html>
  <head>
    <script runat="server">
      void Page_Load(Object sender, EventArgs e)
      {
```

```
              int numtexts = Int32.Parse(DropDown2.SelectedItem.Value);
              for (int i = 1; i <= numtexts; i++)
              {
                TextBox t = new TextBox();
                t.Text = "TextBox" + (i).ToString();
                t.ID = "TextBox" + (i).ToString();
                Panel1.Controls.Add(t);
                Panel1.Controls.Add(new LiteralControl("<br>"));
              }
            }
        </script>
    </head>
    <body>
      <form runat="server">
        <asp:Panel id="Panel1" runat="server"
            BackColor="Beige"
            Height="150px"
            Width="200px">
          Select a number of dynamic controls to add to the panel
          <p/>
        </asp:Panel>
        <br/>
        Generate TextBoxes:
        <asp:DropDownList id=DropDown2 runat="server">
          <asp:ListItem Value="0">0</asp:ListItem>
          <asp:ListItem Value="1">1</asp:ListItem>
          <asp:ListItem Value="2">2</asp:ListItem>
        </asp:DropDownList>
        <asp:Button Text="Show Me" runat="server"/>
      </form>
    </body>
</html>
```

Data Controls

We are now into the realm of the controls that can act as real time savers in ASP.NET, where I feel ASP.NET really comes into its own over JSP are with the list controls – the `Repeater`, the `DataList`, and the `DataGrid` controls.

The `Repeater` control is used in the creation of lists that allow custom layout by repeating a specified template to display each item in a list. The `Repeater` control has no built-in layout or styles; you must explicitly declare all HTML layout, formatting, and style tags within the control's templates.

The `Repeater` control is different from other data list controls in that it allows you to place HTML fragments that will style what the output looks like in its templates:

```
<asp:Repeater id="myRepeaterID"
    DataSource="<% databindingexpression %>"
    runat=server>
  <HeaderTemplate>
    Header template HTML
  </HeaderTemplate>
  <ItemTemplate>
```

```
        Item template HTML
    </ItemTemplate>
    <AlternatingItemTemplate>
        Alternating item template HTML
    </AlternatingItemTemplate>
    <SeparatorTemplate>
        Separator template HTML
    </SeparatorTemplate>
    <FooterTemplate>
        Footer template HTML
    </FooterTemplate>
<asp:Repeater>
```

We can demonstrate this with a simple example that will make use of an XML file, which we will use as a database. Data binding with ASP.NET is covered in detail in the next chapter, but to effectively demonstrate the controls in action, we'll provide a small taste of how we bind a data source to a control. We will bind the contents of the database to the `Repeater` control. When bound, the control knows where to get data from for the items that need repeating, without any requirement to iterate through the data set using code as you would in JSP.

The XML file (called `test.xml`) looks like this:

```
<Elements>
    <Links>
        <Text>Wrox Press</Text>
        <Link>http://www.wrox.com</Link>
    </Links>
    <Links>
        <Text>Microsoft</Text>
        <Link>http://www.microsoft.com</Link>
    </Links>
    <Links>
        <Text>Amazon</Text>
        <Link>http://www.amazon.com</Link>
    </Links>
</Elements>
```

The code we will use is as shown below. Notice that we are importing a couple of required namespaces to help us with handling `Data`, and `IO`. As you'll remember, a namespace is basically the same as a Java package in that it's full of classes, and by using unique namespaces, we can use identical class names as long as each class exists in a different namespace:

You can find information about namespaces back in Chapter 1.

```
<% @Page Language="C#" %>
<% @Import Namespace="System.Data" %>
<% @Import Namespace="System.IO" %>

<script language="C#" runat="server">
    void Page_Load(Object src, EventArgs e)
    {
```

```
        DataSet ds = new DataSet();
        FileStream fs = new FileStream(Server.MapPath("test.xml"),
                                    FileMode.Open, FileAccess.Read );
        StreamReader reader = new StreamReader( fs );
        ds.ReadXml( reader );
        fs.Close();
        DataView Source = new DataView( ds.Tables[0] );
        MyRepeater.DataSource = Source;
        MyRepeater.DataBind();
    }
</script>

<html>
  <body>
    <asp:Repeater id="MyRepeater" runat="server">
      <ItemTemplate>
        <asp:Hyperlink runat="server"
            NavigateUrl='<%# DataBinder.Eval(Container.DataItem, "Link") %>'
            Text='<%# DataBinder.Eval(Container.DataItem, "Text") %>'/>
        <br/>
      </ItemTemplate>
    </asp:Repeater>
  </body>
</html>
```

If this code is run, the output looks something like this:

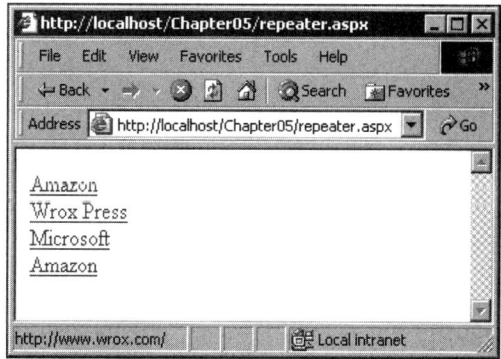

The `DataList` control is like the `Repeater` control, but with more formatting and layout options, including the ability to display information in a table. The `DataList` control, like the `Repeater` control displays the items from a data source by using templates. You can customize the appearance and contents of what is displayed within the control by manipulating the templates that make up the different components of the `DataList` control, such as the `ItemTemplate` and `HeaderTemplate`.

The `DataList` control differs from the `Repeater` control by supporting directional rendering (by use of the `RepeatColumns` and `RepeatDirection` properties) and the option to render within an HTML table:

191

```
<asp:DataList id="myDataListID"
            CellPadding="pixels"
            CellSpacing="pixels"
            DataKeyField="DataSourceKeyField"
            DataSource='<% databindingexpression %>'
            ExtractTemplateRows="True|False"
            GridLines="None|Horizontal|Vertical|Both"
            RepeatColumns="ColumnCount"
            RepeatDirection="Vertical|Horizontal"
            RepeatLayout="Flow|Table"
            ShowFooter="True|False"
            ShowHeader="True|False"
            OnCancelCommand="On Cancel Command Method"
            OnDeleteCommand="On Delete Command Method"
            OnEditCommand="On Edit Command Method"
            OnItemCommand="On Item Command Method"
            OnItemCreated="On Item Created Method"
            OnUpdateCommand="On Update Command Method"
            runat="server">

<AlternatingItemStyle ForeColor="Blue"/>
<EditItemStyle BackColor="Yellow"/>
<FooterStyle BorderColor="Gray"/>
<HeaderStyle BorderColor="Gray"/>
<ItemStyle Font-Bold="True"/>
<PagerStyle Font-Name="Ariel"/>
<SelectedItemStyle BackColor="Blue"/>

<HeaderTemplate>
   Header template HTML
</HeaderTemplate>
<ItemTemplate>
   Item template HTML
</ItemTemplate>
<AlternatingItemTemplate>
   Alternating item template HTML
</AlternatingItemTemplate>
<EditItemTemplate>
   Edited item template HTML
</EditItemTemplate>
<SelectedItemTemplate>
   Selected item template HTML
</SelectedItemTemplate>
<SeparatorTemplate>
   Separator template HTML
</SeparatorTemplate>
<FooterTemplate>
   Footer template HTML
</FooterTemplate>

</asp:DataList>
```

The following code demonstrates the `DataList` in action:

```
<% @Page Language="C#" %>
<% @Import Namespace="System.Data" %>
<% @Import Namespace="System.IO" %>

<script language="C#" runat="server">
  void Page_Load(Object src, EventArgs e)
  {
    DataSet ds = new DataSet();
    FileStream fs = new FileStream( Server.MapPath("test.xml"),
        FileMode.Open, FileAccess.Read );
    StreamReader reader = new StreamReader( fs );
    ds.ReadXml( reader );
    fs.Close();
    DataView Source = new DataView( ds.Tables[0] );
    MyDataListID.DataSource = Source;
    MyDataListID.DataBind();
  }
</script>

<html>
  <body>
    <asp:DataList id="MyDataListID" runat="server">
      <AlternatingItemStyle BackColor="Beige"/>
      <ItemStyle BackColor="Gainsboro"></ItemStyle>
      <ItemTemplate>
        <asp:Label runat="server" Font-Bold="true"
            text='<%# DataBinder.Eval(Container.DataItem, "Text") %>'/>
        <br/>
        Address:
        <asp:Label runat="server"
            text='<%# DataBinder.Eval(Container.DataItem, "link") %>'/>
        <br/><br/>
      </ItemTemplate>
    </asp:DataList>
  </body>
</html>
```

The final control in the list controls is the `DataGrid` control. This is a very advanced control, and given that it is free with the Framework you get an awful lot for your money. This control provides for easily handling of bound data in columns and provides mechanisms to allow editing and sorting. The `DataGrid` control allows you to define various types of columns to control the layout of the cell contents of the grid (bound columns, template columns, and so on) and add specific functionality (such as edit-button columns, and hyperlink columns). The control also supports a variety of options for paging through data. It's a very superior control when it comes to handling and laying out data.

The syntax for the `DataGrid` is as shown overleaf. The number of properties that sit within the `DataGrid` demonstrate how complex, and indeed, how powerful this control actually is:

```
<asp:DataGrid id="programmaticID"
              DataSource='<%# DataBindingExpression %>'
              AllowPaging="True|False"
              AllowSorting="True|False"
              AutoGenerateColumns="True|False"
              BackImageUrl="url"
              CellPadding="pixels"
              CellSpacing="pixels"
              DataKeyField="DataSourceKeyField"
              GridLines="None|Horizontal|Vertical|Both"
              HorizontalAlign="Center|Justify|Left|NotSet|Right"
              PagedDataSource
              PageSize="ItemCount"
              ShowFooter="True|False"
              ShowHeader="True|False"
              VirtualItemCount="ItemCount"
              OnCancelCommand="OnCancelCommandMethod"
              OnDeleteCommand="OnDeleteCommandMethod"
              OnEditCommand="OnEditCommandMethod"
              OnItemCommand="OnItemCommandMethod"
              OnItemCreated="OnItemCreatedMethod"
              OnPageIndexChanged="OnPageIndexChangedMethod"
              OnSortCommand="OnSortCommandMethod"
              OnUpdateCommand="OnUpdateCommandMethod"
              runat="server" >

    <AlternatingItemStyle ForeColor="Blue"/>
    <EditItemStyle BackColor="Yellow"/>
    <FooterStyle BorderColor="Gray"/>
    <HeaderStyle BorderColor="Gray"/>
    <ItemStyle Font-Bold="True"/>
    <PagerStyle Font-Name="Ariel"/>
    <SelectedItemStyle BackColor="Blue"/>

</asp:DataGrid>
```

or:

```
<asp:DataGrid id="programmaticID"
              DataSource='<%# DataBindingExpression %>'
              AutoGenerateColumns="False"
              (other properties)
              runat="server" >

    <AlternatingItemStyle ForeColor="Blue"/>
    <EditItemStyle BackColor="Yellow"/>
    <FooterStyle BorderColor="Gray"/>
    <HeaderStyle BorderColor="Gray"/>
    <ItemStyle Font-Bold="True"/>
    <PagerStyle Font-Name="Ariel"/>
    <SelectedItemStyle BackColor="Blue"/>
```

```
<Columns>
  <asp:BoundColumn
      DataField="DataSourceField"
      DataFormatString="FormatString"
      FooterText="FooterText"
      HeaderImageUrl="url"
      HeaderText="HeaderText"
      ReadOnly="True|False"
      SortExpression ="DataSourceFieldToSortBy"
      Visible="True|False"
      FooterStyle-property="value"
      HeaderStyle-property="value"
      ItemStyle-property="value"/>

  <asp:ButtonColumn
      ButtonType="LinkButton|PushButton"
      Command="BubbleText"
      DataTextField="DataSourceField"
      DataTextFormatString="FormatString"
      FooterText="FooterText"
      HeaderImageUrl="url"
      HeaderText="HeaderText"
      ReadOnly="True|False"
      SortExpression="DataSourceFieldToSortBy"
      Text="ButtonCaption"
      Visible="True|False"/>

  <asp:EditCommandColumn
      ButtonType="LinkButton|PushButton"
      CancelText="CancelButtonCaption"
      EditText="EditButtonCaption"
      FooterText="FooterText"
      HeaderImageUrl="url"
      HeaderText="HeaderText"
      ReadOnly="True|False"
      SortExpression="DataSourceFieldToSortBy"
      UpdateText="UpdateButtonCaption"
      Visible="True|False"/>

  <asp:HyperLinkColumn
      DataNavigateUrlField="DataSourceField"
      DataNavigateUrlFormatString="FormatExpression"
      DataTextField="DataSourceField"
      DataTextFormatString="FormatExpression"
      FooterText="FooterText"
      HeaderImageUrl="url"
      HeaderText="HeaderText"
      NavigateUrl="url"
      ReadOnly="True|False"
      SortExpression="DataSourceFieldToSortBy"
      Target="window"
      Text="HyperLinkText"
      Visible="True|False"/>
```

```
      <asp:TemplateColumn
          FooterText="FooterText"
          HeaderImageUrl="url"
          HeaderText="HeaderText"
          ReadOnly="True|False"
          SortExpression="DataSourceFieldToSortBy"
          Visible="True|False">

        <HeaderTemplate>
          Header template HTML
        </HeaderTemplate >
        <ItemTemplate>
          ItemTemplate HTML
        </ItemTemplate>
        <EditItemTemplate>
          EditItem template HTML
        </EditItemTemplate>
        <FooterTemplate>
          Footer template HTML
        </FooterTemplate>

      </asp:TemplateColumn>
    </Columns>

</asp:DataGrid>
```

The example we will use will be quite simple, utilizing the XML file we used previously. It will demonstrate how to bind to a `DataGrid` and will show you how little code is actually needed in ASP.NET to have the data automatically formatted into a table, and made 'sortable':

```
<%@ Page Language="C#" %>
<%@ Import Namespace="System.Data" %>
<%@ Import Namespace="System.IO" %>

<html>
  <script runat="server">
    string SortExpression;
    DataView getData()
    {
      DataSet ds = new DataSet();
      FileStream fs = new FileStream( Server.MapPath("test.xml"),
      FileMode.Open, FileAccess.Read );
      StreamReader reader = new StreamReader( fs );
      ds.ReadXml( reader );
      fs.Close();
      DataView dv = new DataView(ds.Tables[0] );
      dv.Sort=SortExpression;
      return dv;
    }

    void Page_Load(Object sender, EventArgs e)
    {
      ItemsGrid.DataSource=getData();
```

```
      ItemsGrid.DataBind();
    }

    void Sort_Grid(object sender, DataGridSortCommandEventArgs e)
    {
      SortExpression = e.SortExpression.ToString();
      ItemsGrid.DataSource = getData();
      ItemsGrid.DataBind();
    }
  </script>

  <body>
    <form runat="server">
      <h3>DataGrid Example</h3>
      <b>Product List</b>

      <asp:DataGrid id="ItemsGrid"
          BorderColor="black"
          BorderWidth="1"
          CellPadding="3"
          HeaderStyle-BackColor="#00aaaa"
          AutoGenerateColumns="true"
          AllowSorting="true"
          OnSortCommand="Sort_Grid"
          runat="server">
      </asp:DataGrid>

    </form>
  </body>
</html>
```

The output of this code looks something like this:

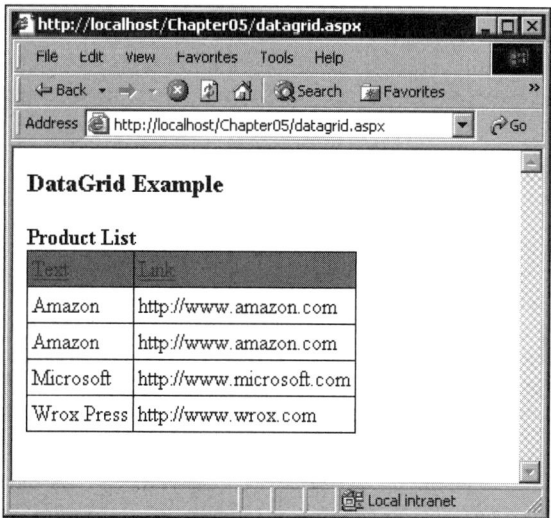

Others

The remaining controls in the web controls collection relate to place holding. They are the `PlaceHolder` control, the `Literal` control, and the `XML` control.

The `PlaceHolder` control allows you to place an empty container control in the page and then dynamically add child elements to it at run time. This control does not produce any visible output and is only used as a container for other controls on the web page:

```
<asp:PlaceHolder id="PlaceHolder1"
    runat="server"/>
```

The code for utilizing the `PlaceHolder` is very simple, as is adding controls dynamically, as shown below:

```
<%@ Page Language="C#" %>

<script runat="server">
  void Page_Load(Object sender, EventArgs e)
  {
    HtmlButton myButton = new HtmlButton();
    myButton.InnerText = "Button 1";
    myPlaceHolderID.Controls.Add(myButton);
  }
</script>

<html>
  <body>
    <form runat="server">
      <asp:PlaceHolder id="myPlaceHolderID"
          runat="server"/>
    </form>
  </body>
</html>
```

While this example does nothing more than add a button at run time, it is clear that it would be quite easy to add, for instance, a series of `Label` controls to represent an unknown range of values returned from a database query.

The `Literal` control renders static text into a web page without adding any HTML elements:

```
<asp:Literal id="Literal1"
    Text="Text"
    runat="server"/>
```

This control is ideal when you want to feed a control something like the data returned from a remote screen scrape for instance, and have no control over the kind of data you expect to display. You may for instance decide to dynamically create a control at run time. Its syntax is as follows:

```
<html>
  <body>
    <form runat="server">
      <asp:Literal id="myLiteralID"
          Text="Hello Java"
          runat="server"/>
    </form>
  </body>
</html>
```

The final control in the web controls collection is the Xml control.

In J2EE there is a confusing number of different approaches to utilizing XML data, and ASP.NET also has quite a few different ways of dealing with this, as you have already seen in this chapter when looking at the data-binding examples. To name a few, JSP has the DOM, where a developer can use classes implementing DOM interfaces such as those found in the org.w3c.dom package to parse and inspect the XML file. There is XPath, where you can use an XPath processor (like Resin) to locate elements in the XML file by path name. You can use XSL to transform the XML into HTML, or you could use the open-source Cocoon Framework, or you could write a wrapper class that uses one of the other techniques to load the data into a custom JavaBean.

In ASP.NET, we have the Xml control. This control can be used to display the contents of an XML document or have the results transformed using XSL code. This control blows simple XML handling in server-side JSP out of the water! We don't even require a single line of code to render XML and have it transformed by an appropriate XSL file, we simply need to correctly declare the control.

The example below shows how simple it is to transform XML tags into output using the XML control:

```
<html>
  <body>
    <asp:Xml id="MyXmlID" runat="server" TransformSource="cost.xsl"
        DocumentSource="cost.xml">
    </asp:Xml>
  </body>
</html>
```

We also need an appropriate XML file to test this, of course, and the contents of the file cost.xml are shown below:

```
<?xml version='1.0'?>
<sales>
  <division id='North'>
    <spending>10</spending>
    <allocation>9</allocation>
    <reserve>1</reserve>
  </division>
  <division id='South'>
    <spending>4</spending>
    <allocation>-3</allocation>
```

```
      <reserve>1</reserve>
    </division>
    <division id='West'>
      <spending>5</spending>
      <allocation>6</allocation>
      <reserve>-1</reserve>
    </division>
</sales>
```

A suitable XSL file is required to format the XML provided:

```
<xsl:stylesheet version='1.0'
    xmlns:xsl='http://www.w3.org/1999/XSL/Transform'>
  <xsl:template match="/">
  <style>
    .value
    {
      width:"25%";font-family:courier new; font-size:.8em; white-space=pre;
    }
  </style>
  <table border="1" cellspacing="0" cellpadding="3" bordercolor="gainsboro">
    <tr>
      <th>Division</th>
      <th>Spending</th>
      <th>Allocation</th>
      <th>Reserve</th>
    </tr>
    <xsl:for-each select='sales/division'>
      <tr>
        <td class="value"><em><xsl:value-of select='@id'/></em></td>
        <td class="value"><xsl:value-of select='spending'/></td>
        <td class="value">
          <xsl:if test='allocation &lt; 0'>
            <xsl:attribute name='style'>
              <xsl:text>color:red</xsl:text>
            </xsl:attribute>
          </xsl:if>
          <xsl:value-of select='allocation'/>
        </td>
        <td class="value"><xsl:value-of select='reserve'/></td>
      </tr>
    </xsl:for-each>
  </table>
  </xsl:template>
</xsl:stylesheet>
```

Running the ASPX page containing the Xml control renders the output, with only a single line of ASP.NET code:

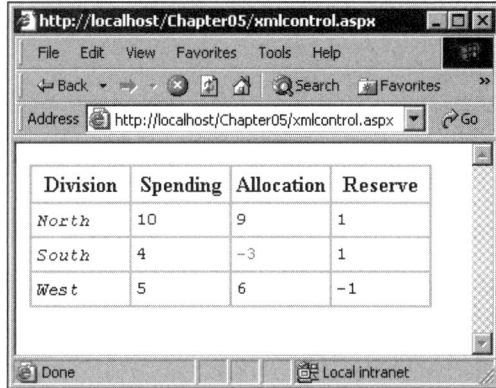

The final set of controls ASP.NET developers need to be aware of are the validation controls.

Validation Controls

Validation controls provide a way to check user input in web or HTML server controls, again using XML syntax control, or by extending the validation controls with code. Again, as with the web controls there is no equivalent in JSP but it is important that you understand these at a simple working level to begin using them in ASP.NET.

There are six types of validation controls to take advantage of and we will see simple examples of each in action:

- ❏ The RequiredFieldValidator
- ❏ The CompareValidator
- ❏ The RangeValidator
- ❏ The RegularExpressionValidator
- ❏ The CustomValidator
- ❏ The ValidationSummary

Let's begin by looking at the RequiredFieldValidator control.

RequiredFieldValidator Control

This control simply ensures that the user does not skip an entry, and it's very useful for mandatory fields. The input control will fail validation if the value it contains does not change from its initial, or default, value at form submission time, or when validation is manually triggered.

201

Here's the syntax:

```
<asp:RequiredFieldValidator
    id="myRequiredFieldID"
    ControlToValidate="ID of control to validate"
    InitialValue="value"
    ErrorMessage="Message to display in Validation Summary control"
    Text="Message to display in control"
    ForeColor="value"
    BackColor="value" ...
    runat="server" >
</asp:RequiredFieldValidator>
```

You don't need any code to enforce required fields; simply setting the validation control to point to a required field is enough, as the example below demonstrates:

```
<html>
  <body>
    <form runat="server">
      Name:
      <asp:TextBox id="myTextID"
          runat="server"/>
      <asp:RequiredFieldValidator id="myRequiredFieldValidatorID"
          ControlToValidate="myTextID"
          Text="<p>Required Field"
          runat="server"/>
      <p/>
      <asp:Button id="Button1"
          runat="server"
          Text="Validate"/>
    </form>
  </body>
</html>
```

We could have fed the validation error to the `ValidationSummary` control we will be looking at shortly, but for now let's simply go with what we have here. Running the example produces output similar to the following if the required field is not present:

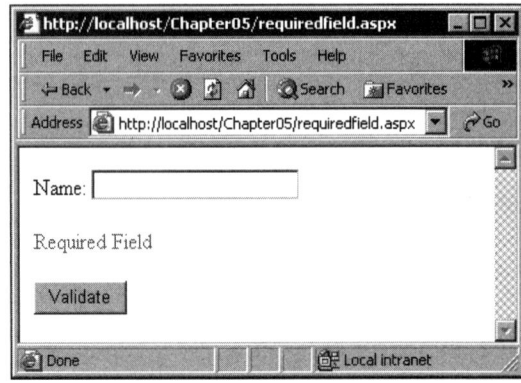

CompareValidator Control

The `CompareValidator` control is used to compare the field entry against a constant value or a property value of another control using the comparison operators, less than, equal, greater than, etc.

```
<asp:CompareValidator
    id="myCompareID"
    ControlToValidate="ID of Server Control to Validate"
    ValueToCompare="value"
    ControlToCompare="value"
    Type="DataType"
    Operator="Operator Value"
    ErrorMessage="Message to display in Validation Summary control"
    Text="Message to display in control"
    ForeColor="value"
    BackColor="value" …
    runat="server" >
</asp:CompareValidator>
```

This example checks that the field entry value is equal to "`Hello`". If it is, an appropriate response is provided, if not then a negative response is provided. We have tied this example to a `RequiredField` validator to demonstrate using more than one type of validation control in action simultaneously:

```
<%@ Page Language="C#" %>

<html>
  <head>
    <script runat="server">
      void Button_Click(Object sender, EventArgs e)
      {
        myCompareID.ValueToCompare = "Hello";
        myCompareID.Validate();
        if (Page.IsValid)
        {
          myResultID.Text = "Hello back";
        }
        else
        {
          myResultID.Text = "That's not polite";
        }
      }
    </script>
  </head>
  <body>
  <form runat="server">
      <asp:Label id="myLabel1ID"
          Font-Name="verdana"
          Font-Size="10pt"
          Text="Say Hello"
          runat="server"/><br/>
      <asp:TextBox id="myTextBox1ID"
          runat="server"/>
      <br/>
```

```
            <br/>
            <asp:Button id="myButton1ID"
                Text="Submit"
                OnClick="Button_Click"
                runat="server"/>
            <br/>
            <br/>
            <asp:CompareValidator id="myCompareID"
                ControlToValidate="myTextBox1ID"
                EnableClientScript="False"
                runat="server"/>
            <asp:RequiredFieldValidator id="myRequiredFieldValidatorID"
                ControlToValidate="myTextBox1ID"
                Text="<p>Required Field"
                runat="server"/>
            <br/>
            <asp:Label id="myResultID"
                Font-Name="verdana"
                Font-Size="10pt"
                runat="server"/>
        </form>
    </body>
</html>
```

The output when the validation fails is shown below:

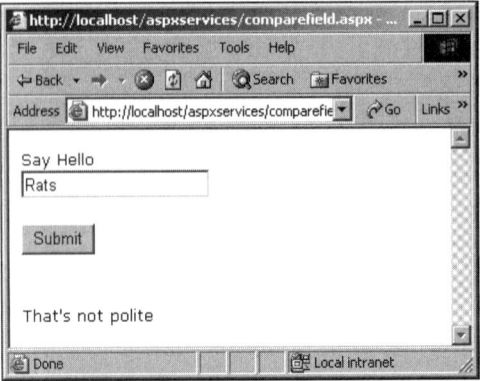

RangeValidator Control

The `RangeValidator` control is used for boundary checking. You can check ranges within pairs of numbers, alphabetic characters, and dates:

```
<asp:RangeValidator
    id="myProgrammaticID"
    ControlToValidate="ID of control to validate"
    MinimumValue="value"
    MaximumValue="value"
    Type="DataType"
    ErrorMessage="Message to display in ValidationSummary control"
```

```
        Text="Message to display in control"
        ForeColor="value"
        BackColor="value" ...
        runat="server" >
</asp:RangeValidator>
```

The example here looks to see if you are between the age of 18 and 65, and reports the result accordingly:

```
<%@ Page Language="C#" %>

<html>
  <head>
    <script runat="server">
      void ButtonClick(Object sender, EventArgs e)
      {
        if (Page.IsValid)
        {
          myResultID.Text="You can join the Pension plan";
        }
        else
        {
          myResultID.Text="You are outside the Pension age range";
        }
      }
    </script>
  </head>
  <body>
    <form runat="server">
      How old are you:
      <br/>
      <asp:TextBox id="myTextBox1ID"
          runat="server"/>
      <br/>
      <asp:RangeValidator id="myRange1ID"
          ControlToValidate="myTextBox1ID"
          MinimumValue="18"
          MaximumValue="65"
          Type="Integer"
          EnableClientScript="false"
          runat="server"/>
      <br/>
      <br/>
      <asp:Label id="myResultID"
          runat="server"/>
      <br/>
      <br/>
      <asp:Button id="myButton1ID"
          Text="Submit"
          OnClick="ButtonClick"
          runat="server"/>
    </form>
  </body>
</html>
```

The results of satisfying the range validation are shown below:

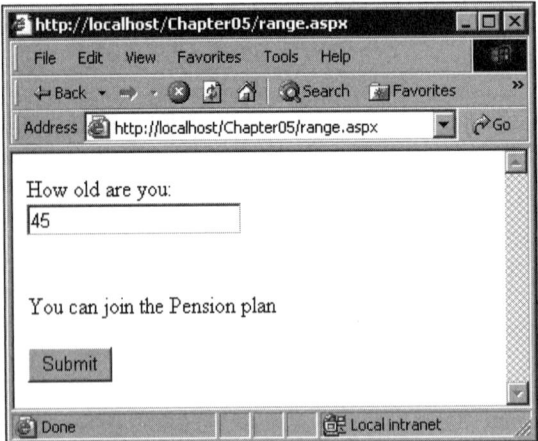

RegularExpressionValidator Control

The `RegularExpressionValidator` control checks that the entry matches a pattern defined by a regular expression following the RegEx patterns found in **Perl 5**. Regular expression syntax is beyond the scope of this book, but you can find information about what Regular Expressions are and the syntax required at:

http://www.perl.com/cs/user/query/q/6?id_topic=63

This type of validation allows you to check for predictable sequences of characters, such as those in social security numbers, e-mail addresses, telephone numbers, postal codes, and so on. If the input control is empty, no validation functions are called and validation succeeds, so you typically need to reinforce this with a `RequiredField` validator:

```
<asp:RegularExpressionValidator
    id="ProgrammaticID"
    ControlToValidate="ProgrammaticID of control to validate"
    ValidationExpression="expression"
    ErrorMessage="Message to display in ValidationSummary control"
    Text="Message to display in control"
    ForeColor="value"
    BackColor="value" …
    runat="server" >
</asp: RegularExpressionValidator>
```

The example below shows the control in action by checking the syntax of an e-mail address to ensure it matches those permitted in the **Validation Expression**. Simply enter an e-mail address (or not) and tab out of the example and you will see a result. The example deliberately leaves out a `RequiredFieldValidator` to demonstrate the vulnerability mentioned above:

Dynamic Web Applications

```
<%@ Page Language="C#" %>

<html>
  <body>
    <form runat="server">
      <asp:Label id="myLabelID"
          Text="Type an E-mail address for syntax validation:<br/>"
          Font-Name="verdana"
          Font-Size="12"
          runat="server"/></br>

      <asp:TextBox id="myEmailID"
          Width="300"
          runat=server />

      <asp:RegularExpressionValidator runat="server"
          id="MailValidation" ControlToValidate="myEmailID"
          ValidationExpression="^([a-zA-Z0-9_\-\.]+)@((\[[0-9]{1,3}\.[0-9]{1,3}\.[0-9]{1,3}\.)|(([a-zA-Z0-9\-]+\.)+))([a-zA-Z]{2,4}|[0-9]{1,3})(\]?)$"
          ErrorMessage = "You must enter an address with a valid mail format"
          Display="Dynamic"
          runat=server>
        <br>That's not a valid address
      </asp:RegularExpressionValidator>
    </form>
  </body>
</html>
```

Running the example and providing an invalid e-mail provides results similar to that shown below.

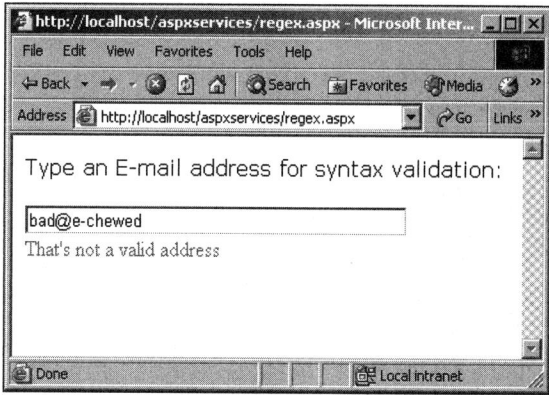

CustomValidator Control

The `CustomValidator` control can be used when none of the out-of-the-box validation controls is inappropriate, and it checks for user entry using validation logic that you code yourself:

```
<asp:CustomValidator
    id="myCustomID"
```

207

```
        ControlToValidate=" ID of Server Control to Validate"
        ClientValidationFunction="ClientValidateID"
        OnServerValidate="ServerValidateID"
        ErrorMessage="Message to display in ValidationSummary control"
        Text="Message to display in control"
        ForeColor="value"
        BackColor="value" …
        runat="server" >
</asp:CustomValidator>
```

This `CustomValidator` example a server-side method called `ServerValidation` to determine if the input value in the field is an even number. We trigger the `ServerValidation` method by calling the `Page` object's `IsValid` property that causes all validation controls on the page to check their state, hence activating the `serverValidation` event:

```
<%@ Page Language="C#" %>

<html>
  <head>
    <script runat="server">
      void start_validation(object sender, EventArgs e)
      {
        if (Page.IsValid) {}
      }

        void ServerValidation (object source, ServerValidateEventArgs
            arguments)
        {
          int i = int.Parse(arguments.Value);
          arguments.IsValid = ((i%2) == 0);
        }
    </script>
  </head>
  <body>
    <form runat="server">
    <asp:Label id=myResultID runat="server"
        Text="Enter an even number:"
        Font-Name="Verdana"
        Font-Size="10pt" />
    <br/>
    <p/>
    <asp:TextBox id="myTextID"
        runat="server" />
    <asp:CustomValidator id="myCustomValidatorID"
        ControlToValidate="myTextID"
        OnServerValidate="ServerValidation"
        Display="Static"
        ErrorMessage="<br>That is not an even number!"
        ForeColor="red"
        Font-Name="verdana"
        Font-Size="10pt"
        runat="server"/>
    <p/>
```

```
        <asp:Button id="Button1"
            Text="Validate"
            OnClick=" start_validation"
            runat="server"/>
    </form>
  </body>
</html>
```

The results of providing an odd number as input to the `TextBox` field "myTextID" and clicking the Validate button will be something like this:

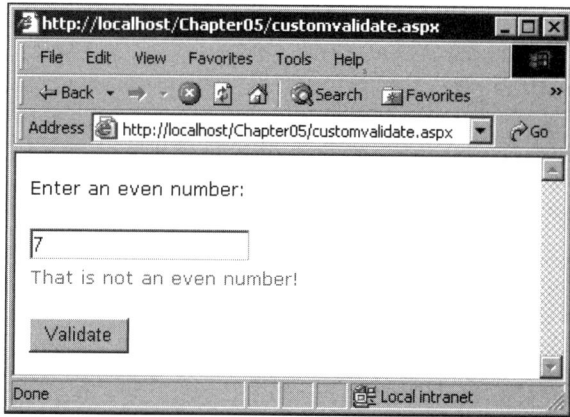

ValidationSummary Control

The final validation control is the `ValidationSummary`, and it is not a validation control, as such. It is a control that can be used to unify the error information presented by multiple validation controls into a single, neat summary. Each of the validation controls can feed the `ValidationSummary`, and looking back through the declaration for each control you will see an `ErrorMessage` property:

```
    <asp:ValidationSummary
        id="mySummaryID"
        DisplayMode="BulletList | List | SingleParagraph"
        EnableClientScript="true | false"
        ShowSummary="true | false"
        ShowMessageBox="true | false"
        HeaderText="Summary Title"
        runat="server"/>
```

The example below demonstrates two required fields in action, populating the `ValidationSummary` control with the error messages passed to it in the `ErrorMessage` property:

Notice we have provided no code in this example, as the summary needs none to demonstrate its action:

```html
<html>
  <body>
    <form runat="server">
      <asp:Label id="myFirstNameID"
          Font-Name="verdana"
          Font-Size="10pt"
          Text="First Name "
          runat="server"/><br/>

      <asp:TextBox id="myTextBox1ID"
          runat="server" />

      <asp:RequiredFieldValidator
          id="RequiredFieldValidator1"
          ControlToValidate="myTextBox1ID"
          ErrorMessage="First name"
          Display="Static"
          Width="100%"
          Text="*"
          runat=server/>

      <asp:Label id="mylastNameID"
          Font-Name="verdana"
          Font-Size="10pt"
          Text="Last Name "
          runat="server"/><br/>

      <asp:TextBox id="myTextBox2ID"
          runat="server" />

      <asp:RequiredFieldValidator
          id="RequiredFieldValidator2"
          ControlToValidate="myTextBox2ID"
          ErrorMessage="Last Name"
          Display="Static"
          Width="100%"
          Text="*"
          runat=server/>

      <asp:Button id="myButtonID"
          Text="Validate"
          runat=server />

      <asp:ValidationSummary id="mySummaryID"
          DisplayMode="BulletList"
          EnableClientScript="true"
          HeaderText="<br><hr>The following fields are mandatory:"
          runat="server"/>
    </form>
  </body>
</html>
```

The result of failing to populate the last name field or the first name field produces a typical `RequiredField` validation error (represented in this instance as an asterisk). The ASP.NET page is then concluded with a summary of errors found:

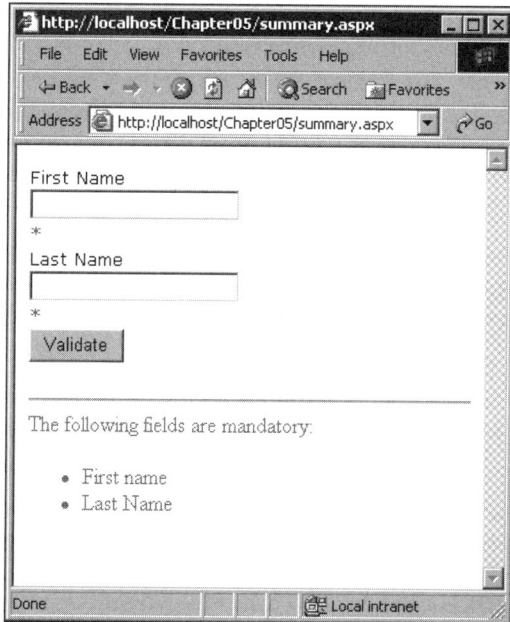

For an experienced JSP or servlet developer, the controls overview we have seen so far should be enough to get you working with ASP.NET. That said, the controls are much more comprehensive than we have demonstrated here and you should refer to the help documentation at MSDN for a more comprehensive explanation of each property.

Before we conclude, there is still another thing we need to cover and that is the concept of Code Behind and Scripting.

Inline or Code-Behind?

ASP.NET supports two modes of page development typically referred to as the **inline** or **code-behind** programming models.

- **Inline** relates to page logic code that is written inside `<script runat=server>` blocks within a `.aspx` file and dynamically compiled the first time the page is requested on the server. This is much closer to JSP development than the code-behind approach, and is how the examples shown so far in this chapter have all been demonstrated.

- **Code-behind** relates to `Page` logic code that is written within an external class that is linked 'behind' the `.aspx` file at run time. This is the equivalent of putting your logic into JavaBeans or TagLibs, or coding directly to a servlet, and passing processing logic from your JSP to the appropriate compiled methods.

It is impractical to use code behind in small pages, with little functionality, as the time taken to get the code working with the code-behind approach can outweigh the benefits. But, in many production environments there are separate teams that work on each part of a Web Application – The design teams design the pages while the programming team looks after the coding, database access, call handling, and so on. With the inline model adopted by JSP this code is mixed throughout the page along with the HTML, and when the design changes the code is easily affected.

In ASP.NET you can work with **separate** design and business logic files. This is quite an elegant solution, since the design team can work on the design page (in peace) and the programming team on their code without undue conflict. This allows the logic or design to change without one breaking the other.

Let's have a quick look at making use of code-behind programming so that you can understand the concept. You will find that it is heavily used in Microsoft's GUI .NET tools, such as Visual Studio (although Web Matrix does not enforce this model).

The following ASPX page has no code in it, but will respond to the button click using code defined in another page. The `Inherits` declaration at the top of the page tells the code to make the `MyCodeBehindClass` available from the source file `CodeBehind.cs`. This file contains C# methods containing our logic:

> It's worth reminding you that this file could just as easily have been written with VB.NET, or any other .NET supported language.

```
<%@ Page Inherits="MyCodeBehindClass" Src="codeBehind.cs" %>

<html>
  <body>
    <form runat="server">
      <asp:button id="myButtonID" text="Show Code Behind in Action"
          OnClick="SubmitBtn_Click" runat="server"/>
      <br/>
      <asp:Label id="myLabelID" runat="server"></asp:Label>
    </form>
  </body>
</html>
```

The source for the `.cs` file is shown below and while it does nothing more than populate a `Label` control, it demonstrates the principle:

```
using System;
using System.Web.UI;
using System.Web.UI.WebControls;

public class MyCodeBehindClass : Page
{
  public Label myLabelID;
```

```
    public void SubmitBtn_Click(Object sender, EventArgs e)
    {
      myLabelID.Text = "hello";
    }
}
```

Unlike preparing JSP beans, which offer a similar approach to separation of business logic, this technique requires no manual compilation. This code will automatically be included in the compilation for the ASP.NET page, and the methods will be made available to the controls that require them. As such, many ASP.NET files could use the same methods by referencing just one code-behind file. Allowing further separation between the interface and the business logic.

Principles of Code Behind

The first lines of our code are the imports. Shown here are the most common imports you would use to access the controls your code may be interacting with. In this instance we are interacting with controls from the `WebControls` namespace, thus we import that namespace, and any others we may be using:

```
using System;
using System.Web.UI;
using System.Web.UI.WebControls;
```

Next, we declare the class we wish to inherit in our .aspx page, which in turn inherits from the Page class:

```
public class MyCodeBehindClass : Page
```

We then declare public instances of the ASP.NET server controls that we plan to interact with in the code-behind file, which makes them accessible:

```
    public Label myLabelID;
```

Finally, we create the methods we need and close the class:

```
    public void SubmitBtn_Click(Object sender, EventArgs e)
    {
      myLabelID.Text = "hello";
    }
}
```

The choice of whether to use inline or code behind is up to you. The current .NET trend is towards code-behind but then every situation is different and you will quickly learn which technique suits your development style.

What we have covered so far in this chapter alone will allow you to develop some fairly hefty ASP.NET applications. The following chapter will take you even deeper into ASP.NET to demonstrate some far more advanced features. But, before moving on, let's quickly clarify where the JSP and ASP.NET technologies stand, in relation to each other, using some small snippets of information.

ASP.NET and JSP

There is not a great deal left to add here that has not been covered in the chapter, with the examples already. To make sure we have covered everything to get you running, there remain one or two things to consider that may help you better appreciate that JSP is not so alien to ASP.NET.

Scriptlets

ASP.NET pages can use the same syntax as JSP for the declaration of **scriptlets** as shown here. If you have read this chapter through from start to finish, however, you should have seen that this approach is much less used, especially with the interaction techniques for controls. In fact, there is not a single example in this chapter that follows this approach and I feel it remains as a legacy from ASP 3.0, although some of you may find it useful:

```
<% for (int i=0; i <8; i++) { %>
    <font size="<%=i%>"> Welcome to ASP.NET </font> <br>
<% }%>
```

What you are more likely to be familiar with is the XML approach that we have been covering from the start of the chapter, which is also heavily utilized in JSP:

```
<jsp:expression>
Java Expression
</jsp:expression>
```

ASP.NET typically uses the `<script runat="server">` expression syntax for the declaration of code blocks, where JSP uses the in-line `<jsp:declaration>`. There is no ASP.NET declaration tag. However, you should now be familiar with the `aspx:Control` approach for declaring controls.

Import Directives

Both ASP.NET and JSP use `import` directives to get access to classes. In C# the correct terminology is `using` (ASP.NET uses `import`, when working with VB.NET).

Error Handling

You can handle exceptions (critical errors) in ASP.NET by making use of `try...catch...finally`, clauses. Exception handling in .NET is almost the same as in Java.

Configuration

Both ASP.NET and JSP use the concept of XML-based configuration files. In ASP.NET we have `web.config` (settings for a specific application) and `machine.config` (settings for the machine). In JSP we have we have `web.xml`. Here is a snippet from `web.config` containing `appSettings` that can be read dynamically in code, and telling one specific web application that the custom error mode is `off`:

```
<configuration>
    <appSettings>
      <add key="AdminContact" value="JohnTimney" />
    </appSettings>
    <system.web>
```

```
        <customErrors mode="Off"/>
    </system.web>
</configuration>
```

Helper Objects

ASP.NET has access to a set of helper objects that, like the equivalent objects in JSP, do a lot of the mundane work for you by storing collections of data relating to that specific object.

- `Response` – encapsulates HTTP response information from an ASP.NET operation.
- `Request` – contains information about the current HTTP request.
- `Session` – stores the current `Session` object provided by ASP.NET for an individual user session.
- `Application` – Stores the `Application` object for the current web request that is shared between all users of that web application.

The next chapter will take you into the realm of User Controls, which like TagLibs, allow the HTML developer to get stuck into developing great layout, and leave code developers to worry about making it all glue together.

Summary

We've worked through a lot of information in this chapter, and I hope I've demonstrated how easy it is to create dynamic web pages within the .NET Framework.

We began by discussing how page requests work, and what goes on behind the scenes. We then went on to consider ASP.NET `Page` events, seeing what the order of events was, and looking at an example based on the `Page_Load` event.

Moving on, we got into the core of ASP.NET with the controls section. First we considered HTML Server Controls, then web server controls, and finally the validation controls, with a series of supporting examples to help jump-start your understanding of the .NET world.

As an addendum to this you might want to look at the **Mobile Controls**, from Microsoft, which automatically allow your controls to render for smart phones, PDAs and so on. At the time of writing they can be downloaded here:

http://msdn.microsoft.com/downloads/default.asp?url=/downloads/sample.asp?url=/
    msdn-files/027/001/817/msdncompositedoc.xml

We also demonstrated the difference between inline and code behind in ASP.NET development looking at how to remove code from your presentation layer and reuse it across pages.

Finally we considered a few commonalities and differences between ASP.NET and JSP, looking at some of the common objects, and the different approaches to handling declarations and application settings.

Experienced JSP developers will realize just how much potential there is in ASP.NET, and how powerful the control-driven model actually is. The next chapter will develop your ASP.NET knowledge even further.

Advanced Dynamic Web Applications

The previous chapter covered the basics of ASP.NET. In this chapter we'll build on that foundation by covering three of the more advanced topics. In particular we'll take a look at:

- Data bound controls in ASP.NET
- Managing session and application state
- Creating Custom Controls

Data bound controls are a concept intimately familiar to Windows programmers, but may well be new to J2EE programmers, so first of all, we'll cover the basics of data-bound controls. Managing session and application state should be familiar territory for JSP/servlet developers, and there are equivalent ASP.NET constructs that we'll move on to. Another thing many JSP developers will be familiar with is the tag library, and finally, we'll examine custom controls, the analog in ASP.NET.

Running the Examples

Before we begin, the following setup tasks must be performed:

- Create a virtual directory in IIS with the name `wrox`
- Place two subdirectories underneath the physical directory that `wrox` maps to, and name them `bin` and `Source`

All source files will be placed in the `Source` directory unless otherwise specified. Now that's done, we can begin our discussion of data bound controls.

Chapter 6

Data-Bound Controls in ASP.NET

ASP.NET controls that expose a `Text` or a `Value` property can be populated automatically by binding them to a data source. Such controls include `TextBoxes`, labels, and buttons. We can also bind controls that maintain collections of data, such as arrays as well as the `DropDownList`, `ListBox`, `CheckBoxList`, `RadioButtonList`, `DataGrid`, `Repeater`, and `DataList` controls.

Bound controls can save a considerable amount of coding, especially when displaying large data sets. We can bind a control property to a single value, which is known as **simple binding**. We can also bind controls to multi-value objects such as collections and `DataTables`, known as **complex binding**.

In this section, we'll show examples of each type of binding. We'll end the section by covering the `DataGrid` bound control. The `DataGrid` provides a simple mechanism for displaying large data sets while giving the developer numerous options for controlling presentation.

We'll come back to the issue of data binding when we look at it in the context of Windows Forms applications in the next chapter.

Properties

A nice feature of ASP.NET is that it allows you to bind properties of a control to the result of an expression, provided that the return type of the expression matches the type of the property. To demonstrate, we'll create a page that displays the current time on a `Label` control. To begin, create a new file in your `Source` directory called `PropertyBind.aspx`. To keep things simple, we'll use inline ASP.NET code rather than code behind. The first thing we do is implement `Page_Load()` so that `DataBind()` is called each time the page loads:

```
<script language="C#" runat="server">
  void Page_Load()
  {
    DataBind();
  }
</script>
```

`DataBind()` executes any data-binding expressions set up on the page. In the page's HTML markup, which follows next, we place a data-binding expression in the `Text` property of our `Label`:

```
<html>
  <body>
    <h1>Binding a Property to a Data Value</h1>
    <form runat="server">
      <asp:Label Text='<%# DateTime.Now.ToLongTimeString() %>'
          Font-Size=32
          runat="server" />
```

In order to display the current time on our `Label`, we've bound the `Text` property of the `Label` to the expression `DateTime.Now.ToLongTimeString()`. Note the special `<%# %>` syntax for ASP.NET data-binding expressions. The expression used in such syntax can be any expression that resolves to a type that the control can handle. In this case, a `String` is expected, and thus we invoke the `ToLongTimeString()` method of `Now` which returns the current time.

Advanced Dynamic Web Applications

The last thing we'll add is a button to refresh the time. All the button has to do is trigger a postback when pressed to fire `Page_Load()` and thus call `DataBind()`, re-evaluating the `DateTime.Now.ToLongTimeString()` expression. Setting the `runat` attribute on the `Button` control to `"server"` is enough to cause a postback:

```
    <asp:Button Text="Refresh" runat="server"/>
  </form>
 </body>
</html>
```

Save the file, and point your browser to `localhost/source/propertybind.aspx`. This is the screen that we will see:

Our label shows the current time, and is updated whenever we hit the **Refresh** button due to the `DataBind()` call in `Page_Load()`. This executes any data-binding expressions that are part of the page. Without this call to `DataBind()`, our data-binding expressions wouldn't be executed. You can demonstrate this by commenting out the method call, which results in a blank label greeting you when you open the page.

Collections

We can populate controls that contain more than a single value by binding them to a collection or other object that implements the `IEnumerable` interface. ASP.NET's `DropDownList` and `RadioButtonList` are two controls that support binding to a collection.

In the next example, we'll populate a `RadioButtonList` by binding to an `ArrayList` collection in an ASPX page called `CollectionBind.aspx`. We use `Page_Load()` to create and populate an `ArrayList` called `Sizes` that represents a collection of font sizes the first time the page loads:

```
<script language="C#" runat="server">
  void Page_Load()
  {
    if(!IsPostBack)
    {
      ArrayList Sizes = new ArrayList();
      Sizes.Add("16");
```

219

```
        Sizes.Add("36");
        Sizes.Add("48");
        Sizes.Add("72");
        Sizes.Add("128");
```

Our radio button control will be called `buttons`, and we bind it to this array like so:

```
        buttons.DataSource = Sizes;
        buttons.DataBind();
    }
}
```

We'll have a button on the page that takes the value chosen in the radio button control and uses it to set the size of the text in a label called `output`. Here is the click handler for that button:

```
    void button_click(Object sender, EventArgs e)
    {
      if(buttons.SelectedIndex > -1)
      {
        output.Text = buttons.SelectedItem.Text + " pt";
        int size = Convert.ToInt32(buttons.SelectedItem.Text);
        output.Font.Size = size;
      }
    }
  </script>
```

The handler checks if the user has made a selection in the `RadioButtonList` according to whether the `SelectedIndex` is greater than -1. If so, we use the `SelectedItem` property to access the selection, and convert it to an integer that we can assign to the `Font.Size` property of our `Label`.

That's the code done. The HTML for the page sets up the radio button and label controls:

```
    <html>
      <body>
        <h1>Binding a Control to a Collection</h1>
        <form runat="server">
          Font Sizes<br/>
          <asp:radiobuttonlist id="buttons" runat="server"/>
          <asp:button id="submit" text="Click to Change Size"
              onclick="button_click"runat="server"/>
```

Notice the `onclick` event. ASP.NET button server controls can react to events such as `onclick`, `oninit`, `onprerender`, `onload`, and `onunload`.

Finish off the HTML as follows:

```
          <asp:label id="output" Text="" runat="server"/>
        </form>
      </body>
    </html>
```

Open the `CollectionBind.aspx` page in your browser, select a font size, and click the button. You should see something like this:

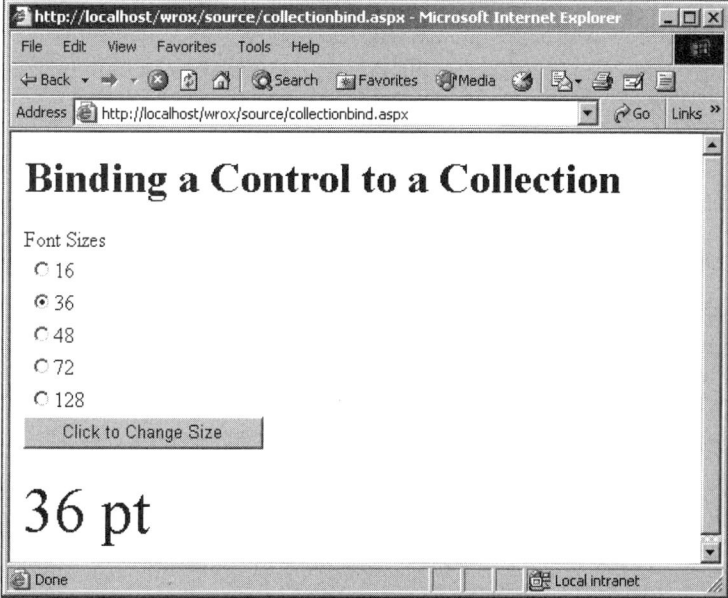

Note that binding a control to a collection involves two steps:

1. Set the `DataSource` property of the control to bind to

2. Call the `DataBind()` method on the control

As long as a control exposes the `DataSource` property, we can bind it to a collection in the same way. In addition to the `RadioButtonList` shown above, the `DropDownList`, `ListBox`, and `CheckBoxList` controls can all be bound to collections.

DataTables

The .NET `DataTable` object is an in-memory data representation in the form of a table. The ASP.NET `Repeater`, `DataList`, and `DataGrid` controls are capable of binding to and displaying the contents of a `DataTable`. The `DataGrid` is useful for displaying data in a tabular layout. The `DataList` is used when you want to display each record in a `DataTable` in list form, where each record makes up a single row in a list of rows. The `Repeater` is a **templated control**. The developer must code templates to control the display of the `Repeater`, which makes it very flexible. For example, we could use a `Repeater` to create a comma delimited or bulleted list.

Rather than binding directly to the `DataTable`, we must bind to a `DataView` associated with that `DataTable`. A `DataView` allows us to filter and sort a `DataTable` to provide a customizable representation of the data it contains. We can use the `DefaultView` property of the `DataTable` to obtain a `DataView` to bind to.

The `Repeater`, `DataList`, and `DataGrid` controls can save a significant amount of coding. We'll have a look at an example that focuses on the `DataGrid`. The `DataGrid` has built-in support for paging (splitting of large data sets into multiple pages), inline editing, and sorting, which can save us a great deal of overhead code. The `DataGrid` is appropriate for displaying data in a tabular format (columns and rows). It can bind to any class that implements `IEnumerable`, and thus `DataView`, `OleDbDataReader`, and arrays are all acceptable data sources for a `DataGrid`. `DataTable` itself however does not implement this interface, and thus we need to convert it to a `DataView` first.

In the example, we'll bind a `DataGrid` to the `Shippers` table of the Northwind sample database that comes with Microsoft Access and Microsoft SQL Server. If you don't already have Northwind, you can download the Microsoft Access version from the following location:

http://office.microsoft.com/downloads/2000/Nwind2K.aspx

The code in this example is broken into two files. The first, `Shippers.cs`, encapsulates the connection to the database and provides methods for selecting, inserting, deleting, and updating data. We'll compile `Shippers.cs` into an assembly called `Northwind.dll` that can be accessed from the second file, `ViewShippers.aspx`.

`ViewShippers.aspx` is responsible for presentation, providing a UI through a `DataGrid` and a series of event handlers that resolve database requests through the `Northwind.dll` assembly.

Let's start with the code for `Shippers.cs`. The first thing we have to do is reference the .NET namespaces we want to use, and then set the namespace for the classes defined in this file:

```csharp
using System;
using System.Data;
using System.Data.OleDb;
using System.Configuration;

namespace Northwind
{
```

`Shippers.cs` will define two classes in this namespace, the first being the `Shipper` class that encapsulates a row in the `Shippers` table (representing a single company):

```csharp
public class Shipper
{
  int id;
  string companyName;
  string phone;

  // Constructor
  public Shipper(int id, string companyName, string phone)
  {
    this.id = id;
    this.companyName = companyName;
    this.phone = phone;
  }
```

```
    public string CompanyName
    {
      get
      {
        return companyName;
      }
    }
    public int Id
    {
      get
      {
        return id;
      }
    }
    public string Phone
    {
      get
      {
        return phone;
      }
    }
  }
```

The other class is `ShippersDB`, which encapsulates the data access logic. First, we'll get hold of the connection string that ADO.NET requires to connect to a database, and place it into a private member called `conn`:

```
  public class ShippersDB
  {
    private static string conn = ConfigurationSettings
        .AppSettings["northwind"];
```

We use the `AppSettings` collection of the `ConfigurationSettings` class to get the connection string from the web.config file. We'll come back to this in a minute. Now we come to the methods, starting with `execCommand` to run non-queries given by the string parameter:

```
    private static void execCommand(string query)
    {

      // Create and open a connection to the database
      OleDbConnection connection = new OleDbConnection(conn);
      connection.Open();

      OleDbCommand command = new OleDbCommand(query, connection);
      command.ExecuteNonQuery();
      connection.Close();
    }
```

If you are using the SQL Server version of Northwind, replace `OleDbConnection` with `SqlConnection` and `OleDbCommand` with `SqlCommand` in the above code to make use of these optimized classes.

Notice how we run SQL commands on the database once we've opened a connection to it: we create a command object using the connection and query, and then execute by calling the `ExecuteNonQuery()` method.

Non-query in our case means an insert, update, or delete operation, and hence `execCommand()` will be called by one of three methods: `AddShipper()`, `UpdateShipper()`, or `DeleteShipper()`. Each of these methods is responsible for creating a string that represents a valid SQL statement for the required operation, which is then passed to `execCommand()`.

Here's `UpdateShipper()`:

```
public static void UpdateShipper(Shipper sh)
{
  string query = @"Update Shippers Set CompanyName='"
                 + sh.getCompanyName();
  query += "', Phone='" + sh.getPhone();
  query += "' Where ShipperID=" + sh.getId();
  execCommand(query);
}
```

This method takes a `Shipper` object as a parameter and uses it to construct the appropriate SQL `UPDATE` command to pass to `execCommand()` so it can update that row in the database. `AddShipper()` and `DeleteShipper()` work in a very similar fashion:

```
public static void AddShipper(Shipper sh)
{
  string query = "Insert into Shippers Values(" + sh.getId() + ",'"
                 + sh.getCompanyName() + "','" + sh.getPhone() + "')";
  execCommand(query);
}

public static void DeleteShipper(int id)
{
  string query = @"Delete from Shippers Where ShipperID = "
                 + id.ToString();
  execCommand(query);
}
```

We've now dealt with the non-query methods, so the last method in this class is `GetShippers()` which creates a `DataSet` object containing all rows in the `Shippers` table, and returns it to the calling ASPX page:

```
public static DataSet GetShippers()
{

  DataSet ds = new DataSet();
  string select = "Select * from Shippers;";
  OleDbConnection objConn = new OleDbConnection(conn);
  OleDbDataAdapter objAdapt = new OleDbDataAdapter(select, objConn);
  objAdapt.Fill(ds,"Shippers");
  return ds;
}
```

We generate the `DataSet` by passing a select statement and a connection object to an `OleDbDataAdapter`. `OleDBDataAdapter` provides the `Fill()` method that we use to populate the `DataSet` with data. `Fill()` takes two parameters. The first is the `DataSet` to be filled, and the second is the name of the `DataTable` we're pulling the data from.

Add the closing braces for the class and namespace, and we're done:

```
    }
}
```

Save the file in the `Source` directory under the name `Shippers.cs`, and compile it from the command prompt at the `Source` directory with the following command:

```
> csc /t:library /out:..\bin\Northwind.dll Shippers.cs
```

This will create an assembly called `Northwind.dll` in the `wrox\bin` subdirectory. Assemblies in this directory are accessible to all ASPX pages under the `wrox` virtual root.

Before we move on to create the ASPX page that uses this assembly, we need to return to the issue of the connection string briefly mentioned earlier. We're going to store it in the XML `web.config` file, which is used by ASP.NET for holding settings that apply to all pages of a particular web application. We can place our own settings here as key-value pairs, and access them through the `ConfigurationSettings` class. The static `AppSettings` property of this class returns the value given for a particular key in the `<appSettings>` element of `web.config`, found under the `<configuration>` element:

```
<configuration>
    <appSettings>
      <add key="northwind" value="Provider=Microsoft.Jet.OLEDB.4.0; Data
        Source=C:\wrox\source\Northwind.mdb"/>
    </appSettings>
</configuration>
```

The `web.config` file may contain information in other elements for other purposes, but for our case, the above is all that we need, so place the above into a file with the name `web.config` in your `Source` directory. Note that the above connection is for the Access version of the Northwind database, which must be copied into the directory specified in the `data source` parameter. If you are using the SQL version of Northwind, you will need to use a connection string of the following form:

```
<add key="northwind" value="Provider=SQLOLEDB; data source=localhost;
  database=Northwind; integrated security=sspi"/>
```

If your SQL Server instance lies on a remote machine, you'll need to replace `localhost` in the `data source` parameter with the UNC name of your data server.

Now we can turn our attention to the presentation logic in the second file, `ViewShippers.aspx`. This file represents a web page consisting of a `DataGrid` called `ShipperGrid` and a button labeled **Add Shipper**. We're going to use the `DataGrid`'s built-in edit and delete functionality, which automatically adds the required buttons next to records in the grid as we'll see later.

The `ViewShippers.aspx` file starts with three ASP.NET directives before we get to the C# code:

```
<%@ Page Language="C#" Debug="true" %>
<%@ Import Namespace="Northwind" %>
<%@ Import Namespace="System.Data" %>
```

The `Page` directive enables debugging to give us more descriptive error messages in the event of an error. The next line imports the `Northwind` namespace giving us access to the code in `Northwind.cs`. Finally, we import the `System.Data` namespace so we can use the `DataSet`.

The code starts by declaring the `DataSet` we'll be using and the `Page_Load()` event. This latter populates the `DataSet` if required by calling the static `GetShippers()` method in the `Northwind.dll` assembly, and calls `BindControls()` the first time the page is opened:

```
<script language="C#" runat="server">

DataSet ds;

void Page_Load(Object sender, EventArgs e)
{
  // Populate the DataSet if not already done
  if (ds == null)
     ds = ShippersDB.GetShippers();

  if (!IsPostBack)
  {
    BindControls();
  }
}
```

`BindControls()` is a simple routine that sets the `DataSource` for the `DataGrid` to the default view of the zeroth table of our `DataSet`, which in this case is the only table it contains, and holds the contents of the `Shippers` table. Then it calls `DataBind()` to display the contents of our `DataSet` in the `DataGrid`:

```
void BindControls()
{
  ShipperGrid.DataSource = ds.Tables[0].DefaultView;
  ShipperGrid.DataBind();
}
```

Note that we're assigning a `DataView` object to the `DataSource`. This `DataView` is what is returned by the `DefaultView` property of the `DataTable` represented by `ds.Tables[0]`.

Next, we need to create the handlers for the button clicks. These buttons are added to each record in a `DataGrid` by ASP.NET, and consist of **Edit** and **Delete** buttons. When the **Edit** button is pressed, the `DataGrid` enters edit mode, and **Update** and **Cancel** buttons appear next to the record in question.

We still need to create the handlers for these `DataGrid` buttons, so let's start with the **Edit** button. Clicking the **Edit** button next to a record fires the `EditCommand` event, which in this example is handled by the `Edit_Click()` method:

```
void Edit_Click(Object sender, DataGridCommandEventArgs e)
{
  ShipperGrid.EditItemIndex = e.Item.ItemIndex;
```

`Edit_Click` uses the `Item` property of the `DataGridCommandEventArgs` object to obtain the index of the row that we want to edit. It assigns the index to the `EditItemIndex` property of the `DataGrid`. This step is required for the `DataGrid` to display the edit view properly.

A `DataGridCommandEventArgs` object is generated when the following events occur on a `DataGrid`: `CancelCommand`, `DeleteCommand`, `EditCommand`, `ItemCommand`, and `UpdateCommand`. In addition to the `Item` property, the `DataGridCommandEventArgs` object has three other properties that provide information for the event:

- `CommandSource` – represents the object that generated the command
- `CommandName` – a string representation of the name of the command that was just generated
- `CommandArgument` – a string that represents an argument for the command

Although we're not doing so here, we can set `CommandName` and `CommandArgument` when we declare a control like so:

```
<asp:LinkButton id="LinkButton1"
            Text="Click here to view cart"
            Command="ViewCart"
            CommandArgument="NewWindow"
            OnClick="OnClickMethod"
            runat="server"/>
```

In this case, when the `LinkButton` is clicked, `ViewCart` and `NewWindow` will be passed to the event handler as properties of the `DataGridCommandEventArgs` object.

We'll finish up `Edit_Click()` as follows:

```
  BindControls();
}
```

After `BindControls()` executes, **Update** and **Cancel** buttons will appear in the `DataGrid`, ready for editing. We'll add the handlers for these two buttons next:

```
void Cancel_Click(Object sender, DataGridCommandEventArgs e)
{
  ShipperGrid.EditItemIndex = -1;
  ds = ShippersDB.GetShippers();
  BindControls();
}
```

Chapter 6

```
void Update_Click(Object sender, DataGridCommandEventArgs e)
{
  string idText = e.Item.Cells[1].Text;
  TextBox companyText = (TextBox)e.Item.Cells[2].Controls[0];
  TextBox phoneText = (TextBox)e.Item.Cells[3].Controls[0];
  int id = Convert.ToInt32(idText);
  Shipper shipper = new Shipper(id, companyText.Text, phoneText.Text);
  ShippersDB.UpdateShipper(shipper);
  ShipperGrid.EditItemIndex = -1;
  ds = ShippersDB.GetShippers();
  BindControls();
}
```

`Cancel_Click` is quite simple, just setting the `EditItemIndex` property of the grid to -1, which takes us out of edit mode. Then it repopulates the `DataGrid`, and calls `BindControls()`.

`Update_Click` is a little more complex, and is ultimately responsible for calling the static `UpdateShipper` method in our assembly to write the update to the database. In order to do this, `Update_Click` must create the `Shipper` object that `UpdateShipper` expects as a parameter, which it does using the `Cells` collection of the `DataGridCommandEventArgs` object. The `Text` property of `Cell[1]` contains our `ShipperID`. During editing, ASP.NET replaces `Cell[2]` and `Cell[3]` in the `DataGrid` with `TextBox` controls for editing the company name and phone number fields. Both these editable cells contain a `Controls` collection that `Update_Click` uses to access the text boxes where the edited data resides.

After the update takes place, we repopulate our `DataSet` using the `GetShippers()` method and then rebind by calling `BindControls()`.

Now let's add the handler for the button that adds completely new records:

```
private void Add_Click(object source, EventArgs e)
{
  ShowGrid.Visible = false;
  AddShipper.Visible = true;
}
```

This doesn't appear to do much, but the key to understanding it is that `ShowGrid` and `AddShipper` are panel controls. The `ShowGrid` panel contains our `DataGrid`, and the `AddShipper` panel wraps the controls that will make up our Add form.

Panels are a great way of coding two (or more) separate modes for a single page. In this case, we can display all controls required for adding by simply making the `AddShipper` panel visible and the `ShowGrid` panel invisible by setting their `Visible` properties.

The principle here will become clearer when our code is done, and we run the page, so let's move swiftly on. The `AddShipper` panel will consist of textboxes for entering the ID, name, and phone number of the new company, along with **Submit** and **Cancel** buttons to commit or cancel the addition. Here's the code for the **Submit** button's click handler:

```csharp
    private void SubmitAdd_Click(object source, EventArgs e)
    {
      int id = Convert.ToInt32(AddId.Text);
      Shipper shipper = new Shipper(id, AddCompany.Text, AddPhone.Text);
      ShippersDB.AddShipper(shipper);
      ds = ShippersDB.GetShippers();
      BindControls();
      AddShipper.Visible=false;
      ShowGrid.Visible=true;
      Response.Redirect("ViewShippers.aspx");
    }
```

This method creates a new `Shipper` object using the values we just entered in the textboxes, and passes the object to the static `AddShipper` method of the `ShippersDB` class. Because the database has changed, we call `GetShippers` and `BindControls` to repopulate our `DataSet`. Finally, we make the `DataGrid` visible again, and call `Response.Redirect()` to refresh the page.

The **Cancel** button on the Add form simply clears any text entered in the textboxes – if we did not do this, any text would still be there next time the **Add Shipper** button is clicked. Then it hides the `AddShipper` panel, and activates `ShowGrid`:

```csharp
    private void CancelAdd_Click(object source, EventArgs e)
    {
      AddId.Text="";
      AddCompany.Text="";
      AddPhone.Text="";
      AddShipper.Visible=false;
      ShowGrid.Visible=true;
    }
</script>
```

Our code's all done now, so we just need the HTML that creates the controls on our page. The first thing we'll do is open the `ShowGrid` panel, and declare our `DataGrid` inside it:

```html
<html>
<body>
<form runat="server">
<h2>Shippers DataGrid</h2>
<asp:panel id="ShowGrid" runat="server">
<asp:DataGrid id="ShipperGrid" runat="server"
     GridLines = "Both"
     CellPadding = "5"
     BorderColor="Black"
     OnEditCommand="Edit_Click"
     OnUpdateCommand="Update_Click"
     OnCancelCommand="Cancel_Click"
     AutoGenerateColumns="false">
<columns>
  <asp:editcommandcolumn
       edittext="Edit"
       updatetext="Update"
       canceltext="Cancel"
```

```
            ButtonType="PushButton"/>
    <asp:boundcolumn headertext="ID" readonly="true" datafield="ShipperId"/>
    <asp:boundcolumn headertext="Company" datafield="CompanyName"/>
    <asp:boundcolumn headertext="Phone" datafield="Phone"/>
</columns>
</asp:DataGrid>
```

The interesting part here is the `<columns>` section, which specifies the column types that control the presentation of our grid. Firstly, we declare an `EditCommandColumn` control. Declaring this for a `DataGrid` enables on-screen editing of the contained data, and is where we specify the text and nature of the buttons that will be used for this purpose. Then we declare three `BoundColumn` controls. Each `boundcolumn` has a `datafield` property that references the column in the `DataView` that populates that column.

Next we declare the **Add Shipper** button, and close the `ShowGrid` panel:

```
<br/>
<asp:button id="add" OnClick="Add_Click" text="Add Shipper" runat="server"/>
</asp:panel>
```

Finally, we create the `AddShipper` panel, and the three textboxes and two buttons that it contains:

```
<asp:panel id="AddShipper" visible="false" runat="server">
<table><tr><td>
ID:</td><td>
    <asp:textbox id="AddId" runat="server"/></td></tr><tr><td>
Company:</td><td>
    <asp:textbox id="AddCompany" runat="server"/></td></tr><tr><td>
Phone:</td><td>
    <asp:textbox id="AddPhone" runat="server"/></td<tr><tr><td>
<asp:button id="SubmitAdd" Text="Submit" OnClick="SubmitAdd_Click"
runat="server"/></td><td>
<asp:button id="CancelAdd" Text="Cancel" Onclick="CancelAdd_Click"
runat="server"/></td></tr>
</table>
</asp:panel>
</form>
</body>
</html>
```

At last our page is complete, so save the file, and open it in your browser. You'll see the following screen:

Advanced Dynamic Web Applications

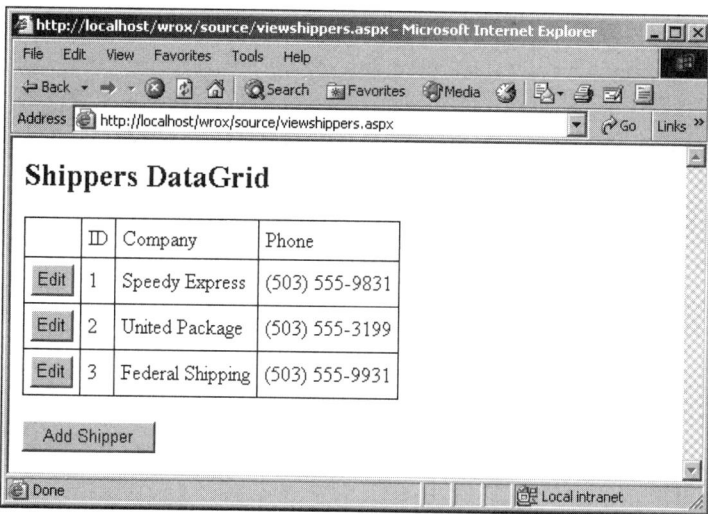

Click on an Edit button, and the buttons and labels will change in preparation for editing:

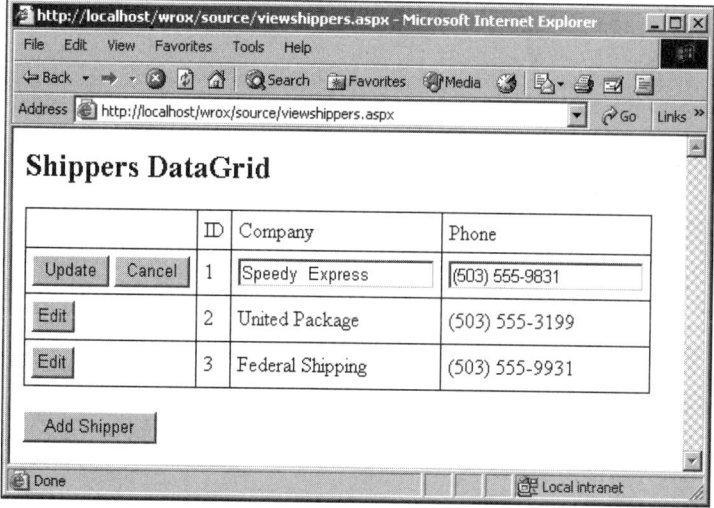

We now have Update and Cancel buttons available. The Company and Phone fields for the record being edited also change from labels to textboxes. This functionality is provided by the DataGrid whenever we include an EditCommandColumn. We have to write handlers for the click events that occur when the user selects Edit or Update or Cancel during the editing process. The buttons are wired to their respective event handlers in the declaration of our DataGrid by the following three parameters:

```
OnEditCommand="Edit_Click"
OnUpdateCommand="Update_Click"
OnCancelCommand="Cancel_Click"
```

231

Chapter 6

Now let's go ahead and click the **Add Shipper** button:

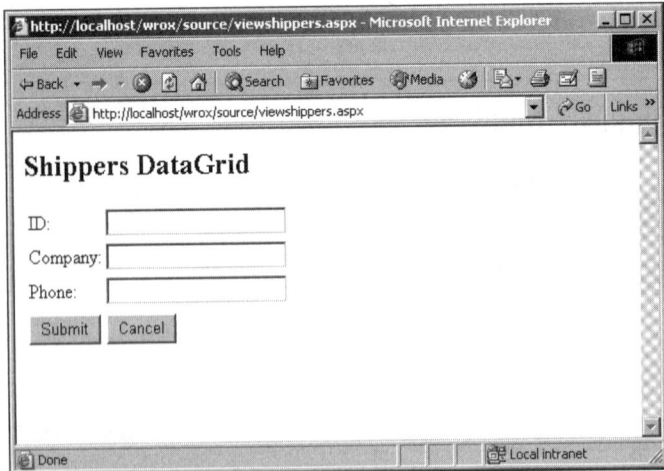

Notice how the view changes. Have another look at the declaration for the **Add Shipper** button:

```
<asp:button id="add" OnClick="Add_Click" text="Add Shipper" runat="server"/>
```

We use the `OnClick` attribute to wire button clicks to the `Add_Click` handler method. Our add form has a textbox for each field in the `Shippers` table as well as **Submit** and **Cancel** buttons. These two buttons are wired to their handlers in the same way.

Deleting Records

We've covered how to view, add, and update our database. Now we'll add another feature: deleting records. We won't be able to delete any of the original records that came with the `Shippers` table, because of dependencies with other tables in the Northwind database, but we will be able to delete newly added records, because no such dependencies exist.

To do this, we'll add a button next to every row in the `DataGrid` that will allow the user to delete the record in that row. We can do this by simply adding a special sort of column to our grid, called a `ButtonColumn`. Open `ViewShippers.aspx`, locate the columns section, and add the line highlighted below:

```
<columns>
  <asp:editcommandcolumn
      edittext="Edit"
      updatetext="Update"
      canceltext="Cancel"
      ButtonType="PushButton"/>
  <asp:boundcolumn headertext="ID" readonly="true" datafield="ShipperId"/>
  <asp:boundcolumn headertext="Company" datafield="CompanyName"/>
  <asp:boundcolumn headertext="Phone" datafield="Phone"/>
  <asp:buttoncolumn ButtonType="PushButton" text="Delete" commandname="Delete"/>
</columns>
```

Advanced Dynamic Web Applications

The three attributes to this control's declaration specify the type of button to use (here, a standard push button – the default is a hyperlink), the text to display on each button, and the name of the command associated with the button. We now need to link this up to a handler for button clicks, which we do by adding another attribute to the `DataGrid` declaration, as highlighted below:

```
<asp:DataGrid id="ShipperGrid" runat="server"
     GridLines = "Both"
     CellPadding = "5"
     BorderColor="Black"
     OnEditCommand="Edit_Click"
     OnUpdateCommand="Update_Click"
     OnCancelCommand="Cancel_Click"
     OnDeleteCommand="Delete_Click"
     AutoGenerateColumns="false">
```

Now, when a **Delete** button is pressed, the `Delete_Click` method will be called, so let's add the code for this method inside the `<script>` block in `ViewShippers.aspx`:

```
  private void Delete_Click(object source, DataGridCommandEventArgs e)
  {
    string idText = e.Item.Cells[1].Text;
    int id = Convert.ToInt32(idText);
    ShippersDB.DeleteShipper(id);
    ds = ShippersDB.GetShippers();
    BindControls();
  }
```

`Delete_Click` extracts the `SupplierID` from the row using the `Cells` collection that we've seen before. Because the `Cell` stores a string, we must convert it to an integer before we can pass it to the static `DeleteShipper()` method. As we've changed the database, we once again make a call to `GetShippers()` and `BindControls()` to refresh our data.

Save your changes, and open the page in your browser, which now looks like this:

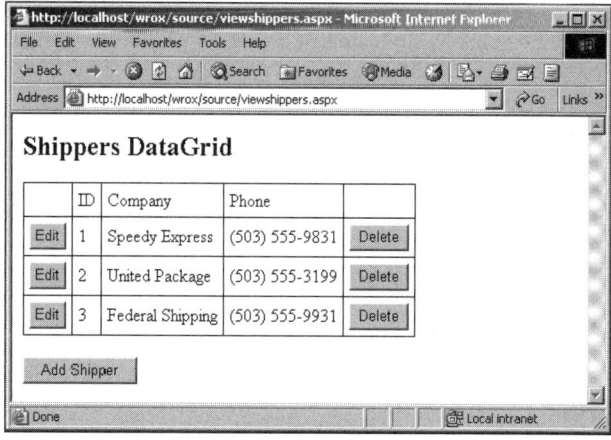

Go ahead and add a record and then press the **Delete** button to delete the record you just added.

233

Chapter 6

Managing Session and Application State

When it comes to **state management**, adjusting from JSP/servlets to ASP.NET should prove no difficulty at all. ASP.NET's `HttpSessionState` and `HttpApplicationState` classes provide essentially the same functionality as `HttpSession` and `ServletContext` on the Java side. In this section, we'll start with a simple shopping cart to demonstrate session state management, and finish with a small web counter application that demonstrates application state.

Session State

Before creating our shopping cart, we need to be aware of the configuration options available in ASP.NET. Session state configuration is placed inside the `<sessionState>` element in the `web.config` file. `web.config` is analogous to the `web.xml` file used by JSP.

Here is the format of the `<sessionState>` element:

```
<sessionState mode="Off|Inproc|StateServer|SQLServer"
  cookieless="true|false" timeout="number of minutes"
  stateConnectionString="tcpip=server:port"
  sqlConnectionString="sql connection string" />
```

The mode Attribute

ASP.NET supports four modes of session state. There is no default here, so this attribute must be specified. `Off` is fairly self-explanatory: if you attempt to make use of session state when `mode` is set to `Off`, the server will generate an exception. The remaining three options determine where state information is to be stored. `InProc` is short for **in process**, and is probably what you expect when dealing with sessions. Storing state information in process ensures the best possible performance but carries the danger of loss of state information in the event of a process crash or restart.

`StateServer` is an out-of-process store for state information provided by ASP.NET. Using this option hinders performance somewhat because ASP.NET must cross process boundaries, but it means we won't lose state in the event of an IIS crash. When the `StateServer` option is used, then we must also complete the `stateConnectionString` property, to specify the server name and port for the remote session (in the form `"tcpip=myhost:42424"`).

The final `mode` option is `SQLServer`, which persists state data to none other than SQL Server. This is the safest possible option but also the costliest in terms of performance. If this option is used, we must also complete the `sqlConnectionString` property (for example: `"data source=cookieStore;user id=sa;password=reallysecretpassword"`).

The cookieless Attribute

Like Java, ASP.NET supports sessions with or without cookies. Set the `cookieless` attribute to `true` or `false` depending on your preference. The default is `false`.

The timeout Attribute

Session timeouts are also supported, and the `timeout` attribute on `<sessionState>` denotes the session timeout in minutes. The timeout is 20 minutes if you don't specify otherwise.

The Shopping Cart Page

Now let's create our `web.config` file for the shopping cart application, in the `wrox` directory:

```
<configuration>
  <system.web>
    <sessionState mode="InProc" cookieless="false" timeout="20" />
  </system.web>
</configuration>
```

To keep things simple, we're going to keep things in process. Later, we'll change the `cookieless` setting to demonstrate how ASP.NET uses the querystring to support state without cookies.

By saving `web.config` to the `wrox` application root directory rather than the `source` directory where our pages are stored, the settings it contains apply application-wide (that is, to any web page under the `wrox` directory). This is necessary because `sessionState` must be set at application level, and cannot be overridden by settings at the child level. If you attempt to set `sessionState` in `web.config` at a child level, the server will generate an exception. For properties other than `sessionState`, settings given in `web.config` in local subfolders will take precedence over those specified at application level.

Our shopping cart application is made up of two files:

❑   `Shop.aspx` displays the products
❑   `ViewCart.aspx` displays the contents of your shopping cart

Let's begin by creating `Shop.aspx` in our editor:

```
<%@ Page Language="C#" Debug="true" %>
<%@ Import Namespace="System.Data" %>
<%@ Import Namespace="System.Collections" %>
```

Again, we turn debugging on to provide a stack trace in the event of an error. Next, we import `System.Data` so that we can use `DataTable` and `DataView`, and `System.Collections` because that gives access to `ArrayList`, which we'll use to populate our store catalog.

Moving on, we begin the script and declare a `DataTable` variable that we'll use to store our shopping cart inside the session cache:

```
<script language="C#" runat="server">
DataTable Cart;
```

Next, we'll implement `Page_Load()`, which will either create our shopping cart, or load it from session if it already exists:

```
void Page_Load(Object sender, EventArgs e)
{
```

If we have already done some shopping then the cart will already be initialized as a `DataTable` and in session. We assign the reference from session to `Cart`, casting it to a `DataTable` like so:

```
Cart = (DataTable) Session["ShoppingCart"];
```

The ASP.NET `Page` class exposes a property called `Session` that holds a reference to an `HttpSessionState` object. Session state is arranged in this object as key-value pairs. If `Cart` has never been initialized, it will be assigned a null value, and so will need to be initialized:

```
if (Cart == null)
{
  Cart = new DataTable();
  Cart.Columns.Add(new DataColumn("Item", typeof(string)));
  Cart.Columns.Add(new DataColumn("Price", typeof(string)));
  Cart.Columns.Add(new DataColumn("Quantity", typeof(string)));
```

If we've never stored the shopping cart, then `Cart` will be null, meaning we should create a new one. We store our cart in a `DataTable`, which we can then bind to a `DataGrid` for display. We configure our `DataTable` by adding three `DataColumn` objects to its `Columns` collection. Once we've done that, we add our cart to the session using the following code:

```
  Session["ShoppingCart"] = Cart;
}
```

The last thing we do in `Page_Load()` is check whether the page is loading for the first time or as the result of a postback:

```
if (!IsPostBack) {
  ItemsForSale.DataSource=GetItemsForSale();
  ItemsForSale.DataBind();
}
```

Our page displays products in a `DataGrid` called `ItemsForSale`, and if we're loading the page for the first time, we use the `GetItemsForSale()` method to populate this `DataGrid`. Now, we'll add the code for `GetItemsForSale`:

```
DataView GetItemsForSale() {

  DataTable items = new DataTable();
  DataRow item;
```

`GetItemsForSale()` returns a `DataView` representation of a `DataTable` of items. To keep things simple, we've stored four items in an `ArrayList` to use as our catalog:

```
  ArrayList Catalog = new ArrayList();
  Catalog.Add("10 Pack of Ballpoint Pens");
  Catalog.Add("1000 sheets printer paper");
  Catalog.Add("Yellow Highlighter Pen");
  Catalog.Add("100 page Wirebound Notebook");
```

```csharp
items.Columns.Add(new DataColumn("ItemNumber", typeof(Int32)));
items.Columns.Add(new DataColumn("ItemDesc", typeof(string)));
items.Columns.Add(new DataColumn("ItemPrice", typeof(double)));
```

We fill the `DataTable` by looping through the `ArrayList` and adding each row:

```csharp
for(int i = 0; i < Catalog.Count; i++)
{
  item = items.NewRow();
  item[0] = i;
  item[1] = Catalog[i];
  item[2] = 2.25;

  items.Rows.Add(item);
}
```

Finally, we return the `DataView` generated from our `DataTable`:

```csharp
DataView view = new DataView(items);
return view;
}
```

The last method we have to write is `AddToCart()`:

```csharp
void AddToCart(Object sender, DataGridCommandEventArgs e) {
  DataRow item = Cart.NewRow();
  TableCell itemCell = e.Item.Cells[1];
  TableCell priceCell = e.Item.Cells[2];
  TextBox qty = (TextBox)e.Item.Cells[3].Controls[1];
  item[0] = itemCell.Text;
  item[1] = priceCell.Text;
  item[2] = qty.Text;
  Cart.Rows.Add(item);
```

`AddToCart()` creates a new `DataRow` object for our shopping cart and fills it with the item description, price, and quantity taken from the `DataGrid`. To get this information from our `DataGrid`, we have to create a `TableCell` object and then copy the data from the `Cells` collection. You'll notice that we're using a `TextBox` rather than a `TableCell` object to store the quantity. This will allow us to customize our `DataGrid` with a template to allow the user to enter an item quantity into a `TextBox`. The `TextBox` is contained within the `TableCell` itself inside a `Controls` collection.

Once the item has been added to the shopping cart, we redirect the user to another page which displays the contents of their cart:

```csharp
  Response.Redirect("ViewCart.aspx");
  }
}
</script>
```

Chapter 6

We'll cover `ViewCart.aspx` in a moment. Before we do, we need to finish `Shop.aspx` by adding the `DataGrid` in the HTML section:

```
<html>
<body>
<h2>Office Supplies</h2>
<form runat="server">
```

Here is where we declare the `DataGrid`:

```
<asp:DataGrid id="ItemsForSale" runat="server"
    AutoGenerateColumns="false"
    BorderColor="Red"
    BorderWidth="1"
    CellPadding="5"
    OnItemCommand="AddToCart"
>
<Columns>
    <asp:ButtonColumn ButtonType="PushButton" HeaderText="Add"
      Text="Add"/>
    <asp:BoundColumn HeaderText="Item Description" DataField="ItemDesc"/>
    <asp:BoundColumn HeaderText="Price" DataField="ItemPrice"/>
    <asp:TemplateColumn>
        <HeaderTemplate>
            Quantity
        </HeaderTemplate>
        <ItemTemplate>
            <asp:TextBox width="50px" runat="server"/>
        </ItemTemplate>
    </asp:TemplateColumn>
</Columns>
</asp:DataGrid>
```

You'll notice that we're using `ButtonColumns` and `BoundColumns` in the `<Columns>` section just as we did previously. This is the first time we've used a `TemplateColumn` however, and it lets us exert precise control over the layout of a column by defining a series of **templates** within the `TemplateColumn` control. In this case, we're using `<HeaderTemplate>` to set the title for our column to the word **Quantity**. The `<ItemTemplate>` defines how cells in the **Quantity** column will be rendered. Here we've specified that each cell should contain a textbox. This provides the mechanism for our customers to enter a quantity for each item. The other useful template is the `<AlternatingItemTemplate>`, which allows us to define the layout of every other cell. We haven't used it in this example, but it lets us create more sophisticated grids quickly.

Notice also, that the **Add** button is wired to the `AddToCart()` method by setting the `OnItemCommand` property of the `DataGrid`.

Finish off `Shop.aspx` by closing off the HTML:

```
<br/>
</form>
</body>
</html>
```

Remember that we're relying on a separate file, `ViewCart.aspx`, to display the contents of the shopping cart after the user adds an item. Let's go ahead and create `ViewCart.aspx` now.

First, we import `System.Data` and declare a few variables:

```
<%@ Import NameSpace="System.Data" %>

<script language="C#" runat="server">

DataTable Cart;
DataView CartView;
```

This `DataTable` will hold the cart that we retrieve from session. We're going to display the cart in a `DataGrid` so we'll need a `DataView` for binding purposes. Next we'll write `Page_Load()`:

```
void Page_Load(Object sender, EventArgs e) {
  Cart = (DataTable)Session["ShoppingCart"];
  CartView = new DataView(Cart);
  ItemsForSale.DataSource=CartView;
  ItemsForSale.DataBind();
}
```

The `Page_Load()` method pulls our cart from the session store and binds it to the `DataGrid` for display. Note that on this page, we haven't checked whether there is a cart in session, as there must be for this page to be reached. You can see from the code that our `DataGrid` is called `ItemsForSale`.

We want to give the user an option to remove an item from their cart. We create a method, `RemoveFromCart()` for this purpose:

```
void RemoveFromCart(Object sender, DataGridCommandEventArgs e) {
  TableCell itemCell = e.Item.Cells[1];
  string item = itemCell.Text;
  CartView.RowFilter = "Item='"+item+"'";
  CartView.Delete(0);
  CartView.RowFilter="";
  ItemsForSale.DataBind();
}
```

The first thing this method does is grab the item description from the table. We then use the filtering capability of the `DataView` object to filter the cart based on the description. After the filter is performed, the item we want to delete will be at the first row of the table, and we can delete this first row by calling the `Delete()` method with a parameter of 0 (this represents the index of the table we want to remove). Setting the `RowFilter` to `""` clears the filter.

We also want the user to be able to empty their cart in one fell swoop. The `Empty_Cart()` method does this:

```
void Empty_Cart(Object sender, EventArgs e)
{
  Session.Remove("ShoppingCart");
```

```
      Response.Redirect("Shop.aspx");
}
```

The `Remove()` method takes a string argument that represents the key to remove from the session store. By passing `ShoppingCart` as the key, we remove the entire `DataTable`. As there are now no items in the cart, the user is redirected back to the shopping page.

Finally, we'll give the user an option to continue shopping. The `Continue_Shopping()` method handles this for us by simply redirecting the user to the `Shop.aspx` page:

```
void Continue_Shopping(Object sender, EventArgs e)
{
   Response.Redirect("Shop.aspx");
}
</script>
```

Now that we have the code in place, we need to work on our presentation. The following code creates a `DataGrid` to display our shopping cart:

```
<html>
<body>
<h2>Thank you for shopping with us</h2>
<form runat="server">
<asp:DataGrid id="ItemsForSale" runat="server"
              AutoGenerateColumns="false"
              BorderColor="Red"
              BorderWidth="1"
              CellPadding="5"
```

We wire an event handler to the button by setting the `OnItemCommand` property of the `DataGrid`:

```
              OnItemCommand="RemoveFromCart"
```

The first column in this grid contains hyperlinks for removing items. This column is implemented in the `Columns` collection as a `Buttoncolumn` (using the implicit default for the `ButtonType` attribute):

```
              >
    <Columns>
        <asp:ButtonColumn Text="Remove"/>
        <asp:BoundColumn HeaderText="Item Description" DataField="Item"/>
        <asp:BoundColumn HeaderText="Price" DataField="Price"/>
        <asp:BoundColumn HeaderText="Quantity" DataField="Quantity"/>
    </Columns>
</asp:DataGrid>
<br/>
```

We also place two buttons below the `DataGrid`. The **Continue** button is wired to the `Continue_Shopping()` method and the **Empty Cart** button is wired to `Empty_Cart()`:

Advanced Dynamic Web Applications

```
<asp:Button id="Continue" Text="Continue Shopping"
            OnClick="Continue_Shopping" runat="server"/>
<asp:Button id="EmptyCart" Text="Empty Cart"
            OnClick="Empty_Cart" runat="server"/>
</form>
<hr>
</body>
</html>
```

Now, we're ready to test our work. Open the `Shop.aspx` page in your browser, and you'll see the following:

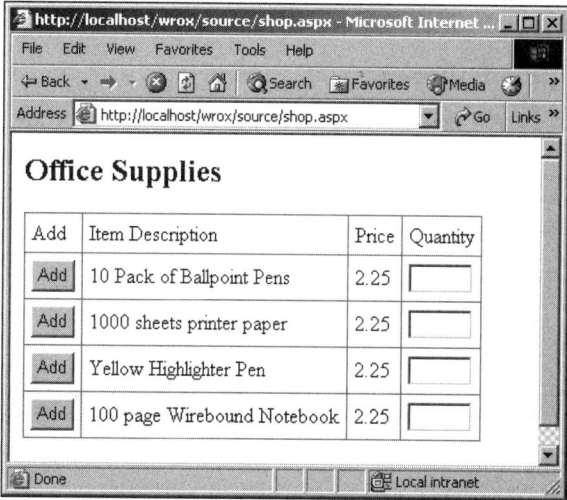

Now try adding an item to your cart. When you do, you'll be redirected to `ViewCart.aspx` which displays your shopping cart:

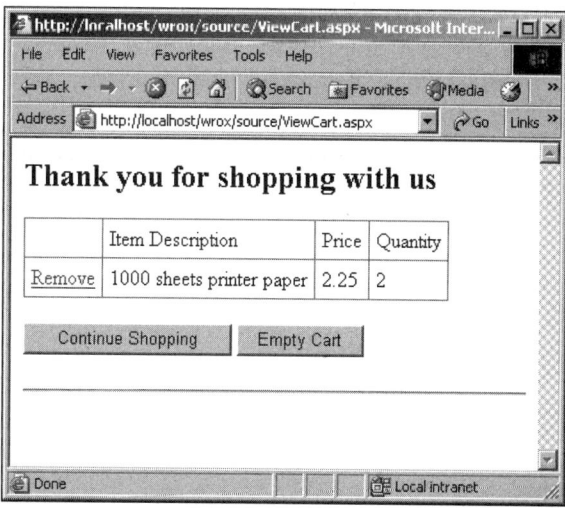

241

Chapter 6

Play around with the cart a bit to demonstrate that it works correctly. Try out the **Remove** link as well as the **Continue Shopping** and **Empty Cart** buttons.

That wraps up our shopping cart. If you're in the mood to experiment, open `web.config` and change the `cookieless` setting to `true`. Once you've made the change, bring `Shop.aspx` up in your browser and you'll see a long string inserted in page's URL:

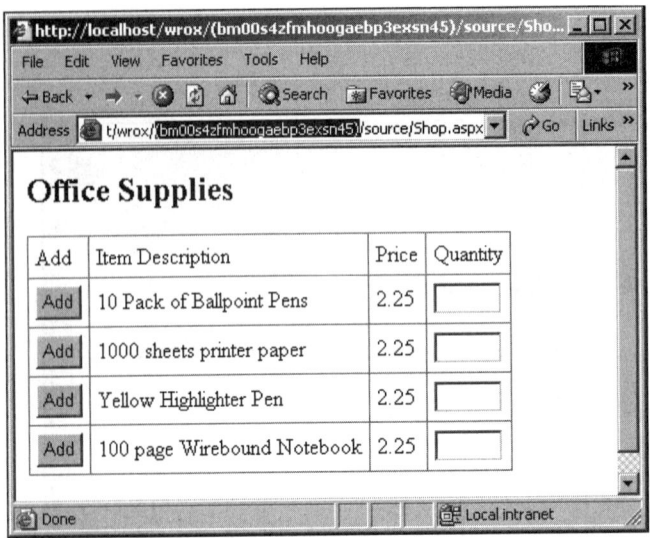

ASP.NET uses the unique identifier in parenthesis (bm00s4zfmhoogaebp3exsn45 in the screenshot above) in lieu of cookies to reference state information for this session.

Application State

When we store objects in application state, we in effect create a global variable that can be accessed by all pages in an application. In Java, we would use the `ServletContext` interface to share attributes between servlets in an application. In ASP.NET, the equivalent class is called `HttpApplicationState`.

To illustrate application state, we'll create a simple web page counter for the `Shop.aspx` page we created in the last example. To get started, make a copy of `Shop.aspx` called `ShopHits.aspx`. Open it up, and add the `Bump_Counter()` method directly above `Page_Load()`:

```
void Bump_Counter()
{
    Application.Lock();
    Object o = Application["count"];

    int count = 0;
    if (o != null)
        count = (int)o;
```

242

```
        Application["count"] = ++count;
        Application.UnLock();
        counter.Text = "This page has been viewed " + count.ToString()
                       + " times.";
    }

    void Page_Load(Object sender, EventArgs e)
    {
        .
        .
        .
```

The ASP.NET `Page` class has a property called `Application` that returns an instance of `HttpApplicationState`. We access application state through this object in the same manner as we accessed session state through `HttpSessionState`.

The first line of `Bump_Counter()` invokes `Application.Lock()`, which prevents other sessions from accessing the application store until `Unlock()` is called. This is necessary when using application state because it is accessible from all concurrent sessions simultaneously, and there is a consequent risk of conflict.

Once we've locked the application store, we check for the existence of an object keyed by the string count. If the object exists, we cast it to an `int` and assign it to the variable called `count`. We then increment the counter and store it using the following assignment:

```
    Application["count"] = ++count;
```

We need to call `Bump_Counter()` every time the page loads, which we can do by adding it to `Page_Load()` as shown here:

```
        .
        .
        .
    if (!IsPostBack) {
      ItemsForSale.DataSource=GetItemsForSale();
      ItemsForSale.DataBind();
    }
    Bump_Counter();
    }
```

The last step is to display the hit count in a `Label` control. Add this control to the bottom of `ShopHits.aspx` as shown below:

```
    </asp:DataGrid>
    <br/>
    <asp:label id="counter" font-size="22" runat="server" />
    </form>
    </body>
    </html>
```

243

Now open `ShopHits.aspx` in your browser and hit refresh a few times to see the counter increment. Open another instance of Internet Explorer (or whichever browser you use), and you'll see that the hit count is shared by both instances:

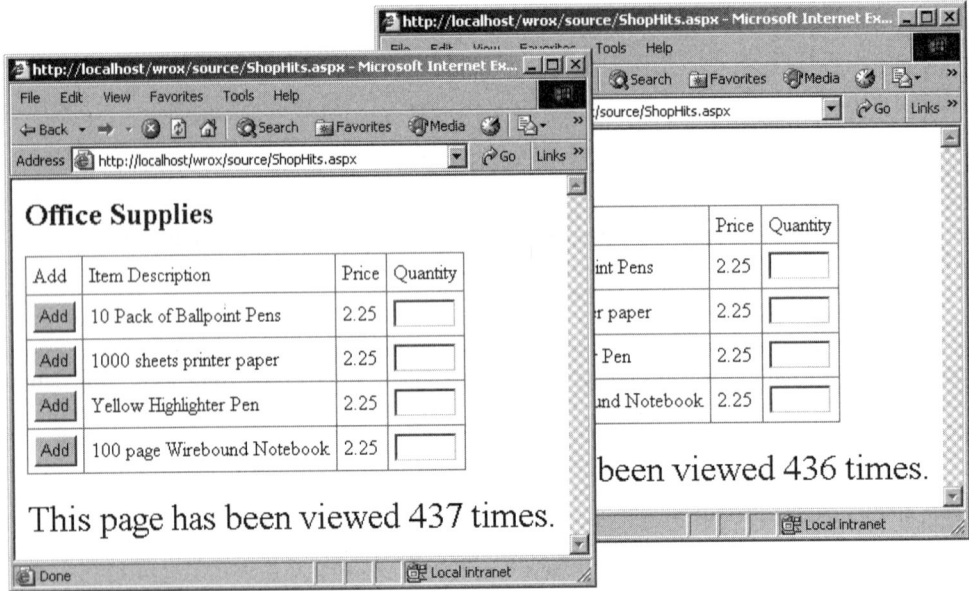

Note that in order for our modified shopping cart to be fully functional, we'd have to modify the `Empty_Cart()` and `Continue_Shopping()` methods of `ViewCart.aspx` so that they redirect to `ShopHits.aspx` rather than `Shop.aspx`:

```
void Empty_Cart(Object sender, EventArgs e)
{
  Session.Remove("ShoppingCart");
  Response.Redirect("ShopHits.aspx");
}

void Continue_Shopping(Object sender, EventArgs e)
{
  Response.Redirect("ShopHits.aspx");
}
```

Building Custom Controls

JSP developers familiar with Custom Tag Extensions will be aware of the benefits of being able to encapsulate functionality within a customized tag. ASP.NET provides the same benefits as custom tags by the mechanism of **custom controls**.

Advanced Dynamic Web Applications

In this section, we'll look at the basics of writing ASP.NET custom controls. Custom controls can be roughly divided into three categories depending on how they are implemented. First, we have controls that derive directly from `System.Web.UI.Control`. Second, we have controls that specialize an existing control by deriving from it. These are called **derived controls**. Finally, we have controls that are made up of two or more existing controls that we call **composite controls**.

We'll show an example from each category as we go along.

A Basic Custom Control

In the previous example, we added some code to a page in order to implement a page counter. It worked well enough, but if we wanted to add a counter to many pages in a site with tens or even hundreds of pages, it would not be the best way to go about it. A better solution would be to create our own control that we then place on every page that requires a counter, and we could create such a control as an ASP.NET server control. In a nutshell, we have to do the following:

- Create a class that derives from `System.Web.UI.Control`
- Wrap that class in a namespace
- Provide an overriding implementation for the `Render()` method
- Compile and deploy the control
- Add the control to an ASP.NET page

Open your editor and create a new file called `SimpleCounter.cs` in your `Source` directory.

First, we need to import a few namespaces that we'll be using later:

```
using System;
using System.Web;
using System.Web.UI;
```

The `System` namespace allows us to instantiate references of type `Object`, `System.Web` exposes the `HttpApplicationState` class, and `Control` and `HtmlTextWriter` are found in the `System.Web.UI` namespace.

After the imports, we begin a new namespace to encapsulate our custom control:

```
namespace CustomControls
{
```

We need to declare a namespace for a custom control as one is required by the ASP.NET page directive that makes our control available on an ASP.NET page, as we will see later. Next, we declare our `SimpleCounter` class, deriving from `System.Web.UI.Control`:

```
    public class SimpleCounter : Control
    {
```

`Control` is the base class that provides common functionality for all ASP.NET server controls. By default it provides no UI features, which is why we must provide an implementation for the `Render()` method.

Next, we create a method called `getCount`. The `getCount()` method is responsible for pulling the count from the application store and incrementing it. You've seen the code in `getCount()` before: it's the exact same implementation used in the previous section on application state, so you should be familiar with its workings:

```
private string getCount()
{

  HttpApplicationState app = Page.Application;

  app.Lock();
  Object o = app["count"];
  int count = 0;
  if (o != null)
    count = (int)o;
  app["count"] = ++count;
  app.UnLock();

  return "This page has been viewed " + count + " times!";
}
```

`GetCount()` returns a string that contains the count, which we'll use when we display the control. To display our control, we must override the `RenderControl()` method of the `Control` base class:

```
protected override void Render (HtmlTextWriter writer)
{
  writer.WriteBeginTag("table");
  writer.AddStyleAttribute(HtmlTextWriterStyle.FontWeight, "bold");
  writer.AddStyleAttribute(HtmlTextWriterStyle.FontFamily, "verdana");
  writer.AddStyleAttribute(HtmlTextWriterStyle.FontSize, "18pt");
  writer.WriteAttribute("border","1");
  writer.Write(HtmlTextWriter.TagRightChar);
  writer.WriteLine();
  writer.WriteFullBeginTag("tr");
  writer.WriteLine();
  writer.WriteBeginTag("td");
  writer.WriteAttribute("valign","top");
  writer.WriteAttribute("bgcolor","yellow");
  writer.Write(HtmlTextWriter.TagRightChar);
  writer.Write(getCount());
  writer.WriteEndTag("td");
  writer.WriteLine();
  writer.WriteEndTag("tr");
  writer.WriteLine();
  writer.WriteEndTag("table");
 }
 }
 }
```

This method provides us with an `HtmlTextWriter` object, which offers methods for writing HTML and raw text to an ASP.NET web form. We use a number of these methods to build a table (`AddStyleAttribute()`, `WriteFullBeginTag()`, and so on). An alternative way to generate the table would be to pass a string of raw HTML directly to the `Write()` method like this:

```
writer.Write("<table border=1><tr> <td valign=top bgcolor=yellow>");
writer.Write(getCount());
writer.Write("</td></tr></table>");
```

In order to use our custom control on a web page, we need to compile the code to an assembly in the `bin` directory by executing the command below:

```
> csc /t:library /out:../bin/CustomControls.dll /r:System.dll
  /r:System.web.dll SimpleCounter.cs
```

Now that we have compiled our control, we can add it to an ASP.NET page and see the counter in action. To make the control available to an ASPX page, we place the following `Register` directive at the very top of the page:

```
<%@ Register TagPrefix="Custom" Namespace="CustomControls"
    Assembly="CustomControls" %>
```

This directive takes three attributes. The `TagPrefix` attribute creates an alias (`Custom`) for the namespace referenced by the `Namespace` attribute (`CustomControls`). The `Assembly` attribute indicates the DLL that contains the compiled control (`CustomControls.dll`).

Using the custom control on a page is then a simple matter of placing the following tag where we want our control to appear:

```
<Custom:SimpleCounter runat=server />
```

To demonstrate our new counter, make another copy of `Shop.aspx`, call it `CustomShopHits.aspx` and add the `Register` directive below the `Namespace` imports as shown:

```
<%@ Page Language="C#" Debug="true" %>
<%@ Import Namespace="System.Data" %>
<%@ Import Namespace="System.Collections" %>
<%@ Register TagPrefix="Custom" Namespace="CustomControls"
    Assembly="CustomControls" %>
```

Finally, declare an instance of our `SimpleCounter` custom control just below the `<br/>` tag:

```
</asp:DataGrid>
<br/>
<Custom:SimpleCounter runat="server" />
</form>
</body>
</html>
```

That's all we need to do to use our custom control on a page. Now point your browser to `CustomShopHits.aspx` and hit refresh a few times to see it in action:

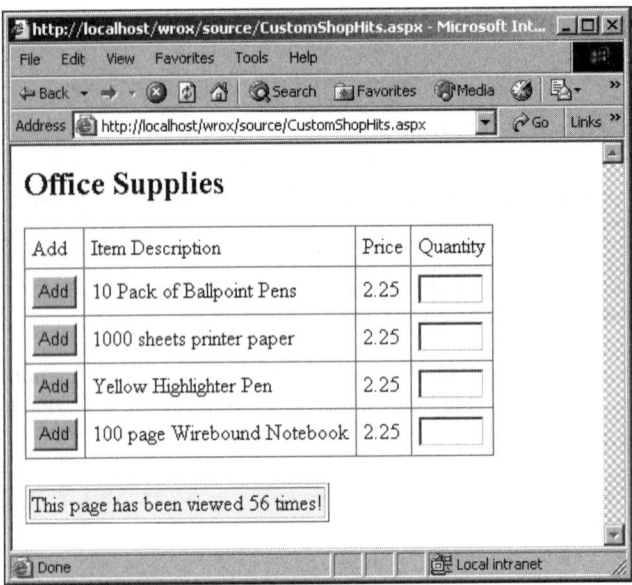

This example shows the basic principle of creating our own custom controls. You should be quick to note however that this control is not very flexible from the page designer's point of view. Any changes to the appearance of the counter (for example, font, border, and so on) must be made in code and recompiled into an assembly.

While this does ensure consistency across pages, it would generally be much better to expose properties of the control that allow the page designer to change the appearance without having to get their hands dirty with code.

Well, ASP.NET provides at least two approaches for creating custom controls that expose attributes that can be set on the custom tag itself. First, we could modify the existing `SimpleCounter` class by adding formatting attributes. This approach would be tedious but is certainly doable.

A preferable approach is to derive our control from an existing control if one is available that already provides the attributes we need. We're in luck because ASP.NET provides a number of controls with the appropriate built-in UI functionality. In our next example, we will do just this, and create a counter as a derived control based on an ASP.NET `Label` control.

A Derived Custom Control

The ASP.NET `Label` control displays text in a set location on a page. As a member of `System.Web.UI.WebControls`, it inherits a number of UI attributes that a page developer can use to set the look and feel of the label. These very same attributes would be ideal for our web counter control. To do this, we follow this procedure:

1. Create a class that derives from `Label` as part of the `CustomControl` namespace
2. Override the `Text` property of the label
3. Compile the control
4. Add our control to any ASP.NET pages we wish

You will notice that we've said nothing about overriding the `Render()` method here: this is because the `Label` control provides its own UI, so we don't have to. The code for `DerivedCounter.cs` is shown below. Once again, we begin by importing a few namespaces:

```
using System;
using System.Web;
using System.Web.UI.WebControls;
```

You've seen `System` and `System.Web` before. `System.Web.UI.WebControls` is required this time because we are deriving from `Label`.

Our `DerivedCounter` class is again part of our `CustomControls` namespace, and it inherits from `System.Web.UI.WebControls.Label`:

```
namespace CustomControls
{
  public class DerivedCounter : Label
  {
```

We access our counter using the `GetCount()` method, which is unchanged from the previous example:

```
    private string GetCount()
    {
      HttpApplicationState app = Page.Application;

      app.Lock();
      Object o = app["count"];
      int count = 0;
      if (o != null)
        count = (int)o;
      app["count"] = ++count;
      app.UnLock();

      return "This page has been viewed " + count + " times!";
    }
```

The most interesting part of the new code lies in the overridden implementation of the `Text` property:

```
    public override string Text
    {
      get
      {
        return GetCount();
      }
      set
      {
        // do nothing
      }
    }
```

The `Label` control's `Text` property allows the message shown on the label to be set either programmatically, or by the `Text` attribute on the ASP.NET `Label` tag. In our implementation, we are going to use the text of the label to display the page count. Consequently, we want to prevent the text from being modified by the page designer, and we can do this easily be overriding the `set` method of the `Text` property to do absolutely nothing. We override the `get` method to return the page count as a string.

We can now compile the control into an assembly like this:

```
> csc /t:library /out:..\bin\CustomControls.dll /r:System.dll
  /r:System.web.dll DerivedCounter.cs
```

After you compile, make yet another copy of `Shop.aspx`, named `DerivedShopHits.aspx` and add the `Register` directive just below the namespace imports as shown below:

```
<%@ Page Language="C#" Debug="true" %>
<%@ Import Namespace="System.Data" %>
<%@ Import Namespace="System.Collections" %>
<%@ Register TagPrefix="Custom" Namespace="CustomControls"
     Assembly="CustomControls" %>
```

This directive is just the same as it was before; the difference comes in the `Custom` tag declaration. As before, add the declaration just below the `<br/>` tag at the bottom of the page:

```
<br/>
<Custom:DerivedCounter BackColor="Green" ForeColor="White"
  Font-Name="Verdana" Font-Size="10" runat=server/>
</form>
</body>
</html>
```

We've set the `BackColor`, `ForeColor`, `Font`, and `Font-Size` properties that are inherited from `Label` to illustrate how the page designer can easily change UI features. Open the file in your browser and you should see something like the following:

Advanced Dynamic Web Applications

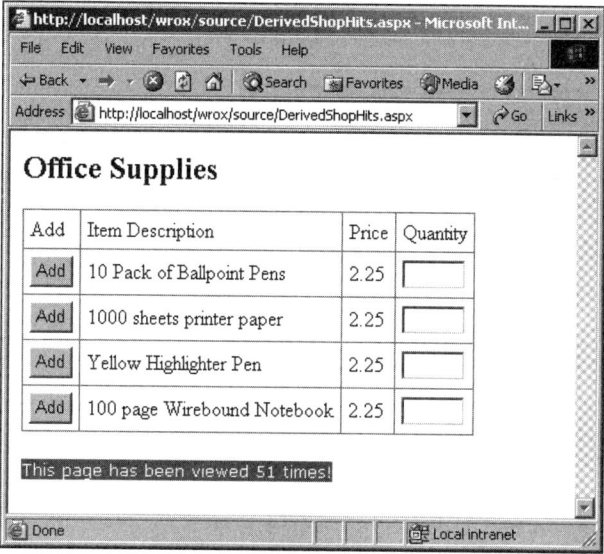

Now change a few properties on the `Custom` tag:

```
<Custom:DerivedCounter BackColor="Green" ForeColor="White"
  BorderStyle="Double" Font-Italic="True" Font-Size="16" runat=server/>
```

Refresh the page in your browser and you'll see that the look has changed:

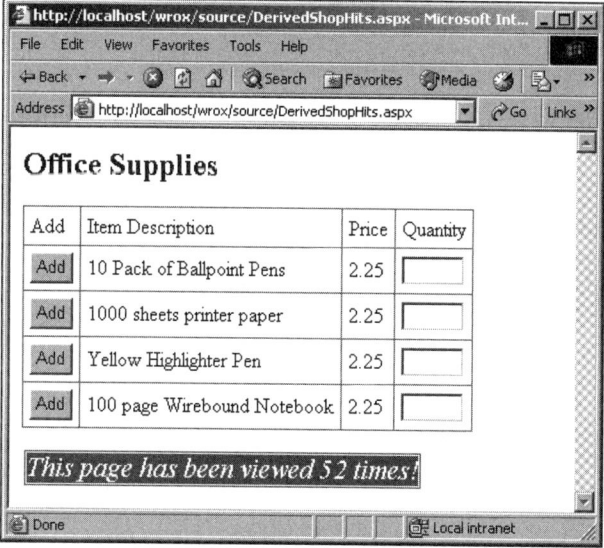

Next, we'll put the web-counters behind us and create a new custom control that combines the functionality of two or more existing server controls. Microsoft refers to these controls as **composite controls**.

A Composite Custom Control

Composite controls are useful in cases where two or more controls are repeatedly used together within an application or applications. A good candidate for a composite control would be a login control. Typically, login details are captured in conjunction with three separate controls: a textbox for the username, another textbox for the password, and a button for submitting the form. We could combine these three controls into a composite so that your page developer can drop a single tag into a page that might look like this:

```
<Custom:GetPassword runat=server />
```

This saves the bother of having to group the controls inside a table every time a password is required.

Another good use of a composite control would be to create online surveys. If you've done much surfing of the web variety, you will likely have been presented with a survey or two such as this one:

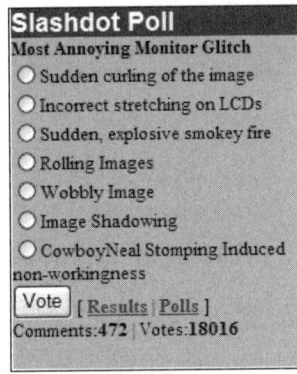

Looking beyond the banal questions they typically ask, we can see that these surveys can be made from a label, a series of radio buttons, and a submit button. This makes the survey control an ideal opportunity to learn about ASP.NET composite controls.

Our composite control will combine three types of ASP.NET server controls: a `Label` control for presenting the question to the user, a series of `RadioButtonList` controls for the possible answers, and a `Button` control for submitting the survey. We will follow this procedure:

1. Create the `SurveyControl` class that derives from `Control` as part of the `CustomControl` namespace.

2. Provide an implementation to override the `CreateChildControls()` method.

3. Expose the `RepeatDirection` property of the `RadioButtonList`.

4. Expose a new property called `Question` that maps to the `Text` property of the label control.

5. Compile and deploy our composite control.

Advanced Dynamic Web Applications

We'll store the questions for our survey in an XML file so we can learn a bit about reading XML under ASP.NET as we go along.

We'll place the code for our survey control in a file called `SurveyControl.cs`. To begin, we have the usual namespaces, and then start `SurveyControl`, inheriting from `System.Web.UI.Control`:

```
using System;
using System.IO;
using System.Data;
using System.Web;
using System.Web.UI;
using System.Web.UI.WebControls;
using System.Configuration;

namespace CustomControls
{
  public class SurveyControl : Control
  {
```

Next we declare the variables we'll need in the class:

```
    RadioButtonList list1;
    Label label1;
    HttpApplicationState app ;
    DataGrid resultsGrid;
    Panel surveyPanel;
    Panel resultsPanel;
```

Our next task is to provide an implementation that overrides the `CreateChildControls()` method of the `Control` class. `CreateChildControls()` is aptly named: its purpose is to create the child controls that together make up the control before the page is rendered. Any time you create a composite control you must override this method. It's quite a long method, so we'll walk through it step-by-step:

```
    protected override void CreateChildControls()
    {
```

To provide two different views for our control, we'll use panels. The first panel, called `surveyPanel`, will hold the controls that present the survey to the user:

```
      surveyPanel = new Panel();
      surveyPanel.Controls.Add(new LiteralControl("<Table style=\"border: "
                    + " 1px solid black\"><TR align=\"Center\">"
                    + "<TD>"));
      label1 = new Label();
      surveyPanel.Controls.Add(label1);
      list1 = new RadioButtonList();
      surveyPanel.Controls.Add(list1);
      Button button1 = new Button();
      button1.Text = "Submit";
```

Chapter 6

```
        surveyPanel.Controls.Add(button1);
        button1.Click += new EventHandler(this.ButtonClicked);
        surveyPanel.Controls.Add(new LiteralControl("</TD></TR></TABLE>"));
```

A `LiteralControl` is a container for raw HTML. We're adding `LiteralControl`s to our panel to wrap our survey inside a table. The `Label` will store the question for our survey, and the `RadioButtonList` will present the possible responses for the survey. Finally, the button will allow the user to submit the survey.

The `System.Web.UI.Control` class has a `Controls` property returning a `ControlCollection` object. The `ControlCollection` represents the children of the composite control and uses the `Add()` method to add members to the collection. Our next step is to add our first panel to the `ControlCollection`:

```
        Controls.Add(surveyPanel);
```

We mentioned earlier that our control would have two views controlled by panels. The second view will display the results of our survey after the user submits their vote, using the `resultsPanel`. Here is the code that creates the `resultsPanel` and its associated controls:

```
        resultsPanel = new Panel();
        resultsGrid = new DataGrid();
        resultsPanel.Controls.Add(resultsGrid);
        Controls.Add(resultsPanel);
    }
```

The `resultsPanel` contains a grid called `resultsGrid` to present the survey results. We'll bind a `DataTable` to the grid at run time. We add the grid to the panel here and add the `resultsPanel` to the `ControlCollection`.

Also notice in the above method that we wired the button's click event to an event handler called `ButtonClicked`:

```
        private void ButtonClicked(Object sender, EventArgs e)
        {
            int row = list1.SelectedIndex;
            RegisterVote(row);
        }
```

Event handlers typically take two arguments. First, an `Object` that represents the sender that raised the event and second, an `EventArgs` object that packages any information that the server might need to process the event. You can create your own events if necessary, in which case you might need to create your own class to encapsulate any required arguments. In this example, we won't use parameters at all.

Our `ButtonClicked` event handler determines what the user selected by looking at the `SelectedIndex` property of the `RadioButtonList`. It passes this value to the `RegisterVote` method:

```
protected void RegisterVote(int row)
{
  app = Page.Application;
  app.Lock();
  DataSet survey = LoadSurvey();
  int votes = Convert.ToInt32(survey.Tables[0].Rows[row]["votes"]);
  survey.Tables[0].Rows[row]["Votes"] = ++votes;
  app["Survey"] = survey;
  app.UnLock();
}
```

`RegisterVote()` takes the vote and updates the dataset accordingly. First, we refresh the dataset by calling `LoadSurvey()`. We then extract the current vote total from the appropriate row based on the index parameter, and increment the vote by one and save the updated survey to the application store.

The survey is stored in an XML file called `survey.xml`. The `LoadSurvey()` method is responsible for loading the survey from disk and adding it to the application store. First, we grab a reference to `HttpApplicationState` and create a new `DataSet`, then lock the application store to prevent concurrent access by other sessions:

```
protected DataSet LoadSurvey()
{
  app = Page.Application;

  app.Lock();
```

If this is the first time the page has loaded, we need to load the survey into memory from disk.

```
DataSet survey = (DataSet)app["survey"];
```

If initialization has already taken place, then all we have to do is load the survey from the application store and cast it as a `DataSet`. Otherwise, survey will be null, so we need to create it. The path to the XML file is held in the `web.config` file, so we use the `ConfigurationSettings` class to find it using the survey key name. Once we have the file name, we can use the `ReadXml()` method which is an expedient way to load an XML file into a `DataSet` in memory:

```
if (survey == null)
{
  survey = new DataSet();
  string source = ConfigurationSettings.AppSettings["survey"];
  survey.ReadXml(source);
  app["Survey"] = survey;
}
```

Now we just need to unlock the application store, and return the survey `DataSet`:

```
  app.UnLock();

  return survey;
}
```

At this point we have the basics of our survey set up. All we need to do now is write logic to control the presentation. It's common practice to display the results of the survey after the answer is submitted. There are many ways to accomplish this; one is to create a button or link that the user can click to display the results. Rather than this though, we'll automatically display the results by dynamically activating the appropriate panel in the `OnPreRender()` method. This method is called just prior to the server control rendering its contents to the page. We start by checking the `IsPostBack` property, and if the page is being loaded for the first time, we display the survey by setting the survey panel to be visible and the results panel to be invisible:

```
protected override void OnPreRender(EventArgs e)
{
  DataSet survey = LoadSurvey();
  if(!Page.IsPostBack) {
    surveyPanel.Visible=true;
    resultsPanel.Visible=false;
    list1.DataSource = survey;
    list1.DataTextField="Answer";
    list1.DataBind();
    list1.SelectedIndex = 0;
  }
```

Remember that `list1` is a `RadioButtonList` object. We bind `list1` to the appropriate data by setting the `DataSource` and `DataTextField` properties. The variable `survey` is a `DataSet` with two columns. We set the `DataTextField` of `list1` to pull its data from the `Answer` column of the `DataSet`.

Finally, we set the `SelectedIndex` property to 0 so that the first answer in the survey is the default choice.

If however this is not the first time the page is being viewed, it means the Submit button has been pressed, and we want to show the results panel:

```
  else
  {
    resultsGrid.DataSource = survey;
    resultsGrid.DataBind();
    resultsPanel.Visible=true;
    surveyPanel.Visible=false;
  }
}
```

In order to give the page designer the ability to change the question text we expose the `Text` property of the `Label` where the question will be displayed. We do this by creating a new property called `Question` and wiring it to the `Text` property of the child label via the `get` and `set` accessors:

```
public string Question
{
  get
  {
    EnsureChildControls();
    return label1.Text;
  }
  set
```

```
        {
            EnsureChildControls();
            label1.Text = value;
        }
    }
```

`EnsureChildControls()` guarantees that the `Label` has been created prior to any attempts to access its properties.

We've now allowed the page designer to set the question from within the tag like this:

```
<Custom:SurveyControl Question="What is your type of survey?" runat=server />
```

`RadioButtonList` controls have a property called `RepeatDirection` that controls whether the list renders horizontally or vertically. We expose this property to the page designer as well:

```
    public RepeatDirection Direction
    {
      get
      {
        EnsureChildControls();
        return list1.RepeatDirection;
      }
      set
      {
        EnsureChildControls();
        list1.RepeatDirection = value;
      }
    }
  }
}
```

This completes the code for `SurveyControl.cs`. Before we can run it, we need to set up `web.config`, and create the survey XML file. Add the following line to the `web.config` file in the `Source` directory, using the path to the `Source` directory on your system:

```
<configuration>
  <appSettings>
    <add key="northwind" value="Provider=SQLOLEDB;data source=localhost;
      database=Northwind;integrated security=sspi"/>
    <add key="survey" value="c:\wrox\source\survey.xml" />
  </appSettings>
</configuration>
```

Now enter the following and save it as `survey.xml` in the `Source` directory:

```xml
<?xml version="1.0" standalone="yes"?>
<Survey>
  <Response>
    <Answer>Surveys about computers</Answer>
    <Votes>0</Votes>
  </Response>
  <Response>
    <Answer>Surveys about TV</Answer>
    <Votes>0</Votes>
  </Response>
  <Response>
    <Answer>Surveys about pets</Answer>
    <Votes>0</Votes>
  </Response>
  <Response>
    <Answer>Surveys about licentious behavior</Answer>
    <Votes>0</Votes>
  </Response>
  <Response>
    <Answer>Surveys about surveys</Answer>
    <Votes>0</Votes>
  </Response>
</Survey>
```

We're all set up, and we can now compile our control to an assembly like so:

```
> csc /t:library /out:..\bin\CustomControls.dll /r:System.dll
   /r:System.web.dll SurveyControl.cs
```

The only thing left is a page to test our survey. Create `SurveyControl.aspx` as follows and save it to the `Source` directory:

```
<%@ Register TagPrefix="Custom" Namespace="CustomControls"
    Assembly="CustomControls" %>
<html>
<body>
<form runat=server>
  <Custom:SurveyControl Direction="Horizontal" Question="What is your
    favorite type of survey?" runat=server/>
</form>
</body>
</html>
```

We again need the `Register` directive that we used before. Our control allows us to set both the `Direction` and the `Question` text. Now open this file in your browser:

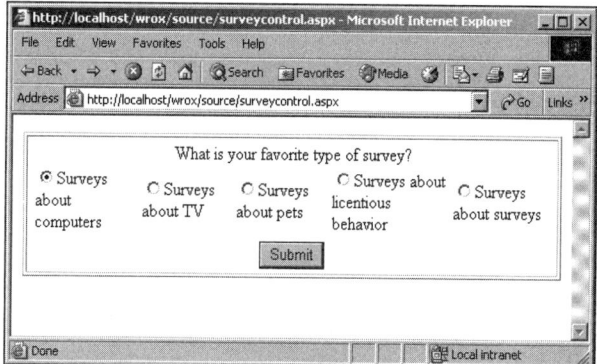

Cast your vote, click **Submit**, and you will see the results appear:

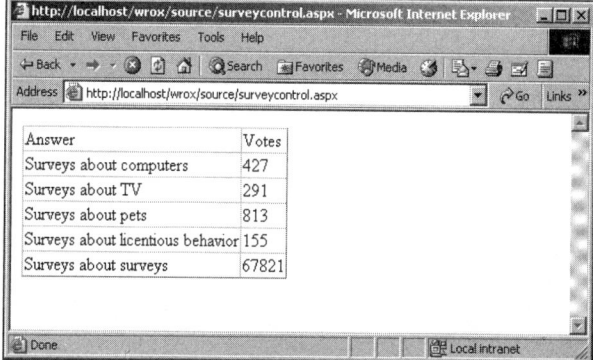

Summary

This chapter has looked at three of the more advanced features of ASP.NET that can enhance your productivity as an ASP.NET programmer.

First off, we looked at data-bound controls. Data binding is ASP.NET's mechanism for linking visual controls to data sources to automatically display data. We can bind any suitable property to compatible data, but the technique really comes into its own when binding to collections and other data sources, saving a lot of coding effort.

The next thing we looked at was the issue of session and application state, and we saw that ASP.NET's state management techniques bear a strong similarity to those of JSP. We can use session state through the `HttpSessionState` object to hold information relating to a single user session. Alternatively, the `HttpApplicationState` object lets us hold data that will be preserved for the lifetime of the application. Unlike JSP, ASP.NET has built-in systems that preserve state in the event of system restarts, using either `StateServer` or SQL storage.

Lastly, we looked at creating custom controls, and experimented with creating one of each of the three categories of ASP.NET custom controls: the basic custom control, the derived control, and the composite control. We saw that these controls offer increasing sophistication, and provide varying degrees of control to the page designer.

7
ASP.NET Web Services

The Java Web Services Developer Pack from Sun provides Java standard implementations of existing key web services standards including Web Services Description Language (WSDL), Simple Object Access Protocol (SOAP), and Universal Description, Discovery, and Integration (UDDI) as well as important Java standard implementations for Web application development in the Java language. The developer pack allows developers to send and receive SOAP messages, browse and retrieve information in UDDI and ebXML (Electronic Business using Extensible Markup Language) registries, and build and deploy web applications based on the latest J2EE standards. If you have worked with J2EE web services, then you'll find much of the ASP.NET web services terminology used in this chapter to be familiar already.

What this chapter aims to do is take you through the basic concepts necessary to become productive in creating ASP.NET web services. In essence, a web service is a programmable entity that provides particular functionality to any system that supports Internet standards such as XML and HTTP.

XML web services can be used either internally by a single application, or exposed externally over the Internet for use by any number of remote applications. One way in which they make themselves accessible is through a standard HTTP interface, enabling multiple systems to easily work together in a single "web of computation", providing a very loose coupling of system component parts.

The alternative, of tightly coupling systems using proprietary mechanisms, is usually at the expense of application interoperability. XML web services deliver interoperability on an entirely new level to negate such counterproductive incompatibilities. XML web services have the potential to become the fundamental means of linking together all computing devices over the Internet.

XML web services are founded on the XML SOAP standard for communications, which permits the XML web service and its client (the **consumer**) to interoperate without any knowledge of each other beyond the web service's inputs, outputs, and location.

If you have experience in working with JSP- or servlet-based web services, you should already have a good understanding of the standards underlying the technology, such as SOAP, UDDI, and WSDL. We won't be covering these in detail here – for more information, check out the following URL:

http://www.webservices.org/index.php/standards/

If you wish to refresh your Java web services knowledge, try Sun's excellent resource on creating web services with J2EE, which can be found here:

http://www.theserverside.com/resources/pdf/J2EE-WebServices-DevGuide.pdf

Creating ASP.NET Web Services

Getting web services to work in Java can be quite tricky – it is not really what you might call an "entry-level" activity. The list of Java enabling products for web services is vast, and there's no clear consensus on the best product. Java has a long way to go before it can be as clear-cut with web services as Microsoft appears to have become with .NET.

At the moment at least, if we wish to develop web services using ASP.NET, there's not much choice in implementation, and in a way, that's a good thing as it encourages commonality between development teams. This can cut down on maintenance problems, training, and so on, which are important considerations in the overall development and maintenance cost of a product. Web services are deeply rooted in the .NET Framework, and they can be created and operated by a very simple model. In contrast to JSP, there's no requirement to install enabling packages onto the web server, such as WASP, or any SOAP framework. ASP.NET web services are implemented as ASMX pages, which are exposed by ASP.NET as web services without our having to do anything.

On the other hand, to create a web service with J2EE requires you to install and configure a range of add-ins, including JAX, SOAP API (SAAJ), the JSP Standard Tag Library, the WSDP Registry Server, and more.

Once your system is set up, you then have to decide how to implement the methods – typically two files are required, one as an interface declaring the service's remote procedures, and the other as the implementation. Next you must configure and deploy the service, which involves creating the WSDL file and packaging a WAR file. Creating a web service in ASP.NET is a breeze by comparison.

Web service capability is provided by IIS by default when the .NET Framework is installed on a compatible system, and no configuration is required for most web service tasks. Writing ASP.NET web services requires just four simple steps:

1. Create a text file with an .asmx extension
2. Place a directive within the file declaring the file as an XML web service
3. Code the methods that implement the web service functionality
4. Deploy the ASMX page by copying it to your web server

Because the ASMX file that represents a web service in ASP.NET is a simple text file, there's no requirement for Visual Studio .NET or similar to create web services. Any text editor such as Notepad or TextPad will suffice, or we could use Microsoft's free Web Matrix GUI tool (discussed in Chapter 2).

It is the `WebService` directive that tells ASP.NET that a particular file represents a web service, and it also specifies the language used (such as C#) along with the name of the class that houses the web service's functionality. Here is a typical directive, for a web service that exposes the functionality of the `HelloJava` class:

```
<%@ WebService language="C#" class="HelloJava" %>
```

We can then follow this directive with the implementation in the same file, or alternatively we can use a separate code-behind file, which we specify in the `WebService` directive with the `CodeBehind` attribute.

The code for a web service must import certain required assemblies (`System`, `Web.Services`, and `XML.Serialization`), and then implement the class and methods required:

```
using System;
using System.Web.Services;
using System.Xml.Serialization;

public class HelloJava {

  [WebMethod]
  public string Hello()
  {
    return "Hello Java";
  }
}
```

Invoking a Web Service

In any .NET language, the only difference between an ordinary method and a web method is the addition of the `[WebMethod]` marker, which unlike the Java approach to declaring web methods is easily identifiable. This attribute simply tells the .NET runtime that the method is to be invoked using XML, and that its return value is to be wrapped as XML. This is all that's needed to make the method callable by remote web clients.

Before we move on to actually creating a web service and a consumer, let's examine the options, or **properties**, that can be set on the `WebMethod` attribute by including them as a comma-separated list in parentheses as shown below:

```
[WebMethod(Description="Says Hello Java", EnableSession=true)]
```

Some of the most useful of these properties are discussed in the following sections.

BufferResponse

The `BufferResponse` property controls how and when data is returned to the consuming client by the web method. This property is `true` by default, which means the entire result is serialized before being returned, rather than being streamed back piecemeal as it is produced. You only need to consider setting the `BufferResponse` property to `false` if a web method is likely to return a substantial amount of data.

CacheDuration

ASP.NET comes with a number of options for caching data on the server, and caching can be switched on for a web method. The default value is zero, indicating no caching. To switch caching on, we simply use this property specifying the number of seconds we wish cached information to be held for.

ASP.NET caches the return result whenever a cached web method is called with a particular set of parameters. When those exact parameters are next used to invoke that web method, ASP.NET will return the cached result instead. This can dramatically improve performance of certain applications.

However, alarm bells should now be ringing in your head, with a flashing message underneath telling you that caching cannot therefore be suitable for every web method. This is indeed true, and caching should only be considered when the **same set of parameters** produces the **same result**. If a web method uses some external, variable data to produce the return value in combination with the parameters, such as a changing field in a database or the time, then caching would not be suitable.

For instance, say we have a method called `SalesOfProduct()` that takes an integer representing a product code and returns the sales data for the specified product. If this sales data comes from a database that changes in real time, and we were to cache this method, it would soon start to return out-of-date results. This won't necessarily be critical, however, and indeed, for certain heavily used applications, may be preferable to overloading the data server. Evidently, methods that themselves update a backend data source can never be cached.

Another consideration when determining whether or not to cache a web method stems from the fact that ASP.NET will cache the result for every set of parameters that are used. Hence, we need to think of the number of permutations of parameters that are likely to occur, and decide whether caching would be worth tying up server resources. For instance, we could have a method called `ProductDetails()`, which returns product details for the specified item. If the only parameter is a product code, this would be a fairly good choice for caching. However, if there were an additional parameter, say `resellerID`, the value of caching the web method would be diminished because there will then be less subsequent hits on that method with exactly the same parameters. To go a step further, let's say the method also takes the current time as a parameter. In such a case, there would be *no* value in caching it, as it would never be called with exactly the same parameters twice – yet each call would nevertheless be dutifully cached by ASP.NET, thus gobbling up resources on the web server with no benefit.

Description

The `Description` property is a simple message that we can provide to describe a web method. This message will then appear on the ASP.NET test interface that we'll be introduced to later in the chapter.

EnableSession

Setting the `EnableSession` property to `true` enables session state. By default web services do not store session state, and the loosely coupled nature of web services tends to encourage stateless operation.

This attribute however allows you to specify that a specific method can interact with the ASP.NET session state for a remote client and query or update the session collection. Like JSP, ASP.NET supports a user session object, as covered in Chapter 6. It is worth noting that session support is not part of the SOAP specification, and is a proprietary addition of the .NET Framework.

MessageName

When we expose a method as a web method, the web method will take the same name as the method in our class. However, web method names must be unique, so if we wish to expose overloaded methods in a web service, we need to change the name that will be used by remote consumers, and we do this through the `MessageName` property.

We might also wish to set an alternative name to give our web method a friendlier name than the one it has in code.

TransactionOption

Transaction support (for database updates and so on) is enabled in ASP.NET by setting the `TransactionOption` property to one of these five choices:

- `Disabled`
- `NotSupported`
- `Required`
- `RequiresNew`
- `Supported`

If transactions are enabled for a compliant method, all code in that method will be executed within the same transaction. Note that transactions are managed by the COM+ transactional services contained in the `System.EnterpiseServices` assembly, which will need to be imported if we wish to enable this feature.

Creating an ASP.NET Web Service

In preparation for our web service, we need to create a new IIS web application (virtual directory) to host it, and eventually the test consumer that we'll write. If necessary, set one up using Internet Service manager with the name `ASPXServices` (if you're using Visual Studio .NET, a virtual directory will be created for you whenever you create an ASP.NET project, and you can skip this step). Also create a subdirectory called `bin` off the physical directory corresponding to the new virtual directory.

Copy `ServicesDatabase.mdb` from the code download to the `ASPXServices` directory. This is an Access database containing just three simple fields:

- `ID` – an autonumber field (the primary key field)
- `Name` – a text field (**Not Null**)
- `Age` – a number field

Now we're set up, create a new text file in your physical directory and name it `DataService.asmx`.

> *If you're using VS.NET, just right-click on your project in* **Solution Explorer***, and select* **Add | Add Web Service***. In Web Matrix, choose* **XML Web Service** *from the* **General Templates** *of the Add New File dialog. Web Matrix users can also specify a class name of* `DataLayer` *and a namespace of* `DOBData` *on this dialog. Such users will find that some of the code described next has already been added by their IDE.*

The first thing our ASMX file needs to contain is the ASP.NET `WebService` directive:

```
<%@ WebService Language="C#" Class="DOBData.DataLayer" %>
```

We'll use inline code rather than code behind – VS.NET users in particular may find code behind more convenient, in which case simply place all the code shown next in the `DataService.asmx.cs` file, adding a `Codebehind` attribute on the `WebService` directive to point to it. If you choose not to use code behind, simply follow the directive with our web service code – there's no need to use `<script>` tags in ASMX files. Our web service will connect to a database and use the `OleDb` classes described in Chapter 4 to talk to an Access 2000 database.

Just after the `WebService` directive, add the following `using` statements:

```
using System;
using System.Web.Services;
using System.Xml.Serialization;
using System.Web;
using System.Web.Util;
using System.Data;
using System.Data.OleDb;
```

These namespaces allow us to work with OLE DB managed data, and the web namespaces allow us to use the `HttpContext` object. Now we can start writing our class that will contain the methods our web service will use:

```
namespace DOBData
{
  public class DataLayer {
```

This class will define the connection string for our data source as a `public` string. This is very similar in layout to the connection strings required by JDBC Bridge DSN Access connections in JSP, so you may recognize the syntax:

```
    public string strDBConn = "Provider=Microsoft.Jet.OLEDB.4.0;Data Source="
                + HttpContext.Current.Server.MapPath("ServicesDatabase.mdb");
```

Now we will put our web methods in place. There are two web methods, called `GetAll()` and `InsertRecord()`. To keep things simple, we won't add any validation of the inputs to the web methods. No upper or lower bounds for the age for instance, or checking for an empty string in the name field. If you have worked with Java web services already, you will probably realize the need to cater for remote clients who are not fully aware of the types required by your methods, or have themselves simply not validated their users' input before requesting a remote method. For the sake of this example though, we'll leave it out, but do be aware of its importance for real-world web services.

```
    [WebMethod(Description="Returns all records from the database as an XML "
                + "Diffgram")]
    public DataSet GetAll()
    {
      return GetDataSet("SELECT * FROM DataRecords");
    }
```

```
    [WebMethod(Description="Inserts new records into the database")]
    public int InsertRecord(string Name, int age)
    {
      return ExecuteNoReturnSQLCall("INSERT INTO DataRecords (name, age) "
                          + "VALUES('" + Name + "', '" + age + "')");
    }
```

Note the `[WebMethod]` attribute required immediately before any method that is to be exposed via the web service. We've set the `Description` property for each to a brief description – we'll return to this later.

These web methods simply call two private methods with an appropriate query, `GetDataSet()` and `ExecuteNoReturnSQLCall()`:

```
    private DataSet GetDataSet(string mySQLString){

      string sqlStr = mySQLString;
      OleDbConnection myCon = new OleDbConnection(strDBConn);
```

As you may note, our code is using the somewhat expensive option of creating a new connection each time the method is called, and closing it as soon as it has completed. For production applications, we would probably want to make use of ASP.NET's sophisticated connection pooling to make our code more efficient. See Chapter 4 for more details on this.

The next step is to populate a `DataSet` from the database:

```
      DataSet dsDataSet = new DataSet();
      try
      {
        OleDbDataAdapter myAdapter = new OleDbDataAdapter( sqlStr , myCon );
        myAdapter.Fill(dsDataSet,"Datarecords") ;
        myAdapter.Dispose();

        return dsDataSet;
      }
      catch(Exception e)
      {
        return dsDataSet;
      }
      finally
      {
        myCon.Close() ;
        myCon.Dispose();
      }
    }

    private int ExecuteNoReturnSQLCall(string mySQLString)
    {

      OleDbConnection dataConnection = new OleDbConnection(strDBConn);
      OleDbCommand DBCommand = new OleDbCommand(mySQLString, dataConnection);
```

```
    try{
      DBCommand .Connection.Open();
      DBCommand .ExecuteNonQuery();

      return 1;
    }

    catch(Exception e)
    {
      return -1;
    }
    finally
    {
      dataConnection.Close();
      dataConnection.Dispose();
    }
   }
  }
 }
```

Make sure the final brackets are there to close the class and namespace, and save the file in the `ASPXServices` directory.

Testing ASP.NET Web Services

To test our web service, we'll use the neat interface that ASP.NET offers for this purpose, which makes web service development much more painless by removing the need for test clients. Simply open your web browser, and navigate to the new web service, using a URL of ASPXServices/DataService.asmx.

> *VS.NET or Web Matrix users can simply press F5 to open the web service's test page in their default browser.*

We see a screen like that shown below:

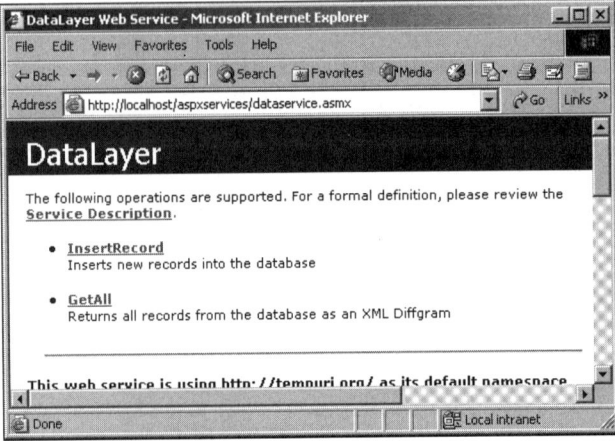

ASP.NET Web Services

Although we have four methods in our web service class, only those marked as web methods are shown, as only they are available remotely. Also notice that the descriptions we added as the methods' `Description` properties appear here.

This interface lets us test our web methods by clicking their names in the browser window and supplying any parameters if required. Click the **GetAll** link, and press **Invoke** on the next screen. The results that the web service obtains from the database are returned in XML format:

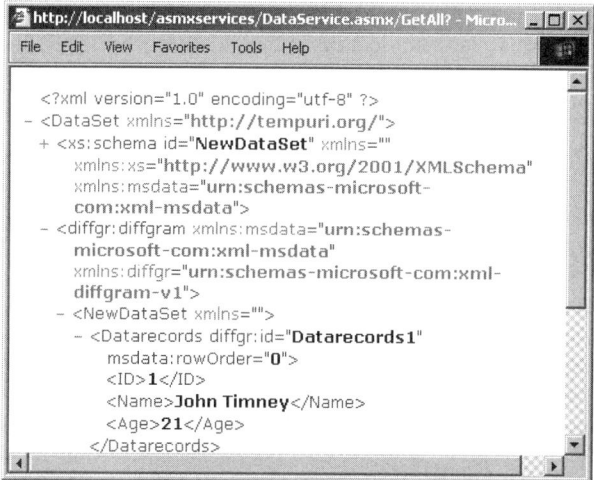

As you can see, this interface allows us to invoke a web service and see exactly what is returned.

Consuming a Web Service

We can build a variety of consumers for web services using the .NET Framework, including ASP.NET, WinForms, and Mobile Forms applications. The Visual Studio .NET IDE does this in a very seamless fashion, as does Matrix with its Web Services Proxy Generator. Here though, we'll see how to build consumers by hand in order to get a more complete feel for what's going on.

The steps we'll follow are:

1. Request the WSDL
2. Use it to create a proxy stub
3. Compile the proxy into a DLL that is placed in the `bin` directory of the consumer

We'll create a simple ASP.NET page to consume our web service to add new records to the database and display its contents by data-binding the results of calling `GetAll()` to a `DataGrid`.

One of the tools you will use frequently in .NET is a tool called `WSDL.exe`. This tool uses the WSDL (Web Services Description Language) file for a web service to create a proxy DLL that .NET consumers can use to call its web methods.

269

To start with, we'll get hold of the WSDL for the web service we'll be using as a local file. Although we can simply pass the web service URL to `WSDL.exe`, there are times when we don't have direct access in this way, and we'd have to take the long-winded route and use a local copy of the WSDL file from the web service provider.

On the ASP.NET test page for the web service, there is a link labeled **Service Description**. Clicking this link shows the WSDL that describes our web service, and we can save a copy locally by choosing **File | Save As** from the Internet Explorer menu bar. Place it in the `ASPXServices` directory with the name `DataService.wsdl`. It's perfectly possible to consume a web service not written in .NET, perhaps using Java Glue from www.themindelectric.com or Perl, although we would then have to get the WSDL another way. Most web service implementations include the WSDL file on the main web service page, but Microsoft has chosen to use an extra link to the WSDL created by ASP.NET.

We can now run `WSDL.exe` on this file as shown below, and it will generate a C# class file (or VB.NET should we wish) that invokes the web methods described in the WSDL:

```
> wsdl /n:DataServiceNamespace DataService.wsdl
```

Here, we've invoked the utility by passing in the filepath to the WSDL document describing the web service we wish to access. Alternatively, we could pass in the URL of the WSDL link for our web service. The above command generates a C# file corresponding to the web service described by the specified WSDL file. It will be named after the name of the web service in question, so that in this case, we get a file called `DataLayer.cs`. `WSDL.exe` offers several options that we can set on the command line should we wish. We've used one above to set the namespace to use in our generated class, and a couple of others include:

- `/l` – the language to use in the generated code, which is C# by default.
- `/o` – the name of the output file if we don't wish to use `DataLayer.cs`.

The complete set of options can be seen by typing `wsdl /?` on the command line. Once `WSDL.exe` has built our proxy class, we can compile it easily enough:

```
> csc /t:library /o:bin\DataService.dll DataLayer.cs
```

This command creates a DLL from our proxy class with the name `DataService.dll`, and places it in the `bin` subdirectory where it will be accessible to our web application's code.

For simplicity, we'll create our consumer in the same virtual directory as the web service, so make sure the DLL is in the `bin` directory off the physical directory we created earlier.

Now we'll create the ASPX page that will consume our web service. Create a new text file called `default.aspx` in the physical directory for `ASPXServices`. The file starts with the usual `Page` directive, followed by two `Import` directives. The first allows us to use our proxy class, and the second lets us use classes in the `System.Data` namespace. We use these classes when working with a `DataSet` that will be populated by the XML diffgram passed back from the web service:

```
<%@ Page Language="C#" Debug="true" %>
<%@ Import Namespace="DataServiceNameSpace" %>
<%@ Import Namespace="System.Data" %>
```

ASP.NET Web Services

Next we have the script that reacts to our button click event:

```
<script runat="server">

void Btn_Click(Object sender, EventArgs e)
{
```

We create an instance of the remote class via the proxy stub:

```
    DataLayer DService = new DataLayer();
```

Once we have the class instance, we can call the proxy methods that handle the details of calling the remote web service:

```
    DService.InsertRecord(Request.Form["Name"].ToString(),
                    Convert.ToInt32(Request.Form["age"]));

    DataSet ds = DService.GetAll();
```

Next we create a view of the returned data and bind it to the grid control for display:

```
    DataView Source = new DataView( ds.Tables[0] );

    resultGrid.DataSource = Source;
    resultGrid.DataBind();

}

</script>
```

Finally, we create the web form controls for our page. After the initial HTML, we start with the `resultsGrid DataGrid`:

```
<html>
<head>
  <title>DataLayer Consumer</title>
</head>
<body>
  <form method="post" runat="server">
    <h1>DataLayer Consumer</h1>
    <p>
      <asp:DataGrid id = "resultGrid"
                runat = "server"
                AutoGenerateColumns = "true"
                HeaderStyle-BackColor = "#00aaaa"
                CellPadding="3"
                BorderWidth="1"
                BorderColor="black" />
      <br />
```

Next we have the label that will identify the purpose of our web page:

```
    <asp:Label id="Title"
            runat="server"
            Font-Size="12pt"
            Font-Name="verdana"
            Text="Add New Record:<br/>"
            ForeColor="DarkGreen"
            Font-Names="verdana"
            Font-Bold="True">Add New Record:<br />
    </asp:Label>
</p>
```

Then we add `TextBoxes` for our user input, each preceded by a descriptive label:

```
<p>
  <br />
  <asp:Label id="NameLabel"
            runat="server"
            Font-Size="12pt"
            Font-Name="verdana"
            Text="Name:"
            ForeColor="DarkGreen"
            Font-Names="verdana"
            Font-Bold="True">Name:
  </asp:Label>
  <asp:TextBox id="Name" runat="server" Width="150" />
  <br />
  <asp:Label id="AgeLabel"
            runat="server"
            Font-Size="12pt"
            Font-Name="verdana"
            Text="Age:" ForeColor="DarkGreen"
            Font-Names="verdana"
            Font-Bold="True">Age:
  </asp:Label>
  <asp:TextBox id="Age" runat="server" Width="50" />
</p>
<p>
  <hr />
</p>
<p>
```

Finally, we add a submit button linked to the `Btn_Click` server event:

```
    <input type="submit"
            value="Submit Request"
            runat="server"
            onserverclick="Btn_Click" />
    </p>
  </form>
</body>
</html>
```

Opening this page in your browser will produce the screen shown below:

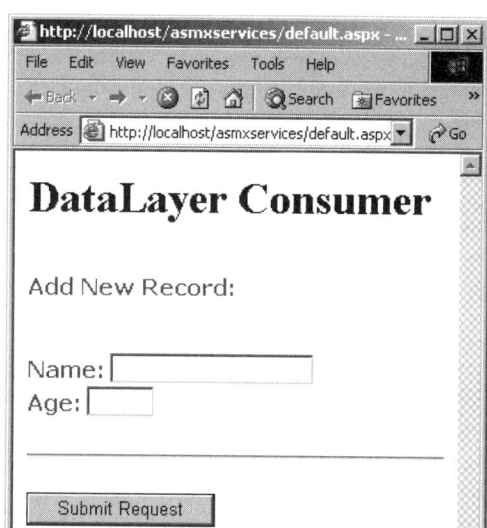

Enter some values and press the submit button, and you'll see results something like this:

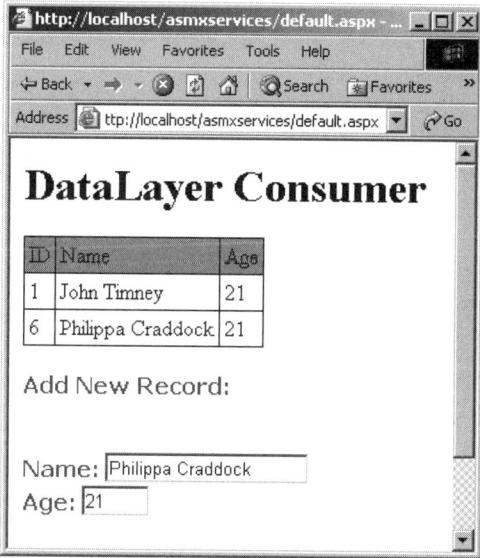

We've now demonstrated creating and consuming a web service using the .NET Framework from the ground up, but one of the founding principles of web services is the dream of platform neutrality, so how easy is it to create .NET consumers for other web services? Let's take a look!

Using External Web Services in .NET Clients

In this section, we will use C# to create a .NET Windows Forms client that accesses a third party web service freely available from the XMethods web site (www.xmethods.com). The site has a range of interesting web services available to incorporate into our applications, from weather reports to virtual file systems.

The web service we will use is the Delayed Stock Quote service, which provides stock quotes delayed by 20 minutes. It is a Java web service built using Glue for the SOAP implementation. To consume it, we need know nothing about the inner workings of its functionality, which incidentally obtains prices from Yahoo, although in a real-world scenario we would want some form of arrangement with the service provider to ensure uptime, accuracy, and so on.

To consume the web service, we simply have to feed its WSDL file to `WSDL.exe`. This time, we'll just pass in the URL. One thing to be aware of here is that the WSDL file in the URL contains hyphens, and this would throw the C# compiler when we tried to create our DLL from the generated proxy class. To avoid this, we use the `/o` switch to specify a different output file:

```
> wsdl.exe /n:quotews /o:xmethodsquotes.cs
        http://services.xmethods.net/soap/urn:xmethods-delayed-quotes.wsdl
```

Now we can compile the proxy class that `WSDL.exe` has just generated like so:

```
> csc /t:library xmethodsquotes.cs
```

The proxy DLL is ready for use, and now we'll create a Windows Forms application to try it out inside a file called `QuotesConsumer.cs`.

As well as the usual .NET namespaces for a Windows Form, this file will need the namespaces for talking to web services, and our own namespace for access to the remote web service through the proxy class we've just generated:

```
using System;
using System.ComponentModel;
using System.Drawing;
using System.Windows.Forms;
using System.Web.Services;
using System.Xml.Serialization;
using quotews;
```

Next we start the class that will contain the methods that talk to the web service:

```
public class QuotesConsumer : System.Windows.Forms.Form
{
```

We then declare a container, called `components`, to house the items that will appear on our form:

```
    // Declare the control container
    private System.ComponentModel.Container components;
```

Now we declare the `TextBox` that will be used for entering the stock symbol to look up, along with a label that will hold a description, and a submit button:

```
// Declare the textbox, label and button
private System.Windows.Forms.TextBox tickerBox;
private System.Windows.Forms.Label description;
private System.Windows.Forms.Button submitBtn;
```

We have to set up a reference to the XMethods web service, using its rather a long object name. We will refer to it as `QuoteService`:

```
// Declare the reference to the remote service
private netxmethodsservicesstockquoteStockQuoteService QuoteService;
```

Now the private members are declared, we can start the class constructor. As the constructor of our WinForm, it is responsible for creating and arranging the controls. First off, it has to instantiate the controls we've declared as private members:

```
public QuotesConsumer()
{
  this.components = new System.ComponentModel.Container();
  this.tickerBox = new System.Windows.Forms.TextBox();
  this.description = new System.Windows.Forms.Label();
  this.submitBtn = new System.Windows.Forms.Button();
```

We must not forget to create an instance of the `QuoteService`:

```
// Instantiate the remote service
this.QuoteService = new
                    netxmethodsservicesstockquoteStockQuoteService();
```

We also need to organize the screen layout, by setting sizes, locations, and text where appropriate:

```
      // Set up the form layout...
      this.Text = "Web Services Sampler";
      this.ClientSize = new System.Drawing.Size(300, 100);

      // the TextBox layout...
      tickerBox.Location = new System.Drawing.Point(100, 15);
      tickerBox.Size = new System.Drawing.Size(180, 20);

      // the Label layout...
      description.Location = new System.Drawing.Point(16, 15);
      description.Text = "Stock Symbol";
      description.Size = new System.Drawing.Size(80, 16);

      // and the Button layout
      submitBtn.Location = new System.Drawing.Point(100, 55);
      submitBtn.Size = new System.Drawing.Size(70, 30);
      submitBtn.Text = "Get Price";
      submitBtn.Click += new System.EventHandler(submitBtn_Click);
```

Chapter 7

Notice that, in the last line, we wire up the button's click handler to a method called `submitBtn_Click()`. Finally, the constructor needs to place the controls on the form by calling `this.Controls.Add()` for each control:

```
    // Add the controls to the form
    this.Controls.Add(tickerBox);
    this.Controls.Add(description);
    this.Controls.Add(submitBtn);
}
```

Don't forget to finish the constructor with the closing brace, and we can add the click event for the button. The value returned (which will be a float if all has gone according to plan) is converted to a string for display, as is any exception should things go wrong:

```
private void submitBtn_Click(object sender, System.EventArgs e) {
    try
    {
        MessageBox.Show(QuoteService.getQuote(tickerBox.Text).ToString());
    }
    catch (Exception Exp)
    {
        MessageBox.Show(Exp.ToString());
    }
}
```

Notice the `try` block around the `MessageBox` call, to catch either empty fields in the submitted data, or errors thrown by the remote service. In a real-world application, we would probably wish to enhance this to show a more useful message depending on the type of exception thrown, or not even calling the web method if the `TextBox` is empty.

We always need to remain conscious that web services are remote objects, and access to them is subject to a range of conditions beyond our control. We need to be prepared for situations where our web service is unavailable, even for web services developed in-house. We may choose to call a different service, or trigger an administrative alert in the event of trouble. In loosely coupled applications, error control should normally form a key part of component design.

Finally, we add the `Main()` method to run the form, and close the class:

```
    public static void Main(string[] args)
    {
        Application.Run(new QuotesConsumer());
    }
}
```

The next step is to compile the form with the following command:

```
> csc /target:winexe /r:xmethodsquotes.dll QuotesConsumer.cs
```

This produces the target file `QuotesConsumer.exe`, which consists of the simple dialog shown in the following screenshot:

ASP.NET Web Services

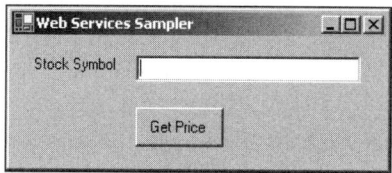

Type in a stock symbol, such as DIS for Walt Disney, and click the Get Price button. The live stock price, delayed by 20 minutes, will then appear in a message box:

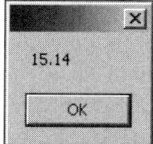

Web Service Chaining

To finish off the chapter, I'd like to quickly mention a design solution known as web service chaining. Many commercial web services, or at least those of real utility, charge a fee for each request. If you have multiple client platforms, such as ASP.NET, Windows Forms, Java applications and so on, controlling access to the remote service can easily become a bit of a nightmare.

One way to cut down on the costs that using such web services can clock up is to employ web service chaining, where we create our own web service that wraps calls to the third party's web service. This provides a single access point for all our client platforms, allowing us – in the case of ASP.NET – to set caching for our web service with a `CacheDuration` property of the `WebMethod` attribute.

As with any web service caching, this is only something we want to do for suitable web methods, as discussed earlier in this chapter. As well as saving time by caching results, it can save time by allowing consumers to get their results off a web server on the intranet, rather than needing to access a remote web service directly, which is often further delayed by an authentication step.

Whether or not web service chaining is suitable for a given situation will be decided by the tradeoff between speed and accuracy. If an application requires the latest up-to-the-minute data, then chaining will probably not be suitable. However, .NET makes web chaining very easy to accomplish, and usually much simpler than attempting to build caching into each consumer application.

Summary

In this chapter, I've attempted to cover all the bases to give a quick feel of the issues when developing web services with the .NET Framework. We started with a quick description of what web services are, and how they have an array of protocol standards for interacting with them including SOAP, UDDI, and WSDL, standards which have been designed for use over HTTP.

We created an actual web service using C#, creating a couple of methods that connect to a database, which we expose as web methods simply by adding the `WebMethod` tag.

Consuming a web service is no harder, thanks to the WSDL standard, which enables us to create code to interact with a web service automatically, using tools such as Microsoft's `WSDL.exe`. The so-called proxy class that such tools generate allows us to create consumer applications that call these remote methods very easily.

Finally, we used this proxy class to consume a remote web service in a .NET Windows Forms application. Following this process should have demonstrated how easy it is to consume third-party web services in .NET: we need no knowledge about the technology underlying the web service.

There really is a great deal of truth in the hype surrounding web services, and they have a lot of potential in the arena of enterprise applications. They are founded on several firm standards that really do make them platform-neutral mechanisms for opening up your functionality to customers, but as Java developers may be aware, there are fundamentally different approaches being followed by different vendors. I hope this chapter has illustrated the simplicity with which we can implement web services in .NET.

One issue that you will need to investigate further should you be interested in making production-quality loosely coupled applications is that of security, because that is a book in itself. A good starting point to find out about such concerns is the security paper *Security in a Web Services World* written jointly by Microsoft and IBM at:

http://www-106.ibm.com/developerworks/security/library/ws-secmap

Alternatively, Wrox Press's *ASP.NET Security* book (ISBN 1-86100-620-9) contains a wealth of relevant information, with plenty of examples using ASP.NET. If you want to find out more on web services using C#, try *C# Web Services*, also from Wrox (ISBN 1-86100-439-7).

Windows Forms and Smart Clients

Windows Forms, or WinForms for short, provide an extensible, object-oriented framework for Windows application development in any .NET language. This chapter takes a look at the WinForms application model in the context of a simple GUI application. Along the way, we'll make a few comparisons with Java Swing and AWT for those of you with experience of creating GUI applications in Java.

GUI building has long been a strength of Microsoft's Visual Studio IDE, and its latest incarnation Visual Studio .NET is no exception. In this chapter, we'll see how that environment simplifies the task of building WinForms applications, although we'll also present instructions for readers using the command-line tools only.

Most of you will think of Windows Forms as the building blocks of standalone .NET applications. However, .NET introduces a new model of application design in the **smart client**. A smart client is a Windows Forms application that combines the advantages of traditional Windows desktop applications with the maintenance and distribution advantages of web applications. In the second part of this chapter, we'll turn our existing Windows Forms application into a smart client.

We'll end the chapter with a discussion of data-bound controls. As we saw in the last chapter, data binding lets us set a given property of a control automatically by linking that property to a data source. We'll show you the basics of data binding in Windows Forms applications along with a couple of examples.

A Simple Windows Forms Application

The Windows Forms application we're going to create in this chapter will be a simple ordering tool for a pizza shop. When a customer calls the shop, the attendant fills in the form with the required information, and submits it to the kitchen for processing. A pizza order has a lot of options. Size, toppings, and pickup or delivery to just name a few. We'll represent these options using different controls from the Windows Forms namespace.

Chapter 8

As I've said, we'll look at how to use Visual Studio .NET to create the application, although a text editor will work just fine, especially for an application as trivial as this one. As we go along, we'll look at the code that VS.NET generates to get a feel for what the IDE does for us, and also so that those of you without VS.NET will be able to follow along. Having said this of course, it's hard to imagine doing extensive GUI work without an IDE in any production environment.

1. Start by firing up Visual Studio .NET. Create a new project by selecting **File | New | Project** from the menu bar, or click the **New Project** button on the Start Page.

2. In the left-hand **Project Types** pane, choose **Visual C# Projects**. In the right-hand Templates pane, select Windows Application.

3. Give your application a name such as `PizzaOrder`, and specify a location, such as `PizzaProject`:

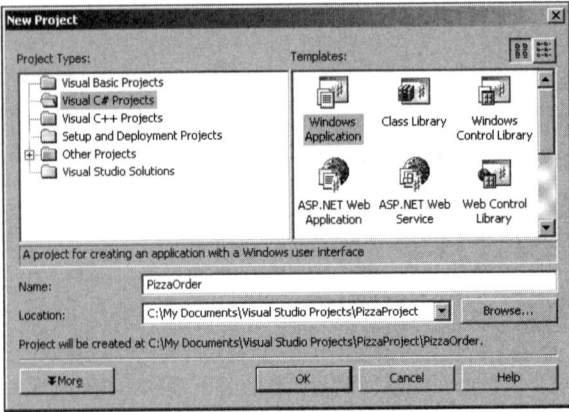

4. Once you've done this click **OK**, and our project is created in the IDE:

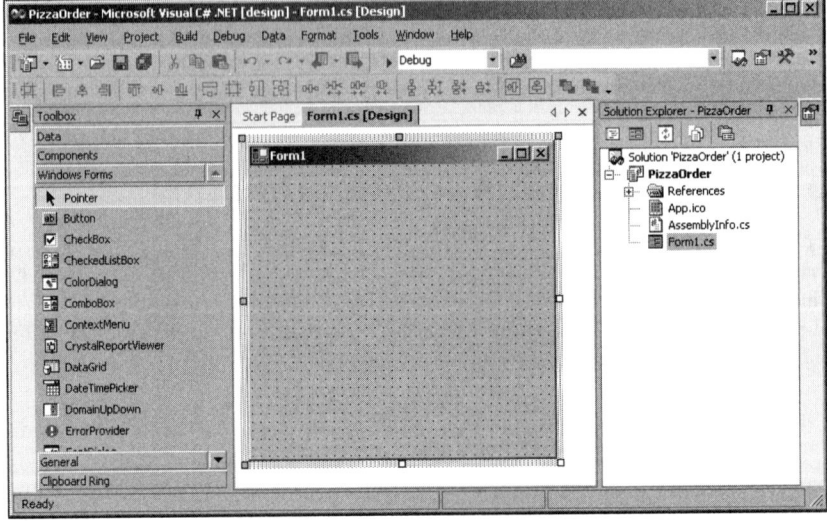

Windows Forms and Smart Clients

The blank form that appears in the IDE, named `Form1.cs`, is a graphical representation of an instance of `System.Windows.Forms.Form`, analogous to a `JFrame` in Java Swing. We add GUI controls to the form to build our user interface. One or more such forms make up all Windows Forms applications, along with additional code files for supporting classes or user controls where necessary.

Its current name isn't very descriptive, so use Solution Explorer (which appears on the right-hand side of the above screenshot) to rename it to `PizzaOrderForm.cs`.

> *If you're following along with the command-line tools, create a suitably named directory for our project files, say* `PizzaProject`*, and create a new text document inside called* `PizzaOrderForm.cs`*. Leave it empty for now.*

Looking Behind the Scenes

So, what does VS.NET do for us when it creates a new form? To find out, right-click on the form in the designer or in Solution Explorer, and choose **View Code**. We are taken to VS.NET's code editor, where we can see the C# code that creates the form:

```csharp
using System;
using System.Drawing;
using System.Collections;
using System.ComponentModel;
using System.Windows.Forms;

namespace PizzaOrder
{
  /// <summary>
  /// Summary description for PizzaOrderForm.
  /// </summary>
  public class PizzaOrderForm : System.Windows.Forms.Form
  {
    /// <summary>
    /// Required designer variable.
    /// </summary>
    private System.ComponentModel.Container components = null;

    public PizzaOrderForm()
    {
      //
      // Required for Windows Form Designer support
      //
      InitializeComponent();

      //
      // TODO: Add any constructor code after InitializeComponent call
      //
    }

    /// <summary>
    /// Clean up any resources being used.
    /// </summary>
    protected override void Dispose( bool disposing )
```

```
    {
      if( disposing )
      {
        if(components != null)
        {
          components.Dispose();
        }
      }
      base.Dispose( disposing );
    }

    #region Windows Form Designer generated code
    /// <summary>
    /// Required method for Designer support - do not modify
    /// the contents of this method with the code editor.
    /// </summary>
    private void InitializeComponent()
    {
      this.components = new System.ComponentModel.Container();
      this.Size = new System.Drawing.Size(300,300);
      this.Text = "PizzaOrderForm";
    }
    #endregion

    /// <summary>
    /// The main entry point for the application.
    /// </summary>
    [STAThread]
    static void Main()
    {
      Application.Run(new PizzaOrderForm());
    }
  }
}
```

The essential parts in this listing have been emboldened above: these are the lines that those of you using Notepad will need to place in your `PizzaOrderForm.cs` file. At the moment, there isn't much there, but as we add controls in the designer, we'll see that code will be added to set them up as required.

One thing that we can see here is the `Main()` method at the end, which constitutes the entry point for our application. It uses the static `Run()` method of the `Application` class to start, passing in our form class as a parameter. To stop an application, we would call `Application.Exit()`.

Working with Properties

If we look at the inheritance hierarchy for `Form`, we'll notice that it is one of the WinForm controls:

```
System.Object
   System.MarshalByRefObject
      System.ComponentModel.Component
         System.Windows.Forms.Control
            System.Windows.Forms.ScrollableControl
               System.Windows.Forms.ContainerControl
                  System.Windows.Forms.Form
```

All controls inherit a common set of properties from the base `Control` class that let us control their look and feel. Some of the more commonly used properties are:

`Name` – the name of the control used to reference it in code.

`Text` – the text label shown on the control. All controls have a `Text` property, although each uses it differently. In the case of a form, the `Text` property determines the text that is to be displayed in the title bar at the top of the form. We want to set the `Text` property to display the name of our application.

`BackColor` – the background color of the control.

`Left` – the x-coordinate of a control's left edge in pixels. When dealing with position properties, keep in mind that the upper left hand corner of your form is the origin, denoted by the coordinates 0, 0.

`Right` – the distance between the right edge of the control and the left edge of its container.

`Top` – the distance in pixels between the control's top edge and the top edge of its container.

`Bottom` – the distance between the bottom edge of the control and the top edge of its container's client area.

`Height`, `Width` – the height and width of the control in pixels.

`Enabled` – a `Boolean` value indicating whether the control can respond to user interaction.

`Visible` – a `Boolean` value indicating whether the control is displayed.

`TabIndex` – the tab order of the control within its container.

`Parent` – the parent container of the control. Typically, this is a form, although it could be an intermediate-level container such as a panel.

`Anchor` – specifies which edges of the control are anchored to the edges of its container.

`Dock` – specifies which edge of the parent container a control is docked to.

Visual Studio .NET makes it easy to set properties for controls using the Properties window. In the VS.NET designer, click once on the form to make sure it's selected and open the Properties window by pressing the *F4* key or by choosing **View | Properties Window** from the menu bar:

At the top of this window is a dropdown that can be used to select the control whose properties you want to view. Below the dropdown, a series of icons appear that allow you to arrange the properties by category or alphabetically, and to switch between viewing the properties of the selected control or events associated with it.

The properties themselves are listed in the main area, with the property names on the left and their values on the right.

Find the `Text` property, and change it to Pizza Order Application and hit enter. Notice that the text in the title bar of the form in the designer changes to match.

If you're using Notepad, just add the following line to your constructor:

```
this.Text = "Pizza Order Application";
```

Adding a Control to the Form

Let's continue the example by adding a control to the form. To start with, we'll just add a simple button that we'll later use as a way to end the application. Visual Studio .NET provides a rich set of GUI controls for our applications, and they can all be added to our form in exactly the same manner as the button we're about to add.

1. If you're still in code view, choose View | Designer to open the form in design mode. Alternatively, click the PizzaOrderForm.cs [Design] tab that should appear above the code editor window, or right-click on the form in Solution Explorer and choose View Designer.

2. We add controls using the toolbox, which by default appears to the left of the VS.NET window. Choose View | Toolbox if it's not there:

For WinForms, the toolbox is organized using four tabs by default: Data, Components, Windows Forms, and General. The control we're looking for is found under the Windows Forms tab.

Windows Forms and Smart Clients

3. To add a button, select it in the Toolbox, and then draw it on the form where it is to appear. Alternatively, we can drag-and-drop it from the Toolbox onto the form, or double-click it. Place the control at the bottom-right corner of the form.

4. Using the Properties window, set the (**Name**) property to **cmdExit**. It appears in brackets at the top of the list of properties because it doesn't actually correspond to a property as such – it simply represents the identifier by which the control is to be accessed from code.

5. Set the Text property to **Exit**. Our form should now look like this:

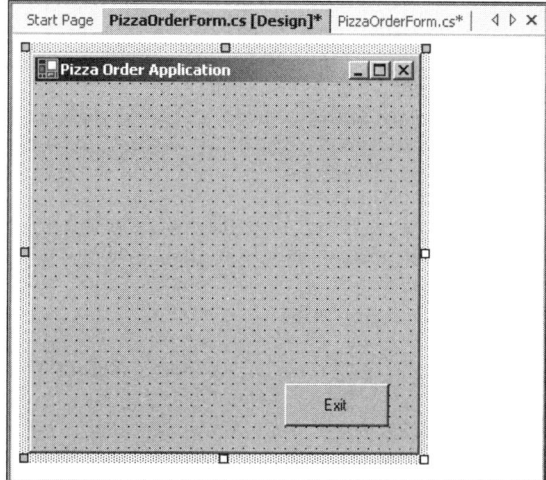

Code for the Button

Right-click on the form and select **View Code** and we'll take a look at what VS.NET has done to create the button on our form. Like a Form, a Button is also a control, and VS.NET represents it as a private member of the PizzaOrderForm that represents our WinForm:

```
public class PizzaOrderForm : System.Windows.Forms.Form
{
    private System.Windows.Forms.Button cmdExit;
    .
    .
    .
```

The button is then set up within the InitializeComponent() method in the **Designer Generated Code Region**. Notepad users should place the code in bold below inside their PizzaOrderForm class constructor:

```
private void InitializeComponent()
{
    this.cmdExit = new System.Windows.Forms.Button();
    this.SuspendLayout();
    //
```

287

```
            // cmdExit
            //
            this.cmdExit.Location = new System.Drawing.Point(192, 224);
            this.cmdExit.Name = "cmdExit";
            this.cmdExit.Size = new System.Drawing.Size(80, 32);
            this.cmdExit.TabIndex = 0;
            this.cmdExit.Text = "Exit";
            //
            // PizzaOrderForm
            //
            this.AutoScaleBaseSize = new System.Drawing.Size(5, 13);
            this.ClientSize = new System.Drawing.Size(292, 273);
            this.Controls.AddRange(new System.Windows.Forms.Control[] {
                                                       this.cmdExit});
            this.Name = "PizzaOrderForm";
            this.Text = "Pizza Order Application";
            this.ResumeLayout(false);

        }
```

Controls under Windows Forms differ significantly from their Java Swing counterparts because they wrap native operating systems controls. In this sense, Windows Forms controls are more akin to Java AWT controls.

Layout Options for Controls

Go ahead and run the application from within Visual Studio by hitting *F5*. If you're using the command-line tools, navigate to the directory containing your form, and run the following command:

```
> csc /t:winexe PizzaOrderForm.cs
```

Then, from Windows Explorer, double-click the executable that will have been created in the same directory.

When our window appears, use the mouse to resize it. As you do, you'll notice that the **Exit** button stays in the same position regardless of how large or small you make the form. We can change this behavior using the `Anchor` and `Dock` properties inherited from the `Control` class.

The Anchor Property

We can secure a control to specified edges of its container by using its `Anchor` property.

1. If you haven't already done so, stop the application by clicking the **x** on the title bar.
2. Select `cmdExit` from the dropdown at the top of the Properties window.
3. Find the `Anchor` property. When you select this property, we see it is in fact a dropdown. Open the dropdown, and highlight the bars along the sides that you want to anchor; in this case choose those on the bottom and the right:

Windows Forms and Smart Clients

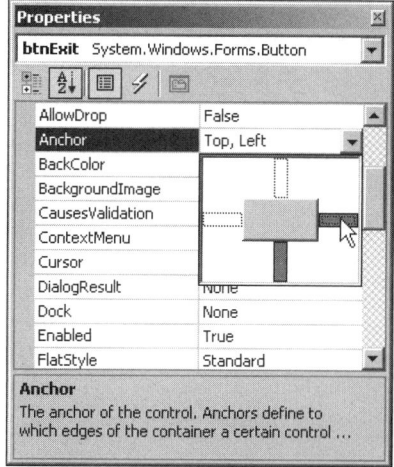

4. This adds the following code to the `InitializeComponent()` method:

```
this.cmdExit.Anchor = (System.Windows.Forms.AnchorStyles.Bottom |
            System.Windows.Forms.AnchorStyles.Right);
```

Notepad users should add this line to their constructor.

5. Run the application again by hitting *F5*, or recompiling if you're using `csc.exe`. Use your mouse to resize the window, and now the **Exit** button moves relative to the form, always staying a uniform distance from its right and lower edges.

The Dock Property

The `Dock` property works a little bit differently. Stop the application if you haven't already done so, and we'll quickly demonstrate how it works.

1. Unselect the right and bottom bars for the `Anchor` property for `cmdExit` so that the property is now set to **None**.

2. Now open the `Dock` property dropdown. This time, you are only able select one area to which to dock your control. Dock the control to the bottom of the form by clicking the corresponding area:

Chapter 8

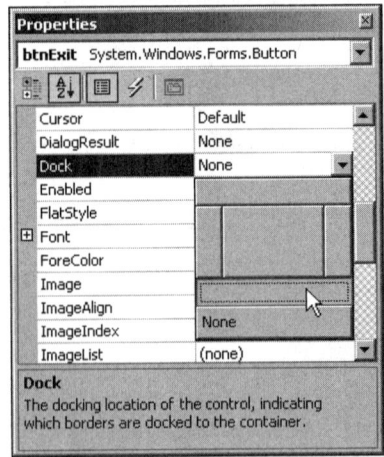

3. VS.NET adds the following line to the `InitializeComponent()` method, which Notepad users should add to their constructor in place of the `Anchor` code:

```
this.cmdExit.Dock = System.Windows.Forms.DockStyle.Bottom;
```

4. Run the application again, and note the new position and behavior of the **Exit** button as you resize the window. Feel free to experiment with the other settings for the `Dock` property – `Fill` is particularly silly, if strangely satisfying, for button controls.

   When you're through playing, reset `Dock` to **None**, and `Anchor` to **Bottom, Right**.

Event Handling

If you attempted to click the **Exit** button while the application was running, you would have noticed that although it moves as you would expect, nothing actually happens. This is because we haven't wired up any code to the button's click event. we need to create an event handler (which simply calls `Application.Exit()` in this case), and associate it with the **Exit** button.

1. In the form designer, double-click the **Exit** button, and you'll be taken to the code editor, with the cursor placed inside a blank method created by VS.NET to handle button clicks:

```
private void cmdExit_Click(object sender, System.EventArgs e)
{

}
```

2. Inside the method, insert a call to `Application.Exit()`:

```
private void cmdExit_Click(object sender, System.EventArgs e)
{
   Application.Exit();
}
```

Windows Forms and Smart Clients

3. When you now run the application, you'll find the **Exit** button works.

If you're used to events from Java Swing, you may be wondering how .NET knows this method is the handler for clicks on the `cmdExit` button, and you'd be forgiven for concluding that it's the name that tells the Framework this. However, there's more to it than this. Let's refresh our memories of how we might create a similar event handler in Java Swing:

```
cmdExit.addActionListener(new ActionListener() {
    public void actionPerformed(ActionEvent e) {
        System.Exit(0);
}});
```

The `actionPerformed()` method contains the event handling code just like the `cmdExit_Click()` method above, but we can see that the event handler is registered with the button object by calling the `cmdExit.addActionListener()` method.

In fact, VS.NET did just this same thing when we double-clicked the **Exit** button in the designer, by adding the following line to the `InitializeComponent()` method:

```
this.cmdExit.Click += new System.EventHandler(this.cmdExit_Click);
```

This code registers the `Click` event of `cmdExit` with an `EventHandler` object instantiated with our event handler method as a parameter. Notice the overloaded += operator syntax to register the event handler as opposed to the inner class used by the Java code.

Notepad users will need to add this line to their constructor, as well as the `cmdExit_Click()` method shown above, before their application will compile and run correctly.

Completing the Application

We now have a foundation for completing the rest of the application. We've seen how to add controls, set properties, manage layout, and create event handlers. To complete the Pizza application, we'll add the following controls:

- Four **RadioButtons** to present the available sizes
- A **GroupBox** to hold the four `RadioButtons`
- A **ListBox** to present the toppings
- A **Label** to serve as a caption for the toppings `ListBox`
- A **CheckBox** to check if the pizza is to be delivered
- Three **TextBoxes** to hold the customer's name, address, and driving directions
- Three more **Labels** to serve as captions for the `TextBoxes`
- A **Panel** to hold the address and directions textboxes
- A **Button** to submit the order

RadioButton and GroupBox

`RadioButtons` are logically grouped together within a `GroupBox` control to offer the user a single choice of several items represented by each button. Our mythical pizza shop sells pizza in four sizes: small, medium, large, and extra large. We're going to create a `RadioButton` for each size and group the buttons together in a `GroupBox`.

The `GroupBox` is an intermediate-level container control, and you use it as you might use a `JPanel` control in Java Swing. It is not the only intermediate-level container, however; the `Panel` control is also an intermediate-level container. We'll use a `Panel` later in the example.

We'll start by adding a `GroupBox` from the **Windows Forms** tab of the Toolbox to our form. Set the **(Name)** property of the `GroupBox` to grpSizes, and its **Text** property to **Size**.

Now we need to drag and drop four `RadioButtons` from the toolbar into the `GroupBox`. Set their properties from top to bottom as shown in the table below:

(Name)	Text
radSmall	Small
radMedium	Medium
radLarge	Large
radExtraLarge	Extra Large

Each of these controls, including the `GroupBox`, is represented by a private member variable of the appropriate type:

```
private System.Windows.Forms.Button cmdExit;
private System.Windows.Forms.GroupBox grpSizes;
private System.Windows.Forms.RadioButton radSmall;
private System.Windows.Forms.RadioButton radMedium;
private System.Windows.Forms.RadioButton radLarge;
private System.Windows.Forms.RadioButton radExtraLarge;
```

As usual, it is `InitializeComponent()` that contains the code to configure these controls, and place them in the appropriate container (the `GroupBox` is contained by the `Form`, while the radio buttons are contained by the `GroupBox`):

```
private void InitializeComponent()
{
    this.cmdExit = new System.Windows.Forms.Button();
    this.grpSizes = new System.Windows.Forms.GroupBox();
    this.radSmall = new System.Windows.Forms.RadioButton();
    this.radMedium = new System.Windows.Forms.RadioButton();
    this.radLarge = new System.Windows.Forms.RadioButton();
    this.radExtraLarge = new System.Windows.Forms.RadioButton();
    .
    .
    .
```

Windows Forms and Smart Clients

```
    this.grpSizes.Controls.AddRange(new System.Windows.Forms.Control[] {
                                                            this.radExtraLarge,
                                                            this.radLarge,
                                                            this.radMedium,
                                                            this.radSmall});
    this.grpSizes.Location = new System.Drawing.Point(8, 8);
    this.grpSizes.Name = "grpSizes";
    this.grpSizes.Size = new System.Drawing.Size(120, 152);
    this.grpSizes.TabIndex = 1;
    this.grpSizes.TabStop = false;
    this.grpSizes.Text = "Size";
    //
    // radSmall
    //
    this.radSmall.Location = new System.Drawing.Point(8, 24);
    this.radSmall.Name = "radSmall";
    this.radSmall.Size = new System.Drawing.Size(96, 24);
    this.radSmall.TabIndex = 2;
    this.radSmall.Text = "Small";
    .
    .
    .
```

The remaining radio buttons are then set up in a similar fashion, but with different positions, names, and `Text` properties. Then note how the `GroupBox` is added to the `Form` control:

```
    // PizzaOrderForm
    //
    this.AutoScaleBaseSize = new System.Drawing.Size(5, 13);
    this.ClientSize = new System.Drawing.Size(292, 273);
    this.Controls.AddRange(new System.Windows.Forms.Control[] {
                                                            this.grpSizes,
                                                            this.cmdExit});
    .
    .
    .
```

Notepad users should alter their constructor accordingly (although don't worry about `TabIndex` and `TabStop` properties). Run the application, and the form should look pretty similar to this:

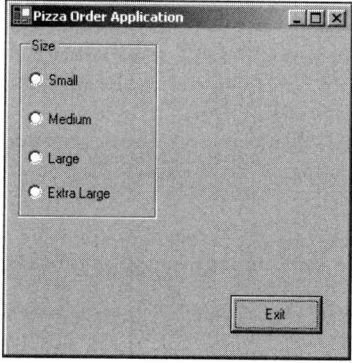

293

Now that the pizza sizes can be chosen from our form, we can move on to the toppings.

Listing Options

The `ListBox` control displays a list of items that the user can select from by clicking with the mouse. The `SelectionMode` property of the `ListBox` determines whether multiple items may be selected. We are going to use a `ListBox` to offer the choice of pizza toppings, and so we'll set the `SelectionMode` property to allow multiple items to be selected.

Items in a `ListBox` are stored inside a `Collection`. We can access this collection using the `Items` property. To access only the selected items we can use the `SelectedItems` property.

We can add items to the `ListBox` through the `Items` property in the Properties windows. An alternative approach is to bind the `ListBox` to a data source. We'll return to look at data-binding techniques later in this chapter.

1. Place a `ListBox` on the left side of your form, below the sizes `GroupBox`.

2. Set the (Name) property to **lstToppings**.

3. Select the `Items` property in the Property window, and click the ellipsis button (...) when it appears. Enter the following items in the String Collection Editor that opens:

    Pepperoni

    Mushrooms

    Anchovies

    Extra Cheese

    Sausage

    Onions

    Feel free to add any extra toppings if you like! When you're done, you may need to resize the `ListBox` so all the choices are visible.

4. Set the `SelectionMode` property to **MultiSimple**.

This last property, `SelectionMode`, has four options. `None` means you can't select anything. `One` means you can only select a single item. `MultiSimple` means a single mouse click selects or deselects an item, and `MultiExtended` means that the user must hold down the *Shift* or *Ctrl* keys to select or deselect multiple items. `MultiSimple` is the most intuitive for novice Windows users so we'll use that for the pizza application.

The only thing missing from our toppings list is a descriptive heading. We'll add that now using a `Label` control.

5. Use your mouse to move the toppings `ListBox` down a bit to accommodate the label we're about to add

6. Drag a label from the Toolbox to the space above the toppings `ListBox`.

Windows Forms and Smart Clients

7. Set the Text property of the Label to **Select Toppings**.

By now, you should be getting a feel for what VS.NET adds when we add controls in the designer. Firstly, our ListBox and Label are represented by member variables:

```
 .
 .
 .
private System.Windows.Forms.RadioButton radExtraLarge;
private System.Windows.Forms.ListBox lstToppings;
private System.Windows.Forms.Label label1;
```

These controls are then initialized in InitializeComponent():

```
private void InitializeComponent()
{
  this.cmdExit = new System.Windows.Forms.Button();
  this.grpSizes = new System.Windows.Forms.GroupBox();
  this.radExtraLarge = new System.Windows.Forms.RadioButton();
  this.radLarge = new System.Windows.Forms.RadioButton();
  this.radMedium = new System.Windows.Forms.RadioButton();
  this.radSmall = new System.Windows.Forms.RadioButton();
  this.lstToppings = new System.Windows.Forms.ListBox();
  this.label1 = new System.Windows.Forms.Label();
   .
   .
   .
```

Items are added to the ListBox in the same way that other controls are added to their container, by calling AddRange(), this time passing in an array of strings:

```
this.lstToppings.Items.AddRange(new object[] {
                                  "Pepperoni",
                                  "Mushrooms",
                                  "Anchovies",
                                  "Extra Cheese",
                                  "Sausage",
                                  "Onions"});
```

The remaining properties of the ListBox, and those of the Label, are set up as you would expect:

```
this.lstToppings.Location = new System.Drawing.Point(16, 176);
this.lstToppings.Name = "lstToppings";
this.lstToppings.SelectionMode = System.Windows.Forms.SelectionMode
                    .MultiSimple;
this.lstToppings.Size = new System.Drawing.Size(120, 82);
this.lstToppings.TabIndex = 2;
//
// label1
//
this.label1.Location = new System.Drawing.Point(16, 160);
```

```
this.label1.Name = "label1";
this.label1.Size = new System.Drawing.Size(112, 16);
this.label1.TabIndex = 3;
this.label1.Text = "Select Toppings";
```

Lastly, the `ListBox` and `Label` controls are added to their container, which is the form itself:

```
this.Controls.AddRange(new System.Windows.Forms.Control[] {
                                                    this.label1,
                                                    this.lstToppings,
                                                    this.grpSizes,
                                                    this.cmdExit});
```

Notepad users should add all the lines highlighted above to their constructor, ignoring `TabIndex` if they wish. Run the application, and the form should look like this:

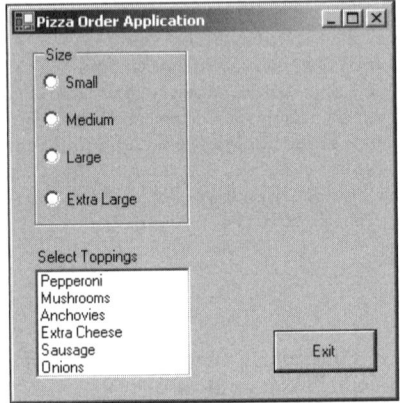

Select and deselect a few toppings to see how the `SelectionMode` property works. If you want, change the property and recompile to see the other options in action.

Our pizza application is now about half-complete. The features that we have yet to incorporate include a text field to capture the customer's name, and a checkbox that specifies whether the order is for delivery. If that's the case then we need the customer's address, which we'll capture in a textbox alongside another textbox where we can add driving directions. We're going to make these boxes invisible to the user unless delivery has been requested, which we can do by grouping the textboxes in a `Panel` control and setting the `Panel`'s `Visible` property to `False`.

Capturing User Input

We use a `TextBox` to capture text input from the user. We can place a `Label` control alongside the textbox for a descriptive caption.

The `CheckBox` normally provides a choice between two options, such as true or false, pickup or delivery, yes or no. However, if we set another property, called `ThreeState`, to `true`, the checkbox can support an additional state, called `indeterminate`. In that state, the checkbox appears grayed out on the form, to denote that it is not available in the current context. `CheckBoxes` have an event called `CheckedChanged` that occurs when the state of the box changes. We'll write a handler for `CheckedChanged` that makes the address and directions panel visible when delivery has been requested.

Let's go ahead and add a `TextBox` and `Label` for the customer name, and a `CheckBox` for delivery.

1. Place a label to the right of the sizes `GroupBox`, and set its `Text` property to **Customer Name:**.

2. Add a `TextBox` immediately below the `Label`, and set its **(Name)** property to `txtCustName`. Clear the `TextBox`'s `Text` property.

3. Drag a `CheckBox` from the `ToolBox` and place it underneath the customer name `TextBox`.

4. Set the **(Name)** property to `chkDelivery`, and set the `Text` Property to **Check here for Delivery**. Resize the `CheckBox` if necessary.

The code for these controls is quite straightforward. First the member variables are declared:

```
private System.Windows.Forms.ListBox lstToppings;
private System.Windows.Forms.Label label1;
private System.Windows.Forms.Label label2;
private System.Windows.Forms.CheckBox chkDelivery;
private System.Windows.Forms.TextBox txtCustName;
.
.
.
```

Then, they are initialized, set up, and added to the form in `InitializeComponent()`:

```
this.label1 = new System.Windows.Forms.Label();
this.label2 = new System.Windows.Forms.Label();
this.chkDelivery = new System.Windows.Forms.CheckBox();
this.txtCustName = new System.Windows.Forms.TextBox();
.
.
//
// label2
//
this.label2.Location = new System.Drawing.Point(152, 16);
this.label2.Name = "label2";
this.label2.Size = new System.Drawing.Size(100, 16);
this.label2.TabIndex = 4;
this.label2.Text = "Customer Name:";
//
// chkDelivery
//
this.chkDelivery.Location = new System.Drawing.Point(152, 64);
this.chkDelivery.Name = "chkDelivery";
this.chkDelivery.Size = new System.Drawing.Size(144, 24);
this.chkDelivery.TabIndex = 5;
this.chkDelivery.Text = "Check here for delivery";
//
// txtCustName
```

Chapter 8

```
        //
        this.txtCustName.Location = new System.Drawing.Point(152, 32);
        this.txtCustName.Name = "txtCustName";
        this.txtCustName.Size = new System.Drawing.Size(120, 20);
        this.txtCustName.TabIndex = 6;
        this.txtCustName.Text = "";
        .
        .
        .
        this.Controls.AddRange(new System.Windows.Forms.Control[] {
                                                    this.txtCustName,
                                                    this.chkDelivery,
                                                    this.label2,
                                                    this.label1,
                                                    this.lstToppings,
                                                    this.grpSizes,
                                                    this.cmdExit});
        this.Name = "PizzaOrderForm";
        .
        .
        .
```

Before we can write the event handler for CheckedChanged, we have to add the Panel and the TextBoxes to hold the customer's address and driving directions.

A Panel is a container, meaning it is a control that holds other controls. It is analogous to a JPanel under Java Swing. We're going to add a Panel to the form, inside which we'll add two TextBoxes, one to hold the customer's address and the other to hold driving directions to the customer's location. The Panel's Visible property will then determine whether all the controls that it contains appear on our form or not, and we'll set this in the CheckedChanged event handler as necessary.

5. Drag a Panel onto your form from the Toolbox, and place it beneath the delivery CheckBox. Set its **(Name)** property to pnlAddress, and its Visible property to **False**.

6. Drag two TextBoxes onto the Panel, and set the **(Name)** property for the first to txtAddress, and that for the second to txtDirections.

Clear the Text property for both.

7. Set the Multiline property for txtDirections to **True**. This will allow us to resize it to create enough space to type the directions.

8. Drag two Labels onto the Panel.

Set the Text property for the first to **Enter Address:**, and that for the second to **Enter Driving Directions:**. Align them above their respective TextBoxes.

The code for these controls is very similar to what we've already seen: private members are created and initialized for each (the Panel is of type System.Windows.Forms.Panel). The Labels and TextBoxes are configured using the same properties that we set for previous controls of that type. The Panel also is nothing new, and we add the relevant controls to it using AddRange() as with other containers:

```
//
// pnlAddress
//
this.pnlAddress.Controls.AddRange(new System.Windows.Forms.Control[] {
                                                  this.label4,
                                                  this.label3,
                                                  this.txtDirections,
                                                  this.txtAddress});
this.pnlAddress.Location = new System.Drawing.Point(152, 96);
this.pnlAddress.Name = "pnlAddress";
this.pnlAddress.Size = new System.Drawing.Size(136, 120);
this.pnlAddress.TabIndex = 7;
this.pnlAddress.Visible = false;
```

Lastly, the `Panel` itself needs to be added to the control collection of the form by modifying its `AddRange()` call. Once all of our controls are in place, we can write the `CheckedChanged` event-handler. This is the default event for `CheckBoxes` in VS.NET, so we can create the handler method signature by double-clicking it in the designer. This opens the code editor with the following new code:

```
private void chkDelivery_CheckedChanged(object sender, System.EventArgs e)
{

}
```

The `CheckedChanged` event fires when the user either checks or unchecks the `CheckBox`. We can examine the `Checked` property to determine the state of the `CheckBox`, and show or hide the `Panel` using its `Visible` property accordingly:

```
private void chkDelivery_CheckedChanged(object sender, System.EventArgs e)
{
    pnlAddress.Visible = chkDelivery.Checked;
}
```

As you may expect, Visual Studio .NET has automatically wired our event handler to the `CheckBox` inside the `InitializeComponent()` method:

```
this.chkDelivery.CheckedChanged += new System.EventHandler(
                                          this.chkDelivery_CheckedChanged);
```

You have to do this by hand of course if you don't have the IDE at your disposal. Now compile and run the application and click on the delivery `CheckBox`. The form should look like this:

Chapter 8

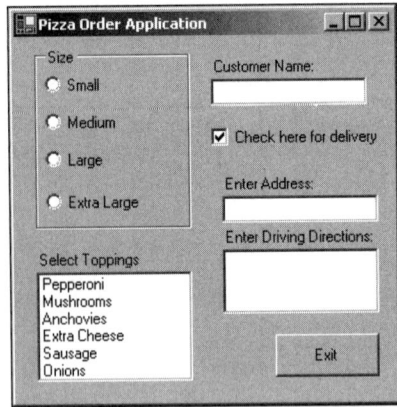

The last thing we're going to add is a submit button. In a normal application, the submit button would send the order to the kitchen for processing. In this case, as only the luckier readers will have a pizza kitchen at their disposal for test purposes, we'll just pop up a message box asking for confirmation of the order and clear the fields ready for the next order if the order is confirmed. If it's not confirmed, we'll return to the order screen.

9. Drag a button from the Toolbox and place it to the left of the **Exit** button. Set its (**Name**) property to cmdSubmit, and its Text property to **Submit**. If you've been following along in Notepad, add this button in the same way that we added the first **Exit** button.

10. Double-click on the new button to bring up the code window, and add the following code for the cmdSubmit_Click event handler:

```
private void cmdSubmit_Click(object sender, System.EventArgs e)
{
    DialogResult response = MessageBox.Show ("Please Confirm this Order",
                                "Confirm", MessageBoxButtons.OKCancel);

    if (response == DialogResult.OK)
    {
      MessageBox.Show("Order Submitted");

      // Add code to send order to kitchen if you have one

      // Clear TextBoxes for next order
      lstToppings.SelectedIndex = -1;
      txtCustName.Text = "";
      txtDirections.Text = "";
      txtAddress.Text = "";
      chkDelivery.Checked = false;
      radSmall.Checked = false;
      radMedium.Checked = false;
      radLarge.Checked = false;
      radExtraLarge.Checked = false;
    }
}
```

Windows Forms and Smart Clients

Don't forget to assign this method as the handler if you're using Notepad. Note the static `Show()` method of the `MessageBox` class that we've used to bring up a dialog. `Show()` has been overloaded a total of twelve times to provide a whole range of options for the programmer. Here is one of these overloads:

```
public static DialogResult Show(string text,
                                string caption,
                                MessageBoxButtons buttons,
                                MessageBoxIcon icon,
                                MessageBoxDefaultButton defaultButton);
```

- `text` – controls the text message that appears in the `MessageBox`.
- `caption` – sets the text in the title bar of the `MessageBox`.
- `buttons` – represents a `MessageBoxButtons` enumeration specifying a maximum of three buttons that are to appear on the `MessageBox`. The available groups are [abort, retry, ignore], [ok], [ok, cancel], [retry, cancel], [yes, no], and [yes, no, cancel].
- `icon` – an icon to indicate the category of the message to the user (this might be different for informational messages and error messages for example).
- `defaultButton` – specifies which button is the default choice for your `MessageBox`. This button will have the focus when the `MessageBox` appears.

This particular dialog asks the user to confirm the order. `MessageBox.Show()` returns a `DialogResult` enumeration that we can check to determine the user's response. If the user selects **OK**, we clear the fields of our form in preparation for the next order, and show a second message box to tell the user that the order has been processed. If they click **Cancel**, we simply return to the order screen.

Run the application now. Make a few selections and click the **Submit** button to verify that it functions correctly.

Building the Application

Once you've determined that everything is working correctly you can go ahead and build the application. Building the application will make a Windows executable out of our pizza application. To start the build process, select **Build | Build Solution** from the menu, and VS.NET will attempt to create an executable underneath the `bin` directory of your project.

> *The exact location of your executable directory will depend on whether debugging is enabled for your project. To enable debugging, select Build | **Configuration Manager** from the menu and choose **Debug** in the configuration dropdown at the top. When debugging is enabled, the compiler includes symbolic debugging information that allows the debugger to do its work. If release mode is selected, the symbolic debugging information is excluded and the application is optimized for speed. Release builds are placed under the `bin` directory in the folder called `Release`, while debug builds are placed in `Debug`.*

301

Smart Clients

Traditional standalone Windows applications, like the one we've just created, have been around for many years. In recent years, thin clients running inside a web browser have been all the rage. With the advent of .NET, Microsoft has created a new type of client called a **smart client**. Smart clients aim to combine the advantages of both the thick and thin client models. In this section, we'll discuss the advantages of each model and convert our pizza application into a smart client.

Thick clients offer two main advantages. The first advantage is client-side processing. Thick-client applications run on the desktop so they aren't robbing cycles from a remote server. The second advantage is a rich user interface. User interfaces for thick clients aren't limited by the capabilities of the web browser. The biggest disadvantage that thick clients have is the issue of distribution. Each time a new version of the software comes out it must be installed on each and every PC. Depending on the size of the organization this can become a serious issue.

Thin clients on the other hand offer easy distribution. Copy the updated application to the web server and you're set – there's no need to run installs on every machine in your corporation, or to distribute and support the update for external customers. The drawbacks of thin clients are the relatively weak UI offered by the web browser, and the fact that the majority of processing occurs on the server side: client CPU cycles are wasted while the server grinds.

Smart clients are a hybrid of thick and thin clients. They offer the easy upgrade path of thin clients with the rich UI and client-side processing of the thick-client model. The model works like this. A Windows Forms application is compiled into assemblies (DLLs) and the assemblies are published on a web server. A second application called a **loader** is created and distributed to each client. The loader is extremely small so it can be downloaded from a web server very quickly. In order to run the application, the user executes the loader, which pulls the required assemblies from the web server and starts the application. The assemblies are cached on the local machine so the download only has to occur once. In the event that one of the assemblies on the web server changes, the loader will detect it and automatically download and cache the new assembly. Thus we have the auto-update features of a thin client with the power of a traditional thick client.

To demonstrate this idea, let's make the pizza application into a smart client. To do this we have to take the following steps:

- ❏ Make an assembly out of our pizza application
- ❏ Publish this assembly to our web server
- ❏ Configure Microsoft .NET to trust the assembly
- ❏ Create the loader application, and publish it to the web server

Making the Assembly

In VS.NET, making an assembly out of our WinForms application is child's play. Right-click on the `PizzaOrder` project in Solution Explorer, and choose **Properties**. Locate the property called **Output Type**, and use the dropdown to change it to **Class Library**. When we next build the project (by selecting Build | Build Solution from the menu), VS.NET will create an assembly called `PizzaOrder.dll` in the `obj\Debug` subfolder off our project directory.

Windows Forms and Smart Clients

If you're not using VS.NET, it's perhaps even easier. We simply compile our pizza project code specifying /t:library instead of /t:winexe on the command line:

```
> csc /t:library /out:PizzaOrder.dll PizzaOrderForm.cs
```

We've also changed the name of the output file so that it's the same as that of the DLL created by VS.NET users.

Publish the Assembly

For this step, we need a virtual directory where we can copy the assembly. The best bet is to create a subdirectory off our `PizzaOrder` project folder, called something like `Web Assemblies`. Set it up as a virtual directory in IIS with a suitable name, such as `Pizza`. Copy `PizzaOrder.dll` into the directory that corresponds to the new virtual folder.

Trust the Assembly

There are security issues to be concerned with whenever you download and execute code from the Internet. To test our example, we have to use the Microsoft .NET Framework Configuration tool to tell client machines to trust the remote assembly. As the idea is that assemblies for smart clients reside on another machine rather than the local host, we need to establish **trust** with the code that we are downloading. Launch the configuration tool now (it is found in the Control Panel under **Administrative Tools**), and undertake the following steps:

1. In the left-hand panel of the tool, expand **Runtime security policy**, then **Machine**, then **Code Groups**, then **All Code**.

2. Right-click on **LocalIntranet_Zone** and select **New**.

3. Enter **TestSmartClient** as the name of the new group, and click **Next**.

4. Select **URL** in the condition type dropdown, and enter the URL for your assembly in the textbox that then appears (http://localhost/pizza/PizzaOrder.dll or something similar). Click **Next**.

5. On the next screen, make sure **FullTrust** is selected under **Use existing permission set**, and click **Next**.

6. Finally, click **Finish** on the last screen.

We now have our assembly published and ready to go. Now we need to create the loader application that will download and execute the code in the assembly.

Creating the Loader

The loader is a very slim executable responsible for downloading and launching assemblies accessed over the Internet or an intranet. In a production environment, we'd create a Microsoft Installer Package to deploy the loader, and make the installer available for download over the intranet or the Web. In this example we won't worry about creating the installer, so we can just concentrate on the loader.

Chapter 8

The loader is a very short program, and we'll create it on the command line for simplicity. You can, if you wish, create it as a C# Windows Application in Visual Studio .NET.

Create a text file called `Loader.cs`, and place the code shown below in it.

> *Note that we don't need a form for the loader, as it will use the one in our assembly. Thus, if you're using VS.NET, delete the form called `Form1.cs` that is created by default, and add a class called `Loader`, by right-clicking the project name in Solution Explorer, and choosing* **Add | Add Class**.

```csharp
using System;
using System.Reflection;
using System.Windows.Forms;

namespace PizzaLoader
{
  /// <summary>
  /// Summary description for Loader.
  /// </summary>
  public class Loader
  {
    static Assembly remoteAssembly;
    static Type remoteFormType;
    static Form remoteForm;

    public Loader()
    {
      //
      // TODO: Add constructor logic here
      //
    }

    public static void Main()
    {
      try
      {
        remoteAssembly = Assembly.LoadFrom("http://Localhost/Pizza"
                                    + "/PizzaOrder.dll");

        remoteFormType = remoteAssembly.GetType("PizzaOrder"
                                    + ".PizzaOrderForm");

        remoteForm = (Form) System.Activator.CreateInstance(remoteFormType);

        Application.Run(remoteForm);
      }
      catch (Exception e)
      {
        MessageBox.Show(e.ToString());
      }
    }

  }
}
```

Windows Forms and Smart Clients

Now I think that's pretty cool. What this code does is call `Assembly.LoadFrom()`, which is a static method of the `Assembly` class that downloads the assembly from the specified URL. Once we have the assembly, we use reflection to determine the type of the `PizzaOrder.PizzaOrderForm` class at run time through the `GetType()` method. This method takes a `string` parameter that represents the fully qualified name of the class that we want to instantiate and returns a `Type` object. The `Type` object contains metadata about the class describing the available methods, constructors, and so on. Next, we pass this `Type` object to `Activator.CreateInstance()` to create an instance of `PizzaOrder.PizzaOrderForm`. Note that we have cast it to `Form` to do so, because `CreateInstance()` always returns an `Object` type for the sake of generality. The last step is a call to `Application.Run()` passing in the form as a parameter. This will launch our application.

Testing the Smart Client

Now compile the loader by running the following command from the directory containing the class:

```
> csc /t:winexe pizzaloader.cs
```

(If you're in VS.NET, choose Build | Build Solution and the `Loader.exe` executable will be created in your project's `bin` directory.) Go ahead and execute this file, and you should see the pizza application pop up just as if it were running as a regular, local Windows application:

Because the assembly is cached locally, the application should start faster when it's next run.

Updating the Smart Client

We'll now change our pizza form to demonstrate how smart clients automatically download newer assemblies when appropriate. We'll also use this opportunity to demonstrate one of the other components .NET provides for GUI applications in addition to controls: the **Menu**.

`System.Windows.Forms.Menu` is the base class for the `MainMenu`, `MenuItem`, and `ContextMenu` classes. As a reminder, context menus are menus that appear when you click the right mouse button on a particular area of a form or control.

We'll add a `MainMenu` to our form. `MainMenu` is the container for the menu structure that appears along the top of a form. The menu is itself composed of `MenuItem` objects that become part of the `MainMenu`'s `MenuItems` collection. Once again, you can hand-code this example if you don't have Visual Studio .NET, but if you do, it makes creating menus very easy.

To keep things simple, we'll just create a very basic menu with two choices, **Submit** and **Exit**, corresponding to the buttons we've already created.

1. Double-click on the `MainMenu` control in the **Windows Forms** tab of the Toolbox. When you do this, an icon called `mainMenu1` appears beneath the form, in the area of the VS.NET designer called the **component tray**. Along the top of the form, the words **Type Here** appear in the place where the menu goes.

2. Click on the words **Type Here** and type in **File**. As you do this, you'll notice that VS.NET then gives the option of adding menu choices both below and to the right:

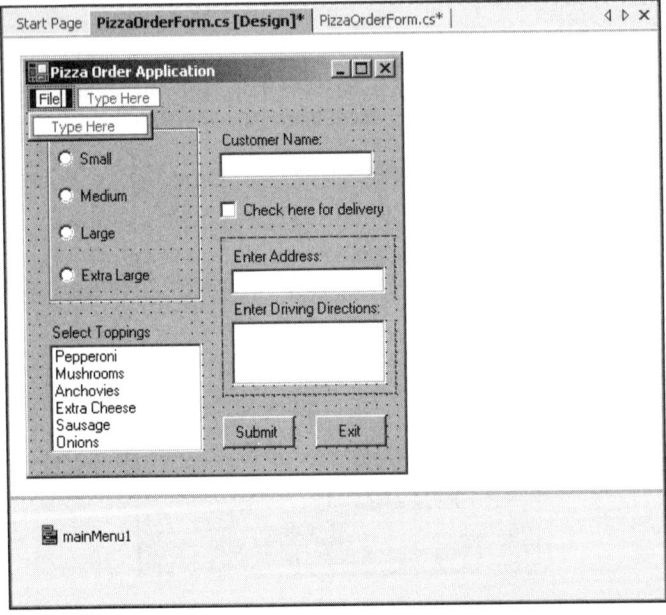

3. Beneath File, type in **&Submit**, and beneath that, **E&xit**. Note that the ampersand is a Windows convention that designates the following letter as the keyboard shortcut for that option.

Now that our menu is in place, we can handle the events that occur when you make a menu selection. Before we do that, we should go back and give our menu choices more descriptive names through the Properties window. Change the name of `menuItem1` to `mnuFile`, of `menuItem2` to `mnuFileSubmit`, and of `menuItem3` to `mnuFileExit`. Adding handlers for menu item clicks in VS.NET is done in the same way as for buttons.

4. In the designer, double-click on **Submit** in the menu. This creates the skeleton handler and associates it with mouse clicks.

Modify `mnuFileSubmit_Click` as follows:

```
private void mnuFileSubmit_Click(object sender, System.EventArgs e)
{
    cmdSubmit_Click(sender, e);
}
```

5. Repeat this for the **Exit** option, adding this code:

```
private void mnuFileExit_Click(object sender, System.EventArgs e)
{
    cmdExit_Click(sender, e);
}
```

We've simply called the corresponding button event-handler inside each menu event-handler.

The C# code for creating these menus is not too complex. As you should expect, the `MainMenu` itself is represented by a `MainMenu` private member, and each option has a corresponding `MenuItem` member in the code added by VS.NET:

```
private System.Windows.Forms.MainMenu mainMenu1;
private System.Windows.Forms.MenuItem mnuFile;
private System.Windows.Forms.MenuItem mnuFileSubmit;
private System.Windows.Forms.MenuItem mnuFileExit;
```

These are initialized in `InitializeComponent()` in just the same way as all the previous controls we've used so far. Now, each of these contains the options immediately below them. That is, the `MainMenu` only contains the **File** menu item, while the **File** item contains both **Submit** and **Exit** options. This is set up by calling `AddRange()`:

```
//
// mainMenu1
//
this.mainMenu1.MenuItems.AddRange(new System.Windows.Forms.MenuItem[] {
                                                    this.mnuFile});
//
// mnuFile
//
this.mnuFile.Index = 0;
this.mnuFile.MenuItems.AddRange(new System.Windows.Forms.MenuItem[] {
                                                    this.mnuFileSubmit,
                                                    this.mnuFileExit});
this.mnuFile.Text = "File";
```

The order of items within a particular menu is determined by the `Index` property, and `Text` of course specifies the label for each item. These properties are set for the **Submit** and **Exit** options at the same time as wiring them up to their handler methods:

```
//
// mnuFileSubmit
//
this.mnuFileSubmit.Index = 0;
this.mnuFileSubmit.Text = "&Submit";
this.mnuFileSubmit.Click += new
                        System.EventHandler(this.mnuFileSubmit_Click);
//
// mnuFileExit
//
this.mnuFileExit.Index = 1;
this.mnuFileExit.Text = "E&xit";
this.mnuFileExit.Click += new System.EventHandler(this.mnuFileExit_Click);
```

Note though that the menu isn't added to the form as other controls, but using this syntax:

```
this.Controls.AddRange(new System.Windows.Forms.Control[] {
                                            this.cmdSubmit,
                                            this.pnlAddress,
                                            this.txtCustName,
                                            this.chkDelivery,
                                            this.label2,
                                            this.label1,
                                            this.lstToppings,
                                            this.grpSizes,
                                            this.cmdExit});
this.Menu = this.mainMenu1;
.
.
.
```

Now recompile, copy the new DLL to the web server over the old one, and execute the loader once more. You will see that the loader downloads and runs the new assembly automatically.

Data-Bound Controls for WinForms

Like their counterparts in ASP.NET, Windows Forms controls support data binding to tie the data in a data source to a control for display. The data source can be almost any structure that holds data, provided that it implements the `IList` interface. All collections implement `IList`, meaning that any control that stores its items in a collection is suitable for binding to, such as the `ComboBox`, `ListBox`, `DataView`, `Table`, and so on.

Any control can bind any of its properties to a data source. Some controls, such as the `DataGrid` and `ListBox`, have the ability to bind to multiple data elements.

In this section, we'll first give an example of binding a property of a control to a single element of a collection, and then we'll bind a control to multiple elements of a collection.

Binding to Single Elements

As mentioned above, any property of a control can be bound to a data source. In this example, we'll bind the `Text` property of a `TextBox` to an `ArrayList`. We'll add a button to step through the contents of the `ArrayList` and update the `TextBox` automatically.

1. Create a new Visual C# Windows application project in VS.NET with the name `BindingExample`.

2. Add a `TextBox` and a `Button` to the form. Clear the `TextBox` contents, and set the `Text` property of the `Button` to **Step**.

3. Switch to code view, and add the code highlighted below:

   ```
   public class Form1 : System.Windows.Forms.Form
   {
     private System.Windows.Forms.TextBox textBox1;
     private System.Windows.Forms.Button button1;
     private ArrayList dataSource;
     /// <summary>
     /// Required designer variable.
     /// </summary>
     private System.ComponentModel.Container components = null;

     public Form1()
     {
       //
       // Required for Windows Form Designer support
       //
       InitializeComponent();

       //
       // TODO: Add any constructor code after InitializeComponent call
       //
       dataSource = new ArrayList();
       dataSource.Add("One");
       dataSource.Add("Two");
       dataSource.Add("Three");
       dataSource.Add("Four");
       dataSource.Add("Five");
       textBox1.DataBindings.Add("Text", dataSource, "");
     }
   ```

We've created an `ArrayList` and populated it with strings. We then bind the array to the `Text` property of the `TextBox` with this line:

```
textBox1.DataBindings.Add("Text", dataSource, "");
```

All controls have a `DataBindings` collection, and we use the `Add` method to add a new binding for any control. In the above line, the first parameter specifies the `Text` property as the property that we wish bind to. The second parameter specifies the object that we are binding it to, and the third parameter represents the "navigation path" to the data within the object.

Chapter 8

We use a navigation path of " ", which in this case causes the `ToString()` method to be called on each `ArrayList` member. This works just fine because we've stored strings in our `ArrayList`. If we had bound to an object with a property, we would specify the navigation path as `Object.PropertyName`.

The last thing to do is implement the logic to step through the `ArrayList` that will be contained in the `Button`'s click-event handler. Double-click on the button in the designer, and add the code below:

```
private void button1_Click(object sender, System.EventArgs e)
{
    BindingManagerBase bmb = this.BindingContext[dataSource];
    int pos = bmb.Position;
    int max = bmb.Count - 1;
    if (pos == max)
    {
      bmb.Position = 0;
    }
    else
    {
      bmb.Position += 1;
    }
}
```

`BindingManagerBase` manages all binding objects that are bound to the same data source and data member. We grab a reference to a `BindingManagerBase` using the `BindingContext` property of the form. The `Position` property of this object tells us the index within the `ArrayList` that we're currently bound to, while the `Count` property provides the maximum index. We use these two properties to step through the `ArrayList` as you will see when you execute the program with *F5*:

Click the **Step** button a few times to see how the binding works. Note that when we hit the top of the array, it resets, and starts over from zero.

Binding to Multiple Elements

To show this, we'll simply add a `ListBox` control to the form we've just created, and one line of code to perform the data binding.

Drag a `ListBox` from the Toolbox onto the form, and place it beneath the **Step** button. You may need to resize the form to accommodate the `ListBox`. Then add the following line of code to the form constructor:

```
public Form1()
{
  //
  // Required for Windows Form Designer support
```

Windows Forms and Smart Clients

```
        //
        InitializeComponent();

        //
        // TODO: Add any constructor code after InitializeComponent call
        //
        dataSource = new ArrayList();
        dataSource.Add("One");
        dataSource.Add("Two");
        dataSource.Add("Three");
        dataSource.Add("Four");
        dataSource.Add("Five");
        textBox1.DataBindings.Add("Text", dataSource, "");
        listBox1.DataSource = dataSource;
    }
```

That's all we have to do to bind to the `ArrayList`. Go ahead and run the application, and the form should look something like this:

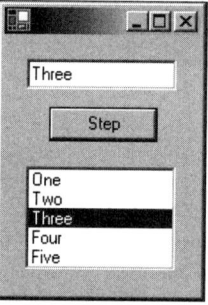

An interesting point to note here is that when you click the **Step** button, the selected item in the `ListBox` changes in sync with the `Text` property of the `TextBox`. This happens because the `BindingManagerBase` object manages **all** binding objects that reference the same data source, and hence the controls stay in sync because they point to the same `ArrayList`.

Summary

This chapter has aimed to provide you with a good overview of the Windows Forms application model. First, we created a small GUI application, introducing the Visual Studio .NET IDE and its Toolbox.

We saw how to work with properties and demonstrated various ways to add controls to a form, and investigated the code VS.NET creates for controls we add in the IDE. We also got a flavor for the event-based model that underpins .NET WinForms applications.

Once our WinForm was up and running, we had a go at turning it into a Smart Client. The smart client offers the best of both the thin-client and thick-client application models, and converting a standalone application into one is far from difficult. The loader application we created is also very simple, yet it allows our users to download the latest version of the client software. It also provided an opportunity to examine how reflection works in .NET a little bit.

Finally, we introduced data binding for Windows Forms, looking at how to bind to both single and multiple data elements. Key items for data binding are the `DataBindings` collection, and the `BindingContext` object, which returns a reference to the `BindingManagerBase`.

Enterprise Components

In this chapter we will be considering how .NET provides enterprise application development support in the form of the `System.EnterpriseServices` library and COM+.

Since there may be a lot of readers that work with some of the J2EE API's but don't really work with all facets of the standard, we're going to start off with a quick recap of what J2EE is and what it offers in the way of Enterprise Support for your applications. This should provide a thorough grounding in understanding the key differences in .NET Enterprise Services as compared to what is offered by the J2EE Specification.

J2EE Support for Enterprise Applications

J2EE is a standard that you can build your application to conform to. This enables your application to take advantage of the enterprise services J2EE-compliant application servers provide. In this section, we will be covering exactly what J2EE provides in the form of enterprise services and how it corresponds to .NET.

> **The goal for J2EE is to provide a simple, unified standard for distributed applications through a component-based application model**

Here is an architectural diagram of the current J2EE 1.3.1 specification:

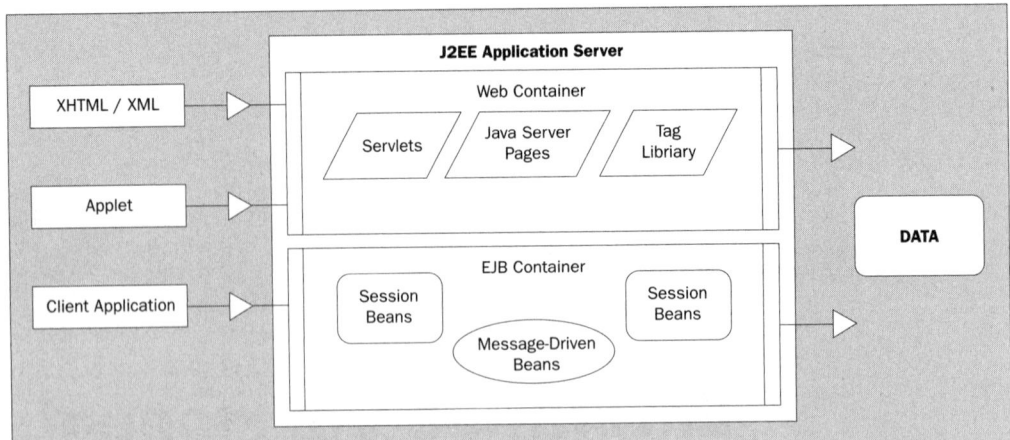

The diagram above illustrates that the J2EE Application Server is where the J2EE standard is implemented. The Application Server provides a standardized means for client applications to communicate with J2EE-compliant application components such as Enterprise Java Beans (EJB), Java Servlets, and Java Server Pages. Two types of containers manage these components:

- The Web Container
- The EJB Container

The web container manages components related to presentation and the EJB container manages components containing your business logic. The containers provide your component with access to a whole host of J2EE-compliant API's and J2EE Application Server Services with which it is able to execute its business logic and communicate with many different types of data sources. These topics will be covered in-depth at a later stage in this chapter.

In this section we will cover:

- The J2EE Platform
- J2EE Technologies
- J2EE Deployment

The J2EE Platform

The J2EE Platform is composed largely of three core components:

- The J2EE Runtime Infrastructure for deploying J2EE applications
- J2EE Container Architecture
- The J2EE API's for building J2EE applications

The J2EE Runtime Infrastructure

The physical implementation of the J2EE Runtime Infrastructure specification is the J2EE **application server**. The J2EE Specification does not explicitly specify how a J2EE application server should, or could, be built but rather abstracts this logic into **roles** and **interfaces** within which applications can interact. This, in turn, results in a clear demarcation between what the application is and what the runtime is, which means that every J2EE Application Server vendor is afforded the creative license to implement the runtime infrastructure as best they see fit, provided they adhere to the standards in the J2EE Specification.

Part of the original design goal of the J2EE specification was application portability. This is provided through each J2EE Application server's conformance to the J2EE Runtime Specification. For example, if your application is J2EE Compliant, you can move it from one vendor's J2EE Application Server to another's with minimal hassle. Thus your J2EE Application is J2EE Application Server agnostic. This is something to keep in mind when evaluating the .NET Framework, as your .NET applications will currently only run on the Microsoft .NET Framework. As has been mentioned before, Microsoft has an effort in place with the ECMA to standardize the Common Language Infrastructure (the .NET Runtime infrastructure specification) in order to have a similar specification concept to that of J2EE where other vendors can build .NET Application Servers that support the CLI. More information can be found on this in Chapter 1.

In J2EE, the core services that the runtime provides are there to minimize the effort developers need to expend on typical enterprise tasks, such as object pooling, distributed transactions, resource management, application security and messaging. These enterprise services are managed by what is known as the **container**, which frees developers from the time-consuming tasks of developing all these services themselves since their application components can simply use the Java Naming and Directory Interface (JNDI) to look up the container-provided services for use within their application. We will hear more about containers in the next section.

J2EE Container Architecture

The J2EE Runtime Specification uses containers to facilitate the abstraction of the application from the Application Server. A J2EE container provides access to the J2EE APIs and assists in managing the application components. In the .NET platform there is only one type of container, which also supports container managed enterprise services. Both the J2EE and .NET containers provide largely the same enterprise services; however, they conform to different implementation specifications. The .NET container is known as COM+ and will be covered in the .NET section of this chapter, later.

The J2EE Container provides runtime services such as:

- Lifecycle management of application components
- Connection and Component Pooling
- Management of the JNDI namespace
- Load Balancing and Clustering
- Client Session Management
- Persistence
- Transaction Management
- Authentication and Access Control

Chapter 9

A comparison will be made between the J2EE Container Managed Enterprise Services and the COM+ Services in the .NET section of this chapter. Now that we have covered what services the containers provide, let's take a look at the two main types of containers:

- Web containers
- EJB containers

The most commonly used containers are the Web and EJB containers that implement the Java Servlet and JSP APIs and EJB API respectively. The containers liaise between your client applications and the custom applications within the containers. Within the J2EE Specification, the custom applications within your containers are known as **application components**.

The container comprises largely the components listed below:

- The Component Contract
- The Container Service API's
- Declarative Services

Component Contracts

Since J2EE specifies that all application components must run within the JVM of the container, the container is therefore responsible for managing the lifecycle of the application components. Component contracts are therefore a set of interfaces and classes your application components are required to implement and extend in order to ensure a standard with which they can be managed by the container.

In .NET this is accomplished in one step by creating a component that extends from the `System.EnterpriseServices` library. Once this has been done and your component registered, you can open the COM+ Administrative console and manage the container-managed services that your component makes use of. An example of this would be modifying the ceiling of your component's object pool.

Container Service APIs

The container service APIs provide a layer of abstraction to enable your application components to make use of the container managed services such as JNDI, JMS, and JCA. The container handles the creation and allocation of these services without you working directly with the services themselves.

The container management provides lifecycle management of application components, resource pooling and application component management. The .NET equivalent of this is the `System.EnterpriseServices` library, which provides programmatic access to the COM+ container services.

Declarative Services

The declarative services include technologies such as the **deployment descriptor**, which enables the developer to specify to the container, via XML files that exist outside your application, how to manage and configure the application components.

Enterprise Components

For example, instead of explicitly developing transactions inside your component, you can specify in the descriptor that you want certain components instantiated within the context of a transaction. In the case of a Java Servlet you can specify which context and URL or URLs you want the Servlet bound to on the Application Server. The descriptor is also used to set up your application security privileges.

.NET accomplishes this task through a number of means:

- Assemblies
- Component Services Manager (COM+ Administration)
- Attributal programming

In brief, Assemblies assist in providing the configuration and deployment on your .NET Application Server and clients for your application as a whole. They are not used to explicitly configure COM+ enterprise services. Actually, that is done via the Component Services Manager, which enables you to use a GUI tool to select your enterprise component and configure it. This is similar in appearance to how some J2EE Application Servers provide GUI tools for configuring your deployment descriptor. The Component Services Manager is covered in more depth in the .NET section of this chapter.

As an introduction to attributal programming, let's give an example as to why it would need to be used. In most cases, certain parts of an application should be configurable and certain parts should not. For instance, you do not want your J2EE Application Server administrator to edit your deployment descriptor and change a method that your core application logic relies on as being transactional, and make it non-transactional. In .NET, attributal programming enables you to add metadata within your code, which is discoverable at application run time, to explicitly define facets of your component's behavior. For example, you could use attributal programming to explicitly state that a particular method must be transactional and therefore guarantee that it will be at run time.

This is quite similar in concept to the Open Source Java Xdoclet tool, however Xdoclet is capable of ensuring this behavior at compile time, while attributal programming provides this behavior at run time.

The J2EE APIs

In order to minimize the amount of work involved interacting with the runtime services, core sets of implementation agnostic J2EE APIs are provided. These are known as the J2EE APIs:

J2EE API	Description	.NET Equivalent or Similar
Java Database Connectivity (JDBC)	This is the API for standard database interaction, connections and connection pooling.	ADO.NET `System.Data.*`
J2EE Connector API (JCA)	This enables you to create portable component drivers that provide support for legacy or unusual data sources.	MS Host Integration Server XA Interoperability, COM Transaction Integrator, and Legacy Data Source Support
Java API for XML Parsing (JAXP)	This API enables you to process XML documents using DOM, SAX, and XSLT.	`System.Xml.*`

Table continued on following page

J2EE API	Description	.NET Equivalent or Similar
Java Server Pages (JSP)	This API provides for template-driven dynamic web applications.	ASP.NET
Java Servlets	This API provides object-oriented abstractions for building dynamic web applications.	ASP.NET
Enterprise Java Beans (EJB)	A framework for multi-tier container-managed server-side components.	COM+ `System.EnterpriseServices.*`
Java Naming and Directory Interface (JNDI)	This enables you to work with a directory service resource and to look up interfaces to resources like EJB's.	Active Directory Services Interface (ADSI) `System.DirectoryServices.*`
Java Message Services (JMS)	This API provides a standard way for Java programs to create, send, receive, and read message in an enterprise messaging system.	Microsoft Message Queuing (MSMQ) `System.Messaging.*`
Java Transaction API	The API for creating, committing, and rolling back a transaction.	`System.EnterpriseServices.*`
JavaMail and Java Activation Framework (JAF)	This enables you to send, retrieve, and compose e-mail messages. JAF is used for working with e-mail attachments.	Collaboration Data Objects (CDO) Messaging API (MAPI) `System.Web.Mail.*`
Remote Method Invocation over the Internet Inter-ORB Protocol (RMI-IIOP)	An application communication protocol for applications distributed over two tiers.	.NET Remoting `System.Runtime.Remoting.*`

In .NET we use the `System.EnterpriseServices` library to interact with COM+ in much the same manner that we'd use the J2EE APIs to interact with the container-managed services in Java. An example of this would be that `System.Xml.*` provides much the same functionality as the JAXP API does. Check out Chapter 8, for more information on this subject.

J2EE Technologies

The J2EE standard comprises three core technologies that enable the developer to build scalable, distributed applications for enterprise:

- ❏ Component technologies
- ❏ Service technologies
- ❏ Communications technologies

Component Technologies

We have already covered the fact that the J2EE standard specifies two types of containers (Enterprise Java Beans and Web containers). The component technologies within the web container are Servlets and Java Server Pages and the component technologies within the EJB container are Enterprise JavaBeans.

Servlets and JSP pages are server-side programs that allow your application logic to interact within HTTP Requests and Responses.

Enterprise JavaBeans take the next step up by allowing you to write distributed, scalable, transactional, and secure applications by separating the application logic from the system services. For example, you would only write your component as an EJB if it needed to make use of the above-mentioned services. If you did not need that functionality you would simply stick to writing either a Servlet or a set of JSP pages (provided that it's a web application that you are developing).

You can choose to implement EJB in one of three models:

- Session beans
- Entity beans
- Message-driven beans

Enterprise JavaBeans are very similar in concept to .NET ServicedComponents which are managed by the COM+ container, and I would say if you wanted an easy way to put COM+ into perspective then look on them as the Microsoft alternative to Enterprise JavaBeans. COM+, however, has no session and entity beans model. All components that you wish to be managed by the COM+ container inherit from what is known as a ServicedComponent; but more of that later.

Sessions Beans

There are two types of session beans:

- Stateful session beans
- Stateless session beans

Stateful session beans are created at the start of the client session and are destroyed when the session is over. They are stateful transient objects that are used to perform application requests on behalf of the client. A good example of this would be the logic behind a shopping cart within an online e-commerce application.

Stateless session beans live up to their name and hold no state on the server. They are generally used to contain business logic that does not contain client state. An example of this would be simple data-tier interaction.

Entity Beans

Entity Beans can be deployed in two fashions:

- Bean-managed persistence (BMP)
- Container-managed persistence (CMP)

BMP necessitates that the developer place all database interaction logic within the bean's code. CMP is designed so that the container manages all the database interaction. For instance, say you had an `item` table that contained data about the items you had in your inventory. You could create a CMP entity bean that would represent your table and fields, by mapping your CMP bean's state to the respective fields in your table. In this way, you could manipulate the data inside your table automatically by changing the attributes of the bean. The J2EE specification allows the developer to choose between CMP and BMP.

One of the really, really cool things that sets J2EE apart is the fact that it has supports Container-Managed Persistence. Unfortunately, the .NET Container has no support for CMP; however, Microsoft is investigating the issue and there are *possibly* plans afoot to include it in a later release of .NET. Thus currently, if you want to implement an equivalent of an Entity Bean in .NET it will have to use Bean-Managed Persistence.

Message-Driven Beans (MDB)

Message-driven beans are stateless, container-managed EJB's that facilitate asynchronous, transaction-aware messaging via message-oriented middleware (MOM). An example of a particular MOM is an IBM MQ Series Application Server. Using the MOM you are able to configure queues, on which applications can place Java Messages (`javax.jms.message`) using the Java Message Service API (JMS). The MOM then facilitates guaranteed delivery to the messages' destination.

The J2EE specification is deliberately MOM-agnostic, and therefore an MDB can communicate with any Vendor implementation of a MOM provided it conforms to the J2EE specification. In .NET this is different in that you are currently restricted to the use of the Microsoft Message Queue (MSMQ) Application Server as your MOM. In J2EE, where the developer uses the JMS API to communicate with the MOM, the .NET developer uses the `System.Messaging` API, which is a part of the .NET Base Class libraries.

The services offered are inherently the same; however, the COM+ container does not manage messaging in .NET, whereas the J2EE Application Server implements container-managed messaging for message-driven beans.

Service Technologies

Although the container run-time services usually provide the means for you to concentrate solely on business logic, there are times when you will need to dig a little deeper into the architecture to access these services directly.

Examples of some of the technologies available at service level are:

- Java Database Connectivity (JDBC)
- Java Transaction API Service (JTA)
- JNDI (Java Naming and Directory Service)

Communication Technologies

In order for a distributed application to truly live up to its name, support for an extensive set of communication technologies needs to be provided. These include the Java Message Service (JMS), JavaMail and JAF, Internet protocols, and Remote Object protocols. I have provided a breakdown of the last two sets of technologies here:

Enterprise Components

Internet Protocols
- Hyper-Text Transfer Protocol (HTTP)
- TCP/IP (Transmission Control Protocol over Internet Protocol)
- SSL (Secure Socket Layer)

Remote Object Protocols
- Remote Method Invocation (RMI)
- JAX-RPC
- Remote Method Invocation over Inter-Orb Protocol (RMI-IIOP)
- Java IDL

J2EE Deployment

The EAR (Enterprise Archive) file is similar to a JAR or a ZIP file with the exception that it contains an archive of your entire application. This file contains the application components as well as their configured properties within their respective containers.

Once an EAR file is ready for deployment, you will need to copy the it onto the application server and install it. This process varies depending upon which vendor's application server implementation of the J2EE standard you are using. A lot of modern J2EE Application Server's allow you to simply select the EAR file and the server will take care of the rest of the installation. Some examples of these are IBM Websphere, JBOSS, and BEA Weblogic.

.NET has a new technology that also eases deployment greatly. Microsoft has finally gotten rid of the Windows registry and replaced it with Application Assembly Files. Deployment was briefly touched upon in Chapter 1.

.NET Support for Enterprise Applications

In the first part of the chapter we reminded ourselves of how J2EE provides enterprise services to applications that make use of its specification. For the remainder of this chapter we will consider how the same results can be achieved under the .NET Framework.

We will be covering the following key topics:

- The `System.EnterpriseServices` library
- COM+ Services

The `System.EnterpriseServices` library enables your application to leverage the runtime infrastructure provided by COM+ Services. Thus COM+ provides the services, while the library provides the means for your class to extend them. Since these two are so tightly interwoven we have chosen to present them to you as one topic, since you will be more interested in programming the services anyway; COM+ is the container that manages the enterprise services that are available in .NET. Thus when you create an .NET Component that extends the `ServicedComponent` class it demarcates your class to the .NET Framework as a class that is to be managed by COM+. COM+ has a GUI available called the Component Services Manager, with which you can navigate to your managed component and adjust the configurations on the services that it is making use of.

The System.EnterpriseServices Library

Below I have included a snapshot of the services that COM+ provides and how they compare to J2EE. There is in-depth coverage of the more important services at a later stage in this chapter:

COM+ Service	Description	J2EE Equivalent or Similar Functionality
Automatic Transaction Processing	Applies declarative transaction-processing features.	J2EE Declarative Services
COM Transaction Integrator (COMTI)	COMTI enables COM+ to execute applications that run under Customer Information Control System (CICS) and Information Management System (IMS).	J2EE Connector Architecture (JCA)
Compensating Resource Managers (CRMs)	Applies atomicity and durability properties to non-transactional resources that are managed by the MS Distributed Transaction Co-ordinator (MS DTC).	No direct equivalent
Just-In-Time Activation	Activates and De-activates objects on an as-needed basis. Once an object is de-activated when new call arrives for the object, it is re-activated 'Just-In-Time', the call is serviced, and the object later de-activated.	J2EE Container Managed Object Activation and Passivation
Loosely Coupled Events	Manages creation of and subscription to object-based (not UI-based) events that are quite similar to the 'publisher-subscriber' model.	No direct equivalent
Object Construction	This enables you to write components with the intention that they will be generic. They are written to be able to be customized for a particular task by their constructor strings, which can be specified by the application administrator at deployment.	No direct equivalent

COM+ Service	Description	J2EE Equivalent or Similar Functionality
Object Pooling	The COM+ Container provides a configurable pool of ready-made objects on the server, for use by calling applications.	J2EE Container Managed Component Pooling
Queued Components	Provides asynchronous component queuing for distributed applications. This is different from message queuing.	Remote Method Invocation (RMI)
Role-Based Security	Applies security permission based on roles.	J2EE Role-Based Security
Shared Property Manager (SPM)	COM+ uses the SPM to share transient state information between multiple objects within a server process. Transient state is state information stored in memory that will not survive a server crash.	No direct equivalent
Synchronization	COM+ provides synchronization and concurrency management that determines when a thread can dispatch a call to an object and prevents more than one caller from accessing a component concurrently.	J2EE Container Managed Synchronization
XA Interoperability	This COM+ Service enables you to write ServicedComponents that can access databases that support the X/Open transaction-processing model.	J2EE Connector Architecture (JCA)

COM+ Overview

> COM+ is the container that manages components that make use of enterprise services.

A Brief History Lesson

Microsoft has revolutionized its existing application architecture models with .NET. So much has changed that in fact, if you are only entering Bill's realm now, I wouldn't really think it worth your while to go back and learn how things were done before! Previously, Microsoft's technology for developing reusable application components was known as the Component Object Model (COM). COM provided basic services such as object location and instantiation and cross-context and cross-process marshaling, but the model required the developer to expend a considerable amount of effort to include functionality required for enterprise applications. COM Developers were later able to make use of the Distributed Component Object Model (DCOM), which extended the original COM principle but enabled developers to write reusable distributed components.

Microsoft Transaction Server (MTS) was then provided so that COM developers could implement additional functionality within their components such as transactions, thread pooling, scalability, database connection pooling, and rule-based security. This made developers' jobs easier.

COM+ then improved on this functionality so that developers could write code that accessed a runtime infrastructure that provided these services, rather than write all the code themselves.

It is important to note that COM+ is not the latest version of the COM; it is rather **a container** that provides an amalgamation of the services provided in COM, DCOM, and MTS, which are made available to COM components, .NET components, and even entities that are not considered components such as ASP pages. Its ease of use is exemplified by the ability to write substantially less code to make the same use of enterprise services. The technology itself is fully compatible with architectures ranging from two-tier to n-tier.

The COM+ services infrastructure can be extended by both managed and unmanaged code and it is important to understand that rather than embedding logic that performs enterprise services, you are actually subscribing your component to those services. It also provides the developer with the ability to write a managed component as if it were single threaded since the infrastructure takes care of object and thread pooling as well as transaction logic.

The Component Services Manager

The Component Services Manager is your administrative console for managing your COM+ Services. You can access it by going to:

Start | [Settings] | Control Panel | Administrative Tools | Component Services

You are now within the **Microsoft Management Console** (MMC). This is a type of shell in which you can initialize snap-ins. If you followed the above route you'll have just loaded up the Component Services snap-in on its own.

There is a second approach, which you as a developer might find useful, however. It is possible to create a display from which you can manage all the services running on your Windows system, through the MMC (SQL Server, IIS, Exchange, and so on).

To do this navigate to Start | Run | Window and then type MMC You can then add the snap-in of COM+ by clicking on File | Add/Remove Snap-in, which will display the console shown:

Enterprise Components

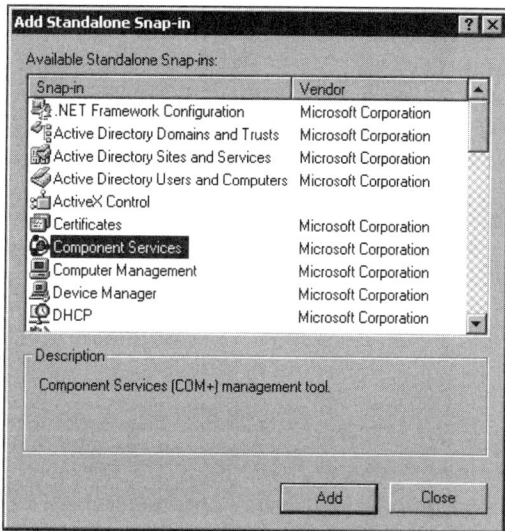

Once you've followed one of these approaches, you are now able to start administering your COM+ components.

I have included the Component Services Manager window below, which displays how you are able to access and administer your COM+ applications. Within each application there are three management tabs for configuring your application **Components**, the **Roles** (security) for your components and your **Legacy Components**:

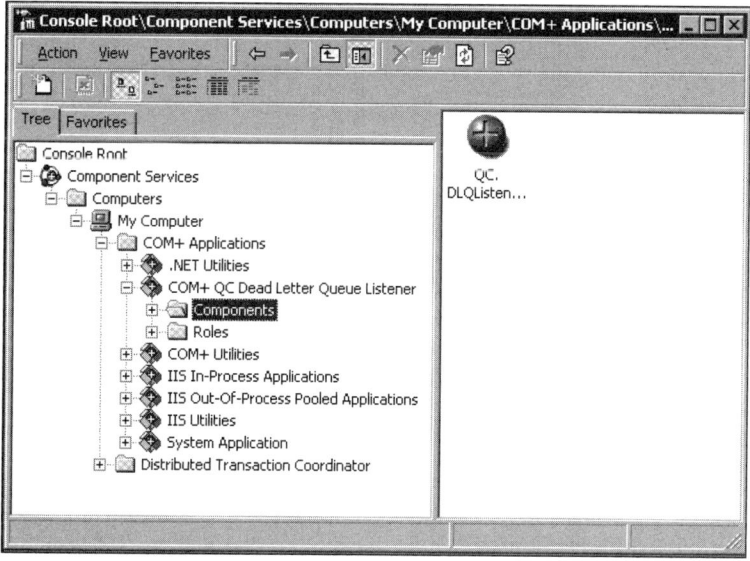

Transactions

Each class you have written that extends a `ServicedComponent` can have transaction support enabled simply by using the Component Services Manager for COM+. By navigating to the **Properties** of your component you can select the level of transaction support you need by selecting one of the options underneath the **Transactions** tab. Here's an example:

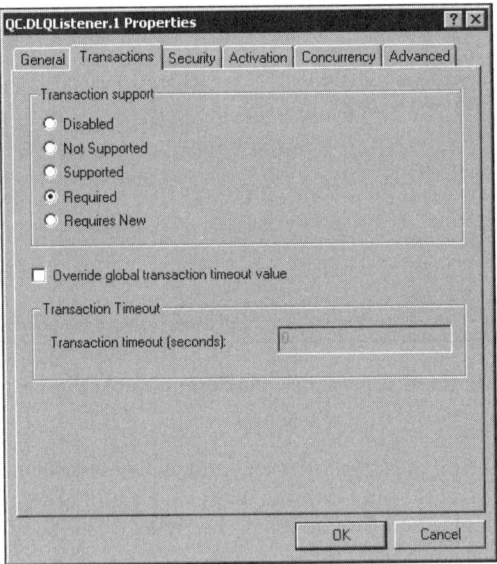

The Distributed Transaction Co-ordinator (DTC) is a core component of the Windows Operating System and it is responsible for managing all transactions. The DTC specifies an interface that all components that wish to make use of it must support; in addition components also need to provide a resource manager that is able to commit or roll back when informed accordingly.

> COM+ encapsulates the DTC functionality within contexts. Every COM+ object that is instantiated exists within its own object context.

Just-in-Time Activation (JIT Activation)

JIT is a pretty cool concept for stateless applications. Later we will learn how resources are managed through component queuing, and JIT goes hand-in-hand with that in the overall task of resource conservation.

When you are developing an enterprise application, the bulk of that application exists on the server making your server resources very precious. JIT is a feature of COM+ that manages the fine line between object instantiation and resource allocation.

What it does is allow your object to be instantiated **once** at the start of your application's use of it and then let you use it at your discretion throughout the application's lifetime. JIT actually de-allocates the space allocated to your objects when they are not being used, and then rudely arouses them from their slumber at the instant they are needed. Thus the memory allocated to your object is freed up while it is temporarily asleep.

This allows the client to hold references to numerous objects without worrying about bogging down the server. Of course, memory de-allocation for managed objects is handled by the Garbage Collector.

Security

Security in application development is largely about access to resources and permission to execute certain logic. COM+ provides two core types of security for your components:

- code-access security
- role-based security

Code-Access Security

Code-access security allows an administrator to assign which code can access a particular resource and which code cannot. It is designed to protect resources from malicious code and manages code depending on how much the Common Language Runtime trusts it. This is an extremely useful state of affairs to have when you're implementing code from un-trusted sources. For example, if a user tried to execute an application that attempted to download and execute some code off the web, the default security policy would throw an exception and the application would fail to start.

When a piece of **unmanaged** code attempts to access a resource, the .NET Framework provides code access permission classes that you can implement to check if the code has the necessary rights to do what it is trying to do. If you like you can even write your own custom permission classes where you can explicitly state how you want the access permissions to be implemented.

This is similar in concept to the Java Security Manager, which a Java application can create and install. Once you have the Security Manager, you can then request permission to approve or decline certain operations. You can write your application to check to see if a particular operation is declined, as it will then throw a `SecurityException`.

Role-Based Security (RBS)

Role-based security allows you to specify roles and assign privileges according to those roles. This means that you can add **Users** and **Groups** from the Windows Security model to your Roles and therefore grant or deny access accordingly. To enable role based security, serviced components largely require roles to be assigned to key resources at deployment via the Component Services Manager.

For example, if you are designing a financial application for a Mobile Home Superstore, in Texas, and you want to provide only certain information to salesman, while providing more extensive information to managers, then you would create a sales role and a manager's role.

You would then add your sales people to the sales role, which would restrict Cletus and Jim-Bob in the Sales Department to access limited to their positions/role while Earl and Junior in Management would have more extensive access in accordance with the role they belong to.

Object Pooling and State Management

Object pooling allows you to exert tighter control over your server resources by creating a pool of objects for a particular component when your application is started. This way your objects are created before they are ever requested, which offers faster response times. This is useful if your object instantiation is an expensive operation such as creating a connection.

327

You can also specify the ceiling of how many objects you want to be created; thus once all the components in the pool are being used, new requests for an object get placed in a queue and have to wait their turn until an object is released. This is really useful in the area of memory management as each object takes up a certain amount of memory, so placing a ceiling on an object pool can be used to limit the amount of memory a particular application can take.

Each object in the pool holds the same state, so no matter which object you get assigned it will be the same as the last one. You typically would use object pooling when instantiation of multiple objects is very costly to you in terms of resources, like an all-expenses paid trip to the database. So you pre-create them and control how many can be created.

This is almost identical in concept to J2EE Container-managed component pooling.

Component Queuing

The .NET Queued Components provide the functionality for you to simply check a checkbox on your component that demarcates it as a queued component.

If you have specified in your client application that you wish to instantiate the component as queued then there is a special kind of proxy on the client with which the application communicates. That proxy sequences every call that is made as well as the parameters of those calls. Once the application signals that its work with the component is done, the sequences are placed on a MSMQ managed queue that is then delivered to the MSMQ Server.

On the server, there are two technologies that facilitate your component being passed the calls. The first is the **asynchronous listener**, which awaits calls arriving on its queue. When the listener receives a message it delivers it to a special stub called the **queued component player** that delivers the calls in sequence to the component as if the client was making them.

Implementation is made easy by the fact that the deployment requirements simply need you to install and configure your component using the Component Services Manager. The COM+ infrastructure will take care of the rest.

Event Support

Eventing is described in a lot of places as the old 'publisher-subscriber' model. It is seen as a way to be able to extend your application at a later stage without having to modify the existing code.

This is accomplished by creating and registering an event interface with the classes that you wish to be able to raise the event. These are known as **publishers**. In turn, you can register classes with the interface that you wish to notify about the event, and these are known as **subscribers**. This enables you to let components interoperate in a very loosely coupled design.

The concept is different, but the implementation seems rather similar to the way exceptions can be built and thrown in Java. Also, Java has the listener model in which you can subscribe to certain events, so that when the event occurs you are notified.

Component Load Balancing

The Component Load Balancing Service provides the ability to spread your application objects out over several servers, which greatly improves your resource management options.

The concept is also known as server farming and is implemented by using a Windows 2000 Advanced Server or Windows 2000 Data Center as a Component Load Balancing Server. The CLB Server uses an algorithm that checks which server currently has the best resources available and assigns the client's request to that server. The algorithm is designed so that it proceeds down a list of available servers, passing the client requests to the first available server. The list is sorted in descending order from the most robust server to the least robust server. Because of this sort order, the most able hosts are more likely to receive the requests.

> *After a client's request has been assigned via the CLB to a particular server, future communication continues unhindered by the CLB. There is no assurance that the client's server object will continue to be hosted on a particular server. Therefore, the components must be stateless and object pooling is deliberately not supported.*

Putting COM+ into Practice

Often, the easiest way to grasp implementation is to review simple examples. So we will start off by creating a simple component that has transaction support. The example will display how one creates a component that is able to make use of the COM+ Container's Enterprise Services. We will build on what we have just learned and investigate how to write a **container-managed transaction** and how to implement object pooling and JIT Activation. We will also detail how to configure your assembly file and create your own strong name key. Finally, we will conclude by writing a client application that is able to instantiate our ServicedComponent and call its transactional method.

> *Remember, all the code examples in this chapter are available for download from www.wrox.com*

Writing your ServicedComponent

You will want to start off by creating a new Visual C# Project in Visual Studio .NET and selecting a new **Class Library Project**. Give your project an appropriate name as it will be used in assigning a name to your type library and entry in the Component Services Manager (we called ours **EnterpriseCOM**). Proceed by clicking on the **OK** button. Below I have attached an example of what this should look like:

> *For readers using the Standard Edition of Visual C#, the IDE does not allow you to create Class Libraries. However it will allow you to open them. There is a skeleton class library available for download with this book's sample code that will allow you to continue this example.*

Now on the right-hand side of the screen in your **Solution Explorer** window you will see two files, `Class1.cs` and `AssemblyInfo.cs`. The former is the file that will contain your COM+ code and the latter is where you specify all your assembly configurations.

You may want to highlight `Class1.cs` in the **Solution Explorer** window and use the **Properties** Window to give it a more suitable filename, such as `Example.cs`, much as you would do in Java when you were naming a class. If the properties window is not in view, you can hit *F4* to bring it up. Now double-click `Class1.cs` (or whatever you renamed it to) and you should see the source code load up in the main body of Visual Studio .NET.

Now before you get coding you will need to add a reference to the `System.EnterpriseServices` library since it provides all the COM+ functionality you are going to need in your component.

Chapter 9

To do this, select **Project | Add Reference** and select `System.EnterpriseServices` underneath the **Component Name** column in the .NET Tab. Make sure that `System.EnterpriseServices` is added to the **Selected Components** and click **OK**:

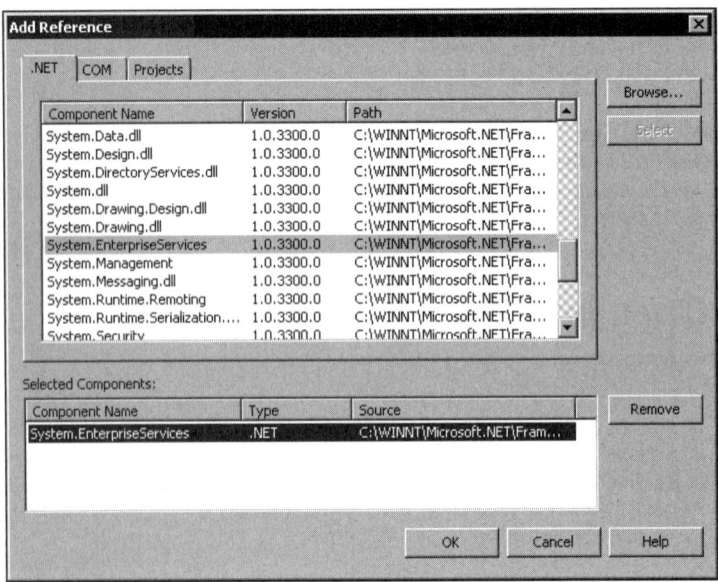

Now that you have the environment configured, let's take a look at the code you need to write to make your component a **serviced component**. The actual code you need to add is fairly minimal and pretty simple so let's go ahead. The Java Equivalent of this simple program would be a Stateless Session EJB with a transactional method that writes certain values passed to it to a table in a database.

Firstly, I will demonstrate a basic serviced component and then elaborate on it for our code demonstration:

```
using System;
using System.Reflection;
using System.EnterpriseServices;
using System.Runtime.InteropServices;

[assembly: ApplicationName("MyComponent")]
[assembly: ApplicationActivation(ActivationOption.Server)]

namespace MyComponent
{
    [Transaction(TransactionOption.Required)]
    [ClassInterface(ClassInterfaceType.AutoDual)]

    public class MyClass: ServicedComponent
    {
        [AutoComplete]
        public bool myMethod( string param1, string param2)
        {
          try
```

```
    {
      if(!ContextUtil.IsInTransaction) throw new
                          Exception("Not in Transaction!");
      if(!ContextUtil.IsCallerInRole("Administrators")) throw new
                          Exception("Security Violation!");
      // write params to the database
      ContextUtil.SetComplete();
      return true;
    }
    catch(Exception e)
    {
      ContextUtil.SetAbort();
      return false;
    }
      }
    }
}
```

The one library that is especially important is `System.EnterpriseServices`, which provides access to COM+. Underneath the using library statements (the C# equivalent of a Java import) we have two assembly metadata tags describing information about our component. The first:

```
[assembly: ApplicationName("MyComponent")]
```

Simply sets the applications name, while the second:

```
[assembly: ApplicationActivation(ActivationOption.Server)]
```

Specifies that the application is a server application and runs in a dedicated server process.

There is a third option, which is to specify it as a library application (an assembly that can be referenced by another application). You could accomplish this by changing its value to `ActivationOption.Library`.

The next thing we need to do is specify that the class requires transaction support. This is done after the namespace and before the class is defined with the statement:

```
[Transaction(TransactionOption.Required)]
```

The transaction support can also be specified once the component is deployed in COM+ by using the management console and going to the properties of your component. However, specifying support directly in the code gives us the added security that it will be pre-configured since the component has methods that require it. If you like, you could choose not to use attributal programming to specify that this method is to participate in a transaction. What I mean is that you could leave the above statement out, and choose rather to configure it to be transactional in the Component Services Manager.

A quick trouble-shooting tip, next. If after your class is registered you are unable to see any of your methods underneath your component in the COM+ Manager, this line of code resolves the issue for me. It is optional though, as you may not have this problem. Once the line is added, I am now able to see all of my methods.

331

```
[ClassInterface(ClassInterfaceType.AutoDual)]
```

Moving on to the class definition, we see that `MyClass` is inheriting from the `ServicedComponent` class. This in turn makes your class a serviced component. Now we will be discussing transaction support in a little more depth.

In order to specify a particular method in your serviced component as required to take part in a transaction, you specify the statement `[AutoComplete]` just before the method, as displayed in the code sample. Before we go any further, let's take a quick look at what the `ContextUtil` class does.

The `ContextUtil` class exposes a transaction's context. Now that your method is part of a transaction it is usually best to write a simple `try...catch` block so that you can isolate whether your code was successful or not. If your code was successful you can then use the static `ContextUtil` class to specify whether you would like the transaction to commit, `ContextUtil.SetComplete()`, or whether you would like the transaction to roll back, `ContextUtil.SetAbort()`. Since the `ContextUtil` is the context within which your transaction operates you can see whether your transaction is in it in the first place by checking the `IsInTransaction` property of the `ContextUtil` class. If it returns `false` then you would want to exit your method before any code executes.

`ContextUtil` can also check the **role** of the call that is presently trying to execute a given method. This is achieved by calling the `ContextUtil.IsCallerInRole` method. This will allow your method to comform to any role-based security that you may choose to implement.

Configuring your Assemblies

Assemblies have been covered in earlier chapters so we'll only be looking at them from a high level, here. You can choose to configure your assembly settings in either your source code or the `AssemblyInfo.cs` file (which can be found in your **Solution Explorer** window). I have already covered the assembly properties I have specified in the source code so let's take a look at the `AssemblyInfo.cs` file.

For your serviced component you really only need to configure one property, which is right down at the bottom of the file. This is:

```
[assembly: AssemblyKeyFile("CodeExample.snk")]
```

This property specifies the location of your **Strong Name Key** (`.snk`) file that you need to create for your serviced component. We're going on to create one now, so firstly think of a suitable name and specify it. (that is, replace `CodeExample.snk` with the name you specified). This strong name key is required so that you can uniquely define your assembly. No two strong name keys are the same.

The next step is to create your SNK. Using the command prompt (type `cmd` at the **Run...** prompt) navigate to your `[Visual Studio Project Folder]\bin\debug` folder. This is the folder in which the `AssemblyKeyFile` property looks for your SNK. Say for example, that you specified the `AssemblyKeyFile` property as "`CodeExample.snk`", you would then type

```
sn - k CodeExample.snk
```

and an SNK file would then be created for you, as follows:

```
C:\EnterpriseCOM\bin\Debug>sn -k CodeExample.snk

Microsoft (R) .NET Framework Strong Name Utility  Version 1.0.3705.0
Copyright (C) Microsoft Corporation 1998-2001. All rights reserved.

Key pair written to CodeExample.snk
```

You are now ready to build your serviced component.

Compiling the Application

To build your component, go to the **Build Menu** and select **Build Solution**. This should output your DLL file in the Visual Studio Project Folder\bin\debug folder. Once this has successfully been completed you will need to register your component. This is done using the `regsvcs` utility.

Using the Command Prompt, navigate to your Visual Studio Project Folder\bin\debug folder. If your DLL file is called `EnterpriseCOM.dll`, like ours, you should type:

```
regsvcs EnterpriseCOM.dll
```

This will register your DLL and create the `EnterpriseCOM.tlb` (Type Library) as well.

```
C:\EnterpriseCOM\bin\Debug>regsvcs EnterpriseCOM.dll
Microsoft (R) .NET Framework Services Installation Utility Version 1.0.3705.0
Copyright (C) Microsoft Corporation 1998-2001. All rights reserved.

Installed Assembly:
        Assembly: C:\EnterpriseCOM\bin\Debug\EnterpriseCOM.dll
        Application: EnterpriseCOM
        TypeLib: c:\enterprisecom\bin\debug\EnterpriseCOM.tlb
```

To verify that all went well, open the COM+ Manager and open up the COM+ Applications folder within it. You should see your application displayed below (it'll be named **EnterpriseCOM**).

Adding Object Pooling and JIT Activation Support

We have already covered what object pooling and JIT activation are, however we haven't covered their actual implementation. We've created a COM Server component as an example for this chapter that you can download from http://www.wrox.com. I am using an excerpt from that download code to illustrate these technologies:

```
    namespace EnterpriseCOM
    {
      [Transaction(TransactionOption.Required)]
      [ClassInterface(ClassInterfaceType.AutoDual)]
      [ObjectPooling (true, 1, 100)]
      [JustInTimeActivation(true)]

      public class Example : ServicedComponent
      {
        public Example(){}
```

```
      protected override bool CanBePooled()
      {
        return true;
      }

      protected override void Activate()
      {
        Console.WriteLine("I am awake !");
      }

      protected override void Deactivate()
      {
        Console.WriteLine("I am asleep !");

      }

      [AutoComplete]
      public bool insertContact(String firstName,String lastName,String address)
```

Adding object pooling and just-in-time activation requires adding two more service attributes after the namespace and before the class definition. The second speaks for itself, while the first requires a little more consideratation:

```
[ObjectPooling (true, 1, 100)]
```

This first parameter specifies whether object pooling is enabled or not, the second parameter specifies the minimum pool size, and the final parameter specifies the maximum pool size. Again, you do not have to use attributal programming in explicitly declaring the object pooling parameters. Instead you could choose to leave it out and configure it in the Component Services Manager.

Furthermore, you are required to override the `CanBePooled()` method and set its return value to `true`, you are also required to override the `Activate()` and `Deactivate()` methods with logic for object activation and deactivation respectively.

These last two methods are also a great way to test your new JIT Activation functionality; by using the `Console.WriteLine` examples above, you will get the equivalent of a `System.out.println` written to your console every time your console is being awoken from its JIT Activation-induced slumber as well as when it is being put to sleep.

Writing the Client Application

When writing a client application that wishes to make use of the COM+ component we just wrote make sure that you **add a reference to your component**. Being a serviced component it should be displayed underneath the .NET tab; however, for some cryptic reason it is sometimes displayed under the COM tab, instead. Selecting your component under the COM tab will not work; besides it's not a COM component anyway. What you need to do is go to the .NET tab, click **Browse**, and manually search for, and select your .DLL file.

You will also need to specify your components namespace in a using statement. We'll see how this works in a moment.

Enterprise Components

As mentioned earlier, I have provided a COM+ Server and Client Example that is downloadable from www.wrox.com. I will illustrate the client logic using these examples. As it's a Windows Client application I'm not going to show all the code here in the book since most of it has nothing to do with interacting with the COM Server. It looks something like this:

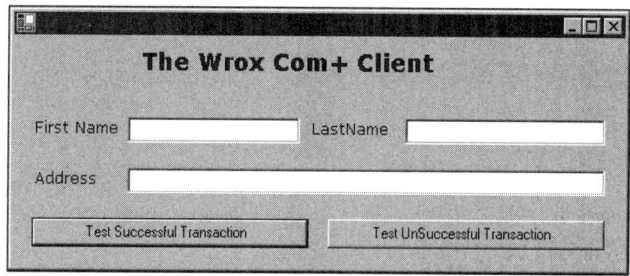

The way the client works is that it allows you to insert the information above and press one of the two buttons. The successful transaction button supplies all three pieces of information to the server component's `InsertContact` method.

The server method then writes the data to the **Contacts** table displayed below (this is held in an Access database for the example):

Contacts Table	
id	PRIMARY KEY NOT NULL
firstname	NULLABLE
lastname	NULLABLE
address	NOT NULL

The **Contacts** table has a NOT NULL constraint on the address column; the unsuccessful transaction button ignores what you enter for the address and therefore triggers the rollback logic when the `insertContact` method is called.

After having set a reference to my COM Server component (called `EnterpriseCOM`), I specified the namespace in my `using` statements:

```
using System;
using System.Drawing;
using System.Collections;
using System.ComponentModel;
using System.Windows.Forms;
using System.Data;
using System.Data.SqlClient;
using System.EnterpriseServices;
using EnterpriseCOM;
```

As you can see overleaf, I call the COM+ Server logic when either one of the buttons is clicked. I then instantiate my Example COM+ Server Component and call the `insertContact` method passing it the required parameters:

335

```
private void successButton_Click(object sender, System.EventArgs e)
{
  Example example = new Example();

   if(example.insertContact(firstNameTbox.Text,lastNameTbox.Text,
      addressTbox.Text))
   {
     MessageBox.Show("Transaction Successfully Completed");
   }
   else{MessageBox.Show("Transaction Error");}
}
```

For the button that causes the transaction to roll back, I simply pass an empty string as the address parameter:

```
private void failureButton_Click(object sender, System.EventArgs e)
{
  Example example = new Example();
  if(example.insertContact(firstNameTbox.Text,lastNameTbox.Text,""))
  {
     MessageBox.Show("Transaction Successfully Completed");
  }
  else{MessageBox.Show("Transaction Error");}
}
```

Summary

As you can see both the .NET and Java technologies provide containers with which your client code communicates. They also both provide a runtime infrastructure to manage those services that are too complicated and time consuming to reasonably write yourself.

COM+ has been around for some time and has proved itself a reliable technology with many successful implementations. Enterprise Java Beans are also reliable and there are many existing implementations making use of the technology too. Also, remember that .NET currently only runs within a Windows environment, although plans are afoot to standardize the CLI (Common Language Infrastructure), while J2EE applications run on any J2EE-compliant application server and can be deployed on any platform.

In my opinion, portability is more an issue for client applications than server applications, especially since the advent of XML and SOAP. These technologies have paved the way for seamless inter-tier communication regardless of the technologies behind the tiers. In addition, since portability is of lesser consequence, it would point to the fact that the EJB and COM+ technologies need to be evaluated upon the following:

- ❑ The Container Services that are provided
- ❑ The efficiency of the Container design
- ❑ How easy it is to write Enterprise Components

The first two points can really be argued both ways, however I feel that .NET really has a lot to offer in regard to how simple it is to write Enterprise Services.

Enterprise Components

10
.NET Remoting

This chapter is intended to give you a clear understanding of remote object distribution concepts for common users of the Java RMI (Remote Method Invocation) migrating to the .NET Framework. Even though we assume the reader has some basic knowledge of RMI and distributed applications, we'll begin at an introductory level to establish an approach that is convenient for both technologies. Along the way we'll be exposing some in-depth examples and techniques that can be used with the .NET Framework.

Here's a breakdown of the most important things we'll be looking at:

- We will introduce the 'big picture' of distributed objects in general implementations, schematically showing the flow of .NET Remoting and RMI, establishing the fundamental goals of both technologies while also covering initial concepts of **serialization**, **streams**, and **channeling**.

- Once we've established the initial ideas, we will start exploring the .NET Remoting architecture getting to know the namespaces and their members that contribute to the .NET Framework.

- We will implement and develop client and server applications using .NET Remoting in order to explore its functionalities.

- With a basic .NET Remoting design implemented, we'll look into some topics that will cover different aspects of execution using Remoting including types of Remoting, Activation, Channels, Marshaling, and so on.

- Finally, we will build a full-featured client-server chat program applying the concepts that we've learned to a practical, real-world, problem.

We will not attempt to create any benchmarking or hard comparison between RMI and .NET Remoting (henceforth 'Remoting'); instead we'll try to make this a pleasant experience for Java developers to use their RMI design skills for implementations on the .NET Framework.

Remote Objects Architecture

Almost every process in modern 'real-world' computing uses data stored within an object's methods and properties. Very often this information will be passed from one process (or application) to another, and become modified along the way. Unless these objects are very well engineered, a situation can arise, where the developer is forced to compromise on the manner of object interaction in order to conform to the architectural designs in place. This can make applications very hard to maintain, re-engineer, or update.

The principal idea behind the use of remote objects is to aid in this modification process, by distributing objects from a domain perspective. Organizing objects in such a manner allows you to make alterations to the object in one place, which can in turn influence many applications (that consume it) at once.

Let's begin by looking at a few important mechanisms that distinguish Java RMI and .NET Remoting in an architectural context.

RMI

As I'm sure you're already aware the Java RMI architecture provides a lightweight Java-to-Java, client-server protocol, and transparent API for the development of distributed objects across networks.

It provides the following benefits:

- Seamless invocation of objects on remote JVMs
- Integration of Distributed Object Model
- Support for callbacks from servers to applets
- Maintains reliability and safety offered by Java runtime environment
- Activation of objects
- Distributed Garbage Collection for remote objects

RMI operates in the following manner – once the client establishes a reference it starts **marshaling** arguments across the connection by invoking **remote calls**. On the server, after **unmarshaling** the arguments the server calls the 'dispatch' method from the **Skeleton** (server-side stub), which, in turn, calls the respective method of the 'real' object – pushing the result back to the client. This might sound a little complicated, so perhaps the following diagram will help clarify things:

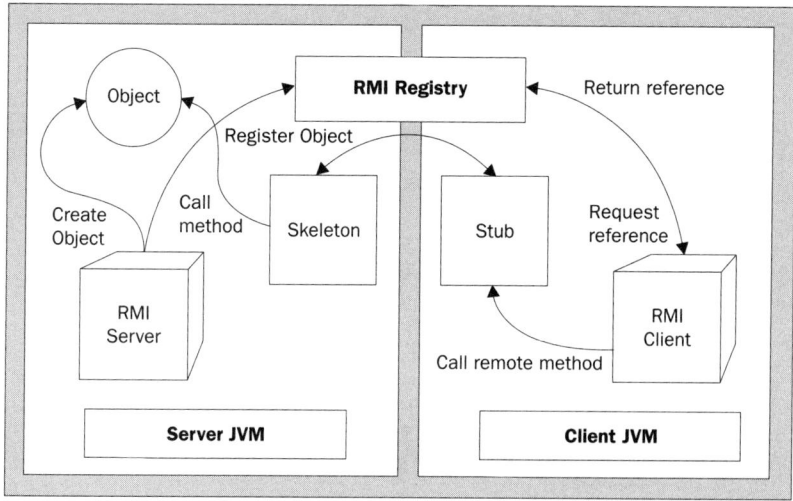

Please try to keep in mind that this is only a basic implementation of RMI, and that there are a great many more, different approaches, that can result from implementing it with other standards and Frameworks to gain more functionality from the process flow.

.NET Remoting

Remoting is provided as part of the .NET Framework, within the CLR, to provide the ability to write distributed applications under .NET. We'll briefly discuss its architecture and operation at this point.

Operating systems and runtime environments usually offer some type of separation among processes. In .NET, this separation is referred to as the `AppDomain`. This isolation is essential to guarantee that running code in one application cannot negatively influence another, unrelated, application. By running each process in its own `AppDomain`, the .NET Framework is able to provide security for each application against its neighbor's possible memory leaks and data corruption.

Remoting can be regarded as communication between two `AppDomains`, or isolated processes. Usually we will execute remote method calls, and pass information, in the form of an object or objects, between `AppDomains` on separate servers (although it is possible to do it locally). This usually means that we'll be communicating over a network, and so we'll need to try and keep traffic to a minimum, in order to ensure efficiency. .NET Remoting has understood this challenge, and a lighter, more network-friendly, architecture has been developed than for its Java counterpart:

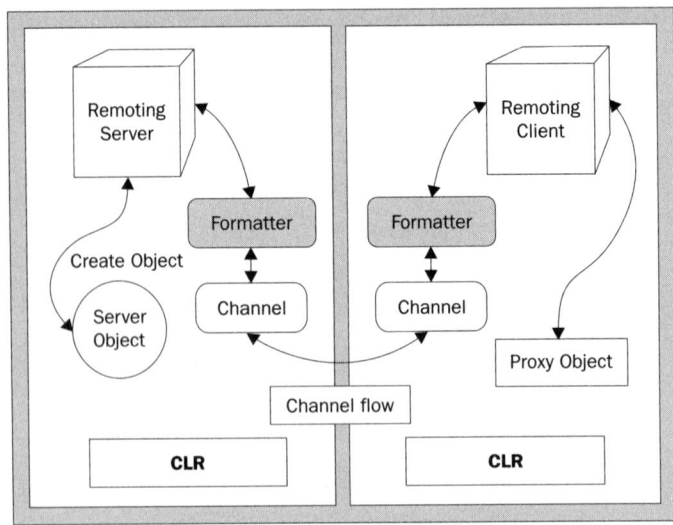

From the client's perspective it is important to understand that we do **not** need to retrieve an object reference from a global registry that defines the remote object. Instead the server application has a service running that is implemented by the Remoting runtime. The client application requests an object from the server, then they are referenced, as a channel is established between the client and server resulting in the activation of the remote object.

Using a server-activation, the client receives a representation of the remote object in the form of a proxy object created by the Remoting Framework. Because the proxy object gives a false impression of being a local resource (**transparent proxy**), the client can now make calls to the proxy object as if it were an actual local object. Once the flow is established, all calls to the proxy object will be routed to the server's process invoking the corresponding method and returning a proxy object supplying the client with the expected result.

Remoting also exposes configurable and extendable protocols and data formatting making it possible to customize interoperability between two different frameworks such as Java and .NET (I think in time we'll see more and more companies bridging across both frameworks).

> *Just a quick reminder: Remoting also benefits from the .NET Framework's ability to instantiate remote objects on the server that were designed and written in different .NET languages, through the use of MSIL.*

Exploring .NET Remoting

To understand Remoting, we'll have to look at the different processes, and dependencies, that are needed to design and build a Remoting system.

The Remoting Namespace

As previously mentioned, Remoting is a framework in itself; organized and packaged into the .NET Framework within a namespace called `System.Runtime.Remoting`. This namespace makes available several classes and interfaces to aid developers in creating distributed applications. In addition the Remoting namespace itself, there are five other namespaces that you need to be aware of:

Namespace name	Description
`System.Runtime.Remoting.Channels`	Comprises classes that support the creation and handling of Channels, used mainly for transporting calls made by the client
`System.Runtime.Remoting.Channels.Http`	Contains channel classes that make use of the HTTP protocol to transport data
`System.Runtime.Remoting.Channels.Tcp`	Contains channel classes that make use of the TCP protocol to transport data
`System.Runtime.Remoting.MetadataServices`	Provides classes that will by used by `Soapsuds.exe` (we will explore this later in this chapter)
`System.Runtime.Remoting.Services`	Contains classes that provide general service functionality to the .NET Framework

Serialization in .NET

Strictly speaking, **serialization** is the process of transforming an object into a stream of bytes that can be transmitted and stored for later use. The reverse process is called **deserialization**. It is very common to use serialization to keep the state of an object and then restore that state at a later date.

The .NET equivalent of Java's `System.To.Serializable` interface is the `ISerializable` interface located in `System.Runtime.Serialization`. This interface has only one member – the `GetObjectData()` method, that populates a `SerializationInfo` object with the information that you are sending to the destination.

It is important to mention here that sometimes we don't want certain members of a class to be stored in the state for serialization – information such as local security settings or full paths that will not make sense when deserialized on a different computer. In this case we would mark that member as a `NonSerializedAttribute`, literally meaning 'do not serialized this'; it is the equivalent of the `transient` keyword in Java.

To have a better understanding how serialization and deserialization work, we will create a class with serializable and non-serializable attributes, then create an instance of this class and serialize it, saving it to the disk before reading it back again to comparing it with its original state. We'll execute this code from the command line, so you can clearly see what is going on.

Chapter 10

```csharp
using System;

namespace SerializationExample
{
    [Serializable()]
    public class BusDriver
    {
        public int driverID;
        public string driverName;
        [NonSerializedAttribute()]
        public int busID;

        public BusDriver()
        {
            driverID = 12;
            busID = 3;
            driverName = "Jervis";
            this.printOriginalState();
        }
        public void printOriginalState()
        {
            Console.WriteLine("---------Original state----------");
            Console.WriteLine("Bur driver Id: {0}",driverID);
            Console.WriteLine("Bur driver Name: {0}",driverName);
            Console.WriteLine("Bur driver Bus id: {0}",busID);
            Console.WriteLine("---------------------------------");
        }
    }
}
```

We've just created a basic class defining a `BusDriver` object. We don't need to import any namespaces in order to use the `Serializable` and `NonSerializedAttribute` attributes.

Note that we flagged the variable busID as NonSerializedAttribute.

Let's look into the writer/reader code:

```csharp
using System;
using System.IO;
using System.Runtime.Serialization.Formatters.Binary;

public class ObjectSerialization
{
    public static void Main(String[] args)
    {
        BusDriver md = new BusDriver();

        Stream st = File.Open("driver.bin", FileMode.Create);
        BinaryFormatter bf = new BinaryFormatter();

        Console.WriteLine("Writing serialized Information");
        bf.Serialize(st, md);
        st.Close();
```

```
            md = null;

            st = File.Open("driver.bin", FileMode.Open);
            bf = new BinaryFormatter();

            Console.WriteLine("Reading Serialized Information");
            md = (BusDriver)bf.Deserialize(st);
            st.Close();

            Console.WriteLine("Bur driver Id: {0} "
              ,md.driverID.ToString());
            Console.WriteLine("Bus driver Name: {0}",md.driverName);
            Console.WriteLine("Bus driver Bus id: {0}",md.busID);
        }
    }
}
```

Here we began by importing the namespaces needed for the job including the namespace `System.Runtime.Serialization.Formatters.Binary` that will provide us with a formatter class, containing the functionality to serialize and deserialized objects. Then we create a `Stream` object pointing to a file called `driver.bin` in `Create` mode to generate the file. Furthermore we create a `BinaryFormatter` object that will serialize the instance of our `BusDriver` class:

```
        Stream st = File.Open("driver.bin", FileMode.Create);
        BinaryFormatter bf = new BinaryFormatter();
```

The next important lines show how simple it is to serialize an object into a `Stream` using the `Serialize()` method. Once the object is serialized in the `Stream` the object is flushed into the file, before we safely close the `Stream`:

```
        bf.Serialize(st, md);
        st.Close();
```

Lastly we reuse the `Stream` object to open the saved file and create a brand new `BinaryFormatter`, using the `Deserialize()` method to deserialize the object casting it back to the `BusDriver` object:

```
        st = File.Open("driver.bin", FileMode.Open);
        bf = new BinaryFormatter();

        Console.WriteLine("Reading Serialized Information");
        md = (BusDriver)bf.Deserialize(st);
        st.Close();
```

Note that the state of the integer busID was reset after the serialization process because it was flagged as non-serializable.

Chapter 10

If you compile and run the code, you'll see something like this:

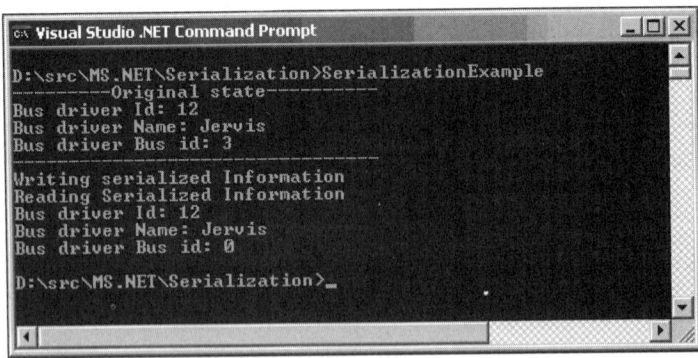

We can also investigate code that's been compiled, by using the `ildasm.exe` utility, which is a tool that explores MSIL code. This tool is distributed with the .NET Framework, and is simply used from the command line, passing in the name of the assembly. For example, here's what you'd see if you were to use it against the `Objserial.dll` file we've included in our download:

> `C:\Ildasm Objserial.dll`

The assembly ObjSerial.dll will be visible at MSIL code level giving us the chance to view the attribute related to `busID` denoted as [NotSerialized]:

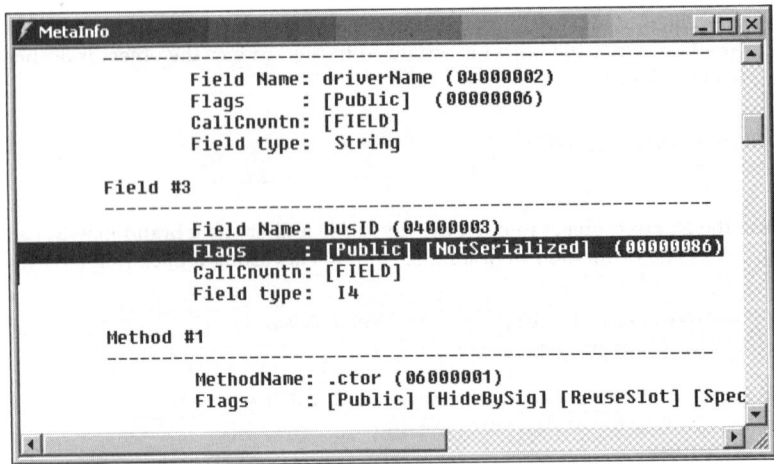

Marshaling Concepts

Remoting makes objects available in one process (client) while residing in a different one; this is actually a very basic definition of **marshaling**. When referring to marshaling objects using the .NET Framework, we must make a distinction between two types of objects: **remotable** and **nonremotable**:

346

.NET Remoting

- **Nonremotable objects**, are objects for local use and are never marshaled (it's prevented by their design). They do not implement the `ISerializable` interface or any methods with a `SerializableAttribute` declared. They also do not derive from `System.MarshalByRefObject` (we'll look into this a little later). Most base classes within the .NET Framework are nonremotable as they define local classes to be used only within the local domain boundary, for security reasons.

- **Remotable objects**, are objects that are designed to be marshaled across domain boundaries. They can either derive from `System.MarshalByRefObject` or implement an `ISerializable` interface (or have methods with `SerializableAttribute` declared). A simple example of a remotable object would be an instance of a `System.Data.DataSet` providing objects with the ability to be marshaled across channels containing relational data from a specific data source.

Once an object has been specified as remotable, it can be marshaled in two distinct ways. We'll look at these now.

Marshal-By-Reference

For an object to be marshaled by reference it must derive from `System.MarshalByRefObject`. The Remoting infrastructure will create a proxy object that communicates with the server's object when invoked. All method calls to that proxy will be marshaled across boundaries and reach the real object on the server:

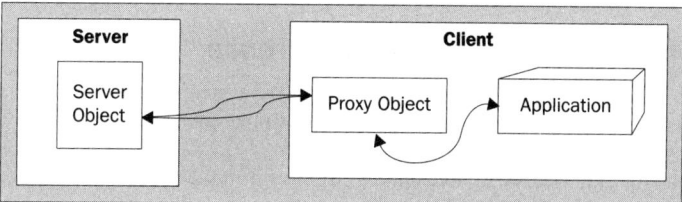

The syntax is as follows:

```
class mySerialClass : System.MarshalByRefObject
{
  public void Message()
  {
    return "Message";
  }
}
```

Marshal-By-Value

Marshaling an object by value is a much simpler concept. The server creates an instance of the object, serializes it, and sends a copy back to the client. The rule remains that the object must be able to undergo serialization by either implementing an `ISerializable` interface or making use of a `SerializableAttribute`:

Chapter 10

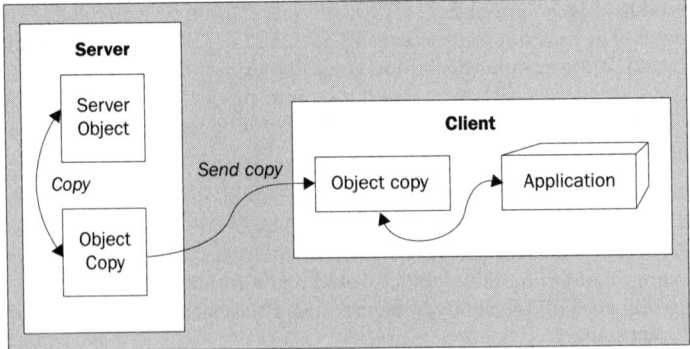

The syntax is as follows:

```
[Serializable()]
class mySerialClass
{
  public void Message()
  {
    return "Message";
  }
}
```

Marshal-By-Value Versus Marshal-By-Reference

When deciding to marshal an object by either value or reference we need to think about the functionality required in the application, in order to optimize processes and avoid bottlenecks.

In many situations the object may be extremely large, so it makes sense to marshal by value if we need transport the object-copy from the server to the client just once. This done the object can be accessed on the client without any further performance hit. However, this can be a considerable job with bulky objects, and if our object needs to make use of server resources (or even other remoting resources) then this isn't possible, and we have to marshal by reference instead, allowing the object to remain on the server, where it can function.

Channels

In RMI a `Stub` internally opens a `socket` connection and tries to open it to the `Skeleton` on the server in order to marshal the information related with the remote call over this `socket`. In Remoting the objects that establish connections are called channels and are not hidden inside a proxy, like the `Stub`.

Channels are objects that carry streams of data between applications, beyond Remoting boundaries, and often between `AppDomains`. A channel has a two-way flow; it can listen on a point for incoming streams, send outbound streams of messages to another point, or both. When creating a Server serving a Remotable object we also define and register one channel or more by using `System.Runtime.Remoting.Channels.ChannelServices` for the class and associate each channel with a specific port. When registering a channel combination we are telling the .NET Framework to listen on that port for messages routed to that channel.

When a message arrives, the Framework directs it to the precise server object it was intended to communicate with. From a client consumer point of view we do not need to worry about whether the object will be marshaled by value or by reference, as the .NET Framework will take care of these plumbing aspects, making Remoting extremely easy.

Generically speaking, RMI applications use an RMI-specific protocol, while Remoting uses the open standards of TCP and HTTP:

- `TcpChannel`: provides a sender and receiver channel using TCP protocol
- `HttpChannel`: provides a sender and receiver channel using HTTP protocol

`HttpChannel` syntax:

```
//Instantiating a HttpChannel
HttpChannel httpChannel = new HttpChannel(1095);
```

`TcpChannel` syntax:

```
//Instantiating a TcpChannel
TcpChannel tcpChannel = new TcpChannel(1095);
```

A very important distinction between these two, is that the `TcpChannel` uses binary encoded messages, while the `HttpChannel` encodes messages using the SOAP protocol which makes use of **formatters** to accomplish its encoding.

Formatters

When a `Channel` is opened from both ends (server and client) it is ready for messages to be serialized and pushed across. As we know an object must meet certain requirements to be serialized. For objects to be streamed across a Channel they need to be serialized using a certain type of encoding. This is where the formatters come in to place: formatters will encode the message and pass it through the Channel to the next end point where it is received by another Channel and deserialized by another formatter on the far side.

There are two common formatters used in Remoting, the `SoapFormatter` and the `BinaryFormatter`. We have already made use of the `BinaryFormatter` while demonstrating our serialization example. The `SoapFormatter` has the same function – serializing and deserializing data – but uses SOAP, rather than binary format.

That's really all that you need to know about formatters, as they are automatically supplied by the Framework behind the scenes. If you create a `TcpChannel`, an equivalent `BinaryFormatter` will be created, while if you create an `HttpChannel`, a `SoapFormatter` will be produced.

Activation

Remote objects must be initialized before being used by the caller (client). Remoting supports two activation types: **server and client activation**. Server activation occurs when the object is automatically created on the server when a client tries to call resources from it, and client activation means the object will be created on the client, as the result of a deliberate activation request from a client.

Server-side Activation

When referring to server-side object activation, its good to understand a bit more about **well-known objects**. The reason they are named well-known is because they are acknowledged by the server. Well-known objects are directly controlled by the server, not created when the client uses the new operator or calls GetObject(); the major advantage with this process is that there is **no round trip from client to server to client** just to activate the object.

Within the context of well-known objects there are two options for activation: **SingleCall** and **Singleton**. We are going to quickly explore these types of activation and demonstrate their usage with some examples.

SingleCall

The SingleCall mode represents the behavior of creating and destroying an object every time a method is called. Most of the time, the object is still alive but a new one is created and if there are several methods to be called from the client each one of them will create, and be served by, a different object. We must remember that because of the nature of the SingleCall process, the object **does not maintain its state**; thus all values must be sent directly when the method is called using the arguments:

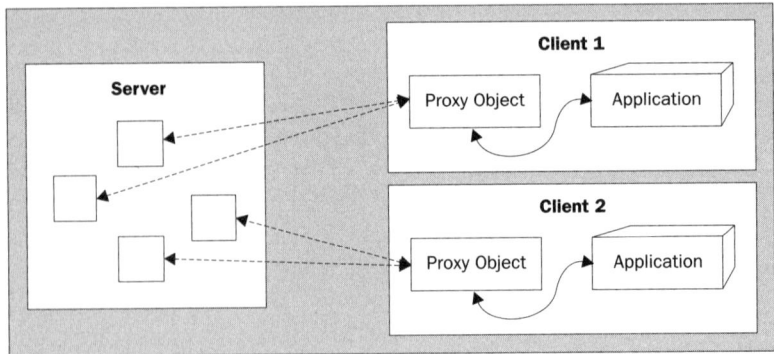

This model is beneficial in a Server Farm situation, as it allows each received message be directed to a different server. Clients denote a type with a URI to detect the object, but no interaction is executed until the very first method is called. During the connection of the call, Remoting just makes use of the type information to manufacture a transparent proxy in order to send information back to the client. Only when a method is actually called does network activity take place.

Now we are going to look at an example that will represent an approach not much different from creating an RMI application. This Remoting application will consist of an interface, an object, a server, and two clients. The interface will be the base for the Remoting object and also will supply the client with enough information about the methods it will be able to call. The interface will only have the signature for one method to be implemented called – GetTaxAmount().Two arguments will be in place: the first is double amount, having a simple tax calculation applied and returning it back to the client, while the second will be string clientName representing the client that called the remote method, it simply goes like this:

```
public interface MyInterface
{
   double GetTaxAmount(double amount, string clientName);
}
```

.NET Remoting

Having created the interface we can now go ahead and code the object, keeping a few Remoting details in mind: this object must inherit from `MarshalByRefObject` in order to be remotable and also implement `MyInterface`.

Once the inheritance and implementation is in place we will place a message to be printed from the constructor to the console every time a new object is instantiated, and finally inside the `GetTaxAmount()` method we'll conduct a calculation from the `double amount` passed and have the `string clientName` sent to the console:

```
using System;

public class MyRemoteClass : MarshalByRefObject, MyInterface
{
  public MyRemoteClass()
  {
    Console.WriteLine("New Object Instance generated");
  }
  public double GetTaxAmount(double amount, string clientName)
  {
    Console.WriteLine("GetTaxAmount() called from client: " +
      clientName);
    return amount * 0.07;
  }
}
```

We now need to build our server that will accept incoming messages from clients and instantiate the objects consumed by the methods called.

Firstly we need to register a `TcpChannel` listening to the port `9999` and register it using the `RegisterChannel()` method from `ChannelServices`. Once we have registered the Channel, we need to register the object that will be listening to the server end of the channel, we'll do this by using a `RegisterWellKnownServiceType()` method, passing the type casting of the object, and the `WellKnownObjectMode`, which will be `SingleCall`. Also we'll keep the server alive by leaving a `System.Read()`, waiting for a character read:

```
using System;
using System.Runtime.Remoting;
using System.Runtime.Remoting.Channels;
using System.Runtime.Remoting.Channels.Tcp;

public class MyServer
{
  public static void Main()
  {
    ChannelServices.RegisterChannel(new TcpChannel(9999));

    RemotingConfiguration.RegisterWellKnownServiceType(
        Type.GetType("MyRemoteClass,MyRemoteObject"),
        "myRemoteObject", WellKnownObjectMode.SingleCall);
```

351

```
        System.Console.WriteLine("Press ENTER to quit");
        System.Console.ReadLine();
    }
}
```

Lastly we are going to create the client that will connect and request methods from the server. It'll be communicating through a TCP channel:

```
using System;
using System.Runtime.Remoting;
using System.Runtime.Remoting.Channels;
using System.Runtime.Remoting.Channels.Tcp;

class MyClient
{
  public static void Main()
  {
    string name = "Client-1";

    ChannelServices.RegisterChannel(new TcpChannel());
    MyInterface m_MyRemoteObject = (MyInterface)
      Activator.GetObject(typeof(MyInterface),
      "tcp://localhost:9999/myRemoteObject");

    Console.WriteLine("Result: "
      + m_MyRemoteObject.GetTaxAmount(200, name));
  }
}
```

After compiling the client and the server we simply run both, in different consoles:

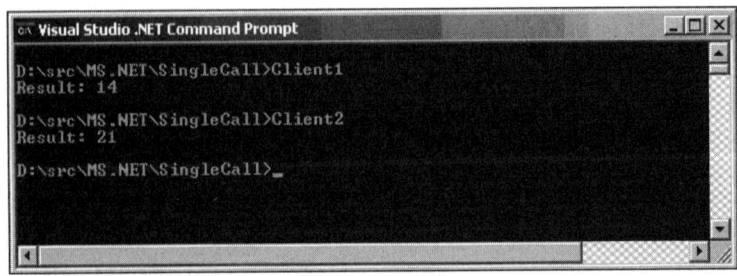

.NET Remoting

By looking at the server we can see that when the first call was made the Framework created an object, before creating the object for the first client call. On the second method call, from a different client, a new instance was generated – even if the same client had continued invoking methods we would end up creating and discarding more and more objects, rather than reusing the ones that we already had.

Singleton

The Singleton is a pattern that relies on the capability to instantiate classes and terminate arbitrary code. This pattern is applied in Remoting where a well-known object can take on that functionality. A Singleton **never has more than one instance at any one moment in time**, meaning that all requests are routed to **the same object from all clients**. If an instance is alive, all client requests are serviced by that object. If there is no object instantiated the server will create an instance.

When the first client calls a method the server checks if there is any object already instantiated, if not it will create a new one, but if there is already an instance, the server will serve any client calling to that object. All clients provide the same URI for a particular type, resulting in connections with the same object instance in the server. Just like `SingleCall` objects, clients cannot pass arguments into the object constructor but they can make subsequent calls to the object, because it maintains its state:

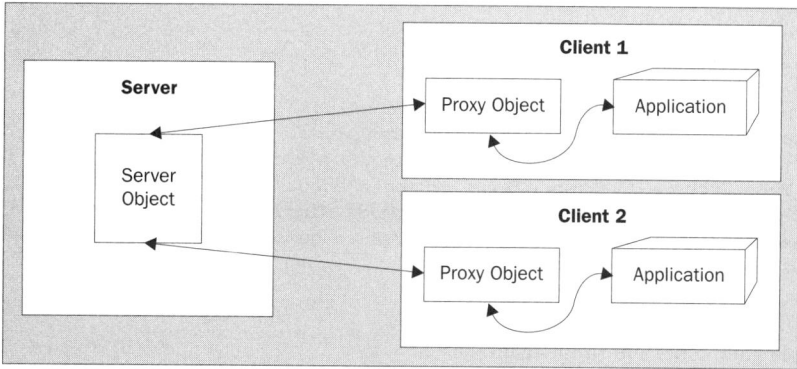

We are now going to look at an example representing the usage of well-known `Singleton` objects. We'll make use of the client and interface from the previous example but making same changes on the object and the server.

Looking at the object:

```
using System;
using System.Runtime.Remoting;
using System.Runtime.Remoting.Channels;

public class MyRemoteClass : MarshalByRefObject, MyInterface
{
  private int m_Counter = 0;
  public MyRemoteClass()
  {
    Console.WriteLine("New Object Instance generated");
  }
  public double GetTaxAmount(double amount)
  {
```

353

```
      m_Counter++;
      Console.WriteLine("GetTaxAmount()- called. Count " + m_Counter);
      return amount * 0.07;
   }

   ~MyRemoteClass()
   {
      Console.WriteLine("Destroying...");
   }
}
```

In the first highlighted part we can see that we are defining and initializing an integer that is increased when the method `GetTaxAmount()` is called subsequently outputting to the console including the counter. Many developers will disagree with using destructors in C# (as we would in any managed framework) but sometimes I find them very useful. Here we just want to know how many objects will be destroyed upon server closing.

Now looking at the server we can see that there isn't much difficulty in changing from a `SingleCall` to a `Singleton`, just change the enumeration `WellKnownObjectMode` to `Singleton`:

```
public static void Main()
{
   TcpChannel m_TcpChannel = new TcpChannel(9999);
   ChannelServices.RegisterChannel(m_TcpChannel);
   RemotingConfiguration.RegisterWellKnownServiceType(
     Type.GetType("MyRemoteClass,MyRemoteObject"),
     "myRemoteObject", WellKnownObjectMode.Singleton);
   System.Console.WriteLine("Press ENTER to quit");
   System.Console.ReadLine();
}
```

Now compile your code, and run it again:

```
D:\src\MS.NET\Singleton>Client
Result: 7
Result: 21
Result: 24.5

D:\src\MS.NET\Singleton>
```

Here, we've made three calls from the client to the `Singleton` object getting back the result from each individual method.

.NET Remoting

```
Visual Studio .NET Command Prompt
D:\src\MS.NET\Singleton>Server
Press ENTER to quit
New Object Instance generated
GetTaxAmount()- called. Count 1
GetTaxAmount()- called. Count 2
GetTaxAmount()- called. Count 3

Destroying...
D:\src\MS.NET\Singleton>_
```

The server proves that the object maintains its state by increasing the counter and not displaying "New Object Instance generated" because the client is making use of only one object; after we close the server we can see that the Garbage Collector only destroys one object.

Client-side Activation

The client-side activation option gives each client an individual reference to an object that is not shared with others. With client activation types, the object is instantiated as a consequence of the client making use of the operator new or an `Activator.CreateInstance()` method. This denotes that the client passes constructor arguments when instantiating the object. Moreover it means that interaction with the object takes place immediately as a result of the activation process. All subsequent method calls made by the client using the resulting proxy will be transmitted to the client's object.

When the client releases the proxy, the object will be discarded:

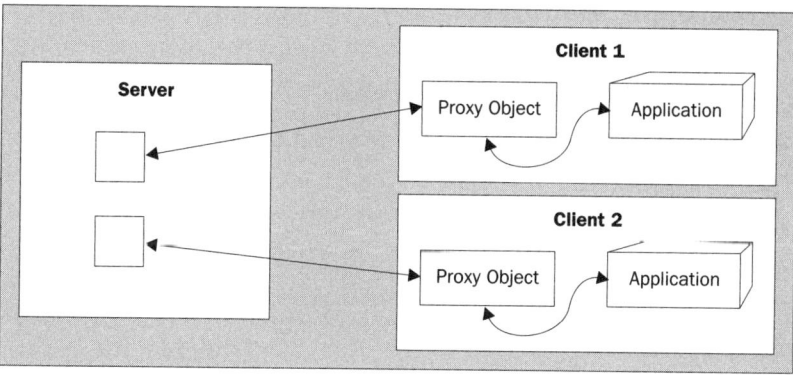

Creating client-activated objects on a server has a major disadvantage. The problem is that we cannot make use of a shared interface; instead, we need to deploy, with the client, a copy of the binary object itself or extract the metadata from it, in the same fashion that there is a stub in RMI (object interface definition). Indeed it is a disadvantage mostly because it's not very convenient to ship a remote object with a client (for versioning purposes).

In our next example we'll write a client, a server, and an object to perform the same tax calculation as we've done previously. This time we'll create the client in such a way that it can access, and have "ownership" of objects on the server, in other words we'll be able to keep the reference, call methods, and persist in calling the same methods and changing properties from our object. Moreover there is no sharing with other clients – if other clients use the object they will be served with a new object.

355

Let's start off by looking at the Server:

```
using System;
using System.Runtime.Remoting;
using System.Runtime.Remoting.Channels;
using System.Runtime.Remoting.Channels.Http;

public class MyServer
{
  public static void Main()
  {
    ChannelServices.RegisterChannel(new HttpChannel(9999));
    RemotingConfiguration.ApplicationName = "Server";
    RemotingConfiguration.RegisterActivatedServiceType(
      typeof(MyRemoteObject));
    System.Console.WriteLine("Press ENTER to quit");
    System.Console.ReadLine();
  }
}
```

This time instead of registering a well-known object we use `RegisterActivatedServiceType` method to register a service that will be promptly waiting for a client to instantiate it. Also notice the `RemotingConfiguration.ApplicationName`, meaning the name of the hosting application such as a Windows Service.

```
using System;
using System.Runtime.Remoting;
using System.Runtime.Remoting.Channels;

public class MyRemoteObject : MarshalByRefObject
{
  private double m_taxRate;
  public MyRemoteObject()
  {
    Console.WriteLine("New Object Instance generated");
    m_taxRate = 0.07;
  }
  public double GetTaxAmount(double amount)
  {
    return amount * m_taxRate;
  }

  public double  TaxRate
  {
    get
    {
      return m_taxRate;
    }
    set
    {
      m_taxRate = value;
    }
  }
}
```

.NET Remoting

This time we are implementing a field property, to set or get the `TaxRate` value. Also notice that there are no interfaces being implemented; as we mentioned before **we cannot share interfaces using client-side activation**, instead we need to either deploy the client with a copy of the binary object or with its metadata.

The major benefit of using `SoapSuds`, is not that you can slim down the assemblies that you are passing to the Client, so much as to keep as much of your IL code as possible on the server for security reasons.

Soapsuds is distributed with the .NET Framework; to run it you can execute the following command in the path where the assembly is located (of course, for convenience you could add it to your machine's PATH statement):

```
> soapsuds -ia:MyRemoteObject -nowp -oa:ObjectMetaData.dll
```

This command will result in the creation of an ObjectMetaData.dll file that should be deployed with your client code. If any changes are made to the server object new metadata should be generated and redeployed to the client.

Now that we have the metadata we can build the client:

```csharp
using System;
using System.Runtime.Remoting;
using System.Runtime.Remoting.Channels;
using System.Runtime.Remoting.Channels.Http;

namespace myObject
{
  class MyClient
  {
    public static void Main()
    {
      ChannelServices.RegisterChannel(new HttpChannel());

      RemotingConfiguration.RegisterActivatedClientType(
        typeof(MyRemoteObject),
        "http://localhost:9999/Server");

      MyRemoteObject m_MyRemoteObject = new MyRemoteObject();

      Console.WriteLine("Current tax rate: " +
        m_MyRemoteObject.TaxRate + '\n' +
        "Tax calculation: " +
        m_MyRemoteObject.GetTaxAmount(1000));

      Console.WriteLine("Changing tax rate to 50%");

      m_MyRemoteObject.TaxRate = 0.09;

      Console.WriteLine("Current tax rate: " +
        m_MyRemoteObject.TaxRate + '\n' +
        "Tax calculation: " +
```

```
                m_MyRemoteObject.GetTaxAmount(1000));
        }
    }
}
```

Looking at the following line we can see that we don't cast any interfaces to activate the object; we merely pass the `typeof MyRemoteObject` to the `RemotingConfiguration` using `RegisterActivatedClientType` and the location of the host application:

```
RemotingConfiguration.RegisterActivatedClientType(
typeof(MyRemoteObject),
"http://localhost:9999/Server");
```

Compile your code and run it:

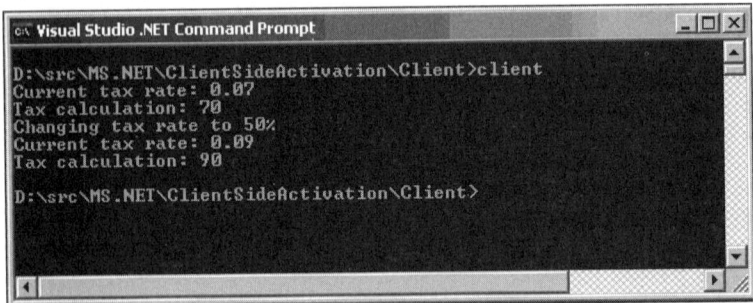

Call Context

Remoting context is a boundary around objects that jointly share the same runtime and are surrounded by objects with similar functional structure; they can be either `local` or `remote`. Objects contained in an application process are denoted as `local` and all other objects that do not reside within the same application process are denoted as `remote`. When a method call takes place within the same application context (`local`) there is no marshaling. When a method calls an object in a different context (`remote`) then marshaling takes place even if both contexts are residing in the same computer.

The `CallContext` class instantiates objects with the functionality to pass data across contexts when a call is made from the client – creating a thread that streams across contexts, working as shared data between the server and client without the need for calling a remote method. This can be helpful when certain data needs to be handled by either the client or server, and not be tied up exclusively by a particular remote method call, for example: data such as IP address can be passed to each remote method call to validate if a call was made from a trusted network without adding extra arguments to the remote method.

We can attach data to the context with `CallContext.SetData()` by passing a string identifier and an object.

.NET Remoting

In order to pass an object to the context it must satisfy the following requirements:

- It must implement the `ILogicalThreadAffinative` interface in order to be identified by the Remoting runtime. This interface does not have any functionality – it is only a way to identify objects that can be added to a context flow.
- The object must be serializable, thus declaring the `[Serializable()]` attribute so it can be streamed across channels.

For example:

```
[Serializable()]
public class InfoClass : ILogicalThreadAffinative
{
  public InfoClass ()
  {
  }
  private string m_infoName;
  public string InfoName
  {
    get
    {
      return m_infoName;
    }
    set
    {
      m_infoName = value;
    }
  }
}
```

Once the object is created we can implement it. The following code shows how this would occur.

Client code:

```
. . .
    InfoClass infoObj = new InfoClass ();
    infoObj.InfoName = "Any Information";
    CallContext.SetData("INFO", infoObj);
    obj.GetTax(1000);
. . .
```

Server code:

```
. . .
    InfoClass contextObject = (InfoClass)CallContext.GetData("INFO");
    if (contextObject!= null)
      Console.WriteLine("Value of context" + contextObject)
    return doubleAmount * 0.05;
. . .
```

359

> We cannot pass primitive types to the context, only objects that implement the
> `ILogicalThreadAffinative` interface and are serializable.

Leases and Sponsors

No matter if we are using Java RMI or Remoting, when creating objects we must deal with a series of different scenarios that will generate several constraints along with a design. Object lifetime is not as straightforward as we would like it to be, mostly because the nature of remote objects is not limited to local processes – creating more than a few opportunities for malfunctions. For example, consider an object *A*, that was referenced by a client, on the server. The client makes some calls here and there but what if:

- The Client computer crashes?
- The Network experiences an outage?
- The person using the client program goes for a long coffee break?

With this in mind, we'll begin on familiar ground, by looking at the JVM and its garbage collector. The garbage collector in a local JVM is a very good mechanism, but when we try to relate two JVMs holding a server and client RMI applications things can definitely get out of control. Ordinarily speaking the problem really starts when a stub references an object and one of the above scenarios occurs, so the stub is no longer using the reference on the server. The RMI runtime on the client must then communicate with the RMI runtime on the server so the server can garbage-collect the object. In Java this is done through a process known as **leasing**, and the terminology is also used in .NET.

In Remoting, when creating an object we start **leasing** its life (determining how long the object should live). By default an object has **five minutes of life**. Every time an object is idle the lifetime counter starts decreasing until it reaches zero and the object suffers disconnection from the Framework, and is disposed of by the Garbage Collector.

Leasing

Firstly all objects and interfaces for Remoting leasing are located in the `System.Runtime.Remoting.Lifetime` namespace. We'll be concerning ourselves mainly with the `ILease` interface. We'll begin by considering the remote object: `MarshalByRefObject` is the base class for our remote object, as it has an `InitializeLifetimeService()` method that returns an `ILease` interface containing leasing properties for the object. We can also set startup values for some `ILease` properties such as `InitialLeaseTime` and `RenewOnCallTime`:

```
using System;
using System.Runtime.Remoting.Lifetime;

public class MyRemoteObject : MarshalByRefObject
{
  private double m_TaxRate = 0.07;

  public MyRemoteObject()
  {
    Console.WriteLine("New Object Instance generated");
  }
```

```
  public override object InitializeLifetimeService()
  {
    ILease objLease = (ILease)base.InitializeLifetimeService();
    if (objLease.CurrentState == LeaseState.Initial)
    {
      objLease.InitialLeaseTime = TimeSpan.FromSeconds(5);
      objLease.RenewOnCallTime = TimeSpan.FromSeconds(2);
    }
    return objLease;
    //This line would give eternal life to the object
    //return null;
  }

  public double GetTaxAmount(double amount)
  {
    return amount * m_TaxRate;
  }

}
```

> If you need the object to have a never-ending lifetime, just override `InitializeLifetimeService()` and return `null`. Then the object will never expire.

The server implementation is a generic design, accepting client-side-activation. For now, have a look at the channel used (this is an `HttpChannel`, so it uses SOAP):

```
using System;
using System.Runtime.Remoting;
using System.Runtime.Remoting.Channels;
using System.Runtime.Remoting.Channels.Http;

public class MyServer
{
  public static void Main()
  {
    ChannelServices.RegisterChannel(new HttpChannel(8085));

    RemotingConfiguration.ApplicationName = "Server";
    RemotingConfiguration.RegisterActivatedServiceType(
      typeof(MyRemoteObject));

    System.Console.WriteLine("Press ENTER to quit");
    System.Console.ReadLine();
  }
}
```

Here's the corresponding code for the client:

```
using System;
using System.Runtime.Remoting;
using System.Runtime.Remoting.Channels;
using System.Runtime.Remoting.Lifetime;
using System.Runtime.Remoting.Channels.Tcp;

  class LeasingClient
  {
    public static void Main()
     {
      ChannelServices.RegisterChannel(new TcpChannel(8087));

      RemotingConfiguration.RegisterActivatedClientType(
      typeof(MyRemoteObject),"http://localhost:8085/Server");

      MyRemoteObject m_MyRemoteObject = new MyRemoteObject();

      ILease m_Lease = (ILease)RemotingServices.GetLifetimeService
        (m_MyRemoteObject);
      try
      {
        for(int icount = 0; icount < 30; icount++)
        {
          if (m_Lease != null)
          {
            Console.WriteLine("Current leasing time: " +
              m_Lease.CurrentLeaseTime);
          }
          System.Threading.Thread.Sleep(2000);
        }
      }
      catch(Exception e)
      {
        Console.WriteLine(e.Message);
      }
    }
  }
}
```

Now, looking at the client we can see that the `System.Runtime.Remoting.Lifetime` namespace must be imported because that is where `ILease` interface resides. On the next line, where the Channel Services are registering a `TcpChannel` on port 8087, we have the Remoting Configuration registering an object on the server. The reason why we have two channels will be explained when we talk about sponsors in a few moments:

```
ChannelServices.RegisterChannel(new TcpChannel(8087));

RemotingConfiguration.RegisterActivatedClientType(
typeof(MyRemoteObject),"http://localhost:8085/Server");
```

Then we get a reference to `ILease` from the object by casting it from `RemotingServices.GetLifetimeService()` returning the `ILease` from the overridden method `InitializeLifetimeService()` in `MyRemoteObject`:

.NET Remoting

```
ILease m_Lease = (ILease)RemotingServices.GetLifetimeService
   (m_MyRemoteObject);
   for(int icount = 0; icount < 30; icount++)
   {
     if (m_Lease != null)
     {
       Console.WriteLine("Current leasing time: " +
         m_Lease.CurrentLeaseTime);
     }
     System.Threading.Thread.Sleep(2000);
   }
```

If you compile this code, and run it:

```
D:\src\MS.NET\Leasing\Client>LeasingClient
Current leasing time: 00:00:04.8497840
Current leasing time: 00:00:02.8368896
Current leasing time: 00:00:00.8340096
Current leasing time: -00:00:01.1788848
Current leasing time: -00:00:03.1917792
Current leasing time: -00:00:05.1946592
Object </ab1d7135_ac96_4502_89bd_745c3ebbd81f/42386548_18.rem> has been disconne
cted or does not exist at the server.

D:\src\MS.NET\Leasing\Client>
```

Looking at the output we can see the `CurrentLeaseTime` decreasing towards zero; even then the object persists until there are no more calls from the client, sending it to its fatal end.

Clients are able to renew the lease if they wish to keep communicating with the same object instance by continuing to make calls within the leasing time; the `RenewOnCallTime` property defined on the object can be set to allow this. But what if the client tries to make a call when the lease as already expired? Well, we can always increase the `RenewOnCallTime` to something like twenty minutes, and then I would refer to another scenario we've defined before "*A person that is using the program goes for a long coffee break.*" In this case we can use sponsors.

Sponsors

We can consider sponsors like a real-estate agency – when we rent a house we make an agreement of payment, such an amount every month or week; frequency of payment is normally agreed at the initial handshake. Then every week we must go to the bank and pay the rent, but if we somehow forget to process the payment the real-estate agency will send us a letter reminding us.

When we create a lease we agree on a certain lifetime that will be the initial `InitialLeaseTime`, then we can also agree on a `RenewOnCallTime` when calls are made within the lease timeframe. The `Sponsor` registers the instance of a remote object, monitoring when the lease expires, then when it does it automatically renews its lease. In the case of a running application where "*a person that is using the program goes for a long coffee break*" while the program is active the `Sponsor` will always renew the lease and if the person then comes back and shuts down the computer the `Sponsor` object will be destroyed along with the client application, letting the lease expire on the server and the object be garbage collected.

Chapter 10

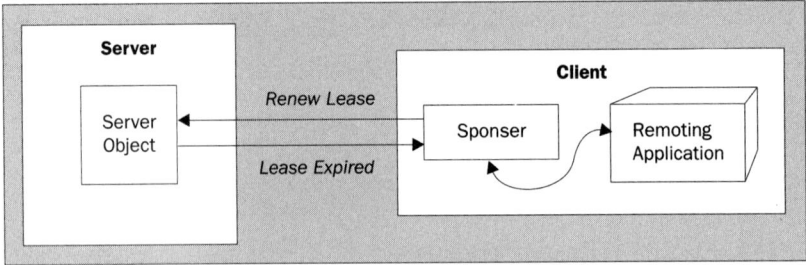

We'll adjust the previous example to take this structure into account:

```
using System;
using System.Runtime.Remoting;
using System.Runtime.Remoting.Channels;
using System.Runtime.Remoting.Lifetime;
using System.Runtime.Remoting.Channels.Tcp;
  class SponsorClient
  {
    public static void Main()
    {
      ChannelServices.RegisterChannel(new TcpChannel(8087));

      RemotingConfiguration.RegisterActivatedClientType(
        typeof(MyRemoteObject),"http://localhost:8085/Server");

      MyRemoteObject m_MyRemoteObject = new MyRemoteObject();

      ILease m_Lease = (ILease)RemotingServices.GetLifetimeService
        (m_MyRemoteObject);

      ClientSponsor m_Sponsor = new ClientSponsor();
      m_Sponsor.RenewalTime = TimeSpan.FromSeconds(8);
      m_Sponsor.Register(m_MyRemoteObject);

      try
      {
        for(int icount = 0; icount < 30; icount++)
        {
          if (m_Lease != null)
          {
            Console.WriteLine("Current leasing time: " +
              m_Lease.CurrentLeaseTime);
          }
          System.Threading.Thread.Sleep(2000);
        }
      }
      catch(Exception e)
      {
        Console.WriteLine(e.Message);
      }
    }
  }
```

As we can see in the highlighted code above, we merely need to instantiate an instance of the `ClientSponsor` class and set the `RenewalTime` to a value represented by the `TimeSpan` type for eight seconds, then we register the object we want to monitor its lease.

If we recompile the code, and run it again, we get this:

```
D:\src\MS.NET\Leasing\Client>SponsorClient
Current leasing time: 00:00:04.6995680
Current leasing time: 00:00:02.6866736
Current leasing time: 00:00:00.6837936
Current leasing time: -00:00:01.3190864
Current leasing time: -00:00:03.3219664
Current leasing time: 00:00:07.7596544
Current leasing time: 00:00:05.7567744
Current leasing time: 00:00:03.7538944
Current leasing time: 00:00:01.7510144
Current leasing time: -00:00:00.2518656
Current leasing time: 00:00:07.7396256
Current leasing time: 00:00:05.7367456
Current leasing time: 00:00:03.7338656
Current leasing time: 00:00:01.7309856
```

Looking at the screenshot we can see that the lease is being renewed each time that it expires completely.

Tracking and Logging

Every distributed application has its merits and demerits within the work it produces. A remote object has a long and arduous journey across domains and processes trying to perform its tasks in order to perform the functionality that it was given. As we have already seen there are constraints that may happen along the way and many times issues may occur making it impossible to detect the problem source because of the nature of the remote object's life. For this reason it is very important to analyze and monitor your object's performance to confirm that everything is running the way it should.

Java RMI's logging facilities, as we know, are fairly extensive when tracking the performance of RMI applications and sometimes very complex in the way they contain three different types of logs: the **standard logs**, **specialized logs**, and **debugging logs**. These logs are easily saved into a stream and dumped to a file.

Remoting does not have as much complexity in its logging. In the namespace `System.Runtime.Remoting.Services` we will look into `TrackingServices` class and `ITrackingHandler` interface.

The `ITrackingHandler` interface is used to create a class implementing three distinct methods:

- `DisconnectedObject` informs us that the existing instance of an object has being disconnected by the proxy object
- `MarshaledObject` informs us that the existing instance of an object has been marshaled
- `UnmarshaledObject` informs us that the existing instance that an object has been unmarshaled

Essentially these are the methods that report on a Remoting object's life. The approach is very simple, we just create a class implementing the `ITrackingHandler`, writing some logging logic to it and then register it on the server using the `TrackingServices.RegisterTrackingHandler()` method.

We are going to create a class called `TrackingHandler` that will implement `ITrackingHandler` interface logging the three methods implemented in the *Windows Event Viewer*. Let's take a look at it:

```csharp
using System;
using System.Runtime.Remoting;
using System.Runtime.Remoting.Services;
using System.Diagnostics;

public class TrackingHandler: ITrackingHandler
{
  public TrackingHandler()
  {
    if(!EventLog.SourceExists("CustomSource"))
    {
      EventLog.CreateEventSource("CustomSource", "RemoteObject");
    }
  }
  public void MarshaledObject(object obj, ObjRef objRef)
  {
    string log = "Remote object" + objRef.URI + " was marshaled\n";
    log += "Type: " + objRef.TypeInfo.TypeName;
      EventLog.WriteEntry("CustomSource",
          log, EventLogEntryType.SuccessAudit);
  }
  public void UnmarshaledObject(object obj, ObjRef objRef)
  {
    string log = "Remote object" + objRef.URI + " was unmarshaled\n";
    log += "Type: " + objRef.TypeInfo.TypeName;
    EventLog.WriteEntry("CustomSource", log,
        EventLogEntryType.SuccessAudit);
  }
  public void DisconnectedObject(object obj)
  {
    string log = "Remote object " + obj.ToString() + " was" +
    " disconnected";
    EventLog.WriteEntry("CustomSource", log,
        EventLogEntryType.SuccessAudit);
  }
}
```

For the implementation of logging in the .NET Framework, we need to import `System.Diagnostics` that will provide us with the `EventLog` class for creating sources and logging entries in the Event Viewer.

For more information on the `EventLog`, consult the .NET Framework documentation.

Examining the first few lines we can see that we are implementing `ITrackingHandler` and adding a default constructor to verify if the `CustomSource` (log information source in the event viewer) already exists, creating a source on demand:

```csharp
public class TrackingHandler: ITrackingHandler
{
  public TrackingHandler()
  {
```

```csharp
        if(!EventLog.SourceExists("CustomSource"))
        {
          EventLog.CreateEventSource("CustomSource", "RemoteObject");
        }
    }
```

Within the rest of the code we merely use the three methods implemented to log the actions occurring on the object within the scope of the server:

```csharp
    public void MarshaledObject(object obj, ObjRef objRef)
    {
      string log = "Remote object" + objRef.URI + " was marshaled\n";
      log += "Type: " + objRef.TypeInfo.TypeName;
      EventLog.WriteEntry("CustomSource",
          log, EventLogEntryType.SuccessAudit);
    }
    public void UnmarshaledObject(object obj, ObjRef objRef)
    {
      string log = "Remote object" + objRef.URI + " was unmarshaled\n";
      log += "Type: " + objRef.TypeInfo.TypeName;
      EventLog.WriteEntry("CustomSource", log,
          EventLogEntryType.SuccessAudit);
    }
    public void DisconnectedObject(object obj)
    {
      string log = "Remote object " + obj.ToString() + " was" +
      " disconnected";
      EventLog.WriteEntry("CustomSource", log,
          EventLogEntryType.SuccessAudit);
    }
```

The `TrackingHandler` class will be created on the server where it will be registered by the `TrackingServices.RegisterTrackingHandler()` method:

```csharp
    ChannelServices.RegisterChannel(new HttpChannel(9999));

    TrackingServices.RegisterTrackingHandler(new TrackingHandler());

    RemotingConfiguration.ApplicationName = "Server";
    RemotingConfiguration.RegisterActivatedServiceType(
      typeof(MyRemoteObject));
```

The client will simply implement a client-activated approach calling the object, then sleeping for ten seconds (considering the object has a lease of five seconds with no sponsor) and trying to call the method again:

```csharp
    ...
        m_MyRemoteObject.GetTaxAmount(1000);

        try
        {
```

Chapter 10

```
        Console.WriteLine("Waiting for object to disconnect");
        System.Threading.Thread.Sleep(10000);

        m_MyRemoteObject.GetTaxAmount(1000);
    }
    catch(Exception e)
    {
        Console.WriteLine(e.Message);
    }
...
```

If we compile this and run it, we see this:

```
D:\src\MS.NET\Tracking\Client>Client
Waiting for object to disconnect
Object </859f8081_7f9a_4618_8422_c0bd11304b27/83620820_5.rem> has been disconnec
ted or does not exist at the server.

D:\src\MS.NET\Tracking\Client>_
```

While the client was disconnected from the object the information was logged in the Event Viewer producing four new entries:

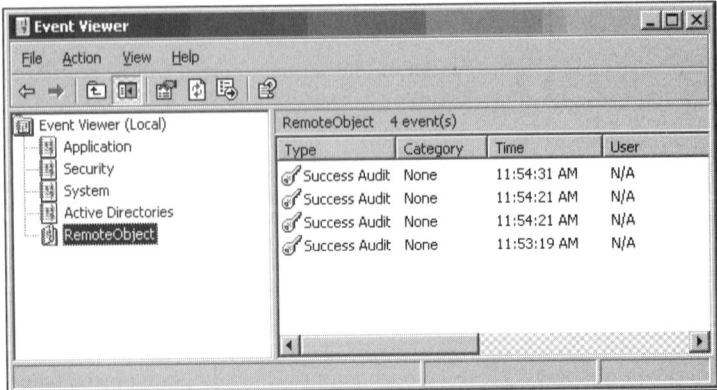

Because of the nature of the client activation process this log indicates that the remote object has successfully marshaled the object and is ready to accept client requests. We can observe it by viewing each of these entries:

.NET Remoting

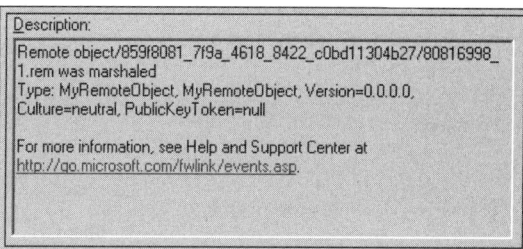

The next log shows when the object is marshaled again from a call made by the client:

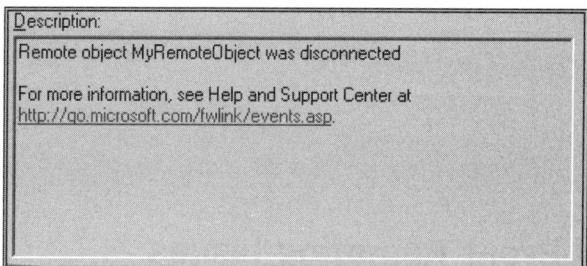

The last log denotes that the object has being disconnected:

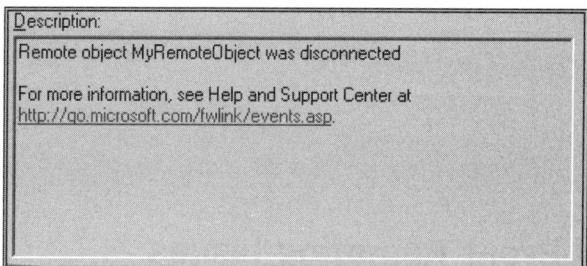

It is also possible to capture the client's IP using a `CallContext` *object for further performance and bug tracking analysis. (We will look into this later in the chapter.)*

Building a Remoting Application

I can still remember when I first stared with Java. The very first program anyone would want to write, just to get the hang of the language was a chat program using sockets (considering prior experience with other languages); at the end of writing the application and getting it to run on different computers it felt just like writing your first "Hello world" in C.

Anyway, we are now going to build a Remoting application consisting of a client and server chat program. This program will make use of asynchronous calls from the client to the server and be able to support several clients calling at the same time; it will also be able to capture each client's IP address for logging purposes. The client will also be aware of the name of the server that it is logging in to.

369

Chapter 10

In order to accomplish these requirements we will be using most of the topics we've already presented in this chapter, together with some new ones, which we'll discuss when we need them. They are:

- Context calls
- Events and Callbacks
- Configuration files

By looking at the diagram below, you can hopefully see, that the intention of this exercise is to create the impression that one client is sending a message to other client(s), when in fact they are just receiving return calls that are being made by any one of them.

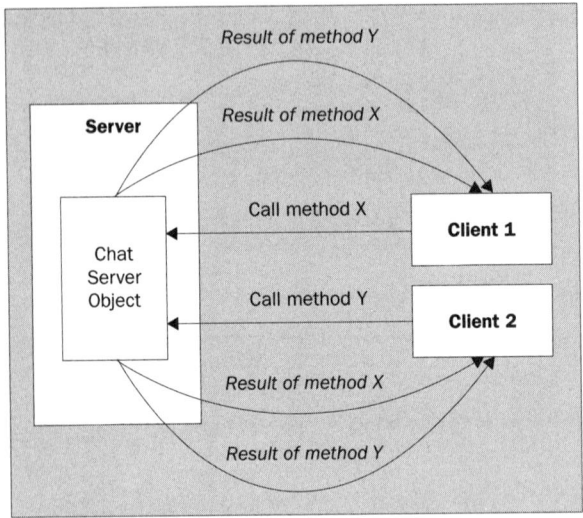

Delegates and Event Remoting Issues

Unfortunately Remoting still has 'issues' with callbacks. If we define a callback function through a delegate to a Remoting server object event, it will work fine as long as the client, server, and assembly containing the server object are residing in the same directory. When split apart in a distributed physical structure it will no longer work, and the server object will throw an exception due to a FileNotFoundException error. To understand why this happens let's revise what happens with callbacks under RMI.

Callback execution under RMI is accomplish by setting the client as an exportable remote object then creating a reference to this with the remote server object. In this fashion, the server can asynchronously call the remote methods of any client, and in the same way, the client can asynchronously call the methods implemented in the server objects.

When using Remoting an error will arise because a delegate needs to be able to obtain the receiving object type information for the class whose method is being wrapped by the delegate (very similar to RMI). Thus, it needs the client assembly to be available for the server object:

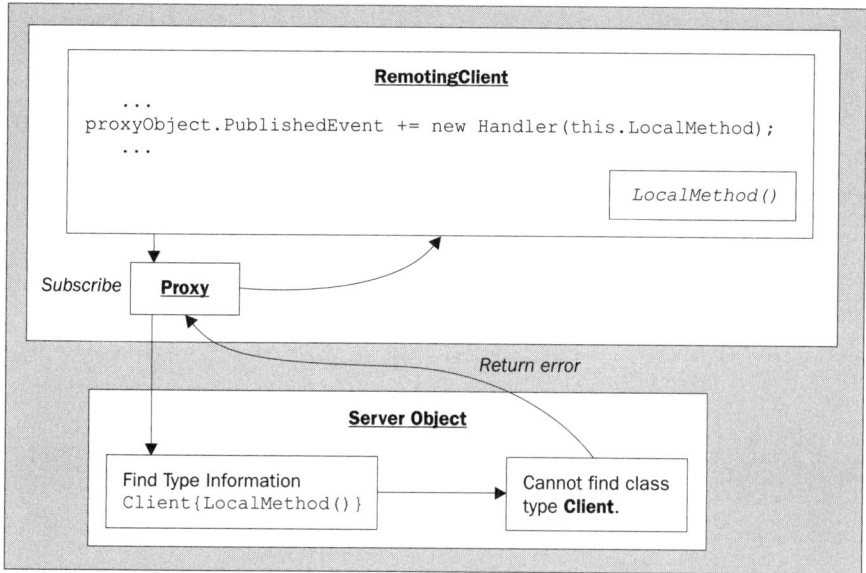

Having exceptions cascaded back to the client will generate the following message (where **Client** is the name of the Remoting client application):

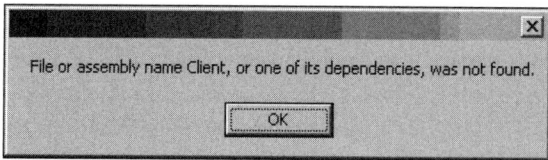

The only way to overcome this issue is by creating a "*shadow*" abstract class that will contain the callback functionality, and must be included in the common assembly that both client and server have access to. This abstract class will need to have a method that will be used for callbacks and it must be a public method that cannot be overridden. By "*shadow*" I mean that this class will be behind **both** ends with the client instantiating an object from a class that derives from the "*shadow*" and the server object having the same "*shadow*" class available within its assembly.

Chapter 10

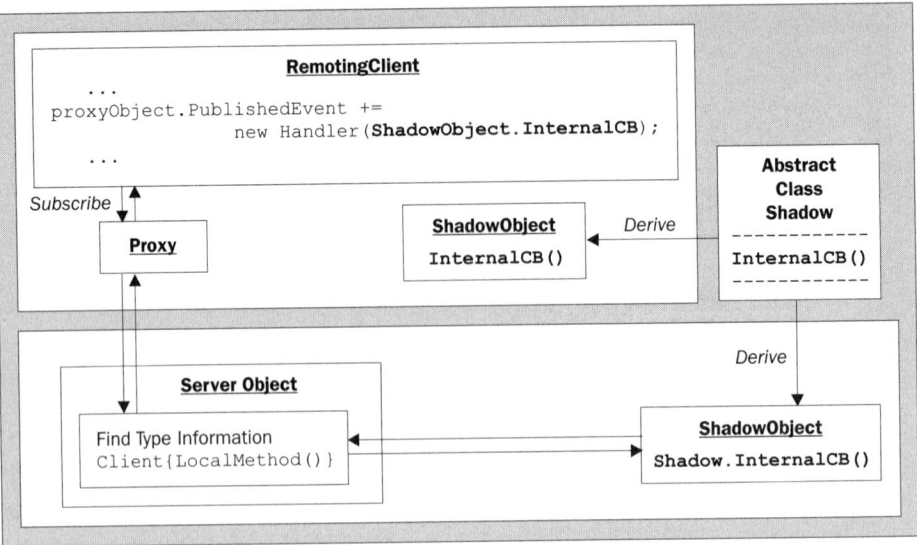

The client will need to create a new custom class and derive from the abstract class that implements the functionality in the callback.

Building the Chat Server

The server will be hosted in a console and will make user of the HTTP protocol, publishing the object on port 9999. Differently from previous examples we will use configuration files to dynamically read settings stored in an XML file.

Configuration files

Using dynamic properties allocation through configuration files we can configure our application's property values using an external XML file, rather then statically compile them into the program's binary code. This is a great advantage for all levels of production, and maintenance, of an application; providing administrators with the procedures for updating property values (such as port numbers) and developers with the ability to deploy and change application settings very easily.

Here is the configuration file we will use for our server, `Server.exe.config`:

```
<configuration>
  <system.runtime.remoting>
    <application name="ChatServer">
      <service>
        <wellknown mode="Singleton"
            type="ChatAdministrator.ChatObject, ChatAdministratorObject"
            objectUri="ChatObject.soap" />
      </service>
      <channels>
        <channel ref="http server" port="9999" />
      </channels>
```

```
        </application>
    </system.runtime.remoting>
</configuration>
```

Just like most XML files it is very straightforward. Looking at the service node pay particular attention to the `<wellknown>` element inside `<service>`, as it contains the `type` and `objUri` attributes with the object scope and the published object name.

Server Application

The server application itself is not very different from our previous examples; the only distinction is the simplicity that we are dealing with because of the configuration files:

```
using System;
using System.Runtime.Remoting;
using System.Runtime.Remoting.Services;

namespace ChatAdministrator
{
  class ChatServer
  {
    [STAThread]
    static void Main(string[] args)
    {
      try
      {
        RemotingConfiguration.Configure("Server.exe.config");
        Console.WriteLine("Chat Server Started.\n " +
          "Press enter to exit");
        Console.ReadLine();
      }
      catch(Exception e)
      {
        Console.WriteLine(e.Message);
      }
    }
  }
}
```

By calling `RemotingConfiguration.Configure` and passing the file name and path of the `Server.exe.config` file we will make the Remoting runtime load all the settings into the application dynamically; and as we can see from the code, we will no longer need to instantiate any objects.

There are two major benefits to this approach. The first, is that the server can be as generic as we want it to be, and the second is that we have no need to import other specific namespaces such as `Channels.Tcp` or `Channels.Http`. If we change the protocol or port, the Remoting runtime will automatically look for those objects.

A downside of this approach is that, I believe, there would be a performance issue arising from the need to constantly keep accessing the physical disk and reading the file into memory. Still, I believe that the maintenance benefits of this dynamic structure supercede minor performance issues.

Chapter 10

As long as the server is running and configured correctly, we can actually type in http://192.168.0.77:9999/ChatObject.soap?wsdl to Internet Explorer and retrieve the SOAP definition of the ChatObject class, which represents the object's interfaces:

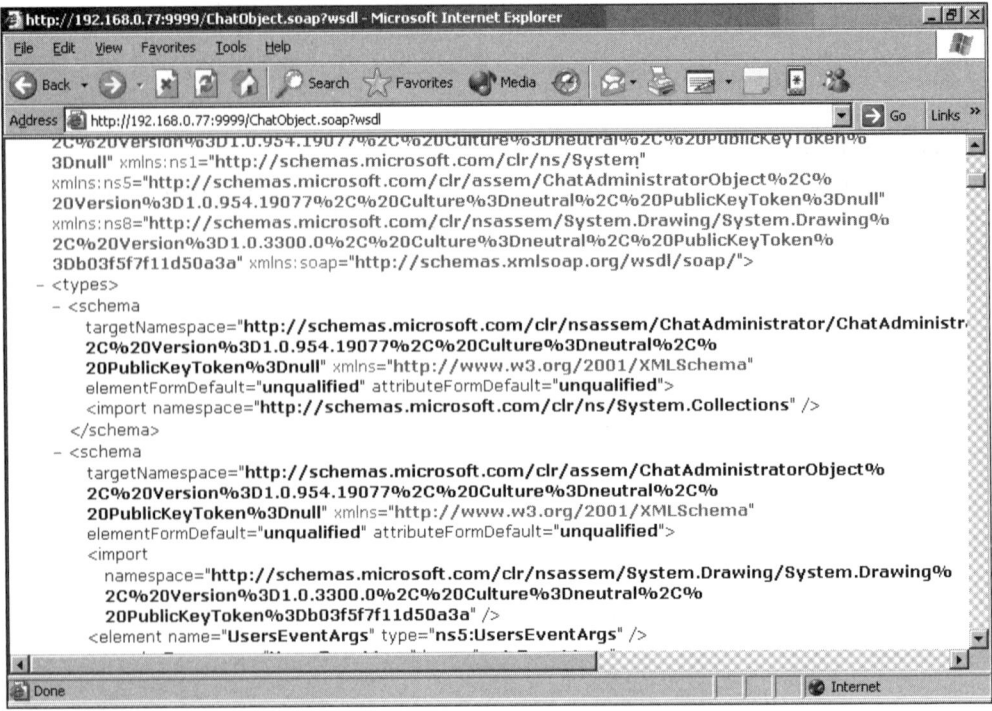

Building the Server Assembly (Remote Server Object)

The assembly ChatAdministratorObject.dll will expose classes needed by both the client and the server; it will include four classes to define their functionality. This is also where the remote server class will reside. We'll also include three callbacks for publishing events to the clients:

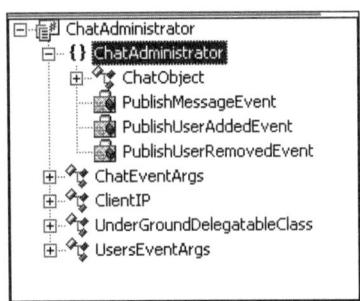

For simplicity this object will be deployed with the clients in order to access the interfaces and request then to the Remoting object.

374

ChatEventArgs Class

This class is made available to `PublishMessage()`. When a message is published the method will raise an event sending a `ChatEventArgs` object instance to all clients, it consists of two properties:

- `message` – a string containing a message from a certain user
- `color` – the color that a user is assigned

In order to make this class serializable, we also declare a `[Serializable()]` attribute:

```
[Serializable()]
public class ChatEventArgs : EventArgs
{
  public ChatEventArgs(string message, System.Drawing.Color color)
  {
    this.message = message;
    this.color = color;
  }

  public System.Drawing.Color color;
  public string message;
}
```

UsersEventArgs Class

This class is made available to `RemoveUser()` and `AddNewUser()`.

When a client calls the `AddNewUser()` method it will create a new `UserEventArgs` object instance that will raise an event to all clients, passing the object containing the username and the color.

When instantiated by the `RemoveUser()` method it will raise an event to all clients asking them to remove that user from the list, otherwise clients would have users showing regardless of whether they were connected. The class contains two properties:

- `username` – a string containing the client username
- `color` – the color that a user was assigned

Again, the class is defined as serializable:

```
[Serializable()]
public class UsersEventArgs : EventArgs
{
  public UsersEventArgs(string username, System.Drawing.Color color)
  {
    this.username = username;
    this.color = color;
  }

  public UsersEventArgs(string message)
  {
    this.username = message;
```

```
            this.color = System.Drawing.Color.Empty;
        }

        public System.Drawing.Color color;
        public string username;
    }
```

The `RemoveUser()` method calls the overloaded constructor with a single string argument since it has no need to relate to the color, unlike `AddNewUser()`.

ClientIP Class

The `ClientIP` class is used to demonstrate the `CallContext` in action. This class will be instantiated by the client and passed to the server via `CallContext.SetData()` then will be read by the server where it can perform IP logging. Remember this class must implement `ILogicalThreadAffinative` and needs to be serializable:

```
[Serializable()]
public class ClientIP : ILogicalThreadAffinative
{
    public ClientIP()
    {
    }

    private string m_ip;

    public string IP
    {
        get
        {
            return m_ip;
        }
        set
        {
            m_ip = value;
        }
    }

}
```

UnderGroundDelegatableClass

We explained before that callbacks with Remoting are not as straightforward as in Java RMI. In order to invoke a callback from the client, we need to create an abstract class that will be available to both the client and the server objects within an accessible assembly.

```
public abstract class UnderGroundDelegatableClass : MarshalByRefObject
{
    public void PublishedMessageCallback (object sender, ChatEventArgs args)
    {
        InternalPublishedMessageCallback (sender, args);
    }
```

```
    protected abstract void InternalPublishedMessageCallback (object sender,
        ChatEventArgs args) ;

  public void PublishedAddUserCallback(object sender, UsersEventArgs args)
  {
    InternalAddUserCallback(sender, args);
  }
  protected abstract void InternalAddUserCallback (object sender,
      UsersEventArgs args) ;

  public void PublishedRemoveUserCallback(object sender,
      UsersEventArgs args)
  {
    InternalRemoveUserCallback(sender, args);
  }
  protected abstract void InternalRemoveUserCallback(object sender,
      UsersEventArgs args);
}
```

As we can see this class has a series of public and protected methods. The first method, `PublishedMessageCallback()`, is public because it is used for the callback and cannot be **overridable** (callback methods cannot be overridable by the Common Language Specification). Within the body of these methods we will be calling a protected method that will be overridden by the client's implementation class.

We also need to remember that this class must derive from `MarshalByRefObject`, otherwise we'll not be able to marshal its subclasses.

ChatObject Class

The `ChatObject` classes will instantiate an object that will be hosted by the ChatServer application serving all client applications that will be establishing a connection. As we've already mentioned, this object will contain three public callbacks for use with asynchronous calls.

Here's the code for the server application. We will be using `System.Drawing` for creating a `Color` object that will be kept in a profile stored in the `Hashtable UsersList` for sending back messages and custom colors associated with distinct users. `System.Threading` is necessary because will using the `Monitor` class for getting a lock on some of the `ChatObject`'s methods. Finally `System.Runtime.Remoting` and `System.Runtime.Remoting.Messaging` are included for Remoting resources.

After the namespace declaration we have declared three delegates that will be associated with events to be subscribed to by the clients:

```
using System;
using System.Drawing;
using System.Threading;
using System.Runtime.Remoting;
using System.Runtime.Remoting.Messaging;

namespace ChatAdministrator
```

Chapter 10

```
{
  public delegate void PublishMessageEvent
      (object sender, ChatEventArgs e);
  public delegate void PublishUserAddedEvent
      (object sender, UsersEventArgs e);
  public delegate void PublishUserRemovedEvent
      (object sender, UsersEventArgs e);

//More code...
```

The method `AddNewUser()` will add a user to the `UsersList` hashtable object and raise an event notifying any connected client that a new user has established a reference.

Let's have a look at the `AddNewUser()` method:

```
public bool AddNewUser(string username)
{
  ClientIP ip = (ClientIP)CallContext.GetData("ipaddress");
  if (ip != null)
  Console.WriteLine("User IP address: " + ip.IP);

  bool ret = false;
    if(!CheckUser(username))
  {
    ret = false;
    if(PublishedNewUser != null)
    {
      UsersEventArgs e = new UsersEventArgs(username,
          this.GetRandomColour());
      try
      {
        Console.WriteLine("Adding new user: " + username);
        Monitor.Enter(this);
        UserList.Add(username, e.color);
        Monitor.Exit(this);
        PublishedNewUser(this, e);
        Console.WriteLine("Ok");
        ret = true;
      }
      catch(Exception ex)
      {
        Console.WriteLine("An error has occurred: " + ex);
        ret = false;
      }
    }
  }
    return ret;
}
```

In the first few lines we can see the casting to `CallContext.GetData("ipaddress")` that is being used to read the data sent from the client. Then we test for the existence of real references in the `ip` object, before the IP address, from the client, is printed to the server host console:

```
ClientIP ip = (ClientIP)CallContext.GetData("ipaddress");
if (ip != null)
Console.WriteLine("User IP address: " + ip.IP);
```

A few lines down we create the `UsersEventArgs` object, initializing the username and color properties. The color property is retrieved by the method `GetRandomColor()` returning an object type `System.Drawing.Color` containing the color that the user will be using when writing in the chat board:

```
UsersEventArgs e = new UsersEventArgs(username,
    this.GetRandomColour());
```

We next get a lock on the object by calling the object `Monitor` class's `Enter()` method and passing the current instance of the object (we can't be too safe). Then we add the name and `Color` object into a `Hashtable` instance.

Finally we notify all connected clients that a user has been added by firing the `PublishedNewUser()` event passing the current instance of the object and the `UserEventArgs` object:

```
Monitor.Enter(this);
UserList.Add(username, e.color);
Monitor.Exit(this);
PublishedNewUser(this, e);
Console.WriteLine("Ok");
ret = true;
```

Once the client has gotten the reference to the remote server object instance it will start processing other methods to perform actions collectively with other clients. After connecting to the server, the only possible action that can be performed by the client is to submit messages to the remote server object. This process is achieved calling the `PublishMessage()` method, which consists of two arguments: a `string` passing the username and a `string` passing the message. Firstly we get the `Color` object that belongs to the distinct user by passing the username to the `GetUsersColor()` method, having the distinct user's `Color` object returned.

Following up, we create an instance of `ChatEventArgs` containing the message received by the callback method and the `Color` object from the sender (user). Then we fire the `PublishedMessage()` event to all connected clients passing the current object and the `ChatEventArgs` object:

```
public void PublishMessage(string user, string message)
{
    Color c = this.GetUsersColor(user);
    ChatEventArgs e = new ChatEventArgs(message, c);
    if (PublishedMessage != null)
    {
        Console.WriteLine(e.message);
        Monitor.Enter(this);
        PublishedMessage(this, e);
        Monitor.Exit(this);
    }
}
```

The very last action from a client should be to call the `RemoveUser()` method. This method will simply remove the user from the `UsersList Hashtable` and notify all clients that a user has been disconnected from the remote server object:

```
public bool RemoveUser(string username)
{
  bool ret = false;
  if(CheckUser(username))
  {
    ret = false;
    if(PublishedRemovedUser != null)
    {
      UsersEventArgs e = new UsersEventArgs(username);
      try
        {
          Console.WriteLine("Removing user: " + username);
          Monitor.Enter(this);
          UserList.Remove(username);
          Monitor.Exit(this);
          PublishedRemovedUser(this, e);
          Console.WriteLine("Ok");
          ret = true;
        }
        catch(Exception ex)
        {
          Console.WriteLine("An error has occurred: " + ex);
          ret = false;
        }
      }
    }
    return ret;
}
```

This code operates in much the same way as the `AddNewUser()` method but with some differences, such as the following code where it gets a lock on the object and calls the `Remove()` method from the `UsersList` hashtable. After that we fire the `PublishedRemovedUser()` event to notify all connected clients that a user has been disconnected so they can remove them from their chatting list:

```
Console.WriteLine("Removing user: " + username);
Monitor.Enter(this);
UserList.Remove(username);
Monitor.Exit(this);
PublishedRemovedUser(this, e);
```

We should also mention that there is a public method available to all clients to get the hosting computer name to display on the remote client application:

```
public string GetServerName()
{
  return System.Windows.Forms.SystemInformation.ComputerName;
}
```

.NET Remoting

The Client Application

Finally we need to implement the client application to connect to the remote server object and perform all actions exposed by it. In contrast to our previous exercises, we'll take advantage of Visual Studio .NET's excellent design features to create the interface.

Here we have the shell of the application in design mode:

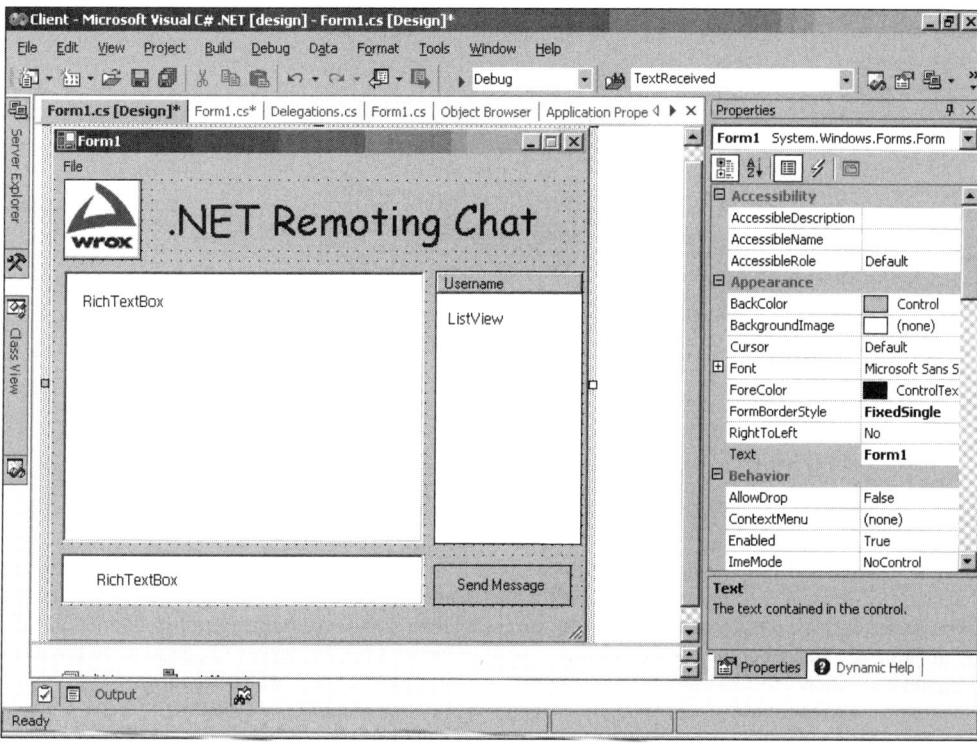

Now let us look at the code behind the form. Firstly we need to create a class that will instantiate objects derived from `UnderGroundDelegatableClass` so we can shadow the callbacks to the remote server through it:

```
using System;
namespace ChatAdministrator
{
  public delegate void MessageReceivedEvent(object sender,
      ChatEventArgs e);
  public delegate void NewUserEvent(object sender, UsersEventArgs e);
  public delegate void RemoveUserEvent(object sender, UsersEventArgs e);

  public class CallbackShadow: UnderGroundDelegatableClass
  {
    public event MessageReceivedEvent ReceivedMessage;
    protected override void InternalPublishedMessageCallback
```

```
        (object sender, ChatEventArgs submitArgs)
    {
      if(ReceivedMessage != null)
        ReceivedMessage(sender, submitArgs);
    }

    public event NewUserEvent UserAdded;
    protected override void InternalAddUserCallback
        (object sender, UsersEventArgs args)
    {
      if(UserAdded != null)
        UserAdded(sender, args);
    }

    public event RemoveUserEvent UserRemoved;
    protected override void InternalRemoveUserCallback
        (object sender, UsersEventArgs args)
    {
      if(UserRemoved != null)
        UserRemoved(sender, args);
    }

    public override object InitializeLifetimeService()
    {
      return null;
    }
  }
}
```

As we know this class was designed to inherit the `UnderGroundDelegatableClass` class to be used as a shadow between the remote server object and the client. At the beginning we simply state the namespace, then we move on to declare the three delegates that will be used to fire events on the client. Again, we will subscribe methods from this class to delegates on the server object and we'll add more delegates and events to this class to fire events on the Windows Form we're creating:

```
using System;
namespace ChatAdministrator
{
  public delegate void MessageReceivedEvent(object sender,
      ChatEventArgs e);
  public delegate void NewUserEvent(object sender, UsersEventArgs e);
  public delegate void RemoveUserEvent(object sender, UsersEventArgs e);
```

Now we can override the `InternalPublishedMessageCallback` (and all the other derived `public override` methods) and add the client implementation, which consists of firing an event on the `Winform`. All `public override` methods derived from the `UnderGroundDelegatableClass` have similar implementation:

```
    public event MessageReceivedEvent ReceivedMessage;
    protected override void InternalPublishedMessageCallback
        (object sender, ChatEventArgs submitArgs)
    {
```

```
    if(ReceivedMessage != null)
    ReceivedMessage(sender, submitArgs);
}
```

Jumping into the form we can see we've added some extra methods to be called right at the constructor of the form:

- ❑ `InitializeComponent()` – generated from Visual Studio .NET custom components
- ❑ `InitConnection()` – will create the connection to the hosting server
- ❑ `InitEvents()` – will subscribe all events to the `CallbackShadow` and remote server object
- ❑ `InitLocalProperties()` – will start some properties for local use.

```
public Form1()
{
  InitializeComponent();
  InitConnection();
  InitEvents();
  InitLocalProperties();
}
```

Staring with the `InitConnection()` method we simply connect to the server using configuration files and creating the remote object `remoteChatObject`:

```
private void InitConnection()
{
  RemotingConfiguration.Configure("Client.exe.config");
  remoteChatObject = new ChatAdministrator.ChatObject();
}
```

Inside the `InitEvents()` method there is a series of subscriptions to events, each one consisting of subscribing events on the server to the `CallbackShadow` object and from `CallbackShadow` object to the form client:

```
. . .
//subscription from the CallbackShadow object to form methods
callback.ReceivedMessage  += new
    ChatAdministrator.MessageReceivedEvent(this.ClientTextReceived);

//subscription from the remoteChatObject object to CallbackShadow methods
remoteChatObject.PublishedRemovedUser +=new
    ChatAdministrator.PublishUserRemovedEvent
    (callback.PublishedRemoveUserCallback);
. . .
```

Then we merely call `InitLocalProperties()` to perform initialization for local properties and contextual objects:

```
private void InitLocalProperties()
{

  ClientIP ipAddress = new ClientIP();
  string objIPAddress =
      Dns.GetHostByName(Dns.GetHostName()).AddressList[0].ToString();
  ipAddress.IP = objIPAddress;
  CallContext.SetData("ipaddress", ipAddress);

  this.rchBoard.Focus();
  this.stsBar.Text =
      "Connected to: " + remoteChatObject.GetServerName().ToString();
  user = SystemInformation.UserName;
  this.Text = "User: " + user + " logged in...";
  this.GetUsers();
  bool r = remoteChatObject.AddNewUser(user);
}
```

It is important to note that we are implementing the `CallContext.SetData()` method, passing a `ClientIP` object to the context to be retrieved by the server:

```
    ClientIP ipAddress = new ClientIP();
    string objIPAddress =
      Dns.GetHostByName(Dns.GetHostName()).AddressList[0].ToString();
ipAddress.IP = objIPAddress;
    CallContext.SetData("ipaddress", ipAddress);
```

Now, let's run the application but firstly remember that if you run more than one client, each one of them must be running on a different computer because if a there is an existing client running the port will be already taken. In order to run the client and server we need to deploy the following files:

ChatServer

- `Server.exe` – executable server program
- `ChatAdministratorObject.dll` – assembly containing the `ChatObject` object and support classes
- `Server.exe.config` – configuration file to be consumed by the Remoting runtime

Client

- `Client.exe` – executable server program
- `ChatAdministratorObject.dll` – assembly containing the `ChatObject` object and support classes
- `Client.exe.config` – configuration file to be consumed by the Remoting runtime

> If we decide to run the client and server on the same computer, don't forget to change the `Client.exe.config` file to `locahost` instead of a remote IP address.

After deploying and starting the server, we can also run the client. Here we have two clients running from two different computers and having a friendly conversation:

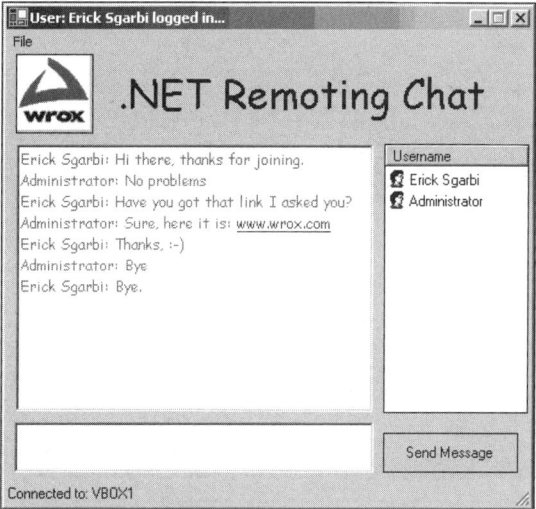

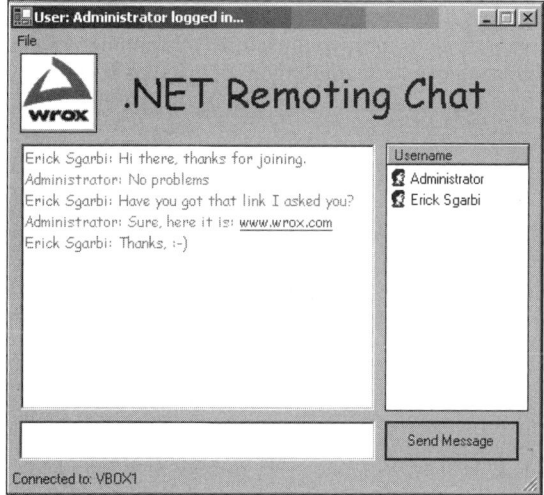

A clever thing about the client's board is that it uses a `RichTextBox` component: note how it highlights, underlines, and make the link's click-able. Of course, in order to click and open an instance of Internet Explorer we need to add some code in the event `LinkClicked` as followed:

```
private void rchBoard_LinkClicked(object sender,
    System.Windows.Forms.LinkClickedEventArgs e)
{
  System.Diagnostics.Process.Start(e.LinkText);
}
```

Chapter 10

After our sample conversation ends, and the user **Administrator** disconnects from the remote server object, we can look at the server console to verify that **Erick Sgarbi** is still connected and making use of the server, consequently waiting for others to join:

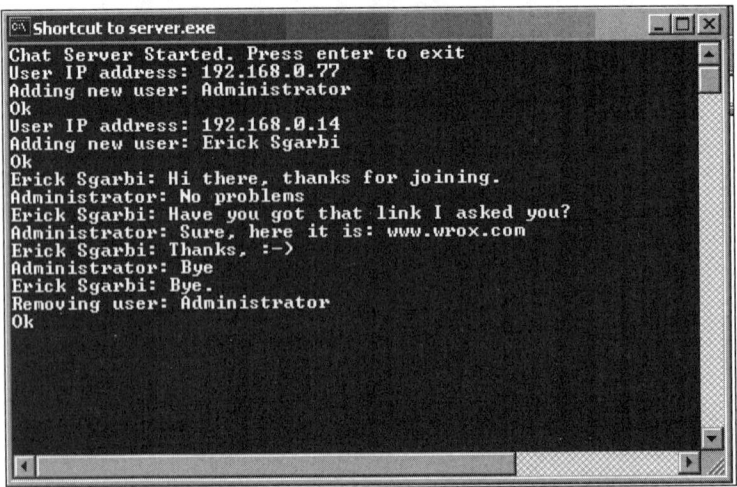

This has been quite a long, and complex example, but its main point has been to show you how we can use .NET Remoting to create three or more applications, all running at the same time, and feeding from the same shared object without conflict. For applications of this type Remoting is a very powerful technology.

Summary

During the course of this chapter we have looked at many aspects of the .NET Remoting Framework. We began on familiar ground, by looking briefly at the flow and architecture of Java RMI, before moving on to contrast it with the simpler architecture of .NET Remoting. This done, we moved on to discuss the theoretical ideas of Serialization and Marshaling, paying careful attention to the differences between Marshaling by Value, and Marshaling by Reference, and the best applications of each.

We also explored the key classes comprised by .NET Remoting. These were:

- Channels
- Formatters
- Activation
- Server-side activation
- Client-side activation
- CallContext
- Leases and Sponsors
- Tracking and Logging

Finally we put together a fully featured client-server chat application to implement many of the concepts we discussed through the chapter. It consisted of:

- Configuration files
- Callbacks and Events
- Winforms
- CallContext

Interoperating with Existing Code

This chapter details how to go about enabling a .NET application to operate with existing applications. Since this book is focussed on Java developers, we'll start by looking at interoperating with Java code, and porting over to .NET. Thereafter, we will focus on interoperating with Component Object Model (COM) components, which formed the crux of Microsoft's *n*-tier application architecture prior to .NET.

Interoperating with Java

If you are a Java developer who has left a firm that uses Java for a firm that prefers Microsoft, the latter half of this chapter will be of primary interest to you. Existing Microsoft shops are unlikely to turf out their existing COM-based applications and re-write them in .NET when they can simply use COM Interop technology to facilitate communicate between the two. For those of you that fall into the second category, this section, along with the previous web services chapter, will be of most interest to you.

Alternatively, you may be a Java developer in a firm that uses Java, but that has decided to incorporate .NET, or even completely migrate to it. In this case, you will most probably be either porting all your Java code to .NET (in which case you will be interested in J# and the JLCA), or you will be writing your own Java interoperation mechanisms with web services, or facilitating them using Microsoft's Biztalk Server. This first section is aimed primarily at you, and we'll be considering the following key areas:

- Microsoft Biztalk Server
- Web Services
- Microsoft Visual J#

Chapter 11

Microsoft Biztalk Server

Microsoft Biztalk Server is part of the .NET Server group and is Microsoft's premier application interoperation and integration tool. It acts as a mediator – a bridge if you will – between one application and any other object that wishes to communicate with it, reminiscent of web services in some ways. In addition, Biztalk provides tools for defining workflow processes for data as it travels from *A* to *B*. Other applications can exchange data with yours using a variety of communication protocols, business processes, and data types, all of which are managed by the Biztalk Server.

Here is an overview of the structure and function of Biztalk Server:

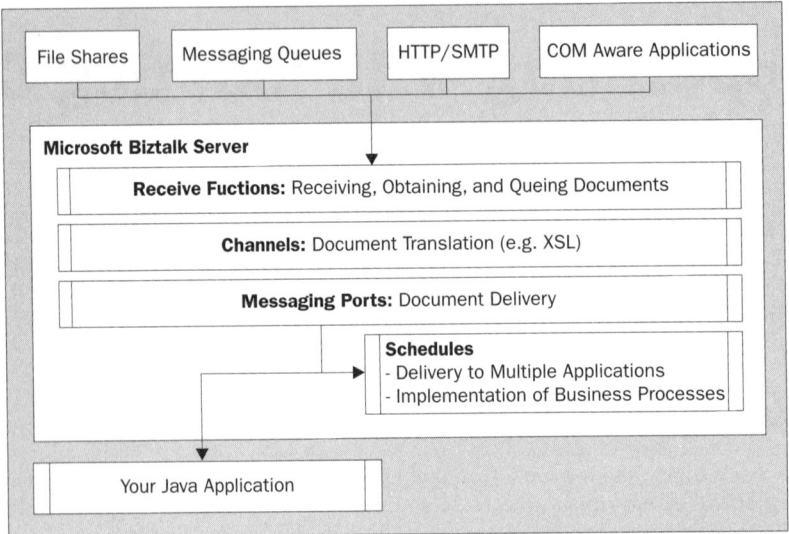

Microsoft Biztalk Server is a good choice for .NET applications that need to communicate with Java apps, when those applications can produce and consume a document, but do not have a web interface and cannot represent their data in XML. If they can communicate in XML over HTTP or another SOAP supported protocol, then I would plump for web services as the tool for interoperation and integration instead. Web services have already been covered in some detail earlier in the book (Chapter 7), but there are a few things I'd like to add to that explanation in the following section.

Integration Using Web Services

One of web services' core goals is integration. Web services implement SOAP (Simple Object Access Protocol), a W3C standardized protocol for XML data transfer.

If a Java application is SOAP compliant, then we can communicate with it quite seamlessly using XML over HTTP. The Java application can make SOAP Requests to our .NET web service, which, depending on what the SOAP Request was asking for, would instantiate the resource required, process the request, and respond with the data requested in the SOAP Response:

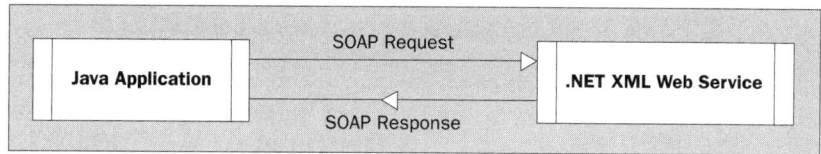

Web services preach code modularity, encouraging breaking functionality into reusable components each of which is implemented as a web service (a SOAP-compliant component). We can use exactly the same approach in existing Java applications and then create a .NET web service to communicate with your Java web service; no mess, no fuss.

Microsoft Visual J#

As we've already stated several times, C# is the preferred language for the .NET platform, and indeed we've used it throughout this book. However, for a quick way to leap up onto the .NET platform, **Microsoft Visual J# .NET**, or simply J#, is worth a look. J# is part of the Visual Studio .NET family, but is not bundled with it. It is currently only available as a separate, but free, download from:

> http://msdn.microsoft.com/vjsharp/downloads/howtoget.asp

The J# language is semantically the same as Java based on **JDK 1.1.4-compliant class libraries**, although J# can also use the regular .NET class libraries. J# provides a tool for **converting compiled Java classes into MSIL**. Nevertheless, one thing J# applications will not do, is run in a true Java runtime environment: they will **only** run on .NET. Essentially, J# is a halfway house where you can write applications using Java-like semantics and most JDK 1.1.4-compliant class libraries, and yet still access the core .NET class libraries.

In my personal opinion, the conversion tools are really the most useful part of J#. C# semantics are not far removed from Java anyway, and it really isn't a great feat to move over to C#. C# also has superior support for the features of the .NET CLR. Having said this, I still would recommend J# for:

- Converting Java or Visual J++ applications to C#
- Fledgling .NET Java developers who want to start off with familiar language semantics while they find their feet

In this section, we'll take a quick look at:

- Creating a Visual J# Application
- The Java Language Conversion Assistant (JLCA)
- The Binary Converter Tool
- A comparison between J# and Java

Creating a Visual J# Application

To write your own J# application, you first need to download and install the setup file (VJSharpSetup.exe) from the URL given before. Once that is done, VS.NET users will find a new Visual J# project type on offer, with some scary purple templates:

Chapter 11

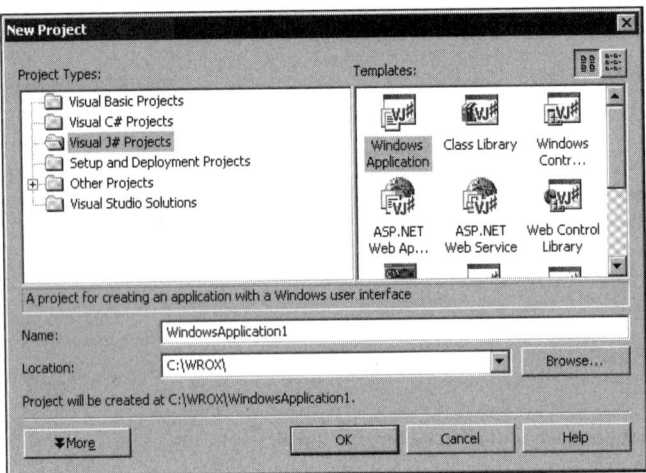

The J# development environment in VS.NET is identical to any of the other .NET development environments and building your applications involves identical processes. For example, to build a simple 'Hello World' type app, one would do exactly the same as in Visual C#. This would involve creating a new Windows Application project, dragging a button onto your form, double-clicking the button on the form, adding a "Hello World" `MessageBox` popup in the `Click` event handler method, and simply pressing *F5* to run your application.

What is different is the underlying code. As you can see from the example below, all code created uses Java semantics coupled with the Windows Forms Designer Code block. Also notice that code files take a `.jsl` file extension, not `.java`. The application entry point, or the `main()` method, is highlighted via the code comments. I created a simple method called `yourMethod()` to give a illustration of how you can add your own methods and extend your application:

```
package WindowsApplication2;

import System.Drawing.*;
import System.Collections.*;
import System.ComponentModel.*;
import System.Windows.Forms.*;
import System.Data.*;

public class Form1 extends System.Windows.Forms.Form
{
  private System.Windows.Forms.Button button1;
  // Required designer variable

  private System.ComponentModel.Container components = null;

  public Form1()
  {
    // Required for Windows Form Designer support
    InitializeComponent();
    // TODO: Add any constructor code after InitializeComponent call
  }
```

```
//Clean up any resources being used.
protected void Dispose(boolean disposing)
{
  if (disposing)
  {
    if (components != null)
    {
      components.Dispose();
    }
  }
  super.Dispose(disposing);
}

#region Windows Form Designer generated code
/*
 * Required method for Designer support - do not modify
 * the contents of this method with the code editor.
 */
private void InitializeComponent()
{
  this.button1 = new System.Windows.Forms.Button();
  this.SuspendLayout();
  //
  // button1
  //
  this.button1.set_Location(new System.Drawing.Point(88, 96));
  this.button1.set_Name("button1");
  this.button1.set_TabIndex(0);
  this.button1.set_Text("button1");
  this.button1.add_Click( new System.EventHandler(this.button1_Click) );
  //
  // Form1
  //
  this.set_AutoScaleBaseSize(new System.Drawing.Size(5, 13));
  this.set_ClientSize(new System.Drawing.Size(292, 266));
  this.get_Controls().AddRange(new System.Windows.Forms.Control[]{
                                                  this.button1});
  this.set_Name("Form1");
  this.set_Text("Form1");
  this.ResumeLayout(false);

}
#endregion

// The main entry point for the application
/** @attribute System.STAThread() */
public static void main(String[] args)
{
  Application.Run(new Form1());
}

private void button1_Click (Object sender, System.EventArgs e)
{
  MessageBox.Show("Hello World");
```

Chapter 11

```
    yourMethod();
  }

  private void yourMethod()
  {
    System.out.println("A method called by the application entry point");
  }
}
```

The Java Language Conversion Assistant (JLCA)

The Java Language Conversion Assistant is a Visual Studio .NET tool that is installed along with Visual J#. It converts Java code to Visual C# .NET code automatically. At the time of going to press, the JLCA was in its beta-2 phase. You can find more information and download the JLCA from:

   http://msdn.microsoft.com/vstudio/downloads/jlca

The JLCA provides a translation service that you can use to port code that is JDK 1.1.4 compliant into C#. Unfortunately not everything can be converted, though Microsoft estimates that on average the conversion rate is roughly 90 percent. For the code that cannot be converted, the tool tags the problem areas and provides links to topics with suggestions on how to complete the conversion. I certainly stopped using JDK 1.1.4 quite some time ago and since this book is aimed at J2EE developers I presume most of you are working with JDK 1.2.2 and up. This essentially means that this tool will be of more use for porting code that you wrote some time ago. According to Microsoft, it is also considering expanding the JLCA to provide a conversion facility for Java Server Pages as well.

The tool also supports conversion of Visual J++ 6.0 applications but my general perception is that there are not very many Java developers that are using Visual J++ to write Java Standard applications today but there are possibly some who use it to write Windows applications in Java. It is my opinion that it would save you a lot of time if you ported your Visual J++ applications to .NET and deployed Web Services functionality in your existing pure Java applications, which would provide the interoperability in its very nature. Otherwise you may expend a lot of time and money porting your code over.

In order to give you a better idea of how to use the JLCA, let's go through a simple example where we convert a simple mathematical Java application into a new C# project. The Java application consists of three source files. The first class initializes the other two and requests that they perform mathematical functions. To give you a better idea, I have provided the source to the Java application's entry point.

```
package wrox.interop.sunexample;

public class Mathematics
{
  public static void main(String[] args)
  {
    AdditionClass ac = new AdditionClass();
    System.out.println("Addition Result:" + ac.add(2,4));

    MultiplicationClass mc = new MultiplicationClass(2,4);
    System.out.println("Multiplication result:" + mc.result);
  }
}
```

Interoperating with Existing Code

Just for comparison's sake, below is the C# result of the JLCA conversion:

```
namespace wrox.interop.sunexample
{
  using System;

  public class Mathematics
  {
    [STAThread]
    public static void  Main(System.String[] args)
    {
      AdditionClass ac = new AdditionClass();
      System.Console.Out.WriteLine("Addition Result:" + ac.add(2, 4));

      MultiplicationClass mc = new MultiplicationClass(2, 4);
      System.Console.Out.WriteLine("Multiplication result:" + mc.result);
    }
  }
}
```

Now, in order for us to achieve this conversion we need to use the JLCA wizard:

❑ Open up Visual Studio .NET and Select **File | Open | Convert**. The JLCA Wizard shown below will open. Select **Create New Solution** and click **OK**:

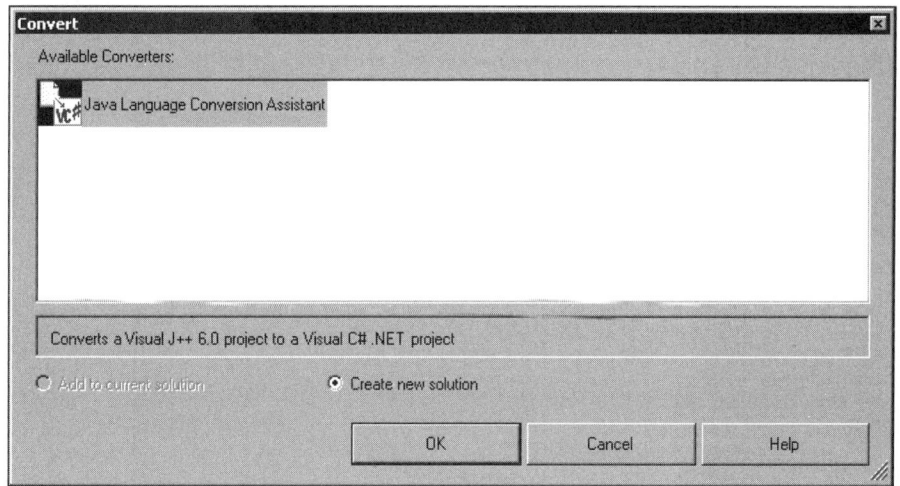

❑ The wizard presents you with an option of either converting a pure Java application or a Visual J++ application. Select **A directory containing the project's files**.

❑ You then specify the directory on your file system where your .java files are located:

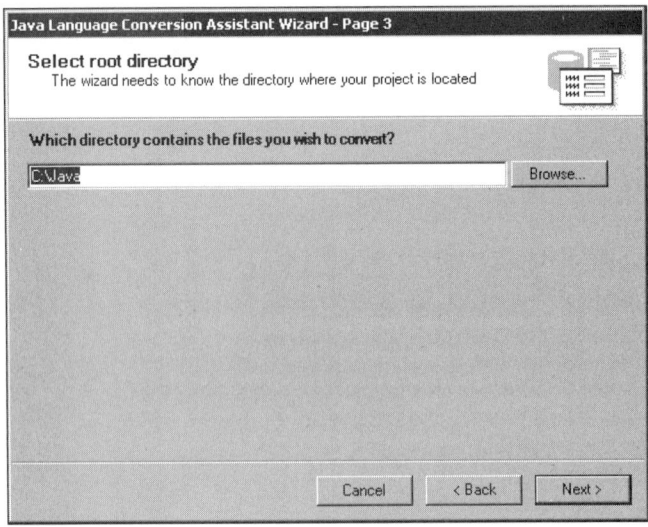

- The next step is to name your C# Project, specify the Java application dependencies (.jars, .zips, etc.), and specify the type of C# project to create (Windows Application, Class Library, and the rest).

    Note: In JLCA Beta-2, in this window, only the name for your .NET project works. The Java application dependencies are ignored and the C# target project type is always a Windows Application .EXE. According to Microsoft, this issue will be remedied at a later stage.

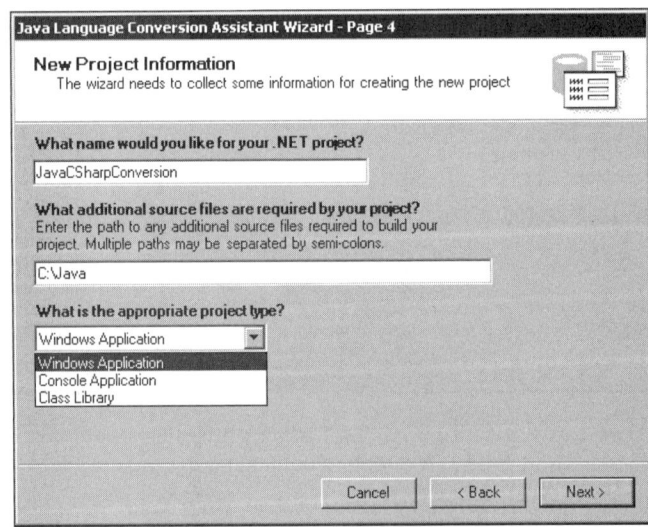

- In the next step, specify the location where your .NET project is to be created, and click **Finish** in the final step to set the application conversion process rolling.

Interoperating with Existing Code

The Java application is then converted into a C# project that appears as shown below if we open it in VS.NET. If you double-click on the `_ConversionReport.htm` file, you will see a report on the conversion:

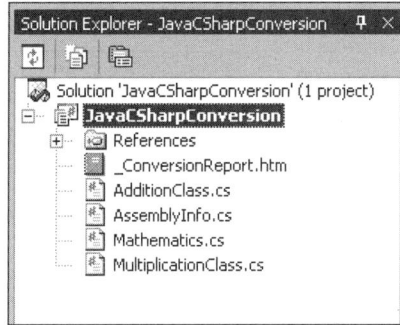

The Binary Converter Tool

This tool (`JbImp.exe`) enables a Java byte code to MSIL assembly conversion. It can port *most* compiled Java libraries into J#, allowing them to be used on the .NET platform. The rule of thumb is simply that, if you have the Java source available then you should use the JLCA for porting your code over. If all you have is byte code (class files) then you should use the Binary Converter Tool. As we have seen above with the JLCA, the .NET conversion utilities only support JDK 1.1.4 or before, thus sadly, if the library of applications you wish to convert uses anything later than JDK 1.1.4, those particular features will not be converted.

In addition certain JDK 1.1.4 class libraries are not supported. Some examples of these are RMI, RNI, JNI, and applets. However, let's take a look at what additional functions the Binary Converter provides:

- ❑ It will convert byte code containing most of the Microsoft Visual J++ 6.0 extensions, such as JavaCOM, delegates, and J/Direct.

- ❑ It enables you to specify an EXE or DLL Assembly for the bytecode being converted.

- ❑ In the conversion process, you are able to create and install a strong-named assembly in the Global Assembly Cache (GAC).

- ❑ You are able to import and use pre-existing .NET Framework Assembly Code.

- ❑ It enables you to search recursively, for `.class` files to convert, through the subdirectories on your file system.

The command line syntax for the tool is displayed below:

```
JbImp [options] <class_files> [[options] <class files> ...]
```

397

A Comparison between Java, J#, and C#

The table below shows how different applications may be migrated from Java to either J# or C#:

Java	Microsoft Visual J# .NET	Microsoft Visual C# .NET
Java language	Java language	C# Language
Applet	Not converted	Windows Forms control
JavaBean	JavaBean	C# Class
		(BeanInfo and ClassInfo are not converted)
ActiveX control	Not converted	ActiveX control
AWT frame	AWT frame	Windows Form
WFC form	WFC form	Windows Form
Compiled library	Compiled library	Not converted
Resource file	ResX file	ResX file

The next table shows how various Microsoft and Java libraries are named in either Microsoft Visual J# or C#:

Package	Microsoft Visual J# .NET	Microsoft Visual C# .NET
`com.ms.awt` `java.awt`	`Java.awt`	`System.Windows.Forms`
`com.ms.com`	`com.ms.com`	`System.Runtime.InteropServices`
`com.ms.dll`	`com.ms.dll`	`System.Runtime.InteropServices` `System.ComponentModel`
`com.ms.dxmedia`	`Not Upgraded`	`DirectAnimation`
`com.ms.fx`	`Not Upgraded`	`System.Windows.Forms`
`com.ms.io`	`com.ms.vjsharp.io`	`System.IO`
`com.ms.lang`	`com.ms.lang`	`System` `Microsoft.Win32.RegistryKey`
`com.ms.object`	`com.ms.vjsharp.object`	`System`
`com.ms.ui`	`Not Upgraded`	`System.Windows.Forms`

`com.ms.util`	`com.ms.util`	`System`
		`System.Collections`
		`System.Diagnostics`

Interoperating with Existing Code

Package	Microsoft Visual J# .NET	Microsoft Visual C# .NET
com.ms.wfc.app	com.ms.wfc.app	System.Windows.Forms System.Globalization.CultureInfo Microsoft.Win32 System.Environment.SpecialFolder System.Threading System.DateTime
com.ms.wfc.core	com.ms.wfc.core	System System.ComponentModel System.Windows.Forms.Design System.ComponentModel.Design System.Resources
com.ms.wfc.data	com.ms.wfc.data	ADODB System.Runtime.InteropServices RDS System.Globalization System System.ComponentModel MSDASC System.Resources
com.ms.wfc.data.adodb	com.ms.wfc.data.adodb	ADODB
com.ms.wfc.data.ui	com.ms.wfc.data.ui	System.Windows.Forms System.Data System
com.ms.wfc.io	com.ms.wfc.io	System.IO System.Globalization
com.ms.wfc.ole32	com.ms.wfc.ole32	
com.ms.wfc.ui	com.ms.wfc.ui	System.Windows.Forms
com.ms.wfc.util	com.ms.wfc.util	System System.Diagnostics System.Collections System.Runtime.InteropServices System.Resources System.Globalization
com.ms.wfc.win32 com.ms.win32	com.ms.wfc.win32 com.ms.win32	*Converted to* PInvoke() *calls*
java.io	java.io	System.IO
java.lang	java.lang	System System.Threading
java.lang.reflect	java.lang.reflect	System.Reflection System
java.math	java.math	System.Decimal

Table continued on following page

Package	Microsoft Visual J# .NET	Microsoft Visual C# .NET

`java.net`	`java.net`	`System.Net`
		`System`
		`System.IO`

`java.security`	`java.security`	*Not Converted*
`java.sql`	`java.sql`	`System.Data.OleDb` `System.DateTime`

`java.text`	`java.text`	`System`
		`System.Globalization`
		`System.Resources`

`java.text.resources`	`java.text.resources`	`System.Resources`

`java.util`	`java.util`	`System`
		`System.Collections`
		`System.Globalization`
		`System.Resources`
		`System.Configuration`

Interoperating with COM

For some of you, you may never need to know the information in the remainder of this chapter. But for those of you that have to use COM-Interop so your .NET components can communicate with COM components, this section should be a useful reference.

COM is the original Microsoft standard for reusable logic in applications and is very similar to Java classes in the way that specific logic is broken up into reusable chunks of code.

This section covers how to:

- Access a COM component from a .NET application
- Incorporate ActiveX into your .NET application

Accessing a COM Component from .NET

There are several scenarios where you could find yourself needing to call a COM component from inside a .NET application. A lot of organizations have large COM class libraries that they have developed over a long period of time, and would be very loathe to do away with, or to expend time porting to .NET. Moreover, many applications may rely on the use of COM components that were developed by a third-party vendor, for which no source code is available – without the source code it is not possible to port the code to .NET.

> *Speaking of porting code, here's a handy tip: Visual Studio .NET offers an upgrade wizard for Microsoft Visual Basic 6 applications and components, so if you find yourself in possession of older code, it might help you upgrade it. However there are obviously going to be scenarios where your components are written in such a way as to make it difficult to port them.*

Runtime-Callable Wrappers

We learned in Chapter 1 of this book that code running within the Common Language Runtime (CLR) of the .NET Framework is known as **managed code**. We also discussed how all other code is known as **unmanaged code**.

The reason unmanaged code cannot execute within the CLR is that it was written for a different architecture: pretty much the same reason you can't run a .NET application (which is compiled into MSIL) in the Java Runtime Environment (which is designed to run Byte Code).

To be able to access unmanaged code from managed code you need a **proxy** to sit between the two and interpret their calls, so that the other can understand. This proxy acts as a translator or interpreter between the two different application architectures. This proxy is known as the **runtime-callable wrapper** (RCW). Metadata is defined as information about other data, and both COM and .NET components have metadata that describe their public interfaces. One of the roles of the RCW is to provide metadata conversion between these applications interfaces. This facilitates and enables the communication between the different application architectures.

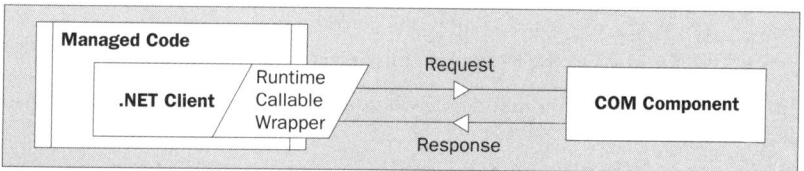

Generating Managed Metadata Using tlbImp.exe

One of the tools that can perform this metadata conversion is the `tlbimp.exe` (Type Library Import) tool. This tool reads the metadata from the COM type library and creates a matching CLR assembly that you can use to call your COM component from within your managed code.

The example below illustrates how to take a COM component named `SimpleCOM.dll` (included in our download) and get `tlbimp` to create a matching .NET assembly called `NETSimpleCOM.dll`. The out parameter lets you specify the name of the .NET assembly that you wish to create. There are several other parameters available that enable you to do important things such as sign the assembly and resolve external references in the type library. These operations can very easily be done using the command prompt or Visual Studio .NET as we'll now see:

Using the Command Prompt

If `tlbimp.exe` is not registered when you first come to use it, you'll need to set a PATH to your .NET SDK directory.

Enter the following at the command prompt:

```
> tlbimp SimpleCOM.dll /out:NETSimpleCOM.dll
```

Chapter 11

```
C:\WINNT\System32\cmd.exe

C:\Java>tlbimp SimpleCOM.dll /out:NETSimpleCOM.dll
Microsoft (R) .NET Framework Type Library to Assembly Converter 1.0.3705.0
Copyright (C) Microsoft Corporation 1998-2001.  All rights reserved.

Type library imported to C:\Java\NETSimpleCOM.dll

C:\Java>
```

Using Visual Studio .NET

Visual Studio .NET integrates this process into the IDE. It makes it quicker and easier, but the disadvantage is the fact that it generates an **unsigned assembly**, which in turn prevents your registering it in the Global Assembly Cache (GAC). This in turn prevents you from using the same .NET component within multiple applications, but in .NET, this is discouraged as it creates unnecessary dependencies (the infamous DLL Hell) and makes the application more brittle. Although this tool has its disadvantages, it does allow you to create batch files to automate the process with large libraries.

To do this in Visual Studio .NET:

- ❑ Open VS.NET and go to the **Project** menu. Select **Add Reference**.
- ❑ A box displaying all your components will appear. It will have two tabs, **COM** and .NET. Select the **COM** tab.
- ❑ Select the component you wish to use (if it is not displayed you can locate it by using **Browse...**). Once you have completed the component selection, click **OK**.
- ❑ Your COM component will be added as a reference to the current .NET project.

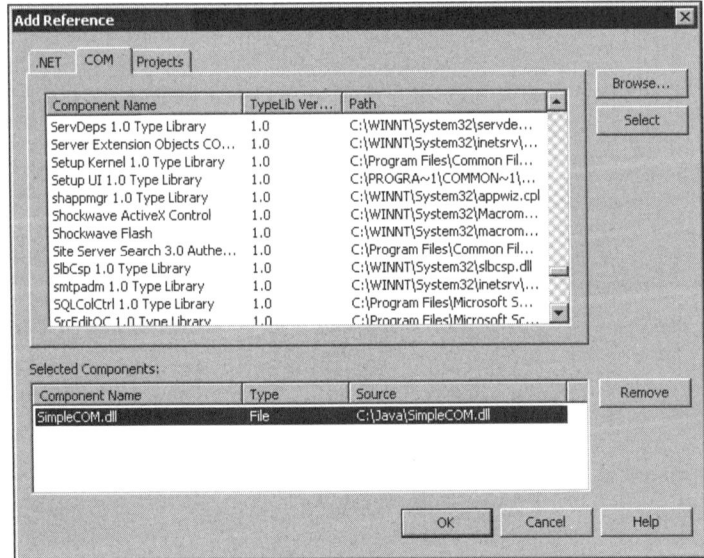

402

Interoperating with Existing Code

Once you've completed the above, Visual Studio .NET will automatically add your component to the list of references in your **Project** window. You are now free to use the original COM component's logic in your .NET application! The following section shows how.

Accessing the COM Component in C#

The `SimpleCOM` component that we've included in our download for you try out these examples contains a simple method called `GetMessage()`.

As with all COM components, you'll have to register it before you can work with it. Do this by navigating to the directory in which it is stored, and entering the following at the command line:

```
> regsvr32 SimpleCOM.dll
```

Let's now build a C# client that calls this method. Start off by creating a new Visual C# Windows application in VS.NET. Once that is done, follow the example above for adding the COM Component to your project.

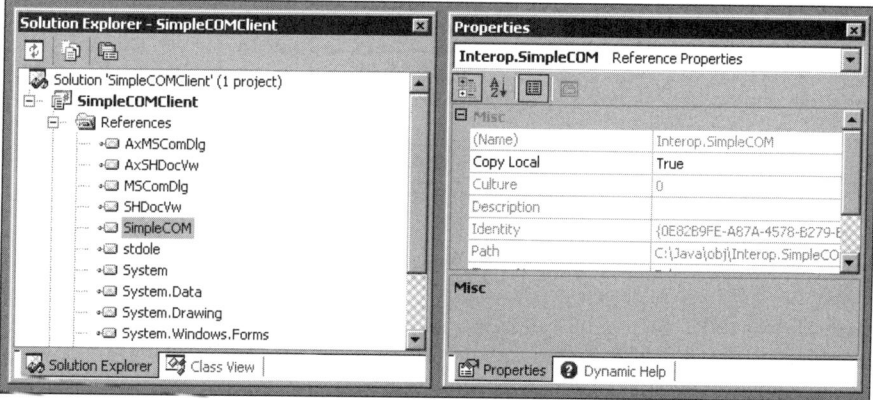

As you can see from the screenshot above, SimpleCOM is added to your project references and when you view the properties for that reference, Visual Studio .NET denotes it as an Interop component (Interop.SimpleCOM).

We looked at building Windows desktop applications in Chapter 8, so we won't cover that ground again. Instead we'll just focus on what you need to do to add a COM component to such an application using VS.NET.

Now we've added `SimpleCOM` as a reference to your project, we need to add a `using` statement for the component like so:

```
using SimpleCOM;
```

In my Windows application I have created a simple form with a button on it called `button1`. When you click the button it calls the click event handler, which is generated automatically for you. I have added two lines of code within it, which are displayed in the code below:

403

Chapter 11

```
    private void button1_Click(object sender, System.EventArgs e)
    {
        SimpleClass simpleClass = new SimpleClass();
        MessageBox.Show(simpleClass.GetMessage());
    }
```

In the code segment above, the `SimpleClass` is first instantiated and a reference is set to `simpleClass`. The next line of code displays a `MessageBox`, which is passed the `string` result returned from a call to the `simpleClass.GetMessage()` method.

If you run the sample, you'll get the following result. For the moment, we're only interested in the upper of the two buttons (we'll look at the second in the next section):

When you click the top button, you get the following:

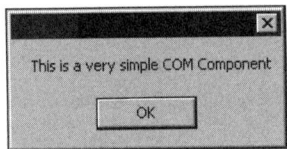

In this example, the .NET client application was launched and the Click me to test the COM Component button called the COM component's `GetMessage()` method. This returns the string (`"This is a very simple COM Component"`) displayed in the `MessageBox`.

Late Binding and Early Binding

Binding involves obtaining information about a component's objects, methods, and properties. Early binding is a faster approach to obtaining this information as it allows clients to obtain compile-time information about a component's type library with stronger type checking; in Java this is the default mechanism and is known as **static invocation**.

Late binding involves clients binding to an object at run time. In this case, the client does not have comprehensive information about the component and relies on the runtime to ascertain the component's method addresses on the run; in Java we call this dynamic invocation or reflection.

Early binding is considered 'safer' because the compiler is able to check the component's type library to make sure all the types that you are calling actually exist. When using late binding this compile-time type checking is not available and leaves your code vulnerable to spelling mistakes on the types you are referring to, which in turn cause runtime errors.

Releasing COM Objects from Memory

Java developers are used to not having to worry too much about memory management, and the nice thing about COM Interop is that you can keep plodding along as usual. Since the runtime callable wrapper is a managed component, when its `Finalize()` method is called by the CLR during routine garbage collection, the RCW will call `IUnknown:Release()` on the COM component as well, releasing it from memory.

For those of you new to all this, `IUnknown` is the default interface of every COM Component.

Incorporating ActiveX Controls in .NET Applications

Adding ActiveX interoperability into your .NET application is really easy.

With the Toolbox visible, right-click an area of open space within it and select **Customize Toolbox**. Scroll down to the **Microsoft Common Dialog Control**, and select it:

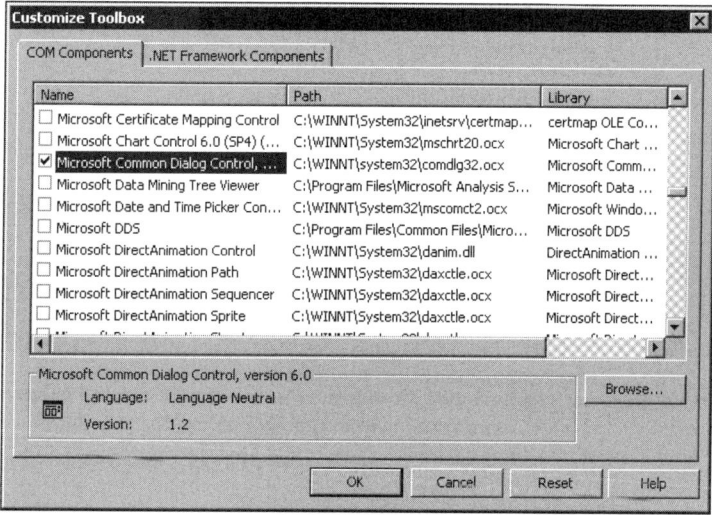

This control provides the functionality you see in Windows when you select **File** and then **Open** in applications, and clicking **OK** above adds it to the Toolbox where it can be placed on a form just as any other control. Once on the form, we can alter it through the Properties window, just as we would for other controls. In my example, I have renamed it to `commdialog`. In the Design window where your Form layout appears, double-click the new button that you've added. This will take you to your code window, and into the event handler for the button. Add the line displayed below so that your code looks like this:

```
private void button2_Click(object sender, System.EventArgs e)
{
   commdialog.ShowOpen();
}
```

Chapter 11

Now when you run your application and click the second button, it should pop up a **common dialog** for you to browse through your file system and select a file. It should look a little bit like this:

When the ActiveX button is clicked, it will pop up the Common Dialog like this:

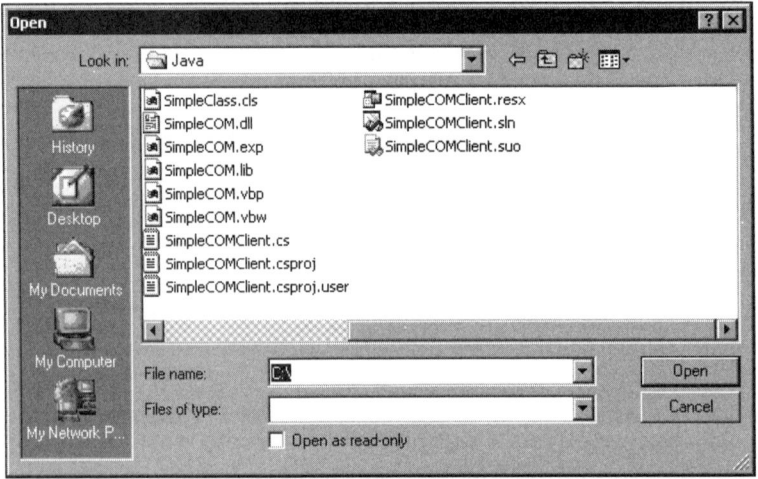

You can also use a manual approach with the Windows Forms ActiveX Control Importer (`aximp.exe`), which is more complicated than the approach above. The code for the conversion of an ActiveX control called `activexcontrol.ocx` *would be:*

`aximp c:\winnt\system32\activexcontrol.ocx`

Summary

In this chapter we learned how to interoperate seamlessly between applications written using Java, COM, and ActiveX architectures and those that use .NET architecture.

Firstly, we covered approaches for migrating your Java Code such as the Java Language Assistant, Visual J# .NET, and interoperating between .NET and J2EE using Web Services and Microsoft Biztalk Server.

We saw how a COM application needs a Runtime-Callable Wrapper to interoperate with .NET. We also saw how easy it was to incorporate ActiveX Controls into your Visual C# .NET Windows Application by Customizing the Visual Studio .NET Toolbox.

Interoperating with Existing Code

Index

More important entries have **bold** page numbers.

.NET enterprise servers (*see* enterprise servers)
.NET Framework, **10-13**, **15-18**
.NET Remoting (*see* Remoting)
\>> shift operator, 72
\>>> shift operator, Java, 72

A

abstract classes, **96-97**
abstract methods, 96
`AcceptChanges` method, ADO.NET `DataSet` class, 135
access modifier keywords, **78-79**
accessors, properties, 84
`Activate` method, COM+ `ServicedComponent` class, 334
activation, **349-58**
 client activation, **355-58**
 server activation, **349-55**
 SingleCall activation, **350-53**
 Singleton activation, **353-55**
`Activator` class, 305, 355
ActiveX controls, **405-6**
`Add` method, ADO.NET `DataRelationCollection` class, 133
`Add` method, ADO.NET `DataRowCollection` class, 137
`Add` method, ASP.NET `ControlCollection` class, 254
`Add` method, Windows Forms `ControlBindingsCollection` class, 309
`AddRange` method, `Items` property, Windows Forms `ListBox` controls, 295
ADO, 114
 cursors, 116
ADO.NET, 18, **113-54**
 events, **143-45**
 exceptions, **146-48**
 managed providers, **116-20**
 serialization, **152-54**
 XML and ADO.NET, **149-52**
`AdRotator` controls, ASP.NET, 176
aliases, namespaces, 66
`Anchor` property, Windows Forms `Control` class, 285, **288-89**
APIs, J2EE, 316, **317-18**
`App.ico` file, ASP.NET, 41

`Application` class, Windows Forms
 `Exit` method, 284, 290
 `Run` method, 284, 305
application components, J2EE, 316
application integration, 18
`Application` property, ASP.NET `Page` class, 243
application servers, J2EE, 315
application state, ASP.NET, **242-44**
`ApplicationName` property, `RemotingConfiguration` class, 356
`appSettings` element, `web.config` file, 225
`AppSettings` property, `ConfigurationSettings` class, 223, 225
`ArithmeticException` class, 101
`Array` class, **88-89**
`ArrayList` class, 309-10, 311
arrays, **86-89**
 jagged arrays, **88**
 multi-dimensional arrays, **87-88**
 one-dimensional arrays, **86-87**
ASP.NET, **19**, 157-58
 `App.ico` file, **41**
 code-behind programming, **211-13**
 configuration files, **214-15**
 custom controls, **244-59**
 data bound controls, **218-33**
 errors, 214
 `global.asax` file, **40**, 43
 helper objects, **215**
 inline programming, **211**
 JSP vs ASP.NET, **214-15**
 state management, **234-44**
 validation controls, **201-11**
 web server controls, **172-201**
 web services, **261-78**
 `web.config` file, **40**, 43, 225, 235, 257
assemblies, **25-26**, **302-3**, **332-33**
 manifests, **25**
 private assemblies, **26**
 shared assemblies, **26**
 unsigned assemblies, 402
`Assembly` attribute, ASP.NET `Register` directives, 247
`Assembly` class, Reflection, 305
`AssemblyInfo.cs` file, 35, **40**, 43, 332
asynchronous listener, COM+, 328
attributes, **104-5**
automatic transaction processing, COM+, 322

B

BackColor property, Windows Forms Control class, 285
base class libraries, 24-25
base keyword, 91-92
bean managed persistence (BMP), 320
BeginEdit method, ADO.NET DataRow class, 139
Binary Converter tool, 397
BinaryFormatter class, serialization, 153, 345, 349
   Deserialize method, 345
   Serialize method, 153, 345
BindingManagerBase class, Windows Forms, 310, 311
BizTalk, 28
   Microsoft Biztalk Server, 390
BMP (bean managed persistence), 320
bool type, 68
Bottom property, Windows Forms Control class, 285
bound controls (see data bound controls)
BoundColumn controls, ASP.NET, 230
boxing, 71
branching statements, 76-77
breakpoints, Visual Studio .NET, 48
BufferResponse property, ASP.NET WebMethod attribute, 263
Button controls, ASP.NET, 182-83
Button controls, Windows Forms, 287
ButtonColumn controls, ASP.NET, 232
byte type, 67

C

CacheDuration property, ASP.NET WebMethod attribute, 264, 277
caching, web services, 264, 277
Calendar controls, ASP.NET, 180
callbacks, 370-72, 376-77
CallContext class, Remoting, 358-59, 376
   GetData method, 378-79
   SetData method, 358-59, 376
CanBePooled method, COM+ ServicedComponent class, 334
casting (see also conversions), 91
catch blocks, 101
chaining, web services, 277
channels, 348-49
ChannelServices class, Remoting, 351
char type, 67
CheckBox controls, ASP.NET, 177
CheckBox controls, Windows Forms, 296-99
   Checked property, 299
   CheckedChanged event, 296, 299
   ThreeState property, 296
CheckBoxList controls, ASP.NET, 177-78, 221
checked keyword, 72-73
Checked property, Windows Forms CheckBox controls, 299
CheckedChanged event, Windows Forms CheckBox controls, 296, 299

class libraries (see also base class libraries), 25
classes, 78-84
   abstract classes, 96-97
CLI (Common Language Infrastructure), 18, 26
client activation, 355-58
client applications, COM+, 334-36
client applications, Remoting, 381-86
client applications, web services, 46-47
Client.exe.config file, Remoting, 384
ClientSponsor class, Remoting, 365
CLR (Common Language Runtime), 20-23
CLS (Common Language Specification), 23
CMP (container managed persistence), 320
code access security, COM+, 327
code editor, Visual Studio .NET, 283
CodeBehind attribute, ASP.NET WebService directives, 263
code-behind programming, ASP.NET, 41, 211-13
collections, 219-21, 308
COM (Component Object Model), 26, 323-24, 400-406
COM Interop, 400, 405
COM Transaction Integrator (COMTI), 322
COM+, 26, 265, 322-36
   client applications, 334-36
   Component Load Balancing Service, 328-29
   Component Services Manager, 324-26
   events, 328
   just-in-time activation, 322, 326-27, 334
   object pooling, 323, 327-28, 334
   Queued Components, 323, 328
   security, 327
   transactions, 326, 331
Command classes, ADO.NET (see also SqlCommand class), 118, 132
CommandBuilder classes, ADO.NET (see also SqlCommandBuilder class), 138-40
CommandText property, ADO.NET SqlCommand, 131
Common Language Infrastructure (CLI), 18, 26
Common Language Runtime (CLR), 20-23
Common Language Specification (CLS), 23
Common Type System (CTS), 21-23
CompareValidator controls, ASP.NET, 203-4
compensating resource managers (CRMs), COM+, 322
complex binding, 218
Component Load Balancing Service, COM+, 328-29
Component Object Model (see COM)
Component Services Manager, COM+, 324-26
component tray, Visual Studio .NET, 306
components
   J2EE, 316, 319-20
composite custom controls, ASP.NET, 252-59
Compute method, ADO.NET DataTable class, 141
COMTI (COM Transaction Integrator), 322
Conditional attribute, 104
ConfigurationSettings class, 255
   AppSettings property, 223, 225
configuration files
   ASP.NET, 214-15
   Remoting, 372-73, 383, 384
Configure method, Remoting RemotingConfiguration class, 373
Connection classes, ADO.NET (see also SqlConnection class), 118
Connection interface, JDBC, 118, 126

Delegate class

Connection property, ADO.NET SqlCommand class, 131
console applications, 32-33
const modifier keyword, 79
constructors, 92-93
consumers, web services, 269
container managed persistence (CMP), 320
containers, J2EE, 315-17
context, Remoting, 358-60
ContextUtil class, COM+, 332
Control class, ASP.NET, 246, 253-54
  Controls property, 254
  CreateChildControls method, 253
  EnsureChildControls method, 257
  RenderControl method, 246
Control class, Windows Forms, 285
  Anchor property, 285, **288-89**
  DataBindings property, 309
  Dock property, 285, **289-90**
ControlCollection class, ASP.NET, 254
controls, ASP.NET (see server controls)
controls, Windows Forms, 284-90
  data bound controls, **308-11**
  layout, **288-90**
  properties, 36, **284-86**
Controls property, ASP.NET Control class, 254
conversions, types, 68-69
cookieless attribute, sessionState element, web.config file, 234
CreateChildControls method, ASP.NET Control class, 253
CreateInstance method, Activator class, 305, 355
CRMs (compensating resource managers), COM+, 322
csc utility, 32
CTS (Common Type System), 21-23
CurrentLeaseTime property, Remoting ILease interface, 363
cursors, ADO, 116
custom controls, ASP.NET, **244-59**
  composite controls, **252-59**
  derived controls, **248-51**
  Register directives, 247, 250, 258
CustomValidator controls, ASP.NET, 207-9

D

data access (see ADO.NET)
data bound controls, ASP.NET, 218-33
  complex binding, **218**
  properties, **218-19**
  simple binding, **218**
data bound controls, Windows Forms, 308-11
data providers (see managed providers)
data types (see types)
DataAdapter classes, ADO.NET (see also SqlDataAdapter class), **119-20**
DataBinding event, ASP.NET Page class, 160
DataBindings property, Windows Forms Control class, 309
DataColumn class, ADO.NET, 122-23, 132
DataColumnCollection class, ADO.NET, 122-23

DataGrid controls, ASP.NET, 193-96, 222, 225-32, 236-40
  DataSource property, 226
  EditItemIndex property, 228
  OnItemCommand property, 238, 240
DataGridCommandEventArgs class, ASP.NET, 227-28
DataList controls, ASP.NET, 191-93
DataReader classes, ADO.NET (see also SqlDataReader class), 119
DataRelation class, ADO.NET, 123-24, 131-34
  constructor, 124
DataRelationCollection class, ADO.NET, **123-24**, 133
  Add method, 133
DataRow class, ADO.NET, 123, 133, 136-37, 139, 140
  BeginEdit method, 139
  Delete method, 140
  EndEdit method, 139
  GetChildRows method, 133
DataRowCollection class, ADO.NET, 123
  Add method, 137
DataSet class, ADO.NET, **120-22**, **124-54**, 140
  AcceptChanges method, 135
  GetChanges method, 135, 140
  GetXml method, 149
  GetXmlSchema method, 149
  HasChanges method, 135
  ReadXml method, 149, 255
  ReadXmlSchema method, 149
  RejectChanges method, 135
  Relations property, 133
  WriteXml method, 149
  WriteXmlSchema method, 149
DataSource property, ASP.NET DataGrid controls, 226
DataSource property, ASP.NET RadioButtonList controls, 256
DataTable class, ADO.NET, 122-23, 132, 136-37, 139, 140-41, **221-33**
  Compute method, 141
  DefaultView property, 221, 226
  NewRow method, 137
  RowChanging event, 144
  Rows property, 123, 137
  Select method, 140
DataTableCollection class, ADO.NET, **122-23**
DataTextField property, ASP.NET RadioButtonList controls, 256
DataView class, ADO.NET, 141-42, 143, 221-22, 226
  Find method, 142-43
  RowFilter property, 143
  Sort property, 141-42
DCOM (Distributed Component Object Model), 323-24
Deactivate method, COM+ ServicedComponent class, 334
Debug mode, Visual Studio .NET, 38
debugging, 48-49
  breakpoints, 48
decimal type, 68
DefaultView property, ADO.NET DataTable class, 221, 226
Delegate class, 105

411

delegates

delegates, 105-7
  Remoting, **370**
Delete method, ADO.NET DataRow class, 140
deployment, **17-18**
  J2EE, **321**
  web applications, **42**
  web services, **45**
  WebMatrix, **56**
deployment descriptors, J2EE, **316**
derived classes (see inheritance)
derived custom controls, ASP.NET, **248-51**
DerivedCounter class (example), 249
Description property, ASP.NET WebMethod attribute, **264**, 267, 269
deserialization, 152
Deserialize method, serialization BinaryFormatter class, 345
DISCO (Discovery Specification), **15**
DisconnectedObject method, Remoting ITrackingHandler interface, 365
Distributed Component Object Model (DCOM), 323-24
DllImport attribute, **104**
do statements, 78
Dock property, Windows Forms Control class, 285, **289-90**
double type, 67
Dreamweaver MX, **57-59**
  templates, **58-59**
DropDownList controls, ASP.NET, 174, 219, 221
dynamic web applications, **157-215**, **217-59**

E

EAR files, J2EE, 321
early binding, 404
ebXML, 28
ECMA, 18
EditCommandColumn controls, ASP.NET, 230, 231
EditItemIndex property, ASP.NET DataGrid controls, 228
EJB (Enterprise Java Beans), 318, 319
  entity beans, **319-20**
  message driven beans, **320**
  session beans, **319**
Enabled property, Windows Forms Control class, 285
EnableSession property, ASP.NET WebMethod attribute, **264**
EndEdit method, ADO.NET DataRow class, 139
EnsureChildControls method, ASP.NET Control class, 257
Enter method, threading Monitor class, 379
enterprise applications, **313-36**
  J2EE, **313-21**
  System.EnterpriseServices assembly, **322-23**
Enterprise Java Beans (see EJB)
enterprise servers, **11-12**
entity beans, EJB, **319-20**
errors, ASP.NET, 214
event handlers, **37-38**, 254, 291
  registration, 37
Event Viewer, 366-68
EventLog class, 366-67

events, 37, **290-91**
  ADO.NET, **143-45**
  COM+, **328**
Exception class, 101, 102
exceptions, **101-2**
  ADO.NET, **146-48**
ExecuteNonQuery method, ADO.NET SqlCommand class, 118, 138
ExecuteReader method, ADO.NET SqlCommand class, 118, 119, 129
ExecuteScalar method, ADO.NET SqlCommand class, 118
ExecuteXmlReader method, ADO.NET SqlCommand class, 118
Exit method, Windows Forms Application class, 284, 290
explicit conversions, 68-69
extends keyword, Java, 89
external web services, **274-77**

F

Fill method, ADO.NET SqlDataAdapter class, 120, 131, 132, 136
finally blocks, 101
Find method, ADO.NET DataView class, 142-43
fixed keyword, **109-10**
float type, 67
flow control, **76-78**
for statements, 77
foreach statements, 78
Form class, Windows Forms, 284
FormatException class, 101
formatters, **349**
fully qualified names, **66**
function pointers, 105

G

garbage collection, 21, **108**
GetChanges method, ADO.NET DataSet class, 135, 140
GetChildRows method, ADO.NET DataRow class, 133
getConnection method, JDBC Connection interface, 118
GetData method, Remoting CallContext class, 378-79
GetLifetimeService method, Remoting RemotingServices class, 362-63
GetObjectData method, serialization ISerializable interface, 343
GetType method, 74-76, 305
GetValue method, ADO.NET SqlDataReader class, 147
GetXml method, ADO.NET DataSet class, 149
GetXmlSchema method, ADO.NET DataSet class, 149
global.asax file, ASP.NET, 40, 43
goto statements, 77
GroupBox controls, Windows Forms, **292**
GUIs (see Windows Forms)

412

H

HasChanges method, ADO.NET DataSet class, 135
Height property, Windows Forms Control class, 285
helper objects, ASP.NET, 215
HTML server controls, 161-72
   id attribute, 162
   runat attribute, 162
   view state, 165-66
HtmlAnchor controls, 164
HtmlButton controls, 163
HtmlForm controls, 163
HtmlImage controls, 165
HtmlInputButton controls, 164
HtmlInputCheckBox controls, 166
HtmlInputFile controls, 169
HtmlInputHidden controls, 165
HtmlInputImage controls, 164
HtmlInputRadioButton controls, 166
HtmlInputText controls, 163
HtmlSelect controls, 165
HtmlTable controls, 166
HtmlTableCell controls, 167
HtmlTableRow controls, 167
HtmlTextArea controls, 163
HtmlTextWriter class, ASP.NET, 247
HTTP, 349
HttpApplicationState class, 242-43, 255
   Lock method, 243
   Unlock method, 243
HttpChannel class, Remoting, 349
HttpSessionState class, ASP.NET, 236
   Remove method, 240
Hyperlink controls, ASP.NET, 185

I

id attribute, HTML server controls, 162
IEnumerable interface, 219
if statements, 76
IL (see MSIL)
ILease interface, Remoting, 360-63
   CurrentLeaseTime property, 363
   InitialLeaseTime property, 360-61, 363
   RenewOnCallTime property, 360-61, 363
IList interface, 308
ILogicalThreadAffinative interface, Remoting, 359-60
Image controls, ASP.NET, 175
ImageButton controls, ASP.NET, 184
implements keyword, Java, 97
implicit conversions, 68-69
Import directives, ASP.NET, 270
import statements, Java, 65
Index property, Windows Forms MenuItem class, 307-8
indexers, 102-3
IndexOutOfRangeException class, 101
inheritance, 89-97
   abstract classes, 96-97
   constructors, 92-93
   interfaces, 97-98
   overriding, 93-96
Init event, ASP.NET Page class, 160
initialization
   multi-dimensional arrays, 88
   one-dimensional arrays, 86-87
InitializeLifetimeService method, MarshalByRefObject class, 360-61, 362
InitialLeaseTime property, Remoting ILease interface, , 360-61, 363
inline programming, ASP.NET, 211
InsertCommand property, ADO.NET SqlDataAdapter class, 136
int type, 67
interfaces, 97-98
   properties, 97
internal modifier keyword, 79
internal naming, 18
Interop components, 403
is operator, 73-74
IsCallerInRole method, COM+ ContextUtil class, 332
ISerializable interface, serialization, 120, 152, 343, 347
   GetObjectData method, 343
IsInTransaction property, COM+ ContextUtil class, 332
IsPostBack property, ASP.NET Page class, 256
Items property, Windows Forms ListBox controls, 294
   AddRange method, 295
ITrackingHandler interface, Remoting, 365-66
   methods, 365
IUnknown interface, COM, 405

J

J#, 63, 391-94
J2EE, 313-21
   APIs, 316, 317-18
   application servers, 315
   components, 316, 319-20
   containers, 315-17
   deployment, 321
   Runtime Infrastructure, 315
J2EE Connector API (JCA), 317
JAF (Java Activation Framework), 318
jagged arrays, 88
Java, 389-400
Java Activation Framework (JAF), 318
Java API for XML Parsing (JAXP), 317
Java Database Connectivity (JDBC), 125-26, 317
Java Language Conversion Assistant (JLCA), 394-97
Java Message Services (JMS), 318
Java Naming and Directory Interface (JNDI), 318
Java Server Pages (JSP), 159, 160, 214-15, 318
Java Servlets, 318
Java Transaction API, 318
JavaMail, 318
JAXP (Java API for XML Parsing), 317
JCA (J2EE Connector API), 317
JDBC (Java Database Connectivity), 125-26, 317
JIT compiler, 23
JLCA (Java Language Conversion Assistant), 394-97

L

JMS (Java Message Services), 318
JNDI (Java Naming and Directory Interface), 318
JPanel controls, Java Swing, 292, 298
JSP (Java Server Pages), 159, 160, **214-15**, 318
just-in-time activation, COM+, 322, **326-27**, 334

L

Label controls, ASP.NET, 173, 249-50
   Text property, 250, 256
Label controls, Windows Forms, 294-95
late binding, 404
layout, Windows Forms controls, 288-90
leasing, 360-63
Left property, Windows Forms Control class, 285
legacy support, 28
LineNumber property, ADO.NET SqlException class, 148
LinkButton controls, ASP.NET, 184
ListBox controls, ASP.NET, 175, 221
ListBox controls, Windows Forms, **294-96**, 310-11
   properties, 294
Literal controls, ASP.NET, 198
LiteralControl class, ASP.NET, 254
Load event, ASP.NET Page class, 160-61
loaders, smart clients, 302, 303-5
LoadFrom method, reflection Assembly class, 305
Lock method, HttpApplicationState class, 243
logging, 365-69
long type, 67
looping statements, 77-78
loosely coupled events, COM+, 322

M

Main method, 80
MainMenu class, Windows Forms, 306-7
managed code, 23
managed providers, ADO.NET, **116-20**
manifests, 25
MarshalByRefObject class, 347, 360, 377
   InitializeLifetimeService method, 360-61, 362
MarshalByValueComponent class, 120
MarshaledObject method, Remoting ITrackingHandler interface, 365
marshalling, 346-48
MemoryStream class, 153
Menu class, Windows Forms, 305
MenuItem class, Windows Forms, 306-7
   Index property, 307-8
message driven beans, EJB, 320
message oriented middleware (MOM), 320
MessageBox class, Windows Forms, 301
MessageName property, ASP.NET WebMethod attribute, 265
metadata, 17, 25-26, **401-3**
methods, 81-83
   abstract methods, 96
   overriding, **93-96**
   web methods, 44, 47

Microsoft Biztalk Server, 390
Microsoft Intermediate Language (MSIL), **23**, 159
Microsoft Management Console (MMC), 324
Microsoft Transaction Server (MTS), 324
MMC (Microsoft Management Console), 324
mode attribute, sessionState element, web.config file, 234
MOM (message oriented middleware), 320
Monitor class, threading, 377
   Enter method, 379
MSIL (Microsoft Intermediate Language), **23**, 159
MTS (Microsoft Transaction Server), 324
multi-dimensional arrays, 87-88
multi-language support, 16
multiple inheritance, 90
multiple interfaces, 98

N

Name property, Windows Forms Control class, 285
Namespace attribute, ASP.NET Register directives, 247
namespace keyword, 65
namespaces, 65-66
   aliases, 66
   fully qualified names, 66
NET Framework (see .NET Framework)
new instantiation keyword, 85, 86
new modifier keyword, 94-96
New Project dialog, Visual Studio .NET, 34, 39, 42
NewRow method, ADO.NET DataTable class, 137
no touch deployment, **17-18**
nonremotable objects, 347
NonSerialized attribute, 343, 344
Notepad, 31-32
NullReferenceException class, 101

O

object construction, COM+, 322
object pooling, COM+, 323, **327-28**, 334
object type, 68
Obsolete attribute, **104**
ODBC, 117
OLE DB, 117
one-dimensional arrays, 86-87
OnItemCommand property, ASP.NET DataGrid controls, 238, 240
Open method, ADO.NET SqlConnection class, 126
operator keyword, 99
operators, 71-76
   overloading, **98-100**
out keyword, 81, **82-83**
overloading, operators, 98-100
override modifier keyword, 93-94
overriding, 93-96
   abstract classes, **96-97**

P

package keyword, Java, 65
packaged classes, Java, 65
Page class, ASP.NET
    Application property, 243
    DataBinding event, 160
    Init event, 160
    IsPostBack property, 256
    Load event, 160-61
    PreRender event, 160
    Session property, 236
    Unload event, 160
Page directives, ASP.NET, 226, 270
Panel controls, ASP.NET, 188
Panel controls, Windows Forms, 298
parameters, methods, 81-83
params keyword, 83
Parent property, Windows Forms Control class, 285
PlaceHolder controls, ASP.NET, 198
pointers, 108-9
    function pointers, 105
populate method, JDBC ResultSet interface, 120
PreRender event, ASP.NET Page class, 160
primitive data types, 67-68
private assemblies, 26
private modifier keyword, 79
Procedure property, ADO.NET SqlException class, 148
projects, Visual Studio .NET, 34-35
properties, 84
    data bound controls, 218-19
    interfaces, 97
    Windows Forms controls, 36, 284-86
Properties window, Visual Studio .NET, 36, 285
Properties window, WebMatrix, 54-55
protected modifier keyword, 79
public modifier keyword, 79

Q

queued component player, COM+, 328
Queued Components, COM+, 323, 328

R

RadioButton controls, ASP.NET, 178-79
RadioButton controls, Windows Forms, 292
RadioButtonList controls, ASP.NET, 179, 220-21, 252-57
    DataSource property, 256
    DataTextField property, 256
    RepeatDirection property, 257
    SelectedIndex property, 254, 256
RangeValidator controls, ASP.NET, 204-6
Read method, ADO.NET SqlDataReader class, 119, 129
readonly modifier keyword, 79-80
read-only properties, 84
read-write properties, 84

ReadXml method, ADO.NET DataSet class, 149, 255
ReadXmlSchema method, ADO.NET DataSet class, 149
ref keyword, 81-82
reference types, 21, 70, 81
Register directives, ASP.NET, 247, 250, 258
    attributes, 247
RegisterActivatedClientType method, Remoting RemotingConfiguration class, 358
RegisterActivatedServiceType method, Remoting RemotingConfiguration class, 356
RegisterChannel method, Remoting ChannelServices class, 351
RegisterTrackingHandler method, Remoting TrackingServices class, 365, 367
RegisterWellKnownServiceType method, Remoting RemotingConfiguration class, 351
registration, event handlers, 37
regsvcs utility, 333
RegularExpressionValidator controls, ASP.NET, 206-7
RejectChanges method, ADO.NET DataSet class, 135
Relations property, ADO.NET DataSet class, 133
remotable objects, 347
Remote Method Invocation (RMI), 340-41
Remoting, 339-87
    activation, 349-58
        client activation, 355-58
        server activation, 349-55
    applications, 350, 369-86
        client applications, 381-86
        server applications, 373-80
    callbacks, 370-72, 376-77
    channels, 348-49
    configuration files, 372-73, 383, 384
    context, 358-60
    delegates, 370
    formatters, 349
    leasing, 360-63
    logging, 365-69
    marshalling, 346-48
    serialization, 343-46
    sponsors, 363-65
RemotingConfiguration class, Remoting
    ApplicationName property, 356
    Configure method, 373
    RegisterActivatedClientType method, 358
    RegisterActivatedServiceType method, 356
    RegisterWellKnownServiceType method, 351
RemotingServices class, Remoting, 362-63
Remove method, ASP.NET HttpSessionState class, 240
RenderControl method, ASP.NET Control class, 246
RenewalTime property, Remoting ClientSponsor class, 365
RenewOnCallTime property, Remoting ILease interface, 360-61, 363
RepeatDirection property, RadioButtonList controls, ASP.NET, 257
Repeater controls, ASP.NET, 189-90

415

RequiredFieldValidator controls, ASP.NET, 201-3
ResultSet interface, JDBC, 119, 120, 127-28
    populate method, 120
Reverse method, Array class, 88-89
Right property, Windows Forms Control class, 285
RMI (Remote Method Invocation), 340-41
RMI-IIOP, 318
role based security, COM+, 323, **327**
RowChanging event, ADO.NET DataTable class, 144
RowFilter property, ADO.NET DataView class, 143
Rows property, ADO.NET DataTable class, 123, 137
RowUpdated event, ADO.NET SqlDataAdapter class, 144
RowUpdating event, ADO.NET SqlDataAdapter class, 144
Run method, Windows Forms Application class, 284, 305
runat attribute, HTML server controls, 162
runtime callable wrappers, **401**, 405
Runtime Infrastructure, J2EE, 315

S

sbyte type, 68
scriptlets, JSP, 214
sealed modifier keyword, **79**
security, 18
    COM+, **327**
Select method, ADO.NET DataTable class, 140
SelectCommand property, ADO.NET SqlDataAdapter class, 131, 132, 136
SelectedIndex property, RadioButtonList controls, ASP.NET, 254, 256
SelectedItems property, ListBox controls, Windows Forms, 294
SelectionMode property, ListBox controls, Windows Forms, 294
Serializable attribute, 344, 347-48, 359, 375
Serializable interface, Java, 343
serialization, **152-54**, **343-46**
SerializationInfo class, serialization, 343
Serialize method, serialization
    BinaryFormatter class, 153, 345
server activation, 349-55
    SingleCall activation, **350-53**
    Singleton activation, **353-55**
server applications, Remoting, 373-80
server controls
    custom controls, **244-59**
        composite controls, **248-51**
        derived controls, **248-51**
    data bound controls, **218-33**
    HTML server controls, **161-72**
    templated controls, **221**
    validation controls, **201-11**
    view state, **165-66**
    web server controls, **172-201**
Server.exe.config file, Remoting, 372, 373, 384

service element, Remoting configuration files, 373
serviced components, 330, 332
ServicedComponent class, COM+, 322, 332
    Activate method, 334
    CanBePooled method, 334
    Deactivate method, 334
ServletContext interface, Java, 242
session beans, EJB, **319**
Session property, ASP.NET Page class, 236
session state, ASP.NET, **234**
sessionState element, web.config file, **234**, 235
    attributes, **234**
SetAbort method, COM+ ContextUtil class, 332
SetComplete method, COM+ ContextUtil class, 332
SetData method, Remoting CallContext class, 358, 376
shared assemblies, **26**
Shared Property Manager (SPM), 323
Sharp Develop, 59-60
    templates, **60**
short type, 67
Show method, Windows Forms MessageBox class, 301
simple binding, 218
Simple Object Access Protocol (SOAP), **13-14**, 390
SimpleCOM component (example), 401, **403-4**
SimpleCounter class (example), 245
SingleCall activation, **350-53**
Singleton activation, **353-55**
sizeof operator, 74
smart clients, **12**, 302-8
    loaders, **302**, **303-5**
SNK files, 332-33
SOAP (Simple Object Access Protocol), **13-14**, 390
SoapFormatter class, 349
SoapSuds, 357
socket connections, 348
Solution Explorer window, Visual Studio .NET, **35**, 39, 329
solutions, Visual Studio .NET, 34
Sort method, Array class, 88-89
Sort property, ADO.NET DataView class, 141-42
source files, 64
SPM (Shared Property Manager), COM+, 323
sponsors, 363-65
SQL Server, 118, 125
SqlCommand class, ADO.NET (see also Command classes), 118, 131, 132, 135-36
    CommandText property, 131
    Connection property, 131
    constructor, 139
    ExecuteNonQuery method, 118, 138
    ExecuteReader method, 118, 119, 129
    ExecuteScalar method, 118
    ExecuteXmlReader method, 118
SqlCommandBuilder class, ADO.NET (see also CommandBuilder classes), 139
SqlConnection class, ADO.NET (see also Connection classes), 118, 126, 131, 132
    constructor, 126
    Open method, 126
    State property, 126
    StateChange event, 143, 144

SqlDataAdapter class, ADO.NET (*see also* DataAdapter classes), 131, 132, 136
   Fill method, 120, 131, 132, 136
   InsertCommand property, 136
   RowUpdated event, 144
   RowUpdating event, 144
   SelectCommand property, 131, 132, 136
   Update method, 121, 137
SqlDataReader class, ADO.NET (*see also* DataReader classes), 128-29
   GetValue method, 147
   Read method, 119, 129
SqlError class, ADO.NET, 147
SqlException class, ADO.NET, 146-48
   properties, 148
SqlParameterCollection class, ADO.NET, 136
state management, ASP.NET, 234-44
   application state, **242-44**
   session state, **234**
state management, COM+, 328
State property, ADO.NET SqlConnection class, 126
State property, ADO.NET SqlException class, 148
StateChange event, ADO.NET SqlConnection class, 143, 144
StateChangeEventArgs class, ADO.NET, 143
stateful session beans, EJB, 319
stateless session beans, EJB, 319
Statement interface, JDBC, 118
static invocation, **404**
Stream class, 345
string type, 68
structures, **85-86**
super keyword, Java, 93
switch statements, **76-77**
synchronization, COM+, 323
System.Data namespace, 114, 116
System.Data.Common namespace, 114
System.Data.OleDb namespace, 114, 117
System.Data.SqlClient namespace, 114, 117
System.Data.SqlTypes namespace, 115, 135
System.EnterpriseServices assembly, 265, **322-23**, 329-30
System.Runtime.Remoting namespace, 343
System.Runtime.Remoting.Channels namespace, 343
System.Runtime.Remoting.Channels.Http namespace, 343
System.Runtime.Remoting.Channels.Tcp namespace, 343
System.Runtime.Remoting.Lifetime namespace, 360-62
System.Runtime.Remoting.MetadataServices namespace, 343
System.Runtime.Remoting.Services namespace, 343, 365
System.Runtime.Serialization.Formatters.Binary namespace, 345
System.Xml namespace, 115

T

TabIndex property, Windows Forms Control class, 285
Table controls, ASP.NET, 186-88
TableCell controls, ASP.NET, 187-88
TableRow controls, ASP.NET, 187-88
TagPrefix attribute, ASP.NET custom controls, 247
TagPrefix attribute, ASP.NET Register directives, 247
TCP, 349
TcpChannel class, Remoting, 349, 351, 362
TemplateColumn controls, ASP.NET, 238
templated controls, ASP.NET, **221**
templates, Dreamweaver MX, 58-59
templates, Sharp Develop, **60**
templates, WebMatrix, **49**
Text property, ASP.NET Label controls, 250, 256
Text property, Windows Forms Control class, 285
TextBox controls, ASP.NET, 173
TextBox controls, Windows Forms, **296-97**
ThreeState property, Windows Forms CheckBox controls, 296
throws keyword, Java, 102
timeout attribute, sessionState element, web.config file, **234**
tlbimp utility, 401-3
toolbox, Visual Studio .NET, **35**, 286-87
toolbox, WebMatrix, 52-53
Top property, Windows Forms Control class, 285
top-level declarations, **64-66**
tracing, data, 134
TrackingServices class, Remoting, 365, 367
TransactionOption property, ASP.NET WebMethod attribute, 265
transactions, **26**
   COM+, **326**, 331
transient keyword, Java, 343
try blocks, 101
type safety, **21-23**
typeof operator, **74-75**
types, **21-23**
   conversions, **68-69**
   primitive data types, **67-68**
   reference types, **70**
   value types, **70**

U

UDDI (Universal Description, Discovery, and Integration), **15**, 46
uint type, 68
ulong type, 68
unboxing, **71**
unchecked keyword, **72-73**
Universal Description, Discovery, and Integration (UDDI), **15**, 46
Unload event, ASP.NET Page class, 160
Unlock method, HttpApplicationState class, 243
unmanaged code, 327, **401**

UnmarshaledObject method, Remoting
  ITrackingHandler interface, 365
unsafe keyword, 108-9
unsigned assemblies, 402
Update method, ADO.NET SqlDataAdapter class,
  121, 137
user interface, web applications, 41
ushort type, 68
using statements, 65

V

validation controls, 201-11
ValidationSummary controls, ASP.NET, 209-11
value types, 21, 70
view state, server controls, 165-66
virtual modifier keyword, 93-94
Visible property, Windows Forms Control class,
  285
Visible property, Windows Forms Panel controls,
  298
Visual J#, 63, 391-94
Visual Studio .NET, 33-49, 282
  breakpoints, 48
  code editor, 283
  component tray, 306
  Debug mode, 38
  debugging, 48-49
  New Project dialog, 34, 39, 42
  projects, 34-35
  Properties window, 36, 285
  Solution Explorer window, 35, 39, 329
  solutions, 34
  toolbox, 35, 286-87
  Watch window, 48
VS.NET (see Visual Studio .NET)

W

W3C (World Wide Web Consortium), 12
Watch window, Visual Studio .NET, 48
web applications, 39-42
  deployment, 42
  user interface, 41
Web Forms, 33
web methods, 44, 47
web server controls, 172-201
web services, 33, 42-47, 261-78, 390-91
  caching, 264, 277
  chaining, 277
  client applications, 46-47
  consumers, 269
  deployment, 45

external web services, 274-77
XML Web Services, 12, 13-15, 261
Web Services Description Language (WSDL), 14-15
web.config file, ASP.NET, 40, 43, 225, 235, 255, 257
  appSettings element, 225
  sessionState element, 234, 235
WebMatrix, 49-57
  deployment, 56
  Properties window, 54-55
  templates, 49
  toolbox, 52-53
  Workspace window, 51-52
WebMethod attribute, ASP.NET, 263, 267
  BufferResponse property, 263
  CacheDuration property, 264, 277
  Description property, 264, 267, 269
  EnableSession property, 264
  MessageName property, 265
  TransactionOption property, 265
WebService directives, ASP.NET, 263, 266
  CodeBehind attribute, 263
wellknown element, Remoting configuration files, 373
well-known objects, 350, 353
WellKnownObjectMode enumeration, Remoting, 351, 354
while statements, 78
Width property, Windows Forms Control class, 285
Windows applications, 33-39
Windows Forms, 20, 33, 281-311
  controls, 284-90
    data bound controls, 308-11
  events, 290-91
Workspace window, WebMatrix, 51-52
World Wide Web Consortium (W3C), 12
Write method, ASP.NET HtmlTextWriter class, 247
write-only properties, 84
WriteXml method, ADO.NET DataSet class, 149
WriteXmlSchema method, ADO.NET DataSet class, 149
WSDL (Web Services Description Language), 14-15

X

XA interoperability, COM+, 323
Xcopy deployment (see no touch deployment)
XML, 33
  ADO.NET and XML, 149-52
Xml controls, ASP.NET, 199-201
XML Web Services, 12, 13-15, 261
XmlWriteMode enumeration, ADO.NET, 149

Notes

Notes

Notes

Notes

Notes

Notes

Notes

Notes

Notes

ASP Today

The daily knowledge site for professional ASP programmers

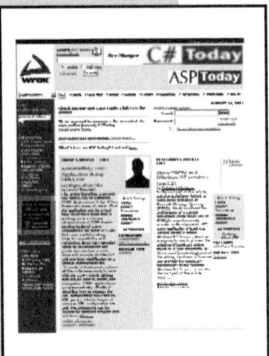

ASPToday brings the essence of the Wrox Programmer to Programmer philosophy to you through the web. Every working day, www.asptoday.com delivers a new, original article by ASP programmers for ASP programmers.

Want to know about Classic ASP, ASP.NET, Performance, Data Access, Site Design, SQL Server, and more? Then visit us. You can make sure that you don't miss a thing by subscribing to our free daily e-mail updates featuring ASPToday highlights and tips.

By bringing you daily articles written by real programmers, ASPToday is an indispensable resource for quickly finding out exactly what you need. ASPToday is THE daily knowledge site for professional ASP programmers.

In addition to our free weekly and monthly articles, ASPToday also includes a premier subscription service. You can now join the growing number of ASPToday subscribers who benefit from access to:

- Daily in-depth articles
- Code-heavy demonstrations of real applications
- Access to the ASPToday Living Book, our collection of past articles
- ASP reference material
- Fully searchable index and advanced search engine
- Tips and tricks for professionals

Visit ASPToday at: www.asptoday.com

C# Today

The daily knowledge site for professional C# programmers

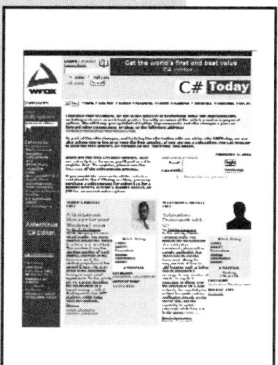

C#Today provides you with a weekly in-depth case study, giving you solutions to real-world problems that are relevant to your career. Each one is written by a leading professional, meaning that you benefit from their expertise and get the skills that you need to thrive in the C# world. As well as a weekly case study, we also offer you access to our huge archive of quality articles, which cover every aspect of the C# language. www.csharptoday.com

C#Today has built up an archive of over 170 articles, in which top authors like Kaushal Sanghavi, Matthew Reynolds and Richard Conway have tackled topics ranging from thread pooling and .Net serialization to multi-threaded search engines, UDDI, and advanced techniques for inter-thread communication.

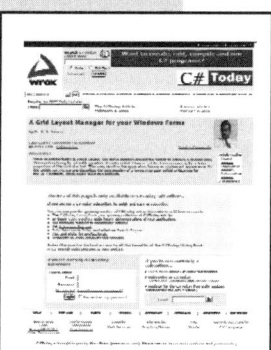

By joining the growing number of C#Today subscribers, you get access to:

- a weekly in-depth case study
- code heavy demonstration of real world applications
- access to an archive of over 170 articles
- C# reference material
- a fully searchable index

Visit C#Today at: www.csharptoday.com

p2p.wrox.com
The programmer's resource centre

A unique free service from Wrox Press
With the aim of helping programmers to help each other

Wrox Press aims to provide timely and practical information to today's programmer. P2P is a list server offering a host of targeted mailing lists where you can share knowledge with four fellow programmers and find solutions to your problems. Whatever the level of your programming knowledge, and whatever technology you use P2P can provide you with the information you need.

ASP — Support for beginners and professionals, including a resource page with hundreds of links, and a popular ASP.NET mailing list.

DATABASES — For database programmers, offering support on SQL Server, mySQL, and Oracle.

MOBILE — Software development for the mobile market is growing rapidly. We provide lists for the several current standards, including WAP, Windows CE, and Symbian.

JAVA — A complete set of Java lists, covering beginners, professionals, and server-side programmers (including JSP, servlets and EJBs).

.NET — Microsoft's new OS platform, covering topics such as ASP.NET, C#, and general .NET discussion.

VISUAL BASIC — Covers all aspects of VB programming, from programming Office macros to creating components for the .NET platform.

WEB DESIGN — As web page requirements become more complex, programmer's are taking a more important role in creating web sites. For these programmers, we offer lists covering technologies such as Flash, Coldfusion, and JavaScript.

XML — Covering all aspects of XML, including XSLT and schemas.

OPEN SOURCE — Many Open Source topics covered including PHP, Apache, Perl, Linux, Python and more.

FOREIGN LANGUAGE — Several lists dedicated to Spanish and German speaking programmers, categories include. NET, Java, XML, PHP and XML.

How to subscribe:
Simply visit the P2P site, at http://p2p.wrox.com/

Got more Wrox books than you can carry around?

Wroxbase is the new online service from Wrox Press. Dedicated to providing online access to books published by Wrox Press, helping you and your team find solutions and guidance for all your programming needs.

The key features of this service will be:

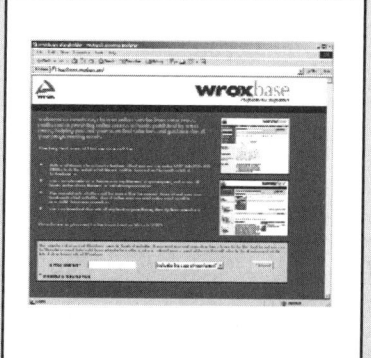

- Different libraries based on technologies that you use everyday (ASP 3.0, XML, SQL 2000, etc.). The initial set of libraries will be focused on Microsoft-related technologies.
- You can subscribe to as few or as many libraries as you require, and access all books within those libraries as and when you need to.

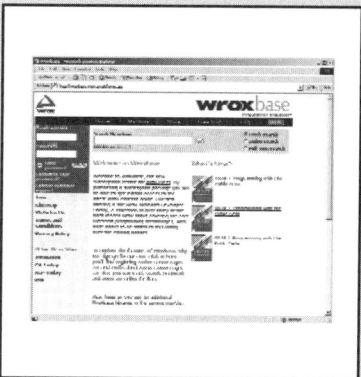

- You can add notes (either just for yourself or for anyone to view) and your own bookmarks that will all be stored within your account online, and so will be accessible from any computer.
- You can download the code of any book in your library directly from Wroxbase.

Visit the site at: www.wroxbase.com

Register your book on Wrox.com!

When you download this book's code from wrox.com, you will have the option to register.

What are the benefits of registering?

- You will receive updates about your book
- You will be informed of new editions, and will be able to benefit from special offers
- You became a member of the "Wrox Developer Community", giving you exclusive access to free documents from Wrox Press
- You can select from various newsletters you may want to receive

Registration is easy and only needs to be done once. After that, when you download code books after logging in, you will be registered automatically.

Just go to www.wrox.com

Registration Code: | 7914EH3274O1Q601 |

Wrox writes books for you. Any suggestions, or ideas about how you want information given in your ideal book will be studied by our team. Your comments are always valued at Wrox.

Free phone in USA 800-USE-WROX
Fax (312) 893 8001

UK Tel.: (0121) 687 4100   Fax: (0121) 687 4101

Professional .NET for Java Developers with C# – Registration Card

Name _____
Address _____
_____
_____
City _____ State/Region _____
Country _____ Postcode/Zip _____
E-Mail _____
Occupation _____
How did you hear about this book?
☐ Book review (name) _____
☐ Advertisement (name) _____
☐ Recommendation _____
☐ Catalog _____
☐ Other _____
Where did you buy this book?
☐ Bookstore (name) _____ City _____
☐ Computer store (name) _____
☐ Mail order _____
☐ Other _____

What influenced you in the purchase of this book?
☐ Cover Design ☐ Contents ☐ Other (please specify): _____
_____
How did you rate the overall content of this book?
☐ Excellent ☐ Good ☐ Average ☐ Poor
What did you find most useful about this book? _____
_____
What did you find least useful about this book? _____
_____
Please add any additional comments. _____
_____
What other subjects will you buy a computer book on soon?
_____
What is the best computer book you have used this year?
_____

Note: This information will only be used to keep you updated about new Wrox Press titles and will not be used for any other purpose or passed to any other third party.

Check here if you DO NOT want to receive support for this book ▮

wrox

Programmer to Programmer™

Note: If you post the bounce back card below in the UK, please send it to:

Wrox Press Limited, Arden House, 1102 Warwick Road,
Acocks Green, Birmingham B27 6HB. UK.

Computer Book Publishers

NO POSTAGE
NECESSARY
IF MAILED
IN THE
UNITED STATES

BUSINESS REPLY MAIL
FIRST CLASS MAIL   PERMIT#64   CHICAGO, IL

POSTAGE WILL BE PAID BY ADDRESSEE

WROX PRESS INC.,
29 S. LA SALLE ST.,
SUITE 520
CHICAGO IL 60603-USA